"Sarah Arthur's meditations provide a year of thoughts and prayers that offer more than dull pieties and bland devotional language. The freshness of her life and thought on these pages will help make the love of God appear 'new every morning.'"

Kent Gramm
Professor of English, Wheaton College, and author of *November*

"Sarah Arthur weaves everyday life with a call to look more deeply and discover God. It's inviting and open for readers. She concludes each reflection not in finality but in a search. She is on a pilgrimage to carve out places where God is sublime—bigger than we can stab at everyday, yet we are called to make a stab and live in a way that we value something more than life itself—that we lift up our eyes to the heavens even as our hands and feet are at work. Its conversational tone suggests a community effort in the task of devotion to God. Her call to past saints, their thoughts and experiences, and her push to spur on the Kingdom of God in the here and now create an earnestness for more devotion and to think beyond the daily grind."

Zach Kincaid
Director of the Matthew's House Project

Tyndale House Publishers, Inc.
Carol Stream, Illinois

SARAH ARTHUR

THE

ONE

YEAR®

DAILY

GRIND

Visit Tyndale's exciting Web site at www.tyndale.com

www.saraharthur.com

TYNDALE and Tyndale's quill logo are registered trademarks of Tyndale House Publishers, Inc.

The One Year is a registered trademark of Tyndale House Publishers, Inc.

The One Year Daily Grind

Copyright © 2007 by Sarah Arthur. All rights reserved.

Front cover photo copyright © Tariq Dajani/Getty Images. All rights reserved.

Back cover photo copyright © by Nathan Watkins/iStockphoto. All rights reserved.

Author photo copyright © by Tom Arthur. All rights reserved.

Designed by Jacqueline L. Nuñez

Edited by Stephanie Voiland

Unless otherwise indicated, all Scripture quotations are taken from the *Holy Bible*, New Living Translation, copyright © 1996, 2004. Used by permission of Tyndale House Publishers, Inc., Carol Stream, Illinois 60188. All rights reserved.

Scripture quotations marked NIV are taken from the HOLY BIBLE, NEW INTERNATIONAL VERSION®. NIV®. Copyright © 1973, 1978, 1984 by International Bible Society. Used by permission of Zondervan. All rights reserved.

Scripture quotations marked TLB are taken from *The Living Bible*, copyright © 1971. Used by permission of Tyndale House Publishers, Inc., Carol Stream, Illinois 60188. All rights reserved.

Scripture quotations marked NKJV are taken from the New King James Version®. Copyright © 1982 by Thomas Nelson, Inc. Used by permission. All rights reserved. *NKJV* is a trademark of Thomas Nelson, Inc.

Scripture quotations marked *The Message* are taken from *The Message* by Eugene H. Peterson, copyright © 1993, 1994, 1995, 1996, 2000, 2001, 2002. Used by permission of NavPress Publishing Group. All rights reserved.

Library of Congress Cataloging-in-Publication Data

Arthur, Sarah.
   The one year daily grind / Sarah Arthur.
      p. cm.
   Includes bibliographical references.
   ISBN-13: 978-1-4143-1139-5 (sc)
   ISBN-10: 1-4143-1139-7 (sc)
      1. Devotional calendars.   I. Title.

BV4811.A79 2007
242'.2—dc22   2007020438

Printed in the United States of America

13   12   11   10   09   08   07

7   6   5   4   3   2   1

ACKNOWLEDGMENTS

Many thanks to whoever invented coffee and the other visionary people who made this book possible. To Jan Axford, who had the crazy idea in the first place, and to Carol Traver and Stephanie Voiland for thinking it wasn't so crazy after all. To my ever-gracious family and friends, whose stories I tell in this book—including my housemates at Isaiah House, who weren't told ahead of time that our community would become a major theme because I didn't know it myself. Also, to the people who created those foldable file boxes with handles: You are the reason I'm still sane after moving four times during the writing of this book. But above all to Patsy and Phil Morrissette for their last-minute hospitality to a desperate writer in need of uninterrupted quiet to finish this thing. I raise a cup (regular breakfast blend with a dash of cream, no sugar) in your honor.

To Isaiah House of Hospitality:
"Salvation will surround you like city walls,
and praise will be on the lips of all who enter there."
Isaiah 60:18

—

WELCOME TO THE DAILY GRIND

Welcome to this collection of daily ramblings on the spiritual life. I say "ramblings" because the thoughts in this book are not your usual devotional material. You may wonder why they're so chatty and personal, or why they wander aimlessly at times, or why they often end with a question rather than a neat, tidy thought that ties everything together. You'll notice they aren't always cheerful or inspiring; sometimes they have an ironic edge. That's because, in my own spiritual journey, I've come to realize that the Christian faith isn't always neat and tidy. Nor is it always cheerful and inspiring. It's not easy to get up in the morning and fix my eyes on Jesus through prayer or devotional reading. The spiritual journey takes work. It's a daily grind.

But it isn't a grind in the same way that other daily rituals are, like getting stuck in traffic on the way to campus or work or whatever we do to survive during the week. It isn't a grind like taking medicine. Technically speaking, I can survive without the spiritual life, and of course millions of people do (though their souls are shrinking every day). In that sense, the spiritual life is more like my first cup of coffee for the day—another kind of daily "grind," if you will. I don't need it to survive, but if I go without it, I'm muddled and grumpy and unproductive. Something in my soul needs that shot of spiritual caffeine every day.

If you have a personal relationship with coffee, you get the metaphor. If not, it's going to be a long year for both of us. But bear with me: I have a feeling God is up to something with these daily writings (for me) and readings (for you), and I'm willing to stick it out if you are. Somehow I think it'll be worth it.

Commitments are like that. Have you noticed?

Sarah

To Do

I woke up this morning in a panic about all the things I have to do. This is not a new experience. It happens roughly 357 days a year. The times it doesn't are when I'm on vacation hiking in the wilderness, when the only things on my to-do list are:

1. Wake up.
2. Eat.
3. Walk in one direction for a really long time.
4. Stop. Set up camp.
5. Eat again.
6. Go to sleep.
7. Repeat steps 1–6.

I'm not on a hike right now, which means my list of things to do is ridiculously huge. At the top is the line item, "Write one devotion for *Daily Grind*," so when I get to the bottom of this page, I can check off my first item. Do you know how tempting it is to simply blather on about nothing in particular, periodically checking my watch, my word count, my location on this blank white space, until I'm done?

Maybe you've never had to write one devotion a day for an entire year, but you know what I'm talking about. Work and school, errands and exercise are like this. We go through the motions and then mentally check them off. Church is like this too. And small groups. And daily devotions, whatever we think those are. Let's be honest: We often treat faith like another thing on our to-do list—albeit somewhere toward the bottom so we don't feel all that guilty if we don't get to it. But then we come across a quote like this:

> I used to write in my daily calendar 7–7:30 a.m.—Prayer. But many times I passed that up. It was one more thing to pass by that day. Now I write 7–7:30 a.m.—God. Somehow that's a little harder to neglect.[1]

So it's not devotions that we're putting on our to-do list, it's a Person, and what would *any* person think if we failed to show up for a prearranged get-together? God isn't just one more thing "to do." Rather, he's the air we breathe, our daily bread, the Spirit that gives us eternal life beyond the frenzied activity of this world.

What if God's not on *our* to-do list . . . but we're on *his*?

Ecclesiastes 5:1-5

The Real Calendar

My calendar is crammed full of stuff, and not just the stuff I put in there, either. The one I bought for this new year had things written on the pages already: national holidays and celebrations and observances—in short, more things for me to *do*. Grr. And thanks to businesses like Hallmark, which continually remind us of all the obscure holidays out there (such as Sweetest Day, whatever that means), mandatory shopping is also on the schedule.

The truth is, my calendar isn't really *mine*. A lot of things are already planned for me as a member of this culture, and I'm just along for the ride.

But there's another calendar out there, one that once governed Western society. It includes holidays and celebrations and observances too, except the focus is on Jesus. Starting with the prophecies about Christ's birth (Advent), the calendar works its way through the various events of his life, death, and resurrection, culminating with the season of Pentecost, when the Holy Spirit swept through the disciples and sent them into the world as the first Christian evangelists (see Acts 2).

Advent to Pentecost. That's what we call the church calendar. It was created over a thousand years ago as a way for communities to retell and remember the greatest story ever told.

Most people are unaware of the church calendar these days, except when some yahoo makes a stupid movie like *40 Days and 40 Nights*, about a guy who tries to give up premarital sex for Lent.// Our culture also still celebrates things like Christmas and Easter— even All Saints' Day, though most people don't know that's where the word *Halloween* comes from (see November 1). Every once in a while, the civic calendar and the church calendar collide in a bizarre train wreck of values and beliefs, and I'm left realizing I'd better stick with the church calendar if my schedule is going to have any real spiritual significance.

So I suppose it's no surprise that this devotional book is organized around the church calendar more than anything else. But have no fear: I won't therefore ignore such vitally important events as, say, International Talk Like a Pirate Day(!?).

Acts 2:41-47

// In case you're wondering, Lent is the season of personal repentance leading up to Easter. Which begs the question: Does giving up premarital sex for only forty days and nights fix the *real* problem? ("NEXT, on Dr. Phil . . .")

The Spiritual Life

Okay, so I should probably try to define "the spiritual life" before we get too far, since that's what this book is about.

I'll start by telling a story. One time I was sitting in a coffeehouse reading a book of daily prayer. The book was small, dark blue, and completely plain except for a tiny cross on the front cover. It must have been the cross that caught the attention of the person sitting at the table next to me, because she leaned over and said in all seriousness, "Hi. I'm curious: Are you a very spiritual person?"

How would you answer that question?

On one level, I believe every human being is a spiritual person in the sense that each person has a spirit. It's the part of our beings that has no material substance but that constitutes life. The word for spirit in Hebrew (the ancient language of the Old Testament of the Bible) is *ruwach*, which is sometimes translated as "breath" or "wind." So when we read in the first chapter of Genesis that the *Spirit* of God hovered over the unformed earth, it's the same word that we see in places like Job 12:10, where "the *breath* of every human being" comes from God (italics added). Take that spirit or breath away, and the human being dies. So in a sense, we're all spiritual people, whether we're conscious of it or not.

But there's also Spirit as in *Holy Spirit*: the power and presence of God that dwells in us when we claim the eternal life God offers through Jesus Christ. It's like connecting a cell phone to a charger and plugging it into an electrical outlet because the battery will die sooner or later. Like a battery, the human spirit doesn't have the power to last for eternity separated from the true source of its life: the Holy Spirit. The Bible promises that those who claim Jesus as Lord are plugged into the only power source that will outlive and outlast this world (see John 3:16, which you maybe know by heart anyway). This means that as we continually seek to put Jesus in charge of every aspect of our lives, we are *very* spiritual people: intentionally, consciously, eternally. That's the spiritual life.

And yet none of this matters if I don't know what the woman meant by "spiritual." How come she didn't ask if I was very "religious," for example? or "faithful"? What does popular culture mean by that word?

More on that later. At the moment, the unspiritual part of me is begging for caffeine.

Genesis 1:1-2; Job 12:7-10

The Best Stuff

It took me a couple of months, but I think I've found the best coffee on campus. (Side note: Hubby Tom is a grad student in seminary at Duke University, so we live in a dinky apartment one block from school.)

At first I went to this really cool place around the corner that has wireless Internet and funky artwork and a girl named Courtney, who began to recognize me after about a week of watching me shuffle in every day, another sad junkie on the hunt for a lift. But eventually I realized I don't like dark roast, which is all they serve besides decaf.

So then I went to this other café, where I meet with my friend Enuma every week to talk about writing. It feels very scholarly to sip our Starbucks and gaze at the glass architecture of the Biological Genetics building or whatever it's called and discuss things like editing. But I must say, the coffee isn't nearly as inspiring as the conversation.

Next I tried the cafeteria in the center of the campus, the one that looks like the main hall of Hogwarts in Harry Potter. I half expected to be greeted by the Sorting Hat at the checkout and sent to the Slytherin section of the room with my muffin and coffee. But instead I was greeted by a very chipper, very deaf cashier who seemed unperturbed when I handed her the wrong change.

Me [mumbling]: Oh, sorry about that. I'm not awake yet.

Cashier [kindly, in a loud voice]: Now, don't you get down on yourself like that, ma'am. Don't you go saying that kind of thing, calling yourself retarded. You're not retarded.

[Entire cafeteria stares.]

Me [mortified]: No, you're right. Absolutely. Thanks. [Grab coffee and make quick exit.]

I don't go there anymore. Besides, the coffee was terrible. It's always lousy in a Styrofoam cup.

Finally, I found the best stuff. It's at the organic café near the chapel where we go for morning prayer during the semester. I'm not sure if the organic-ness has anything to do with it, but they serve the coffee in a china cup and then leave me alone to read and write while the place fills and empties between classes. The café is closed during Christmas break, and I'm beginning to miss it.

Unlike my search for the best coffee, I haven't been very diligent about finding the most helpful routine for spending time with God every day. When a certain devotional book or prayer service or Bible study doesn't work out, I tend to give up on the whole idea. What if I were to search just as earnestly for a devotional routine that works as I have for the best coffee on campus?

John 6:22-27

Addicted

My kind relatives gave me a coffeemaker for Christmas, which is in one sense like giving a heroin addict a syringe and in another like giving a Christian a devotional book and saying, "Here, I know you're gonna need this." (Hold on, cowboys: I don't use metaphors lightly.) My family knows I'm addicted to caffeine, which is clear when I go without it for even one morning. I feel foggy and crabby and get a headache by midafternoon. If I'm traveling someplace where coffee isn't on hand for breakfast, it's something of a crisis until I find a drive-through Starbucks or whatever—and then of course there's always a long line of irritated junkies just like me. Sad, really.

The funny thing about it is I hated coffee for a long time and couldn't understand why people drank the stuff. It's the kind of thing you have to develop a taste for. It doesn't come naturally, but then when it's finally part of your routine, you'll move mountains to get your hands on it.

Kind of like the spiritual life, when you think about it. We know it's important to spend time every day reading the Bible and praying, but it's not the kind of thing that comes easily to us at first. We have to develop a taste for it. But once we get in the habit of it, life feels out of sorts if we go without it for any length of time. We can't think straight. We feel crabby and start growling at the people we love. Then when it finally occurs to us what the problem is, we wonder, *How could such a tiny ritual be so important?* And yet it is. We're not really content again until we've spent some time each day nurturing our spirits with the revitalizing presence of God.

What would happen if I got as addicted to God as I am to coffee? How can I move heaven and earth to carve out time for him every day?

Psalm 63:1-5

The *Really* Spiritual People

When the woman asked me if I was a very spiritual person" (see January 3), I suppose compared to most people in the coffeehouse, I appeared more overtly spiritual than the average customer. But that wouldn't be a fair judgment of our hearts, which only God can see. Is the quasi-Buddhist with the nose rings any less "spiritual" because she follows a religion of empty promises? Or rather, does her earnest search for balance, peace, and enlightenment put my own sloppy routine to shame? And what if no one has ever introduced her to the real Jesus? What if someone did?

Today is Epiphany, the day in the church calendar when we remember the journey of the wise men who followed the star from an Eastern country to baby Jesus. Matthew is the disciple who writes about what happened (see Matthew 2), and when we read his story closely, we realize that the travelers most likely didn't arrive on the night Jesus was born, as most of our crèches depict. They probably arrived weeks or months or even up to two years after Jesus' birth. So that's in part why Epiphany comes twelve days after Christmas: to signify the passing of time.

We often forget that the wise men were not "Christians" when their search began; they were probably of an Eastern religion and would have been considered pagans by our standards. But did that make them any less spiritual than the Scripture-reading believers of the day? Any less than the folks who, for example, pointed out the prophecies of Bethlehem as the Messiah's birthplace (see Matthew 2:3-6) but didn't bother to go see for themselves? If anything, the wise men's earnest search for enlightenment— for an *epiphany*—for the true Lord to worship, makes them some of the most profoundly spiritual people in the Bible. They didn't give up the search until they were kneeling at the feet of Jesus.

Could I say that about myself? Could you?

Isaiah 49:5-7

Down the Road

I talk a lot about the "spiritual journey," and that's because the Christian faith isn't merely a onetime statement of the truth so we can go to heaven when we die. It's an intentional decision to *follow* Jesus every day for the rest of our lives, which implies fixing our eyes on him as our trail leader and putting one foot in front of the other just to keep up. He expects us to move from point A (spiritual baby) to point B (spiritual grown-up) over the long haul, and that's why we do daily devotions like this.

One of the ways we stick to the journey is by learning from the folks who've taken this trail ahead of us. When I consider the many deeply devoted Christians I've met or read about in my life, I'm always painfully aware of how small my faith is, how much farther I have yet to go down the path to maturity. Am I a "very spiritual person" compared to any of them? No. But they're willing to share their experiences with those of us who are a ways behind, and that's a great comfort.

Besides the people I've known personally (some of whom you'll read about this year, no doubt), the spiritual heroes who've most influenced me have been, among other things, writers (go figure!). People like Oswald Chambers, author of *My Utmost for His Highest*, and C. S. Lewis, author of *Mere Christianity* and The Chronicles of Narnia. The little blue book I was reading that day in the coffeehouse (see January 3) is entitled *A Guide to Prayer for Ministers and Other Servants* and includes excerpts from authors throughout the centuries: folks like George MacDonald, Evelyn Underhill, Dietrich Bonhoeffer, Richard Foster, and so on. Lately I've also been reading my contemporaries like Lauren Winner, particularly her book *Mudhouse Sabbath*.

So don't be surprised if I talk a lot about these folks this year. If you've never heard of them, I'll introduce you.// Even as I write devotions for other people, these are the devotional readings that keep me focused in my own journey. They remind me that I'm not alone, that the Christian faith is larger than my narrow little view of it, that there are bends around the path I haven't yet seen. Hopefully their thoughts will be an encouragement to you as well, pushing you a bit farther down the road.

In the meantime, consider: Who in your life keeps you focused on your Christian journey? Who helps you put one foot in front of the other?

Hebrews 12:1-2

// Check "More Spiritual Caffeine" in the back of this book for suggestions.

Spirituality or Whatever

Our postmodern culture isn't that big on religion, I've noticed, but likes to talk about "spirituality," a loosely defined term that, at best, admits there's more to our human experience than just our bodies, minds, and emotions—and at worst, seems to be nothing more than a selfish attempt to gain more control over our lives.

For a lot of people spirituality has to do with things like meditation, organic foods, prayer beads, yoga, and deep breathing, the purpose of which is apparently to achieve balance and peace, not necessarily to commune with a higher power. Call it Eastern meditation, call it New Age religion, call it whatever you like—but I think this is what the woman at the coffeehouse wanted to know when she asked if I was a "very spiritual person" (see January 3). Was I aware there's more to life than eating, drinking, sleeping, thinking, making friends, and running around from place to place? Was I seeking balance and peace by reading a little book with a cross on it in the middle of a busy coffeehouse?

The bald answer to those questions is yes. Yes, I'm aware there's more to me than my body, brain, and heart. There's a dimension of me that participates in another realm altogether, an invisible plane of existence that's eternal and unchanging. It's from this realm that I get the true Power, the Spirit, the Life that gives purpose to my everyday experiences. That's what gives me balance and peace. But this Life isn't just a series of spiritual exercises meant to make me feel better about myself. It's a Person. And his name is Jesus.

But how do you explain this to a stranger?

John 4:19-26

Small Ideas

Classes start back up this week, which is a good thing because Tom and I are driving each other nuts. Christmas break does that to roommates stuck together in tight quarters for weeks at a time—and our grad school apartment must set some kind of record for smallest number of square feet per capita. But then again, having my husband around day after day is a good reminder that the world does *not* revolve around me. When I'm alone with my laptop and MP3 player all the time, it's frighteningly easy to start thinking that I really am the center of the universe, that this spiritual life really is about *my* ideas and *my* personal maturity and the development of *my* character.

Then I pick up a book like Evelyn Underhill's *The Spiritual Life*, and I'm mortified by my own silliness. She writes:

> Any spiritual view which focuses attention on ourselves, and puts the human creature with its small ideas and adventures in the centre foreground, is dangerous till we recognise its absurdity.[2]

And:

> Our own feelings and preferences are very poor guides when it comes to the robust realities and stern demands of the Spirit.[3]

Ouch. So this week I'm back to the daily routine that saves me from descending into self-centered absurdity. I get up early enough to walk into campus with Tom for morning prayer in the chapel. We sit in the wintry light with a handful of students and follow the beautiful daily ritual from *The Book of Common Prayer*, reading aloud from the Psalms, the Old Testament, and the New Testament, and repeating ancient prayers that have been said by God's people for hundreds of years. In hearing those ancient words and listening to the voices of our fellow students, my focus gradually shifts away from my own "small ideas and adventures" and onto the bigger, higher, holier life that is God's Kingdom at work in the world. He's been at it since long before I took my first breath and will continue long after I'm gone, just as he worked through the people who wrote those words in the prayer book so many centuries ago.

Which means that my own small ideas on this page aren't really mine at all, and the spiritual life is most definitely not about me. Hurrah!

Isaiah 55:6-9

Pessimism and Wobble

Sometimes I get so familiar with the words of the Bible that they lose their meaning in my brain. How many times have I read Jesus' statements about worry—for example, when he asks, "Can all your worries add a single moment to your life?" (Matthew 6:27)? I've read that passage dozens, if not hundreds, of times. And what about when Paul says, "Don't worry about anything; instead, pray about everything" (Philippians 4:6)? I just typed that sentence mostly by heart; that's how often I've read it and quoted it. But it doesn't seem to matter how much I memorize the words if my actions don't reflect the truth of them in my life.

That's why sometimes I need to have those old biblical truths reinforced through the words of Christians who have been walking this journey for a long time. I said last week that a lot of my spiritual mentors are writers (see January 7), and I think part of the reason for that is because they know how to say old truths in new ways that my ears are open to hearing. They startle me into a fresh awareness of what my heart once knew.

When I wake up every morning in a panic about all the stuff I have to get done before the end of the day, I rehearse the words of Jesus and Paul about worry and anxiety—and those biblical reminders are lifelines. But I also turn to the words of my fellow journeyers and mentors like Evelyn Underhill, who has a knack for grabbing me by the shoulders (metaphorically speaking) and shaking me awake again.

"Fuss and feverishness," she writes, "anxiety, intensity, intolerance, instability, pessimism and wobble, and every kind of hurry and worry—these, even on the highest levels, are signs of the self-made and self-acting soul. . . . The saints are never like that. They share the quiet and noble qualities of the great family to which they belong."[4]

Worry I've heard about too many times. *Anxiety* I know by heart. But "pessimism and wobble"? That's like a smack upside the head. Suddenly I'm alive to Jesus' words again. Now I'm listening.

Matthew 7:24-27

Fuss and Feverishness

Evelyn Underhill's quote from January 10 brings to mind two kinds of streams. One clatters and burbles and catapults its noisy way over rocks and branches—a shallow, fussy, obnoxious thing. The other is a great, slow, quiet river of immense depth, ponderous in its movement but powerful in its potential. Of course, the noisy creek draws our attention as perhaps more lively in its personality or more excitable when confronted by any small obstacle; but by contrast, the powerful depth of the quiet river puts a hushing spell on our spirits. We are awed by the presence of something so mighty, so eternal, the sources of which stretch to the farthest corners of our imagination.

Which stream am I?

Too often I'm the noisy, shallow stream. I chatter on and on about the spiritual life when my commitment is only a few inches deep. And I know I'm not alone. Most of us are content with the fussy, chattering kind of spirituality, because it requires so little of us— and perhaps because we get more attention that way. But our very shallowness betrays us in those moments when, in the mildest of dry periods, we trickle to a standstill. And yet the great call and challenge of the saint is to allow the Spirit of God to well up like a deep river within our souls until we overflow our banks—not with noisy complaints but with a quiet, unassuming depth of peace that rolls on unshaken, unbeatable—easily moving past any obstacle that comes our way, ripples barely breaking the surface. To be hardly heard but to be felt in all our immensity, power, and depth—that is the spiritual life of a saint.

Underhill writes, "All our action . . . must be peaceful, gentle and strong."[5] How can I become such a river? How can I grow in depth and quietude and steadiness?

Isaiah 48:17-18

Winter Morning

During my junior year of college I began writing free verse poetry in my prayer journal. Some of the poems took the form of psalms, starting with phrases I found in places like Psalms 103, 104, and 106, while other poems simply explored biblical themes I was pondering at the time. I thought it'd be fun to include some of them in this book, just to offer a different perspective than straight prose.

I wrote this particular poem one gray January morning while sitting at the window of the dining hall on campus, looking out at the bare trees. Even in winter they seemed joyful, their branches lifted up to the sky in praise. And I thought, *That's how I want to be!*

Praise the Lord!
Praise him when the Illinois clouds
streak layered across
the gray January sky
and the bare brown trees
sprawl up and out and
praise their Maker,
as trees do:
with every limb and branch
and twig and nub.
In winter they praise him
as if it were summer all the same;
they praise him for the promise
of buds and leaves and wild rustling things;
for wind, tossing in the high blue sky,
warm and alive.
They lift up their arms and hands
in thanks for hope kept alive
even in the cold;
even when the frozen ground
is bleak and worn and tired—

Praise the Lord!

1 Chronicles 16:31-34

Ordinary Time

I think I've finally hit my postholiday slump. Since Thanksgiving, everything has been fun and exciting, with parties and performances and presents and piles of food and everybody in a holiday mood. Even until just the other day we still had treats left over from our Christmas stockings. But now it's really and truly over. We're back to the same old, same old: back to the usual routine of school and homework and deadlines and dishes, forever and ever until spring break, amen.

I'm guessing that's why this particular season of the church calendar is called Ordinary Time." This is the long, mostly boring stretch between Christmas and Lent, when nothing special is going on, just one ordinary day after another.

The guy sitting next to me in church the other day asked if the color of the altar cloth means anything. "It's like, white at Christmas, right? But then sometimes it's purple. So why is it green right now?" It seemed to be the clue to a very important puzzle. I vaguely remembered having learned about it in Sunday school when I was a kid. There are traditional colors that go with each season in the church calendar: white and purple are for special events like Christmas and Easter, red is for Pentecost (see Acts 2), and green is for most of the rest of the year, which is now. Most of the colors seem obvious: white for the purity and holiness of Jesus; purple for Jesus the King; red for the flames of the Holy Spirit; green for . . . well, what *is* green for, anyway?

I'm guessing it's for the season when we get into a rhythm of slow growth, like plants in a greenhouse. If you sit and watch a plant, you can't see any changes. But if you leave it for a day or two and come back, you see the new growth that happened while you weren't looking. That's kind of like Ordinary Time for all of us. At first glance there's nothing very spectacular going on. But over time, as we stick to the spiritual journey, we're slowly but surely transforming into something stronger and more mature, like green, growing plants.

The holidays might be fun and exciting, but my guess is the really important time is right now. Ordinary Time.

Ecclesiastes 3:9-13

// Ordinary Time comes from the term *ordinal* and means "counted time." You might call it the "season between the seasons"—the weeks between the main events on the church calendar (like Lent, Pentecost, and Advent).

Kairos

Sometimes I feel as though time is less like a measuring stick—where the lines are equally spaced—and more like a rubber band, which can be stretched. From a scientific standpoint, I suppose this syncs with Einstein's theory of relativity and the whole space-time continuum (ask your science geek friends if you don't get that); but from a personal standpoint, I don't need to climb into a spaceship to experience how time seems to drag on some days and race on others, depending on what I'm doing and how into it I am.

But it gets weirder. Occasionally I'll have an experience when time seems to be suspended altogether—when I'm completely unaware of the clock or the world outside. It's usually when I'm watching a movie or reading a great book or doing something artistic. It's like I've stepped through a magic wardrobe or fallen down a rabbit hole. Time, very briefly, seems to have no hold on me at all. And then when I come back to the "real" world, I feel more relaxed and sane.

Modern theologians have borrowed an ancient Greek word to refer to the steady passing of earthly time, the kind you can mark or measure: They call it *chronos* (or *kronos*). That's where we get words like *chronological* and *chronic*. But theologians have also borrowed an ancient Greek word for the sense of timelessness that comes over us when we're deep in thought or inspired with creativity or overcome with awe: They call it *kairos*.

For Christians, *kairos* is closely linked to the presence of God, because God doesn't inhabit time the way we do. If you picture time or human history as a long line with a beginning and an end, God's reality is a huge circle that encompasses the line and everything else. He's not bound to our calendars. He exists in the timeless realm of eternity, where no clocks are ticking. And sometimes, when we're feeling especially close to him, we step for a little while into that eternity. Our souls take a deep breath and relax, because we've temporarily escaped from the tyranny of the clock. *Kairos* is true "time."

Obviously, if I'm going to function in this world, I can't ignore my watch or my calendar. But I also need to remember that *chronos* doesn't govern my life; *kairos* does.

Where are those moments in my day when I can step into God's unhurried eternity?

Psalm 90:3-12

True Character

This week the banks and schools will be closed for Martin Luther King Jr. Day, the national remembrance of the civil rights leader who was assassinated in 1968 for leading peaceful protests against racial discrimination. On campuses across the nation there will be speeches and rallies to mark the occasion. Commentators will assess how far our country has come in realizing Dr. King's original dream, his vision that one day God's children won't be judged "by the color of their skin but by the content of their character." And I will look around at the wise faces of the older folks in my congregation—some of whom were arrested during the early civil rights protests—and think, *Will I have that kind of character when I'm their age? Do I now?*

I always find it interesting, whenever Dr. King's legacy is discussed by the media, that his other title—Reverend—is rarely mentioned. It's like the world conveniently forgets that this man was more than just a civil rights leader; he was a *Christian* leader first. Many of his speeches were not just speeches but sermons preached from the pulpits of prominent churches all over the South and elsewhere.

And meanwhile, our Christian subculture seems to forget this detail too. We celebrate Christian bands that make it big on secular radio or Christian athletes who are lifting weights for Jesus—and we make sure all our nonbelieving friends know that these famous people are Christians too, as if to say, "See, *some* of us are cool." But for some reason when it comes to King, we clam up. Either we don't realize he was quoting Old Testament prophets like Amos and Isaiah in his world-famous "I Have a Dream" speech, or we choose to ignore it.// Either we've never heard that he was a biblically and theologically trained minister of the gospel, or we'd rather forget that the gospel may just possibly cost you your life.

Amos 5:21-24

// For the full text of this speech online, visit http://www.usconstitution.net/dream.html.

How Wide, How High, How Deep

This week I'm looking around for where I see God in the everyday world. Here's what I see:

Right in the heart of our campus is a gigantic cathedral (though it's technically called a chapel). It's situated at the top of a hill, so you can see the spire for miles around; and when I say it's in the heart of everything, I mean you have to walk all the way around it to get from one side of campus to another.

Which I find intriguing, actually. Here's this secular university that's just like any other state school you've ever heard of—parties and everything—and yet at the center of the main quad is a simply enormous structure built to the glory of God. Not only does it command every field of vision with its impressive size, but the sidewalks are constructed in such a way that you have to walk through the cloisters on either side of the sanctuary in order to get to the student center or the biology building or the school of engineering.

So here are all of us in our frayed jeans and flip-flops (yes, even in January), chatting on our cell phones, obsessing about our small lives, and meanwhile—strangely enough— we're walking toward the chapel as if we really mean it. By the trajectory of our progress, you'd think we were headed to worship. We brush past the doors in spite of ourselves, and I can't help wondering: Do we sense the presence of God in that moment? Do we hear a whisper, like someone calling our names?

Not that God's presence is limited to a church building, obviously. Though the chapel is built in his name and for his glory, does this massive pile of stone and mortar give the student body even an inkling of the height and depth and breadth of God's love for each person here?

Or is it up to the individuals, like me, who say we know him?

Ephesians 3:18-19

Living Symbols

I believe symbols can be more powerful than we often give them credit for. By this I don't mean they have some kind of magic power in and of themselves, as if a Nazi swastika could actually *make* my grandpa feel sick to his stomach." I mean that our hearts can be stirred by the realization or memory of what a symbol stands for. Take a cross, for example. Sometimes the mere sight of a cross can be a profound reminder of what it cost Jesus to save us from our sins. A cross isn't magical, but it is powerful.

So what about the chapel here in the heart of campus?"" Does it point people to God by itself? There it is, rising in all its massive glory above the buildings and trees, its spire pointing into the blue sky. The bells ring out from one end of campus to another, reminding us of the hours but also of the presence of God in every minute of every day.

From inside the sanctuary, we see the stained-glass windows full of symbols: crosses and crowns and roses and robed men; a lamb here, a dove there. We sit beneath the enormous arches, our eyes drawn upward into the elegant curves of the distant ceiling. And even if no one tells us what the symbols in the stained glass mean or why the ceiling is constructed so high, we get it. Our imaginations somehow understand that God is bigger, higher, holier, and more mysterious than we often think. The symbols speak their own language.

But I don't think that's enough all the time. A building can't express the love of God the way a human being can. A building can't hug you, it can't help you with your problems, it can't look you in the eye and say, "Jesus loves you." This chapel can't listen to your questions when God seems far away and uncaring.

When God seems too big and too high and too mysterious for the student on campus who's struggling to make sense of this life, who will be there to show him or her Jesus?

Acts 17:24-25

// See January 21.
<< See January 16.

Dusty Knees

On most days after morning prayer on campus, I walk from the chapel to the student center, where I do various errands before heading home. Today I was on my way to the student center as usual, but for some reason people kept looking at me funny, as if I'd dyed my hair green or forgotten to wear shoes or something. After receiving a couple of strange glances, I looked down and realized that the knees of my hip black pants were completely white with dust. Since I was also wearing a dressy black coat and sleek boots, it must have been an odd sight to those passing me on the sidewalk: a stylish and "together" young woman in every respect—except, what's up with her knees?

I'd been kneeling on the chapel floor in prayer, that's what. I'd never noticed before that when you kneel for the prayer of confession, your knees get dusty. Duh. And of course the temptation when I saw my white knees was to bend over and wipe the dust off so I would look "together" again, so I'd appear stylish and even cool—so people wouldn't stare. But as soon as I did I wished I hadn't. Why pretend I have it all together when the very fact that I kneel every day and confess my sins to God proves that I don't? Why pretend I'm the perfect princess of my own little material world when the very act of confession means to acknowledge that Jesus is really the one in charge of my life?

Today is the day in the church calendar when we remember the confession of Saint Peter—the moment when this disciple acknowledged or confessed that Jesus is "the Messiah, the Son of the living God" (Matthew 16:16). We can picture Peter kneeling in the dust of that ancient land and then standing up again with his knees all white and powdery with the truth of his confession. People probably stared afterward as he walked along the roads of Caesarea Philippi, eyeing that undignified guy with the proof of his human frailty and submission to God written all over his knees.

Why wipe off that kind of honesty?

Matthew 16:13-20

Crazy Towel Guy

Last night Tom and I went to the men's basketball game at Duke University's Cameron Stadium. For those of you who aren't sports types or don't live in the South, such an event may not mean much, but the rest of you know that Duke is usually considered one of the top Division I teams in the ACC (as I write, the women's team is undefeated). Students camp out for days just to get in the lottery for season tickets—just the *lottery*, mind you, meaning only about a third of them will actually get in. A couple of our friends got season tickets but couldn't make it to last night's game, so we were the lucky winners.

Yep, we were the lucky ones who got to spend two hours on our feet in the student section of the bleachers, hollering, chanting, heckling, and generally acting like chimpanzees on happy pills. We quickly learned there's a canon of traditions in Duke basketball, including Crazy Towel Guy, the die-hard season-ticket holder who—on cue—stands up and whips a towel around above his head while everyone chants, "Cray-zee Towel-Guy [clap, clap, clap-clap-clap]." Then there's the standard "you-you-you-you-you!" accompanied by finger-pointing whenever an opponent fouls one of our guys. The list of sophisticated traditions goes on.

We had a blast. And it wasn't so much about the basketball—even though that rocked too—as much as it was the excitement of being in a huge crowd of people who all love the same thing and know they're lucky to be there. Hundreds of them stood in the cold for hours, hoping for a chance to get in, and once they were in, they didn't take it for granted. They participated with every bone in their bodies, at the top of their lungs, for two hours straight—Crazy Towel Guy included.

Which makes me wonder: Why isn't church like that? I mean, we're the lucky ones who've discovered the greatest human experience on the planet. We're witnesses of the very Kingdom of God in our midst! And yet so often we sit in church like dental patients under heavy anesthesia. What's wrong with this picture? Where's Crazy Towel Guy on Sunday morning?

2 Samuel 6:13-22

God in the Details

Today I made a new friend. His name is Griffin, and he's seven months old. I never used to think of people who were so much younger or older as *friends*, but I've begun to realize that if the only people I know are the same age as I am, then my view of the world is limited to a very small, very narrow perspective. After all, we're merely one generation out of the hundreds of thousands who have walked this planet, and it's not like we're any more intelligent or experienced. We're not even necessarily *cooler*—Griffin being a case in point. Today he was wearing a lime green velour pantsuit like the Grinch who stole Christmas. How cool is *that*?

Anyway, I met Griffin because his mom was looking for someone to watch him on Friday mornings while she was in class, and I volunteered to help. It's not that I've been looking for something to do in my spare time, because I have no spare time. And it's not simply that I want to help somebody out because Jesus asks us to—I have plenty of other opportunities for that. In this case, I've begun to realize how important it is to have diverse friendships in my life—people who challenge my self-centered view of the world and help me see God at work where I couldn't see him before.

Today was my first morning with Griffin, and right away I was learning new stuff. For one thing, I learned that babies get bored, just like we do. When they sit on the floor with only three little plush toys, while their babysitter tries to read because she's extremely busy and important, they sigh deeply and mutter in baby speak, "This stinks. Isn't there anything better to do?" Griffin did this, I swear. So I picked him up and wandered around the hallways, pausing at bulletin boards and drinking fountains and mirrors and other items that aren't all that fascinating to the rest of us but Griffin finds startling in their newness. He's never seen a drinking fountain before. He's transfixed by the idea that when you're thirsty you can walk down a hallway, stop by a square metal box, push a little button, and—*voilà!*—water pops up out of a hole. Magic. Grace. A gift from God.

What other details am I missing in God's amazing world that my new friend Griffin can teach me to see?

Psalm 8:1-2

The Big Picture

If seven-month-old Griffin helps me see God in the details (see January 20), then my grandfather helps me see the big picture.

Grandpa is ninety-something years old. He defies all stereotypes for a person his age. He lives in his own home with my ninety-something-year-old grandmother and takes care of everything himself: driving, grocery shopping, making dinner, washing windows, running the vacuum cleaner, taking Grandma to Bible study, reading good books, and turning on the nightly news to keep up with what's going on in the wide world.

But even more amazing is his mind, which is sharp as a scholar's, though he doesn't consider himself an academic. He was born in 1911, before World War I, and remembers life in Detroit, Michigan, before automobiles were common. He chuckles as he remembers the day a huge cart full of beer barrels pulled by Clydesdale horses crashed in the street and the beer ran down the gutters like rainwater. He grins as he recalls courting my grandmother at the Lutheran church where her father was a pastor, and how Great-Grandpa forgot to register their marriage license with the city until almost a year later ("so we were living in sin all that time and didn't know it!"). He grows grave when he thinks of World War II; even today, the sight of a Nazi swastika makes him feel nauseated. He doesn't easily forget what such things meant: the darkness that threatened to cover the earth, the triumph of the Berlin Wall coming down in his lifetime.

Yet the thing I admire most about him is his ability to see and share how he has experienced the hand of God at work in his life over the past century. As he said the other day, "Jesus gives life in abundance."// My grandfather pays attention to God's work in the lives of other people too. He repeatedly tells us, his beloved children and grandchildren (and now great-grandchildren), how much he loves us and how amazed he is at all God is doing. He helps us see the big picture.

When my mind gets too narrow, when I become too obsessed with my own small ideas, I call my grandpa. He reminds me I'm part of a story that's bigger than I am, a story that—as I've said before—started long before I was born and will continue long after I'm gone. That's the big picture, the story God is telling through the sweeping centuries of our human history.

That's something I don't want to forget.

Psalm 71:17-18

// See John 10:10.

Listening for God

Last week I was looking around for where I saw God on campus, in my life, and in the lives of the people I know. This week I'm *listening*.

Whenever I ask a certain friend of mine how I can pray for her, she almost always says, "Pray that I'll be able to really hear God." One time I asked what she meant. Did she mean an audible voice? Did she mean a passage from the Bible that seems to speak directly to her situation? Or perhaps the pastor's sermon? What about those moments when people just *feel* God's presence or *know* exactly what they're supposed to do? Is that what she wanted?

She paused and then said, "Yeah, all of that. Except maybe not the audible voice. That would freak me out."

This week I want to explore some of the ways God speaks—even the audible ways. I want to pay attention to how he speaks in the everyday world around us, even through people or events or things we never would have expected. I want to hear him in the small things, like the whisper of the wind, as well as the big things, like the booming of the chapel bells on campus.

The trouble is, all around us there's noise. We're simply drowning in it. Music and ring tones and traffic and chatter and news anchors . . . the crush of sound never seems to stop. Even when I'm home alone in the apartment, there's still the hum of appliances, the swish of traffic, the high-pitched buzz of the computer monitor, the ever-alluring MP3 player plugged into our sweet new speakers.

The more I think about it, the more I'm beginning to suspect that hearing God has less to do with whether or not God is actually saying anything to me and more to do with whether or not I'm actually listening.

When my ears are ringing with everything else, how do I know when it's God calling?

Isaiah 42:18-20

You Belong to Me

My freshman year of college was a tough one. I had such high expectations of myself—to have a fun social life, a profound spiritual life, and a successful academic life—that it was inevitable I would end up disillusioned and disappointed. I was alone a lot more than I liked. I struggled to figure out where I fit in my new surroundings and who my real friends were. I had to push myself really, really hard to keep up with work and school and volunteer commitments. And in the midst of all this, I felt like my quiet time alone with God (when I managed to get it) was mostly unproductive. I complained. A *lot*.

Then one evening, after yet another frustrating day, I came back to the dorm room to find myself alone—again. And that was it. I couldn't handle the silence and the emptiness and the loneliness anymore. I wanted to be able to *enjoy* the silence, to treasure those moments alone with God. But I couldn't. Instead I dropped to my knees by my bed and did all the classic things people do when they're worn out, lonely, and sad. I cried. I pounded on the mattress with my fists. I prayed things like, "Who am I, Lord? Why am I alone again? Where are you? Why can't I hear you? Speak to me. Speak to me. Speak to me."

Strangely enough, in the midst of this high melodrama, I was also vaguely aware of muffled music drifting from the room next door. It was a song I knew well, a remix of "Every Breath You Take," by the Police. The lyrics weren't audible, but I still could tell what song it was. Then all of sudden it was as if my neighbor cranked the volume or the wall between the rooms melted away, because these words came blasting into my head like the bass line from a subwoofer:

"Oh, can't you see? You belong to me. . . ."

Now, some may call it coincidence. Some may insist that Sting never meant the song to be about God's relationship with us (and they're probably right). Some may assert that God can't possibly speak to us through "non-Christian" music. But for me in that moment, it was the voice of God speaking directly to my heart.

I *did* see that I belonged to him. And I knew I would never, ever be alone.

Isaiah 43:1-7

The Word Speaks

Last weekend I had dinner at a friend's house, and we ended up talking about how and why we decided to move to this city. His reason was quite simple: God had spoken to him through a particular verse of the Bible, confirming his sense that God wanted him to make this huge transition to a new life in a new city. Not an easy decision, but the Scripture verse seemed as clear as if God had spoken directly.

The same thing has happened to me at different points in my life. I can't say that I've opened my Bible for the express purpose of finding specific answers to specific issues or problems or decisions, but occasionally in my daily Bible study a verse has startled me with its obvious implications for my life. For example, there was a time when I was so burned out from full-time youth ministry that I knew something had to change. I knew I probably needed to quit, but the question was, what would I do instead? Various friends and family members were encouraging me to take a sabbatical—a break of several months, like an extended Sabbath—but that sounded too much like giving up. Then one morning, while reading the book of Isaiah, a verse I'd never noticed before suddenly seemed to jump off the page:

> The Sovereign LORD, the Holy One of Israel, says: "Only in returning to me and resting in me will you be saved. In quietness and confidence is your strength."
>
> Isaiah 30:15

And although the original author of that Scripture most likely intended another meaning when he penned those words, it was as if I'd been given the green light from God to take a much-needed break. So I did.

While the Bible may not have specific answers to every problem that comes our way, God often speaks to us through his Word, offering guidance and confirmation when things seem unclear (more on this later). This is why the apostle Paul could tell a young minister named Timothy that God uses Scripture to "prepare and equip his people to do every good work" (2 Timothy 3:17).

What has the Bible been telling you lately?

2 Timothy 3:14-17

JANUARY 25—THE CONVERSION OF SAINT PAUL

The Whispering Gallery

The summer I studied in England, a group of us went to St. Paul's Cathedral in London. It's considered the center of worship for the Church of England (the official denomination of the country) and draws millions of visitors every year. With a huge dome rising 355 feet from street level, St. Paul's is a massive and breathtaking work of art, especially considering the fact that it's more than three hundred years old!

While I was gaping up at the murals and mosaics on the vast ceiling of the dome, my friend Elizabeth asked if I'd been to the Whispering Gallery yet. Intrigued, I followed her up the 259 steps to a narrow balcony that runs around the interior of the rotunda.

"Okay," Elizabeth said. "Apparently there's something about the design of this dome that allows sound waves to travel around the circle without interference. So here's what we'll do: I'll walk around to that side of the dome, and you walk around to the opposite side and put your ear really close to the wall and see if you can hear me whispering."

Skeptical, I did as she said. At first, all I could hear were the hundreds of voices and footsteps echoing up from the ground floor. I squinted at Elizabeth way on the other side. Her lips were moving, but I couldn't hear her.

"This is ridiculous!" I muttered.

"No, it's not," her lips mouthed on the other side of the dome.

"I can't hear anything," I said, a little louder.

"There's no need to shout," she said. "I can hear you just fine."

"Well, I can't hear *you*," I replied. But then it hit me that I *could* hear her voice, soft and low and perfectly normal, weaving in between the layers of all the other sounds. Somehow my ears had adjusted to a new way of listening.

Today is the day in the church calendar when we remember the conversion of Paul, the first Christian missionary. Before he converted to Christianity, Paul was a devout Jew who persecuted Christians because he believed they were leading people astray from the true God. But while on the road to Damascus, he experienced the voice of Jesus addressing him personally, and the encounter left him temporarily blind. His sight was gone, so all he had was the memory of that voice—not a whisper, but a loud, clear call that turned his world upside down.

Sometimes God speaks to people in ways we can't ignore, like when he spoke to Paul. But other times we have to seek those whispering galleries (such as quiet times reading a devotional book) in order to hear his voice in the midst of all the other noises of this world. Perhaps that's why the cathedral built in Paul's honor teaches us a new way of listening.

Acts 9:1-9

Inner Noise

I will never forget my senior year of college. That's when I lived and studied for a semester in Nairobi, Kenya—in East Africa—two degrees south of the equator near the Indian Ocean.

Nairobi is a huge and dangerous city full of buses, cars, markets, dust, and nonstop noise. The cheapest forms of transportation are the *matatus*, or minibuses, most of which are equipped with blaring sound systems to get customers' attention. (I could tell which matatu belonged to which bus route by whether it played reggae, rap, hip-hop, techno-rave, or R & B!) Each matatu also has a *taut*, or attendant, who hops onto the sidewalk at the bus stop, hollering for your attention, and then collects your fare once you're on board. Needless to say, in a city like that you can't even hear yourself think.

But Nairobi is also surrounded by a wilderness of empty grassland, like a huge prairie stretching for hundreds of miles in every direction. Since my university had both a city campus and a rural campus, every other day I hopped on a bus and rode for an hour into the grasslands, where the impalas and giraffes grazed in the distance. I would sit on a porch for hours between classes, drinking in the sunshine and the silence. One day I even followed a trail off the grounds to a rock formation—only to be told afterward by my concerned African friends that I could have been eaten by the old lion that lives out there(!).

To this day, I've never been anyplace where the silence is so complete. No buses or matatus or hollering tauts, no airplanes overhead. Even the wind died down and the crickets stopped buzzing during the noon heat. When I was out in the grasslands, it was like I'd gone deaf—all I could hear was the blood rushing in my ears.

But even so, it wasn't perfectly quiet. Unlike the city, the grasslands are a place where you can hear yourself think. And I suddenly realized just how noisy my inner mind is. It's like an amplifier of constant worries, complaints, and running commentary. I could be in the quietest place on earth and still be nearly deafened by my own interior noise.

When God admonishes us to "stand silent! Know that I am God!" (Psalm 46:10, TLB), I think that mental chatter is part of what he's talking about. Not only do we need to seek times of silence away from earthly noise, but we need to still our inner voices too. Otherwise, how will we be able to hear him?

Psalm 46

A Divine Scolding

I know people who have *audibly* heard God speak to them. This is different from hearing him through song lyrics or Scripture or the wise words of other Christians. This is a unique voice that seems to come out of nowhere, saying things these people never would have thought up on their own. Now I suppose the really hard-core skeptics might argue that these people are hallucinating or lying or demon possessed or whatever, but when they describe their experiences, it doesn't sound as strange or freaky as you might think.

For example, my brother-in-law was all stressed out about a huge exam he had to take in school, but then just as he was walking through the school parking lot, he heard a voice, clear as a thunderclap, saying, *My child, why do you doubt me?*—or something along those lines. It stopped him in his tracks. He knew instantly it was God speaking because the voice didn't seem to travel through the air like other sounds; rather, it came into his head like a thought. Except it was stronger than any thought he'd ever had on his own—it was definitely from another Person.

"And God was definitely scolding me," he explained when attempting to describe the experience. Not a bad scolding but a loving scolding, like the kind a good parent would give. Instead of being frustrated and angry (like most of us feel when our parents scold us), this guy felt instantly calm, went in and took the test, and passed without any problem.

At some point or another, most of us have prayed for God to help us with a test or some other issue. Sure, we know that if we fail it's not the end of the world, but we also hope that God cares about the little things too. It's comforting to imagine his voice saying something like, *It's gonna be okay. I'll still love you, even if you fail.* But a scolding? That's a little tougher to take.

Yes, God cares about the little things in our lives. He even cares about the tests we take. But he's not afraid to scold us when we get *way* too wrapped up in the stuff that isn't all that important in the grand scheme of things. Somehow that's comforting.

Isaiah 40:27-31

The Sender

For reasons too complicated to explain on this small page, my Web-hosting service is presently messed up, along with all the e-mail addresses associated with it. My primary e-mail address temporarily doesn't exist, which means everyone who has tried to contact me for the past three days has received a message in their in-box that says something like, "This message was undeliverable." Meanwhile, every time I try to send something, I get this notice:

> THE MESSAGE COULD NOT BE SENT BECAUSE IT REJECTED YOU
> AS THE SENDER.

Okay. Now I can understand if the cyber cops reject my e-mail address since it no longer works. I can even understand if they've rejected the message itself for some reason. But reject *me*? To make it personal like that? As if the Internet were some kind of social clique: "Uh-oh, girlfriends, here comes that cyber loser with the weird e-mail. Look the other way." Not only has my address failed and my message been cut off, but I, the sender, have been rejected.

Bear with me: There's a spiritual point to all this. I'm sensing a connection here to what I read in the Gospel of John, as unlikely as it sounds. Jesus was teaching in the Temple in Jerusalem, and the people were naturally skeptical about his message (see John 12:37-38). Not only did he make what sounded like outrageous claims ("He says he's the Messiah?"), but he had a knack for irritating the religious authorities while he was at it. People weren't sure whether to reject him or drop everything and follow him for life.

But one thing was clear: If they rejected him, they were not simply rejecting his message. They weren't even simply rejecting his address (after all, he was from the region of Galilee, which to city folk was the equivalent of the backwoods). No, if they rejected him, he said, they rejected the One who sent him—they rejected God himself, the Sender.

The same is true whenever we choose to ignore something Jesus says. I mean, who really wants to hear, "Whoever divorces his wife and marries someone else commits adultery" (Matthew 19:9)? Or "Sell all your possessions and give the money to the poor" (Matthew 19:21)?

We must be careful not to dismiss the message he speaks when it sounds old-fashioned or impossible or even unfair, because when we do, we're actually rejecting God. Yikes.

John 12:44-50

Take Heart

Most of the time the daily news depresses me. It never seems to change. Journalists should just boil it all down to one basic headline:

WORLD TERRIBLY MESSED UP, EXPERTS SAY

That's every news story in a nutshell. Take Iraq, for instance. That country has been in turmoil since long before most of us were born, and it won't be fixed overnight. Then there's Pakistan, still reeling in the aftermath of a massive earthquake that killed almost 80,000 people—though the event mostly went unnoticed by the rest of the world. And then there's my home country, the USA, which is already bracing itself for yet another wild hurricane season this coming summer even as it cleans up after previous seasons. And last but not least is my own city, a place of increasing gun violence and homelessness. The whole thing is just plain depressing.

Whenever we experience the overwhelming darkness of this planet and feel helpless to do anything about it, that's depression. Maybe you know what it's like. I certainly do. I've gone through seasons when all my small efforts to battle the darkness of the world— or the darkness in my own soul—seemed pointless, so why bother? Depression isn't simply feeling sad (though sadness is part of it); it's like being paralyzed. We feel helpless and weak, unable to make changes for the better, so we shut down and stop functioning.

And yet as Christians, we're called to be people of joy. Jesus knows we face tough circumstances. Thankfully, we're not asked to be happy about it—joy and happiness are not the same thing (happiness is the birthday present you weren't expecting; joy is the ability to praise God even when people forget your birthday). But we *are* asked to seek Jesus in the midst of our troubles so he can fill us with *his* joy, with the knowledge that he loves us and that our lives are in his hands. No matter how discouraging things may seem, we can take heart because of what Jesus has done for us. This is the joy that gives us the strength to get out of bed in the morning when we don't have the power to do it on our own.

So there's at least one other daily headline that never changes:

TAKE HEART, MESSIAH SAYS: I HAVE OVERCOME THE WORLD.

Nehemiah 8:10; John 16:31-33

ALL the Time

When I lived in Africa for a semester, I learned a joyful church ritual that goes like this:

Leader: THE LORD IS GOOD . . . ?

Congregation: ALL THE TIME!

Leader: ALL THE TIME . . . ?

Congregation: THE LORD IS GOOD!

[Everyone hollers, "Amen!" and applauds.]

Almost every church I went to in Africa included this ritual at some point in the worship gathering, often right before the offering. I got so used to it every Sunday that I really missed it when I came back to the USA. Not many churches here seem to know it, except those with African roots.

Which is ironic, actually. There I was worshipping with some of the poorest people in the world—many of whom had lost family members to bloodshed, war, or curable diseases—and yet they were able to say, without hesitation, that the Lord is good. He's good even when there's drought and the crops fail and the babies are hungry. He's good even when there's war and neighbors kill each other. He was good yesterday, and he's good today, and he'll still be good tomorrow. The Lord is good *all* the time.

But here in the United States—the world's wealthiest and most powerful nation—even Christians seem pretty skeptical about God's goodness. "How could God possibly be good," they ask, "when my day has gone so badly or when there's so much evil and suffering? Sure, maybe he has a good *side*, but what if he has a bad side too? Or perhaps he's not as powerful as we think, because then wouldn't he stop all this violence?" We may live in luxury, dress like celebrities, and eat like kings, but don't ask us to call God *good*, much less ALL the time.

So the very people who, on the surface, have the greatest reasons for celebrating God's goodness are the ones most reluctant to do so, while those who endure some of the greatest suffering on the planet are the first to give God the thanks and praise.

What's up with that?

Psalm 136:1-9

The Lord Is Good

Praise the Lord in the morning,
when all is still, Africa-dark,
and the rooster has crowed
beyond three times,
and the traffic has begun
with all its alarm and noise and pollution,
and the workmen are already laughing
outside our window as they walk.
Praise the Lord, who created
this great, wide-open plain,
this mysterious tangled maze of city.
Yes, let these people of his
—let all of us—
praise the Lord!
On this cloudy new day,
in this early morning chill,
let the redeemed of the Lord
stand up and say so.
Let each tribal language
in all its rhythm and dance
be raised to the cloud-sky
while the people testify
that the Lord is good—ALL the time;
ALL the time—the Lord is good.
He is good when they are hungry,
he is good when they are sick,
he is good when they have nothing.
Their circumstances do not
change the eternal nature of his character,
the very God of very God in all his goodness.
Surrounded by evil, God's people
cannot help but taste and see
that the Lord is good
—ALL the time!

So . . . what's something you've been neglecting to praise God for lately?

Psalm 34:1-10

The Sacrifice of Praise

I reached a point during my freshman year of college when I got really sick of going to church. Not only had I gone to church for most of my life (my dad being a pastor and all), but it was tough to get up early on Sundays after such late nights on Fridays and Saturdays. Sitting there nearly comatose in the sanctuary, exhausted and numb, I couldn't exactly muster a worshipful attitude—not to mention I found all those perky, happy, perfectly groomed grown-ups really annoying. They sang with smiles on their faces and clapped to the music (offbeat, most of the time) as if they were cheering on a marathon runner. One song they particularly liked was a happy little praise chorus that went, "We bring the sacrifice of praise / into the house of the Lord," and all I could think was, *Please, please— your perkiness is killing me.*

Half the time I was emotionally miserable because of some frustrating friendship or thwarted romance or (more nobly) a genuine concern for this hurting world we live in. It just didn't seem right or even honest to praise God when I didn't feel like it. So one day I said so to my roommate, a young woman who'd been a Christian for only three years. And she said something I'll never forget: "Well, maybe that's why the Bible talks about bringing the *sacrifice* of praise. Because it costs us. It doesn't come easily. We don't want to do it, but we do it anyway as a kind of offering, like giving up our money or possessions or time."

I remember this now on all those mornings when I wake up and don't feel like praising God. First, my feelings don't change the fact that God is deserving of my praise—just as he is deserving of my time and money and anything else I may sacrifice to give him. Second, it's my own fault if I'm crabby because I didn't get enough sleep the night before. It's *my* job to get to bed at a decent hour so the Sabbath actually *means* something: a day of *rest*, not *recovery*. And third, I've learned in time that God honors the sacrifices we make, including the sacrifice of praise. Our spirits are lifted a little bit—probably because we're forced to get our minds off ourselves for once and concentrate on something worthwhile.

So those perky grown-ups were onto something after all. . . .

Hebrews 13:15

No Exemptions

Several years ago I went through a season in which my future was up in the air. I didn't know what God wanted me to do next with my life. If only God would pick up a micro-phone and announce, in very clear tones, "I want you to turn left, take ten steps forward, and—do you see the door I've unlocked for you? Go through it!"

But of course, that's not what God did. I felt like a hiker lost in a cave, groping around in the dark. And it made me feel panicky. My anxiety was so high at times, I could hardly pray.

Eventually I got through that difficult time. But I learned an important lesson along the way that I cling to whenever another tough season comes along.

The lesson is this: Christians are not exempt from difficult seasons in life. We can expect them regularly. Now, you're probably wondering how this could possibly be comforting, especially since popular culture often depicts God as some kind of magic genie who shows up when we need help and fixes all our problems. After all, Jesus is a healer, right? We've all heard of miracles in which this or that person survived a car accident or cancer; and these are truly amazing events for which we can praise God. The problem comes when we begin to *expect* preferential treatment from God, as if God owes us our health and well-being in exchange for faithfulness. But if that were the case, our relation-ship with God would be built on a sense of obligation rather than love and mercy.

In the end, I'd rather have a loving God by my side through the difficult times—even if my problems don't go away—than an annoyed genie who shows up because he must and says, "Well, what do you want *now*?"

Hebrews 12:5-13

When the Going Gets Bad

Sometimes God wants us to choose suffering. Yes, I'll say that again. Sometimes God wants us to *choose* suffering *on purpose*.

Now, don't get me wrong. I don't mean that he wants us to put up with domestic abuse or that he wants us to stay home from the emergency room when we break a leg. I mean that Jesus often asks us to do something that we'd rather not do—such as live in a neighborhood that isn't the nicest so people can experience God's love, or sit with a dying friend in the hospital so she can feel the touch of your hand, or on the milder side, take shorter showers in order to be a better steward of God's creation.

Just because a situation really stinks doesn't mean God is telling you to leave. If anything, he calls us into the fray more often than he calls us out of it. Perhaps that's why I'm uneasy with how some people depict the end times—that somehow Christians will be snatched up into heaven and therefore be exempt from suffering while the rest of the world struggles on until Christ returns. When has God ever called the church *out* of the world when things get tough? If Jesus set any kind of example(!), Christians are supposed to be the spiritual firefighters of the universe, sent *into* the burning building at the first sign of emergency, not ushered out of it by a side door to a waiting limo. But I digress. Or maybe not. Maybe I'm onto something.

Most of us Americans don't have a very good understanding of suffering, generally. We tend to think of it as something we must get through as quickly as possible so we can go back to our vaguely happy, comfortable, spiritually comatose existence. The early Christians had a better idea.// Suffering is exactly where God meets us. It's what puts us in touch with the One who gave us this life in the first place and has a plan for where things are going. Too often we fail to seek Jesus out until things are really bad and we're pretty sure they'll only get worse before (if) they get any better.

But if you were God, which would you rather have: a mildly content person who's oblivious to your existence or a hurting person who seeks you out because there's no other place to go?

Mark 10:35-40

// See Hebrews 12:1-13.

The Job Factor: Part 1

I've been attending daily morning prayer at the chapel on campus (where my husband is a graduate student), and a few months ago we read through the book of Job. I've probably read portions of that book a dozen times, but for some reason hearing it read aloud day after day by different voices—men, women, young, old, black, white—had an amplifying effect on passages I'd never noticed before. And today's text was the most profound of all.

Job 42:10: "When Job prayed for his friends, the LORD restored his fortunes."

In all my readings of Job, I swear I've never heard that verse before. I suddenly find myself in unfamiliar territory within a story that's all too familiar. Most of us recognize Job as that guy whom God allowed to suffer horrible losses—the death of every single one of his children, bankruptcy, health problems, etc. And even though his friends tried to diagnose Job's spiritual problem as sin or rebellion or pride, Job refused to accept their assessments of his situation—he knew he was righteous. But neither was he willing to "curse God and die," as his wife encouraged him to do.

Okay, so most of us know the story. But have you ever noticed that little verse tucked away at the end of it? "When Job prayed for his friends, the LORD restored his fortunes." Note that it doesn't say, "When his friends had prayed for *him* . . ." It doesn't say, "When Job cried out to God in repentance . . ." No, it's entirely counterintuitive to the way we usually think about prayer—especially when we consider that the list of prayer concerns in most churches includes many, many, many Jobs. People who are hurting. People who are in broken relationships. People who are "down on their luck." People who are weak. And so on.

Something is going on with this passage that runs counter to everything we've assumed about suffering and weakness. *Job* is the one whose prayers matter—Job, the hurting one. Job, whose wife told him to curse God and die. Job, who was as down on his luck as any figure in classic literature. Job, who was weak. Job, who would've been on his church's list of prayer concerns week after week until they were tired of praying for him.

So *what* is going on here?

Job 42:1-17

The Job Factor: Part 2

We've been talking about that surprising little verse toward the end of the book of Job that says, "When Job prayed for his friends, the LORD restored his fortunes" (Job 42:10—see February 4). I'm still working through the implications of this snippet. Remember: Job is the main character in this story because every possible bad thing has happened to him. He's at the lowest point of his life. His friends, meanwhile—the ones who have it all together—come to be with him in the midst of his pain and anguish. They reach out a helping hand. But when they make the mistake of trying to solve Job's problems, God steps in. He tells them to repent and go to Job for prayer.

I'm simply blown away by the whole concept. I mean, when our friends are suffering, we're supposed to pray for *them*, not the other way around, right? When was the last time an inner-city food pantry asked the homeless guests to pray for the ministry? When was the last time a pastor asked a hospital patient to pray for the church? When was the last time we repented by asking the poor to pray for *us*, for once?

I think it goes back to our natural resistance to suffering in general. We think we're supposed to be exempt from it somehow, because we're not *that* bad. We think we can take certain shortcuts in order to attain the kind of wisdom that only comes from walking in the way of the Cross. But what if it's not the ones who are suffering who need to repent? What if it's those of us who supposedly have it all together? What if we went to *them* and said, "Please pray for me because you alone are wise enough to intercede on my behalf"? Shouldn't we be making pilgrimages to cancer wards in order to receive a blessing from the saints in Christ who are there?

It slowly becomes clear from our encounters with Job—and elsewhere throughout the Old and New Testaments—that it's not the people who have it "all together" that have the ear of God. Think of our psalm for the day, Psalm 34. Verse 18 says, "The LORD is close to the brokenhearted; he rescues those whose spirits are crushed." God is near to the brokenhearted, which means that if the rest of us want to get close to God, we seek out the hurting because they're the ones who are nearest to him. We seek them out—not because of what we could possibly offer *them*, as if we're the spiritual first responders on the scene to save the day, but because we recognize how much they have to teach *us* about who God really is.

Psalm 34:17-22

Blessed by Those Who Suffer

Often we're embarrassed, uncomfortable, or downright fearful of spending time with someone who clearly needs help. We'd rather not visit the hospital. We really don't like hanging out with dying people. We avoid the sick, the lonely, the broken, the oppressed. I'm one of the worst culprits in this department. I'm terrified that I won't be able to help them, that I'll say something stupid, that I'll fail them utterly. So we find ourselves avoiding those who are suffering because we think we can't help them or because their vulnerability makes us uncomfortable. But the fact is, we should be seeking them out for a blessing— because they have experienced God in ways the healthy, vibrant, robust, and just plain lucky have not.

The truth is, God meets people in their suffering, which means that the ones among us who have seen God, who are closest to God, aren't the ones who seem to have it all together but the ones who daily battle pain and battle it graciously—our Christian brothers and sisters who know what loss and tragedy are. Those who have suffered well have learned wisdom. They have seen the face of God. So if we want to be blessed by those who are close to him, we should seek out the elderly widows in our churches and say, "Please, please—you who have spoken face-to-face with God—I beg you to pray for me." And what better person to ask than one who, like Job—even in the midst of tremendous pain and loss—can say, "But as for me, I know that my Redeemer lives, and he will stand upon the earth at last" (Job 19:25)? That's the person I want to bless me. That's the one I want to learn from.

We've been talking about Job, the suffering one, and his friends, who seemed to have it all together. And on a certain level his friends are to be commended: They didn't avoid him. Instead, they came and sat with him and shared in his grief. The problem was that they attempted to help by philosophizing about why he was suffering in the first place. But all the same, they didn't abandon him. They stuck around long enough to be a nuisance, sure, but they also stuck around long enough to be blessed.

Are you sticking it out with your hurting friends long enough to experience a blessing? Or are you so busy trying to help them that you miss those moments when *they* want to pray for *you*?

Job 19:21-27

Side Trip with a Blind Man

Remember Jesus' statement about the sick being the ones who know they need a doctor (see Mark 2:13-17)? Today's Gospel story speaks of the blind man Bartimaeus, who had no shame about asking Jesus for help. He hollered out loud until he got everyone's attention, including the ear of the Master. Sure, Bartimaeus was suffering and wanted help from someone he thought held tremendous power—the Healer. But the interesting thing is that this story takes place as Jesus is on his way to Jerusalem for the last time. In fact, just a few verses earlier, Jesus took his disciples aside and very clearly told them what would happen to him once they got to Jerusalem:

> The Son of Man will be betrayed to the leading priests and the teachers of religious law. They will sentence him to die and hand him over to the Romans. They will mock him, spit on him, flog him with a whip, and kill him, but after three days he will rise again.   Mark 10:33-34

So Jesus was well aware of the suffering that was in store for him. He tried several times to convince his own friends that what they would face in Jerusalem was apparent defeat, not victory. Then tucked into these conversations about greatness versus weakness (see Mark 10:35-45) is this little story about a blind man who wouldn't take no for an answer. But what Bartimaeus didn't realize was that he was asking for help from one who would soon suffer far more than the blind man could possibly imagine. Bartimaeus sought Jesus because he thought Jesus was a man of power, but Jesus reached out to help because Jesus is a man of sorrows. He reached out because he knows what it's like to face a future that is dark and without earthly hope.

What about us? When we face our own kinds of suffering, does it occur to us that others might need our help in the midst of it all?

Mark 10:46-52

The Secret of Weakness

So far this week we've been discussing a concept I call "the Secret of Weakness." It's the counterintuitive idea that the ones among us who are weak or suffering—who are the "least of the least"—are in fact the ones closest to God. They are the people God uses to bless the world. Let's explore this concept for a moment through the eyes of someone we usually think of as a strong and unwavering Christian of towering intellect, the author C. S. Lewis.

For the uninitiated, C. S. Lewis was a twentieth-century British scholar and is best known for the children's series The Chronicles of Narnia. He was also famous in his day for his ability to build a logical defense of the Christian faith (*Mere Christianity*). And when you read those writings, it's easy to assume that this was a man of unstinting faith who whipped weak Christians into shape by his robust apologetics and rich imagination. And certainly his writings have done that for many of us, including me.

But one of the things that strikes me about Lewis is his humility, particularly in how often he asked his fans—especially children—to pray for him. Clearly this man knew the Secret of Weakness. In a snippet from the book *C. S. Lewis: Letters to Children*, he wrote to a class of fifth graders, "Best love to you all. When you say your prayers, sometimes ask God to bless me."[6]

At first glance this sounds a bit egotistical. But there he was, one of the intellectual giants of his time, a toweringly brilliant apologist for the Christian faith, and yet he humbly asked the least of the least to pray for him. He never discounted someone's experience of grace, particularly grace in the midst of suffering. I mean, he married a dying woman who was in constant pain for most of their few years together![//] Meanwhile, his brother was an alcoholic, and Lewis himself, toward the end of his life, lived with daily pain from various ailments. But in the midst of it all, his writings blessed millions of readers around the world.

So have you learned the Secret of Weakness?

Isaiah 53:1-6

[//] See the 1993 movie *Shadowlands*, starring Anthony Hopkins and Debra Winger.

Struggling Together

In all this talk about suffering (see February 2–8), we've been focusing on how individuals deal with their personal struggles. But I don't want to forget that we as Christians are part of a larger group of believers called the body of Christ—and when one part of the body is hurting, the others suffer too. Churches go through rough seasons together in which everyone is struggling, and the trick is to not lose sight of the Secret of Weakness (see February 8). What might God be doing through all of us as we suffer together?

It's easy for churches to think of their group struggles as some sort of spiritual liability, as if God will only work through us if we've got it all together. You hear this in meetings, when people say things like, "Well, if only we had more money" or "If only we had a bigger building" or "If only we had a singles' ministry" and so on, blah, blah, blah. We think if only we can become like that vibrant new "seeker" church down the road, then maybe we'll grow. Or if only we did worship in a certain way. Or if only we could come to some sort of theological consensus. Or if only we weren't hit with one tragedy after another. If only, if only . . .

But the Secret of Weakness is not primarily about what God is trying to teach *us* in the midst of our struggles but how God wants to bless *others* in the midst of our struggles.

People seek out the church, not necessarily because Christians are strong and vibrant and healthy and have it all together, but because the honest Christians have known what it is like to be weak. They have known suffering. They have felt the stab of pain and loss. They have held each other in their sorrow—they have knelt at the beds of dying friends, prayed in the ER, handed tissues to someone at the end of a rough day. And the reason people come through the sanctuary doors week after week is not because Christians have it all together or have eliminated suffering from their schedules but because they are still able to say, after all this, "We know that our Redeemer lives."//

The world is looking for saints to pray with who have known the depths of weakness, because that's where this world is. It doesn't want light, fluffy spirituality. It wants to kneel next to the Jobs who have seen the face of God. And that's what we as a Christian community can be for the hurting. Our pain and suffering are not some kind of spiritual liability. They're how God positions us to bless others.

1 Corinthians 12:12, 22-27

// See Job 19:25.

Obsessed

Okay, enough dark and serious stuff! It's time to switch gears. February, as we approach Valentine's Day, seems an appropriate time to tackle the subject of love and relation-ships. There was a season in my life when this was the *only* subject I could concentrate on—okay, obsess about—so I've raided my college journals to see what kinds of spiritual lessons I was learning in the midst of my general boy craziness. And I stumbled upon an incident that I'd almost forgotten from my freshman year, an incident that my husband, Tom, now claims was an act of God, steering me away from stupidity so Tom could marry me later. A rather flattering spin on the whole thing, actually. But it was mortifying at the time.

Here's what happened. One Saturday I decided to fast—go without food for the whole day—so I could concentrate on prayer and devotions. For some unknown reason I decided to read in the dining hall during the lunch hour, even though I couldn't eat anything. There I was, trying to be deeply spiritual, when I looked up and a guy was stand-ing next to my table. We'll call him Nick. Nick was someone I'd noticed before, mostly because he'd developed the unnerving habit of staring at me from across crowded rooms. At first I had thought it was merely coincidental, but eventually it became obvious. I had even asked my friends, "Okay, am I crazy, or is that guy staring at me?" They'd glance at him for a moment and then say, "You're not crazy. He's definitely staring." So Nick was no stranger, though I don't think we'd ever formally met.

(I should add parenthetically that it wasn't like I was used to being stared at. I hadn't once been asked on a date since arriving at college. Tom says this was all part of God's plan, of course.)

Okay, so there was Nick, standing nervously by my table. And before I could say, "Hi," he blurted out, "Um, some friends and I are going downtown for dinner and stuff tonight—would you like to come with me?" There was an awkward pause. I put down my book, being enough of a literary geek to catch the irony in this situation. Here I was *fast-ing*, and I had just been asked out to *dinner* by my first potential college date ever.

I took a deep breath and babbled something like, "I don't mean to sound hyper-spiritual or anything, but I'm fasting today. I just wouldn't be a very fun person to have around." I babbled some other stuff too, after which he nodded and shrugged and said, "Okay, well, another time, then," and walked back to his table.

I'd like to say I was able to return to my book and concentrate on prayer and devotions for the rest of the day. Not quite.

Isn't it amazing how easily we let the thrill of potential romance derail us from whatever spiritual headway we think we're making?

Proverbs 4:20-27

Rash Promises

In the reading for February 10, I described a whacky romantic, er . . . awkward encounter that happened during my freshman year of college, in which I turned down a dinner date because I was, of all things, *fasting*. Oh, the irony! Here's an excerpt from my journal at the time, after I'd spent several days thinking how nice it might've been to go out with Nick after all:

> I keep wishing for Nick to call and ask me out a second time, so I neglect to make plans for Friday or Saturday because I just assume I'll be busy—on a date with Nick. Then when I sit and think about it, I realize it's entirely possible that he'll never ask again, and my gut response is what a nuisance it was that I happened to be fasting the day he asked me out. What a twisted thought! Spending time with God is a *nuisance*? And me feeling so pious at the time because I refused to go when I had made a prior spiritual commitment, and then feeling the gnawing regret afterward. . . . Ah, yes: Sarah, the martyr. Well, if I had entered into the fast with the right attitude in the first place, I wouldn't have felt regret about the things I had to refuse along the way.
>
> I should feel *joy* that God has called me to be totally his, that I can express my dependence on him by giving up other distractions! I wouldn't have been totally God's if I had gone on the date. And what is so odd is that I had no desire at the time to go, because my desire to stick with my fast was stronger. The temptation came *afterward* in the form of self-satisfaction that I had been asked, frustration that I couldn't go, expectancy that Nick would ask me again (or shall we say self-confidence), and even a little spark of pride that thought, *Oh, I was so good for refusing; surely God will reward me by allowing me another opportunity.*
>
> The writer of Ecclesiastes was right: "It is better to say nothing than to make a promise and not keep it" (Ecclesiastes 5:5).

This all seems like such a long time ago, and yet I still have that same gut reaction whenever I have to give up something fun because I've made a prior spiritual commitment. First comes the smug self-satisfaction that I'm such a good person; then comes the irritation that I'm missing out. If I can't have the right attitude, what's the point of making the commitment in the first place?

Ecclesiastes 5:1-7

The Testing Ground

If you're wondering whatever happened to my potential relationship with "Nick," the guy who asked me out during my freshman year of college, the answer is nothing. At least, nothing happened with Nick. A whole lot happened with *me*, however. Here's another excerpt from my journal at the time:

> So now I've been given a new option for a romantic adventure, a new possibility in the relationship arena, a new face to watch for, a new gaze to catch, a new set of friends to observe, a new voice to strain to hear, a new person to imagine is watching me as I stroll into the dining hall, a new feeling to feel when the phone rings, a new schedule to stealthily figure out, a new name to listen for, a new character to catch tidbits and passing comments about . . . a whole new obsession.
>
> In all the people I see or imagine are watching me, in all these people I imagine a little Nick. I'm constantly wondering, *Am I being watched? Am I being thought about, speculated about, talked about, and generally found interesting from afar?* And it strikes me how backward all this is. Instead of seeing every person as a little Nick, I should be seeing every person as a *little Jesus*—because, as Jesus himself said, whatever I do unto them, I do unto him (see Matthew 25:37-40). Whenever I treat others with respect, take interest in their character, listen to them, care for them (feed them, clothe them, take them into my home, in other words), I am doing so as if they were *Jesus*, not someone else. My perspective is so warped!
>
> Elisabeth Elliot[7] was right in saying there is no greater testing ground for faith than the arena of love and relationships.

I had just discovered firsthand how a love interest can derail our spiritual journeys. Every ounce of energy that we once threw into our relationships with God we now throw at a human being who will ultimately disappoint us. We worry about how to please this new person rather than how to please God, and thus our spiritual lives come to a screeching halt.

The only cure is to fix our eyes on Jesus and, through him, to reach out to those in our hurting world who need his love. Romance is a testing ground for this kind of faith.

1 Corinthians 7:32-35

Slow Growth

The "dating" saga from my college journals continues with one final installment (this is the last one, I promise!):

Well, so much for my ridiculous imaginings. Much dreaming is meaningless (see Ecclesiastes 5:7, NIV). Last night I sat next to Nick at a movie (dumb idea in the first place), and we didn't really talk. In fact, he turned his back to me and talked down the row and didn't even say, "See ya" when he left, a million little wisps of fortune cookie slips fluttering after him in my mind. And there I was, miserable with myself, sick of it all, desperately seeking a friend who is real . . . wanting Jesus to be a reality that I can feel.

So this morning in church I found myself kneeling before the cross at the prayer rail during Communion, sobbing my heart out and being comforted by two wonderful women I'd never seen before in my life. I keep thinking it's got to be me, that I've got to work harder, try harder at this relationship thing, and all the while I'm stunned by the failures, by the sense of shame that I'm somehow embarrassing to people once they get to know me. And meanwhile I know I'm growing and maturing spiritually on the inside, but it doesn't seem fast enough.

What the women reminded me today is that internal spiritual growth may seem lightning fast, but the external takes time, and you must not be trapped by thinking that it's all going to happen quickly or that you'll see visible signs of change overnight. If your outward faith is struggling—particularly in the relationship department—be patient with yourself. In the midst of it all, *you* are to be the one who is receptive, humble, open, selfless—and Jesus will come the rest of the way to meet you. To learn how to walk, you must have his hand removed and take a few falls before you can walk on your own.

Part of me still has the emotional bruises from all those falls, but the women were right. Spiritual maturity takes time, but eventually we begin to walk on our own, with our chins up, following in the footsteps of Jesus.

Ephesians 3:14-21

Valentine

One of the main reasons I'm able to hold my head up and not feel ashamed about who I am in Christ is due to the loving support of my husband, Tom. We've been married now for almost ten years (yes, we were just kids when we got engaged—ha!), and each day I'm reminded by my wonderful husband that Jesus loves me just the way I am, that I'm intelligent and beautiful and worth being around day after day.

And even though my parents told me all those things while I was growing up, it was easy to forget that kind of love in middle school, where everyone tells you daily just how stupid and worthless you are. High school wasn't much better. That's why I was so excited to go to a Christian college, because I thought maybe people there would be saner, more loving. And to some extent they were, but it's hard to shake all those cruel habits from junior high. There were still cliques and clubs, snubs and slights, self-centeredness and jealousies. After a while I began to wonder how anyone could ever find someone to marry in the midst of such silliness.

Then one Saturday morning during the spring semester of my senior year, I hopped into the van that took our group of volunteers to an inner-city ministry once a week. I'd been in Africa for the previous semester, so there were some new volunteers I hadn't yet met—just kids, really, including a sophomore named Tom, who sat in the seat behind me. Apparently Tom took one look at my sun-browned skin, my carefree attitude, and the long dreadlocks hanging down my back and found the whole package rather intriguing. So he yanked on one of my braids. Hard.

If this sounds like an *Anne of Green Gables* flashback, don't worry: I didn't smash anything over his head. But I *was* annoyed and hollered, "Ow!" And so began our legendary romance.

We progressed quickly from silliness to serious conversations and eventually to lifelong commitment, which we still believe is worth diving into sooner rather than later when it's clear this is the person God has for you. God's love is the web that binds us together from year to year, and in the meantime we're not afraid to verbalize how beloved the other is. I can hold my head up high because my husband believes I'm "more precious than rubies" (Proverbs 31:10)—and he tells me so daily.

Are there other treasured people to whom I can express my love this Valentine's Day?

Proverbs 31:10-31

The Relational Bank Account

Grad school hasn't been easy for my husband lately. He's inundated with papers and quizzes on a daily basis, with no end in sight. So I don't see much of him. He goes off to school early in the morning, comes home, eats dinner, and then studies until bedtime. Which is why the spouses of seminarians have been nicknamed "seminary widows," I suppose. Not a pleasant image, but it's awfully close to reality, in my experience.

Of course, my husband feels bad about it. But this isn't the first time one of us has been overly busy. Back in the days when I was a full-time youth director, I would be gone for weeks at a time on mission trips and camp trips, service projects and retreats. You might say Tom was a "youth ministry widower." Neither of us liked it very much, and eventually I realized it wasn't the vocation for me. (I'd rather be a youth ministry volunteer anyway!)

All marriages will go through stressful times. One or the other spouse will be extended beyond his or her ability to contribute much to the relationship, and unless you've spent significant time pouring love into one another, the emotional well can dry up. That's why from the beginning Tom and I envisioned what we call our Relational Bank Account (I can't remember where we got this idea, but it wasn't ours. Tom thinks it was from a marriage guru named Gary Smalley). We make lots of "deposits" in the account when we can—through date nights and time alone, through snuggling and talking and being affectionate—so that our account is full to overflowing. Then when the busy times come, the stressed-out spouse can make "withdrawals" as needed—while the other takes care of household chores, runs errands, rearranges the schedule to fit the other person's, etc.—and hopefully the account is never depleted.

It's not hard to transfer the concept of the Relational Bank Account to our relationships with God. Have you deposited anything in your spiritual account lately, or is God your "vocational widower" (or "school widower" or "sports widower" or "Internet widower" or "fill-in-the-blank widower")?

Hosea 2:19-20

The Little Things

In the reading for February 15, I talked about how my husband and I keep what we call a Relational Bank Account: We make emotional deposits on a daily basis so that when times are stressful, we can make withdrawals without depleting the account.

What amazes me is how the little deposits are the ones that actually give us the biggest bang for our buck. Greeting each other with a hug and a kiss when one of us comes home or praying together in the morning is sometimes all it takes to fill the account right up. My husband doesn't have to take me on an anniversary trip to the Florida Keys, and I don't have to cook a six-course meal every evening in order to put our account in the black (which is a good thing because not only are we broke most of the time, but *I can't cook at all*). Unlike what popular culture would like us to believe, we don't have to spend hundreds of dollars on each other to make ourselves feel all mushy inside.

Once again, let's transfer this concept to our relationship with God. All throughout Scripture, the relationship of God to believers is that of a divine marriage. Starting with the nation of Israel, in the Old Testament, God has loved and taken care of his people with "an everlasting love" (Jeremiah 31:3); his people, meanwhile, have attempted (well, sort of) to live as a faithful spouse in return. The same is true for us today. Too often we seem to think God is only impressed when we do something financially huge for him, such as support a missionary in Bolivia or donate money to build a gym onto the church. But then I can't help thinking about the poor widow in today's Gospel story, who gave just two small coins—which was everything she had. . . .

So if you were God, which would you rather have: a spouse who throws money at the relationship once or twice a year in the hopes that it will impress you, or a spouse who checks in with you daily, tells you how much you're loved, asks your opinion on small matters, and generally sticks close by?

Luke 21:1-4

Hold Tightly

I remember when my parents first sat me down and had the "sex talk" with me. (Honestly: Who could forget it?) Unlike my friends' parents, who talked as if sex were an "act," like brushing your teeth or taking out the garbage, completely disconnected from the rest of life, my parents made it clear that sex is so much more: It was designed by God to happen within a committed marital relationship. You're not just a free agent, doing this on your own because it feels good. You're in a relationship with someone. Sex is communication—that's what the word *intercourse* means, after all—and genuine communication can't happen unless two people are fully connected with one another. Connected, committed, married.

In the midst of the conversation, my dad pointed to his wedding ring and said something like, "When you get married, there will be people who don't respect this ring. They will try to seduce you into being unfaithful to your spouse. But don't fall for their lies. This ring means you're committed, period. That's the promise you make before God and everyone. Stand on the side of your marriage."

Now that I've been married for a while, I realize just how wise my father was in preparing me for how the world operates. Popular culture definitely doesn't stand on the side of marriage. All around us—in the media, especially—is the glorification of infidelity. Married people flirt with other married people. Both my husband and I have dealt with people who have no respect for the rings we wear. Divorce is considered normal. But in the midst of it all, I hear the words of Paul, the first missionary, admonishing us to "hate what is wrong. Hold tightly to what is good" (Romans 12:9).

Because if we don't hold tightly to our marriage, who will?

Romans 12:9-11

Weak Desires

The ancient Greeks had a legend about the island of the Sirens, a place of foul creatures that sang like angels to lure men from their ships, only to devour them in cold blood. According to the stories, no man could resist their song; it was a seductive spell that forced all men to jump overboard. Knowing this, the hero Ulysses (of *Iliad* and *Odyssey* fame), while sailing home from war, learned of the way to save his crew: He plugged up their ears with wax so they wouldn't be lured by the music. He, however, wanted to hear the Sirens, so he had his men tie him to the mast. They did so, and sure enough, as they passed the island, Ulysses strained at the ropes and begged to be freed. But soon the Sirens were out of hearing, and Ulysses was himself again.

Another tale speaks of young Orpheus, the greatest musician and poet of ancient Greece. His music had the power to enchant all living things, so when he joined another hero named Jason and his shipmates on their journey past the island of the Sirens, he wasn't worried. He simply played music more beautiful and more enchanting and more worthy of attention than anything the Sirens could have sung. And so he saved the entire crew.

Harry Emerson Fosdick calls the image of Ulysses tied to the mast "a picture of many a man's pitiful attempts after negative goodness."[8] In other words, people try to resist sin by creating elaborate systems to protect themselves, often to their own detriment. They concentrate so much on the negative allure of sin that they forget how powerfully compelling God's promises are to those who walk in righteousness.

So the issue isn't the lure of surface vices but our lack of desire for all that God promises us—for the abundant life Jesus offers. C. S. Lewis wrote:

> Our Lord finds our desires, not too strong, but too weak. We are half-hearted creatures, fooling about with drink and sex and ambition when infinite joy is offered us, like an ignorant child who wants to go on making mud pies in a slum because he cannot imagine what is meant by the offer of a holiday at the sea. We are far too easily pleased.[9]

And so I pray:

> *Lord, help us to seek the abundant life you offer, so we are no longer attracted by sin but are able to "[conquer] sin by surpassing it."[10] Amen.*

Galatians 5:19-25

Again

I've been reading through the book of Judges—or rather, reading a chapter now and then as time and memory allow (you know how it goes)—and recently the opening line of chapter 13 got my attention: "Again the Israelites did evil in the Lord's sight. . . ." It was the *again* that jumped out at me. Obviously there was a pattern developing there, but I'd been reading the book so slowly that I'd lost track of the thematic thread.

So I skimmed back through Judges from the beginning and realized what I'd been missing was a phrase that's used over and over to introduce each new episode—"Again the Israelites did evil" (see Judges 3:7, 12; 4:1-2; 6:1; 10:6-8; etc.)—always paired with this curious little phrase: "So the Lord handed them over to [insert enemy here]." This is significant. The point isn't just that the Israelites kept messing up. The point is that every time they did, they lost their freedom.

How many *agains* are to be encountered in our lives? We turn away, and God steps in and helps us—he brings people into our lives who tell us the truth, for example—and for a while we repent and attempt to get ourselves on track. But then the material attractions of the world glitter before our eyes, or we receive the attentions of popular people, and before long we are no longer interested in spiritual things but start chasing after the things of this world. *Again* is a lifestyle, an ongoing pattern of resistance to the living God. And it's not without consequences: Sooner or later he turns us over to the things we crave. He hands us over to other masters who do not love us—to what we thought we wanted.

Are material possessions what you're chasing after? Fine, God says—I'll hand you over to those things until you're a modern-day slave trapped in bondage to credit card debt. Is it sexual pleasure that you crave? Okay, God says—I'll hand you over to every indulgence until you can no longer feel anything at all. Or what about romance? Sure, God says— I'll hand you over to another human being until you experience how similar love can be to hatred in the end. Is it popularity you want? Go for it, God says. I'll hand you over to your heroes until you can no longer speak or breathe without needing their permission.

And so on and so forth. How many *agains* are there to be in my life before I recognize my worthless idols for what they are?

Judges 13:1

Inner Strength?

If you've been reading through this devotional over the past few weeks, you've probably begun to notice that I've shifted from the theme of romance and relationships to the subject of righteousness, or being in right relationship with God and others. While I'm at it, I'd like to debunk the popular notion that we all have an "inner source" of strength or life force or whatever, which we must discover in order to be good or overcome the problems in our lives. It's the subtle distortion of the Christian truth that we must turn to no one but God for true strength—and since God is supposedly inside all of us, we must turn inward to discover the source of strength we need, right?

To me it seems the opposite. I believe it's when we turn inward, only to find our spiritual well is dry and empty, that we finally realize just how desperate our situation really is. When a person look insides herself and discovers (to her horror) that she is in fact nothing, it is precisely this horror that drives her either to take her own life or to fall on her knees before God's throne of grace, begging to be filled. If a person *does* find some kind of "inner strength" inside, it's most likely nothing more than the will to survive—something which every living creature is born with. But it is only power for the moment, like spiritual adrenaline, and then the individual moves back into the same complacency that lulled her into ignoring her inner vacuity in the first place.

Jesus tells us that he is the vine, and we are only branches; apart from him we can do nothing (see John 15:5). It is only when we, like beggars, have seen in ourselves the horror of spiritual emptiness and turned to the God who fills us that we can say, like Paul, "I can do everything through Christ, who gives me strength" (Philippians 4:13). Long afterward—once we have continually put ourselves in God's presence, day in and day out—is when our spiritual wells begin to fill with living water and overflow into any circumstance or problem we encounter.

John 15:1-8

Spiritual Discipline vs. Legalism

It's easy to beat ourselves up about all the ways we fail to do what God has commanded for our spiritual health or the renewal of our communities. We make commitments and then bemoan our inability to keep them. We vow to read the Bible and do our devotions every day, but instead we cram all the readings into one frantic morning a week (or less). Pretty soon our lack of initiative feels hopeless, and we give up trying altogether.

On the one hand, it's important that we don't take ourselves too seriously or become legalistic about this whole faith thing. The last thing we want is a kind of "works-righteousness" mentality, in which we try to win God's approval by doing good deeds—and if we fail to keep it up, we're afraid God will be furious and punish us. If we ever reach that state, it's important to take a step back and say, "Okay, stop. This isn't about what I do for God but about what God has done for me." Because Jesus lived a sinless life and died on our behalf, said the apostle Paul, we have freedom from the bondage of religious legalism (see today's text). Jesus *is* our righteousness.

But this doesn't mean we become spiritual slugs either. Over the centuries, Christians have identified several spiritual practices, or intentional behaviors, that bring us into the presence of God and help us grow. These include prayer, Bible study, worship, solitude, silence, fasting—all of which Jesus himself did during the course of his life and ministry. These practices are also known as spiritual *disciplines*—not because they're some kind of punishment, but because this is what *disciples*, or followers, do (notice that *discipline* comes from the root word *disciple*).

In the end, we don't practice the spiritual disciplines because we're trying to make God happy, like yet another form of religious legalism; we practice them because they draw us closer into a personal relationship with the living God.

How can we expect to get to know him if we never spend any time in his presence?

Romans 3:21-28

Vanity, Vanity

During my semester in East Africa, I washed all my clothes by hand on the rooftop of the dorm and then hung them to dry. I remember feeling especially crabby one morning about my inability to overcome the persistent sin in my life, despite all the "good deeds" I kept stacking up in my calendar. And this crabbiness deepened as I tackled the mundane task of laundry. So I wrote:

I'm doing my good works today.
That's what my little self is thinking
as she plunges her hands into water and soap,
washing clothes.
These good works,
this self-righteousness, this careful
scrutiny of my spiritual actions
in everyone's eyes
—this is all filthy rags.
I am scrubbing,
Lord knows.
I'm scrubbing and bending
fingernails and watching my fingers
turn dead-white at the tips
while the water gets darker and darker
till it's no longer water,
and I say to my little self in the mirror
dimly, "What are you doing?
You love this dirt, this sin,
and yet you do what you can
to scrub it all out—
and for what?
Only to get dirty all over again?"

Vanity, vanity, all is vanity . . .

I plunge my hands into the water

. . . all is filthy rags.

Isaiah 64:5-7

The Means of Grace

I've already mentioned the importance of the spiritual disciplines—those daily practices that bring us into the presence of God, such as prayer, Bible study, worship, silence, service, etc. (see February 21). This is different than legalism, which is an attempt to do good works in order to somehow "earn" God's approval. Unfortunately, a lot of people seem to think we can earn our way to heaven this way too, by chalking up more good points than bad points on God's cosmic ledger or whatever. I'm not kidding—I seriously heard a member of my local congregation turn down an opportunity to volunteer because, he claimed, "I've done my time this week already."

As if this is prison or something. Anyway, Christians throughout the centuries have affirmed that there's no possible way we could chalk up enough good deeds. The Bible says that on our own power we are incapable of living holy and righteous lives, because "everyone has sinned; we all fall short of God's glorious standard" (see Romans 3:23). Only by surrendering our lives to Jesus can we enter the Kingdom of Heaven with a clean slate; because it's *his* slate God is reading, not ours.

Yeah, yeah, I'm sure you've heard all this before. So now the operative question becomes (if we're really honest): Why do any of these spiritual disciplines matter if I'm "saved" and going to heaven anyway?

Hmm. Good question. The eighteenth-century evangelist John Wesley tackled it this way: He affirmed that our salvation from sin is indeed important—he called it "justifying grace," in which God gives us a clean slate through the death and resurrection of Jesus Christ. It's a free gift that we can't earn and don't deserve. But Wesley also affirmed that *after* we're saved, there's still important spiritual work to do. We are to be holy "just as God . . . is holy" (1 Peter 1:15), which means we are to become more and more like Jesus over the course of our many years on this earth. Wesley called this "sanctifying grace"— *sanctification* being the process of becoming more holy, more like Jesus. Just as our salvation from sin was a free gift, so is the pursuit of holiness.

Sanctification happens through God's Holy Spirit at work in us whenever we participate in the same spiritual disciplines that Jesus himself practiced. Wesley called these practices the "means of grace," or the ways we experience the transformative power of God's grace in our everyday lives. The spiritual disciplines aren't the doorway to heaven, but they are the doorway to the presence of God here on earth. What if others followed us through it?

1 Peter 1:15-16

Courageous Action

> What we failed to understand was that a life incapable of significant sacrifice is also
> incapable of courageous action.   Urban T. Holmes III[11]

The profundity of the above sentence always strikes me when I read it in *A Guide to Prayer
for Ministers and Other Servants* each year, but it's particularly cutting this morning for
some reason. I hear and stand convicted—convicted of my inability and unwillingness to
sacrifice, convicted, too, of my own cowardice and fear. Courageous action has rarely char-
acterized my life, and this fault is more and more evident the longer I am married.

My husband is a man of extraordinary integrity—this I can truly say even as I'm
fully aware of his faults (albeit endearing ones). He strives for purposefulness and inten-
tionality. He sees very few decisions as spiritually neutral—for example, we no longer shop
or stop for gas on Sundays if we can possibly help it, because that would mean someone
else is unable to keep the Sabbath due to our greed(!). He makes people uncomfortable by
exposing their self-centeredness *without saying a word*. He does this simply by how he
lives and how he reflects on that living.

And while everyone around him—including me—is telling him to stop being so
uptight or so hard on himself, it soon becomes obvious that our complaining is, again, self-
ishly motivated. We're uncomfortable in the presence of such integrity; it makes us all too
aware of our own moral laxness. But he plunges ahead in his practical pursuit of righteousness anyway, and I find myself plunging along with him—mostly by default, since I'm still
naturally selfish, generally speaking.

He is a gift to me. He makes me a better person than I would ever be on my own.
It's an honor, a challenge, and a spiritual discipline to be married to this man. I'm not
saying this lightly. Christians throughout the centuries have called the sacraments a
"means of grace," or one of the spiritual disciplines that brings us into an experience of
God, and generally the sacraments are limited to baptism and Communion. But in some
traditions, marriage is also a sacrament. As far as the way marriage brings me into God's
presence, convicts me of sin, shows me grace and forgiveness, and crafts me ever more
fully into the image of Christ—it is indeed a sacrament, a way to enter into the presence
of Jesus.

So Tom is not only my spouse but a means of grace to me.

Who is a means of grace in your life? How can you play that role for someone else?

Philippians 2:12-16

You Can't Take Credit for This

How much of my spiritual growth depends on me—on my commitment, hard work, and tears—and how much depends on the Holy Spirit?

I'll attempt to make sense of this question by telling a story. When I spent a semester as an exchange student at a university in Nairobi, Kenya (East Africa), several of us American Christians became involved in an indigenous ministry to street children. In the meantime, we also made friends with our fellow students and various middle-class families who seemed oblivious to the poverty on their own streets. They were intrigued by our work with poor children. "Why would you want to do that?" they'd ask, as if the kids were somehow less than human and not worth our time.

I remember having a picnic with two of our friends one Sunday afternoon after they'd observed us buying groceries for the little boy who stood begging at the church exit every week. "You're not like the other Americans," one of our friends said to us. "And you're not like us. You do things we never would have thought of. Why are you different?"

This was one of those moments when the Holy Spirit must have given me the words to say, because I'm usually a flustered, bumbling fool whenever someone asks about my "Christian hope" (see I Peter 3:15). Without hesitation I picked up my Bible, turned to Ephesians 2:8-10, and read aloud these verses:

> God saved you by his grace when you believed. And you can't take credit for this;
> it is a gift from God. Salvation is not a reward for the good things we have done,
> so none of us can boast about it. For we are God's masterpiece. He has created us
> anew in Christ Jesus, so we can do the good things he planned for us long ago.

I explained that what they saw in us was Jesus, nothing more and nothing less. We couldn't take credit for any of it.

The next weekend they joined us at the ministry center, lugging a huge duffel bag of clothes they didn't need anymore.

Ephesians 2:8-10

For His Name's Sake

It strikes me lately in reading the biblical prophets and psalms that God's insistence on our personal righteousness isn't for our sake at all, but *for the sake of his name*. The psalmist wrote, "He guides me along right paths, bringing honor to his name" (Psalm 23:3), which indicates that if I *don't* follow the right paths, God's name is dishonored in the world. His reputation is threatened by my actions. His name is debased because of the selfish and sinful behavior of his own people—the people who claim his name as the defining identity of their lives, the people of God, followers of Christ, Christians.

So his interest in our spiritual growth isn't really about us in the end. He isn't *primarily* interested in our good behavior or emotional health, much less our personal happiness—although those are often by-products. Rather, he transforms us so we can be light in a dark world, leading people to him, so that when people see our good works, they don't see us at all but praise our Father in heaven (see Matthew 5:1-16). Our actions are to be utterly selfless so his name is exalted in all the earth. In the meantime, he *does* change our lives for the better, renewing our sense of identity and purpose, restoring us emotion-ally, even allowing us deep and abiding moments of joy. But what is *really* at stake is his reputation.

I may be operating with the right intentions and in complete honesty, but if I give others the impression that I'm living otherwise, it's not just *their* problem. The visible life of the individual Christian—and of Christians together—should be markedly different from that of the world. Observers shouldn't have to probe beneath the surface to find where the differences are. Certainly, beneath the surface is what really matters in the spiritual life—inner holiness and conviction are where the spiritual rubber meets the road. But ulti-mately, righteousness is not a private matter. The goal of righteous living is not to benefit ourselves, in the end, but to give glory to the One whose name we bear. It is for the sake of his name—his reputation in the eyes of the world—that we live as we do.

Ezekiel 36:16-23

What Am I "Working On"?

Periodically I become concerned that I'm not "working on" anything in my spiritual life, that I'm not concentrating on a certain spiritual project, such as practicing the fruit of the Spirit or holding my tongue or going through a prayer list. But perhaps that's not what I'm being called to right now. Perhaps I'm simply being called to soak myself in Scripture and other spiritual writings and to at least get my thoughts on paper.

And maybe that is enough: to marinate myself in these things for so long that in time I begin to take on their flavor. Eventually I do begin to hold my tongue, not because I've made some vow that I can't possibly keep on my own strength, but because the Spirit is at work in me. Eventually I do begin to intentionally intercede for others in prayer, not because I've made some list of prayer requests that I'll eventually forget about, but because the Spirit compels me. And aren't these changes, even now, already happening?

As the darkness outside this window gradually shifts to lighter hues, imperceptibly moving to dawn, so too our spirits, nurtured and bathed and marinated in God's presence, gradually grow and change—even if we can't mark the changes.

Work on me, O God, when I am too weary, too scattered to work on myself. Change me like a predawn sky that slides into sunrise through no effort of its own but rather by your bidding. I love you. Amen.

Philippians 2:12-13

Getting in Shape

This time of year people seem to wake up a bit from their winter hibernation and decide they should probably start eating better and getting some exercise. I see more people jogging on campus now than I did during the holidays. After all, spring break isn't that far off, and people probably decide it's a good idea to shake some of the leftover holiday fat before squeezing into that bathing suit. Of course, eating healthy is good for us all year round, but there's something about the onset of winter that turns us into bears and badgers, stuffing ourselves during the holidays and then sleeping it off for the next couple of months until spring. Isn't it odd how animal-like we can be?

Maybe that's why Christians in ancient times established the season of Lent for this time of year in the church calendar. The word *Lenten* is linked to the Old English word for spring and signifies the forty days leading up to Easter Sunday (not including Sundays). In ancient times, new converts to Christianity were baptized on Easter, so those forty days were a time of repentance, self-denial, and training. Basically, they were getting in shape for the big event when they publicly confessed their faith in Jesus and joined the church family. They shook off their spiritual hibernation and began a new life in Christ.

To this day, the season before Easter is a time when many Christians repent from and change those ways in which they've failed to give themselves fully to God. Many Christians fast, or go without food (or particular kinds of food), on and off throughout those seven weeks, which is why the day before Lent begins has become known as Fat Tuesday. In other words, people pig out before the long stretch of self-denial.

Lent begins this week, and I'm trying to decide what spiritual (and even physical) exercises to do as my commitment to God for the next forty days. Should I fast from lunch once a week? Should I stop drinking coffee (*gasp!*)? Should I get up early and pray more? Should I limit myself to one hour online a day? If I try to tackle it all, I'll be overwhelmed and won't do any of it. But if I don't tackle anything that would help me grow spiritually, what does that say about my genuine commitment to Jesus?

1 Corinthians 9:24-27

Ashes to Ashes

It was 77 degrees and sunny, and all the trees were flowering as I drove to church for the noon Ash Wednesday service today—a strange irony, since the first day of Lent is about sin, death, and repentance, not sunshine and new life. When I arrived, there were only six of us plus the pastor. Four old ladies, a young grandson, and me. Not exactly a hyped-up, plugged-in, rocking-out worship experience, but then again, neither is Lent.

Lent is the season when we remember the sacrifice Jesus made for us on the cross, which is why it begins with ashes. Ashes symbolize death: the death that all of us will face one day, the death our sins bring, the death that Jesus died for us. When the first humans committed the first sin against God, their punishment was clear: "You [will] return to the ground from which you were made. For you were made from dust, and to dust you will return" (Genesis 3:19). Since we're their spiritual great-great-great-great (times 1,000 or so) grandchildren, we are the heirs of that choice. Ashes to ashes, dust to dust.

Sin costs. It consumes whatever it touches, like a flame to a pile of wood. It turns beautiful things to ashes. Because of this, I know that being a Christian means becoming a firefighter against the sin in my own life. I can't become lazy and let the "small" sins smolder just because they don't seem to be hurting anyone. And I can't just sit there and let injustice or poverty or suffering go unnoticed either. Lent is the time when I suit up in my firefighting gear and attack even the small blazes in my own life and in my community before they get out of control.

That's why I go to the Ash Wednesday service on the first day of Lent, even though there's hardly anyone else there, and it's a beautiful sunny day, and I'd rather be outside. I go to church, and the pastor puts his thumb in a little bowl of ashes and makes the messy mark of a cross on my forehead. For the rest of the day I look like a firefighter who just battled a blaze.

It's a reminder of how much my sin cost the Savior.

Genesis 3:1-19

Turn Our Plates

Yesterday a friend of mine suggested we "turn our plates" and give up lunch today in order to concentrate on all the prayer requests that keep piling up in our church. I'd never heard that phrase "turn our plates" before, but it makes a lot of symbolic sense. When we fast, instead of piling our plates with food, we are in essence turning them over and placing them facedown on the table. The overturned plate becomes a visible symbol of our self-denial and reminds us to pray for the requests before us. We can do this wherever we are: at school, at work, at home.

But of course, that's easy to say. Now comes the hard part of actually doing it.

I've already mentioned that fasting—going without certain things, such as food or TV—is a big part of Lent (see February 28). In the past I've experienced how difficult it is for me to fast from a meal when I'm home alone, how it gives me a headache and makes me crabby and causes me to be generally unproductive all day. Well, it's all still true. I'm feeling it right now.

Yet it seems a little easier today than it has in the past, and I think it's because I've taken the idea of "turning my plate" literally. At noon—instead of merely trying to ignore that it was lunchtime like I usually do when I'm fasting—I went into the kitchen, pulled a plate out of the cupboard, poured myself a glass of water, and sat down at the table with my empty plate in front of me. Then I prayed a prayer of thanks for my fast(!) before taking the plate in my hands and very deliberately turning it over. Sitting there during the lunch hour sipping water, looking at my overturned plate, and praying through the list of prayer requests was a powerful reminder that I am, in fact, *giving up* food, not merely trying to *ignore* it.

As I go through the rest of the day, my plate is still over there on the table, face down, visible from every part of our main living space. Does it stop my stomach from growling? No. Does it make the full cupboard any less tempting? No. But it visibly reminds me that I've made a decision. And somehow that helps.

What other visible reminders can I put in my life to represent the decisions I've made for God?

Isaiah 58:1-7

Giving and Giving Up

Today I received an e-mail from an old friend. She wrote, "The beginning of Lent always makes me think of you, and I hear you say that it isn't necessarily about giving up something; it is just as much about giving something. And then I think fondly of breakfast and the gathering and sharing that took place during my senior year." The memory makes me grin.

That was the year a handful of girls from church decided we needed to meet weekly during Lent to encourage each other in our faith. Since everyone was already extremely busy with extra commitments, we decided to get up early and have breakfast together before class—even though some of us were definitely *not* morning people. So that first week of Lent, the eight of us met at the local pancake house to kick off six weeks of mutual commitment.

Funny how much easier it is to get up early and spend time reading the Bible and praying when you know seven other people are counting on you! Not only do they expect you to show up at 6:30 a.m. for breakfast, but they expect you to share something worth getting together and praying about. I know faith isn't supposed to be a legalistic list of rules and behaviors—as if God were a genie who only responds when we say the magic words in the right order—but I do know this: I'm a healthier and more mature Christian when I've set myself some spiritual goals and others have promised to keep me accountable to those goals. It's easier to keep running a marathon when you know your best friend is waiting at mile ten to cheer you on.

It's no surprise that once Lent was over, the group decided to keep meeting through the end of the school year. Sure, Lent is about giving up things. And that year we gave up some sleep to meet for breakfast once a week. But Lent is also about giving things. My friends gave me their time and support, but they also shared their honest struggles and doubts—they gave *themselves*.

How could I take that for granted?

Colossians 3:5-10

Spiritual ADD

I'm not sure what happened to my afternoon. One moment it was lunchtime and I was casually checking my e-mail, and the next moment it was almost dinnertime and I was *still online*. It's like I followed a white rabbit and fell down a tunnel into Wonderland.

The Internet is its own magic world. Somehow all my talk of "spiritual discipline" and Lenten commitments become awfully easy to ignore when, say, the Oscar speeches are posted on Yahoo.

I'm reminded of some of my friends who've been diagnosed with ADD (attention deficit disorder). They find it really hard to concentrate in school or to focus on their work without being distracted by other things. My one friend loves the Internet because she can open up six separate windows, log on to three different chat sessions, play online Risk, and download a bunch of podcasts—all at the same time. This is while she text-messages her friends via cell phone, checks iTunes for updates, and listens to her MP3 player—during the commercial breaks for *Lost*. She freely admits that this is a problem and hopes her new medication will help her concentrate on the important things, such as her studies and prayer. But in the meantime, she's chasing one rabbit after another, never sticking to a healthy path long enough to help her grow into a better person.

When I think of it that way, I can't help wondering if I have spiritual ADD. Too often I treat spiritual exercises such as Bible study, prayer, serving, and worship as if they're boring chores; I look for any distraction to keep from having to do them. The more distracted I get, the harder it is to get back into the stuff I really need to be doing, so I look for more distractions, and the vicious circle goes round and round.

Maybe that's why monks and nuns shut themselves up in cloisters, completely focused on God and away from the outside world. They know how easy it is to be distracted from the things that help us draw closer to Jesus.

I can't go live in a cloister, but maybe I can fast from the Internet tomorrow. . . .

Proverbs 4:18-27

Make Me Be Still

Some of the most restless moments of my life are when I'm attempting to pray or read Scripture and my mind is chasing a million unspiritual thoughts, like a gerbil on a wheel. I'm sure I'm not alone. What would happen if we were honest to God about those moments and turned them over to him?

God, make me be still.

My mind is full of words and pictures
and ideas I imagine to be true.
My heart is full of desires
I wrongfully feel I'm entitled to.
My body is full of sleep
and cobwebs and dust.
My soul is empty.

Now I know that when
my rambling, fast-forward,
high-powered mind
and my creative, unrealistic imagination
take over my life,
my relationship with you suffers.
And when my body is sleepy,
I'm not awake to your presence.
When my soul is empty,
I have nothing to give others.

So if my mind is taking over,
let my thoughts be full of you, Jesus.
And if my imagination is taking over,
let it be baptized and sanctified by you, Jesus.
And if my body is taking over,
may it be awakened and energized by you, Jesus.
And if my soul is empty,
pour in your Holy Spirit till I'm full to overflowing.
Be the conscious control
over every aspect of who I am,
for it is in you that I live
and move and have my very being.

Psalm 131

Holding My Tongue

Of all the spiritual practices—including prayer, Bible study, worship, and serving others—
silence is definitely the hardest for me. This is no surprise to the people who know me.
I'm a talker, and it has gotten me in trouble more times than I care to remember. (Ugh.
I don't even want to *think* about it. . . .)

On the one hand, I'm glad my parents encouraged me to be a confident and articulate person. On the other hand, I wish holding my tongue were as simple as taking a vow
of silence. I've tried that before. A couple of years ago I decided I would exercise verbal
self-control during Lent. As I babbled on about my decision to a friend, she looked at me
with amusement and said, "Well, you're not doing a very good job so far, are you?"

Ouch.

What's really at issue here is *why* I—or any of us—feel this compulsion to speak.
What is the purpose of talking? Why do we learn language in the first place? When we're
small children, it's so that we can articulate what we want. Instead of crying for a bottle,
we learn to say, "I want my bubba." When we're older, we use language to share ideas and
ask questions, which is *still* mostly self-centered, unless we're also learning how to value
and respect the people we're communicating with, rather than viewing them in terms of
what they can do for us.

Choosing to be "quick to listen, slow to speak, and slow to get angry" (James 1:19)
doesn't come naturally, even if we're naturally quiet or shy. It's something we learn over
time through repeated practice as we grow more and more like Jesus. So holding my
tongue isn't merely about exercising self-control with what comes out of my mouth. It's
about learning to put the other person first. That's what Jesus has done for us, and what
greater silence could a person possibly choose than the Cross?

James 1:19-27

Vow of Silence

I have a friend who is a Mennonite (sort of a distant cousin to the Amish, except he's allowed to use electricity, drive a car, and wear regular clothes. He can also camp out for season tickets to Duke University basketball, which he did with relish last fall). One of the things I admire about him is that he rarely speaks unless someone asks him a question—not because he's naturally quiet and shy but because he's practicing the spiritual discipline of silence according to his Mennonite tradition.

This is a different kind of silence than simply the absence of noise. This is about self-control when it comes to the words we choose to speak. At first it may seem odd, especially since we live in a culture that encourages us to be ourselves and speak our minds. In fact, sometimes we wish we had a quicker wit to say what we mean or to amuse our friends. But we've also experienced the devastating effects of careless comments or cruel remarks, and we all wish we could take back some of those things we've said without thinking.

That's why the spiritual exercise of verbal self-control makes sense. Not only is my friend extremely kind because he refrains from saying mean things, he also means what he says when he does speak. As he told me, "The disciplined speech that I use is integral to my commitment to nonviolence. I strive to reject those forms of speech that are hasty, cruel, or manipulative. This will hopefully enable me to carefully attend to another on his or her own terms without seeking to control either the person or the conversation." In short, he's a very good listener. He isn't merely nodding until he can interrupt with his own opinion; he's actually paying attention to what people are saying. The practice of silence doesn't make him disconnected from what's going on around him; instead, it allows him to be *more* in tune with who people are. It's a way of loving them the way Jesus does.

If only it were an easy task! The amazing thing about my friend is that he has practiced this spiritual discipline for so long that he's really good at it, like a star basketball player at the free-throw line. I can only watch in awe and wish I could be like that some-day. But it takes practice, which is why I've chosen to give up unnecessary words for Lent this year. I'll take it one day—one sentence—at a time, with God's help.

James 3:2-10

Undulations

After a brief review of this devotional so far, I'm struck by how my attitude shifts and changes with the seasons. Perhaps it's the time of year, early March, when winter still clings to much of the northern regions of this land and the days seem grayer than gray. Now I understand what C. S. Lewis meant in chapter 8 of *The Screwtape Letters* when he described the "law of Undulation," or the unfortunate reality that human beings are like waves. We can't sustain a spiritual "high" for very long before we lose interest or energy and are quickly drawn into the valley again.

How true. My "spiritual melancholy" is so profound lately that I can hardly pull myself out. The oddest thing (or perhaps a comfort?) is that so many others around me are experiencing the same prevailing mood—it's like we share the same internal weather. Unfortunately there is no one, then, who has the energy or spirit to lift me out of myself.

And so I pray:

Lord, we languish here, needing your joy and the presence of your Holy Spirit. We need you to give us a sense of purpose and diligence in all our work and all our doings. Gently show us your loving grace as often as you convict us of the sin so apparent, so blatant these days. Do not let guilt overwhelm us, but spur us to meaningful action and loving communion with you.

And I hesitate to ask, because it seems cheeky . . . but can we please have some sunshine? Thanks.

Amen.

James 1:22-25

Obedience Anyway

I keep coming across flashes of insight from my college journals that remind me of God's faithfulness. Here's one:

I learned something very important today from the woman named Ginger who picks us up and takes us to church. This morning the topic of school Bible studies came up, and I mentioned how once upon a time I had wanted to start one in my high school. "So did you?" Ginger asked. And I said, "No, it just wasn't my thing." I offered a bunch of excuses as to why I didn't do it, such as my inadequacy as a leader, my poor skills at evangelism, the various friends who told me a Bible study was a dumb idea, and so on. Ginger listened patiently, and when I was done she said something I'll never forget. She gently reminded me that I may not have felt equipped to lead a Bible study or witness to the non-Christians in my school, and I may have even botched both things up pretty badly, but God would have honored my obedience—if he desired me to do it in the first place and if I had obeyed, no matter how I felt about it.

Immediately I knew she was right. In retrospect I now realize I *was* supposed to start a Bible study back then, but I didn't obey, even though prayerful people said that a campus Bible study was an answer to prayer. Instead I listened to the opinions of people whose input didn't have any bearing on the situation and shouldn't have derailed my obedience. The whole idea makes me sad.

So now I have another opportunity to start up a new study, and I may have a lot of anxieties and it may be very frustrating. But God honors obedience anyway. And above all, his will and desire should rule in my life, which means that if he wills it, there's nothing legitimately stopping me. Any other response is to fall short of the mark.

How easily we forget the truths we once knew!

Colossians 2:6-10

March Revival

A strange but not wholly unexpected thing happened during the spring semester of my senior year of college. Spiritual revival swept our campus in the form of late-night worship services and public confession of sin. It was strange because it engulfed almost everyone, not just individuals here or there; and yet it didn't transform us into an unthinking mass the way a rock concert or stampede might—it had the air of sanity as well as sanctity.

But although it was unplanned (it broke out during the regular student-led worship service one Sunday night), it was also not wholly unexpected, as I said. That's because revivals have happened regularly on college campuses for centuries, and people had been praying that one would break out soon in our generation. And break out it did—not just at our school, but all over the country. For at least a week students on my campus gathered for evening worship, confession, and prayer, often lasting until the early hours of the morning. After years of wearing our hip, happy Christian masks, it was finally time to be honest with God and one another about the deep-rooted sins that held us in bondage. It was time to come clean.

Of course not every student was there, and not everyone thought this whole revival business was genuine. But no one could avoid the sudden wind that came blasting over the Midwestern plains that week. Every time you turned a corner, there it was. Eventually the spiritual significance of it became too obvious for me to ignore. I wrote:

> Praise the Lord!
> Praise him on this
> wet, windy, wild March day
> when the trees toss high,
> rocking back and forth from the roots,
> and the air is alive
> with the hints and blasts
> of the promised, inevitable spring.
> There's no avoiding this wind:
> it invades our personal space,
> snatches our hair,
> pushes against us as we walk.
> We have the urge to holler at it—
> to exert our wills over it,
> to resist each blast and shock.
> But the wind blows where it wills.
> So with sudden relief
> we turn to face it head-on,
> realizing there's no exerting
> our human strength against such power anymore.
> There is only giving in.

John 3:6-8

Just like Dad

Whenever I'm around an older Christian whom I admire, I tell that person, "I want to be just like you when I grow up." My dad is one of those people. Today is his birthday, and I honor him because I want to be like him someday—a down-to-earth example of lifelong commitment to Jesus, an example of Jesus himself.

"What would Jesus do?" That's what we're taught to ask in any given situation, because Jesus is our ultimate example. And on a certain level it's an important question, because it trains us to pause and think before we act. But the problem is, we're so disconnected from Jesus most of the time that we actually *have* to pause and think. Our instincts are all messed up. This worldly society has conditioned us to follow our naturally self-obsessive habits to the point that a Christlike response doesn't even register on our behavioral radars.

But the goal of the Christian life isn't simply to acknowledge that Jesus died for our sins so we can go to heaven. The goal of the Christian life is to gradually transform our very beings so we *instinctively* act and think and talk like Jesus. We spend so much time with him and with his people that we no longer have to stop and ask ourselves, *What would Jesus do?* We simply do it. We put our own petty preferences and small desires aside so that Jesus can shine through us.

The apostle Paul wrote, "Imitate God, therefore, in everything you do, because you are his dear children" (Ephesians 5:1). The verse calls to mind a young child who wants to be big and strong, just like Dad. I picture a toddler wanting to use grown-up-size spoons and eat at the table like everyone else, or a little girl clomping around in her mommy's shoes holding a cell phone to her ear. Paul is saying we should imitate God in this way! God is our hero, our Daddy, our favorite person in the whole wide world. We should want to be like him when we grow up.

Just like my dad.

Ephesians 4:30–5:2

Playing Dress-Up

For one of my first jobs in high school, I was an interpreter at a historic pioneer village, which means I dressed up in old-fashioned clothes and worked at pioneer crafts and talked with tourists all day long. "Welcome to the Burns family farmhouse, built in 1867," I would say over and over again with each new batch of visitors, and I would take them on a tour through the building. Sure, it got boring sometimes, but what job doesn't? It was better than cleaning bathrooms, like some of my friends were doing.

In fact, the really cool part was learning the pioneer crafts. Usually I was stationed in the farmhouse kitchen, where my assigned task was to fire up the old cookstove for baking. Yep, build a fire and keep it going at just the right temperature all day—do you know how hard that is? I would churn butter and make cookies from scratch for the tourists—and somehow I managed to do it expertly, even cheerfully, though in "real life" I can't cook *at all*.

Seriously: I'm a disaster in the kitchen. I generally end up cutting myself, burning fingers, forgetting major ingredients, losing track of time, and making everyone else miserable before we finally sit down to eat. There are roughly two meals I can make without bursting into tears (so my husband is the official cook in our family). Which is why it's so strange that for an entire summer, I somehow managed to simultaneously keep a fire going, churn butter, and make batch after batch of perfectly shaped little sugar cookies that melted in your mouth—and I *enjoyed* it.

I think the reason I succeeded is because I was able to imagine I wasn't Sarah at all, but Mrs. Burns, the farmer's wife, a strong pioneer woman for whom baking cookies was an effortless hobby in the midst of all the other difficult tasks of keeping a farmhouse operative. I stepped into my pioneer clothes and became someone else for the day. I played dress-up, like we did as kids, all summer long. And as Mrs. Burns, I could tell exactly when the cream turned to butter by the sound of it in the churn. I could gauge, simply by hovering my palms over the burners, whether or not the stove was hot enough for baking. Something about putting on that pioneer apron transformed my attitude and gave me abilities I didn't even know I had. The question is, if I could do that as Mrs. Burns, what's to stop me from doing that as everyday Sarah?

"Clothe yourselves with tenderhearted mercy, kindness, humility, gentleness, and patience," wrote the apostle Paul to his friends in Colosse. Maybe we fail at those things God wants us to do because we forget how to play dress-up.

Colossians 3:12-14

Just Pretend

A guest musician visited my college one day and led a workshop. He sat us all down and, without saying much, helped us regain our sense of playfulness and fun with music. He had us repeat lines of rhythm after him with our hands or fingers, following his lead with vocal scales and generally acting silly. For a bunch of serious academic types who'd forgotten how to laugh at ourselves, it was a welcome relief.

For instance, he led us in singing an ordinary warm-up exercise—"ee-ay-ah-oh-oo"—right up the scale until we were higher than we felt comfortable. We didn't sound very convincing, either, most of us a bit breathy and trying not to screech.

"Now, how many of you can sing opera?" he then asked. No hands went up. "Well, it doesn't matter," he said. "Let's do that warm-up again, except this time pretend you're opera singers."

So we did. Grinning, giggling, then sitting up straight and becoming very stern, we opened our throats and belted out a glorious noise like the cast of *Carmen*. Our eyes grew wide, we glanced at each other in astonishment, and then we sang like kings and queens of the grand stage until we collapsed in laughter. It was marvelous. We didn't know we had it in us. And not one of us screeched.

Funny how *pretend* opera sounds an awful lot like the *real thing*, you know? Many of us, if someone were to tell us we'd just been given the lead in Verdi's *Aida*, would protest, "But you don't get it—I can't sing!" And yet if we're just playing around, pretending to be opera singers, we sound like opera singers. The problem is that we rarely imagine what we're capable of because we can't seem to get over ourselves and just plain have *fun*.

What would happen if we were to do the same in our spiritual lives? My guess is that God's Kingdom is full of laughter when everyone is trying his or her hardest and best to be like Jesus—and it's not laughter *at* each other but laughter from the sheer joy of not taking ourselves so seriously and instead attempting those things we didn't know we could do. What if I were to pretend to be Joan of Arc (minus the sword)? Or Mother Teresa? Or any of the great saints of the church throughout time and history? What if I were to think of myself as a missionary or a preacher? What would happen if I got over myself and acted like a Christian for once?

Romans 14:8-9

God's Own Armor

"Put on the full armor of God," wrote the apostle Paul to his friends in Ephesus, "so that you can take your stand against the devil's schemes." Ephesians 6:10-17 contains one of the most famous images or metaphors in the Bible: putting on spiritual armor like a Roman soldier of ancient times, dressed for battle from head to toe. The belt of truth, the breastplate of righteousness, the shoes of the gospel of peace, the shield of faith, the helmet of salvation, and the sword of the Spirit, "which is the word of God." When I was growing up, my mom taught us hand motions to go with this passage, and we said it together as a family before we left the house each morning.

For most of my life, I've thought of this spiritual armor as a kind of cookie-cutter outfit that all foot soldiers are given, as it would have been in the Roman army. If you wished to join, they'd take you into the armory and rummage through the belts and shields and helmets until they found some that fit and then suit you up to look just like the other soldiers.

But this time around I'm struck by the phrase "*God's* armor"—as if this is no ordinary suit but *God's own outfit*, given to me to wear. "Here," Jesus says. "Since you have no protection of your own, try on my helmet and see if it fits. And take my chain mail." I can just picture him unhooking his belt and slinging it around my waist—"How does that fit?" He hefts his shield and hands it to me—"Try that." Then the sword, ringing as he unsheathes it. He doesn't stop until he's standing in a plain robe, barefoot, while I'm glittering from head to toe in his own armor. "There," he says, smiling, nodding his approval. "Now you're ready."

"What about you?" I say, but he's already ushering me outside into the sunshine and waving me off. I look back at his vulnerable figure, standing there unprotected and alone, while the rest of the army goes about its business around him.

And I can't help wondering: How many blows will my Lord take for me while I'm out there conquering evil using his own armor?

How many hits has he already taken?

Ephesians 6:10-17 (NIV)

The Pilgrims' Way

In medieval times a route called the Pilgrims' Way led from Canterbury, England, to Rome, Italy, where those who were taking spiritual pilgrimages could worship at the center of Christendom, the holy city of the Catholic church. The route connected the dots from church to church throughout Europe and was often paved with white stones or marble so pilgrims could travel at night by moonlight. Some sections of the trail are still intact today.

A few years ago my husband and I had the privilege of spending a week in Tuscany, a region in Italy just north of Rome. I had read about the Pilgrims' Way in various guidebooks, but we weren't familiar enough with the countryside to track down any parts of the trail. *Maybe someday,* I thought to myself.

Toward the end of the trip we took a hike in a mountainous region of Tuscany known as the Apuane Alps. The Apuanes are famous for their white marble—in fact, that's where Michelangelo got the marble for his statue of David. As we began hiking up an old road toward the trailhead, it became clear our road led to a working quarry. But before we reached it, the footpath cut away to our left and began a long, slow ascent to an abandoned village high in the mountains. We followed the path.

The village was perched on the terraced slope of a steep valley. On each side of the valley were stone churches, still intact and who knows how old. In the foggy gloom of those high peaks, with the ancient cedars lining the trails, it was easy to picture medieval priests carrying water up from the creek, chanting the psalms. Surely they took in travelers such as ourselves, tired and hungry wanderers worn out from the spiritual journey. The whole place made me feel like praying.

Then in the midst of my daydreaming I noticed the trail. White pebbles paved the way through the gloom, smooth stones of marble that glowed in the near-dusk of that mountain pass. We had found the Pilgrims' Way.

Sometimes we know we're on the right path when it's clear the saints have come this way before. God doesn't expect us to carve new trails in the spiritual life: We follow in the footsteps of those who've gone before us. We pray as they prayed, we serve as they served, we seek after righteousness just as they did, we soak ourselves in God's Word, which stays true from generation to generation. We follow others along the Pilgrims' Way, knowing that in the end it leads to the heart of God.

Psalm 25:4-10

Back in Step

My husband and I are hikers, but I'll admit: I'm hopelessly out of shape most of the time (sitting in front of a laptop all day might have something to do with it . . .). As my hiking partners effortlessly stride up a mountain, chatting and laughing, I'm the one in the back of the line, wheezing like a cat with a fur ball. So is it all that different when it comes to the spiritual life? Am I keeping pace like I should be?

Father, I want to walk with Jesus.
Somehow I got out of step,
sat down, figured I'd
catch up later or something.
He's so far away now
I can't hear the sound of his voice,
only my own thoughts in my head
rambling on undisciplined,
unholy, fruitless.
But I'm not going to stay seated,
even though I know
it's humanly impossible to catch up.
I'm going to get up, here on this
narrow mountain track.
I'll follow the footprints,
though by now
they're nearly obliterated and mostly blurred.
I'll get back in step,
put one foot in front of the other,
repeating the Prodigal's speech,
putting my hope in the promise
that if I keep on plodding along,
if I just push myself to try, to hear
his voice, to walk as he does,
then a long way off
he'll see me—
a straggling, selfish little girl—
he'll turn
and begin to run full tilt
to meet me where I am.

Hebrews 12:12-13

Saint Patrick's Breastplate

My godson was born in March, so I decided to reclaim the only March holiday—Saint Patrick's Day—as a reminder of his Christian heritage. Unfortunately, this day is now associated with silly leprechauns and tacky shamrocks and getting totally plastered at the local pub. But originally it was a time to remember Ireland's patron saint, the fifth-century evangelist who converted almost the entire island to Christianity before he died.

Patrick was born in Scotland but was captured by Irish marauders when he was about sixteen. He was a slave for six years in Ireland, where he learned the Celtic language and druidic practices of his masters. Later he escaped back to Britain and became a Christian monk and priest, only to be commissioned by the church as a missionary to his former enemies. Previous attempts to evangelize Ireland had not gone well—missionaries had fled in terror, threatened by the pagan chieftains. But Patrick was a powerhouse. He regularly went head-to-head with the druidic priests, challenging their cultural practices that had kept the land in fear and bondage for millennia. Confrontations led to conversions, lives were transformed, and churches were established all over the island. But it wasn't easy. The story goes that on the night before his biggest confrontation, Patrick prayed a prayer that is now known as "Saint Patrick's Breastplate." Here's an excerpt that I used as the border of the picture I created for my godson:

> I bind unto myself today
> The virtues of the starlit heaven,
> The glorious sun's life-giving ray,
> The whiteness of the moon at even,"
> The flashing of the lightning free,
> The whirling wind's tempestuous shocks,
> The stable earth, the deep salt sea,
> Around the old eternal rocks.
>
> Christ be with me, Christ within me,
> Christ behind me, Christ before me,
> Christ beside me, Christ to win me,
> Christ to comfort and restore me.
> Christ beneath me, Christ above me,
> Christ in quiet, Christ in danger,
> Christ in hearts of all that love me,
> Christ in mouth of friend and stranger.[12]

So as my godson grows up surrounded by silly leprechauns each Saint Patrick's Day, I hope he remembers this prayer instead—that our battle against evil is very real indeed and that he is protected by the same Christ who protected Patrick all those centuries ago.

Ephesians 1:15-20

// Old-fashioned shorthand for "evening."

Confessions of a Lazy Slob

When it comes to prayer, I'll admit it: I'm a lazy slob. For you to read anything I've written about prayer is basically the spiritual equivalent of hiring a personal marathon trainer who shows up wheezing in a purple velour jumpsuit, weighing in at just under three hundred pounds and on the verge of a coronary. This is not something I'm proud of. I am constantly in a state of bemoaning my lack of focus and self-control. And yet even an overweight personal trainer knows how important self-discipline is and will probably give you the lecture about diet and exercise at some point. Then the onus is on *you* to follow up on what you know will be the healthiest possible approach to fitness.

The analogy of physical fitness isn't a bad one, actually. People write all kinds of stuff about prayer, recommend all sorts of prayer "diets" (think *Jabez*), and give retreats and seminars and classes on the subject. But the actual *practice* of it is a different matter altogether. That's why prayer is considered a spiritual discipline: It takes intentional planning, determined effort, perseverance, and let's be honest, a little bit of the work ethic of America's pioneers.

It's difficult at first for me to feel any sense of connection with God when I'm deliberately trying. I know others who experience the same thing, especially nocturnal types who are suddenly compelled after Sunday's sermon to get up at a ridiculously early hour and sit comatose on Monday morning over a Bible and a mug of coffee. Such efforts usually last about three days. That's because prayer, as I've learned through fits and starts, isn't about *feeling* anything; it's about doing what God has asked me to do. Diet and exercise. Obedience.

1 Thessalonians 5:14-18

Personal Trainer

Somewhere in the process of prayer is the help of the Holy Spirit. Perhaps that's a better visual than imagining me as your coach (see March 18). Picture the Holy Spirit as your personal trainer, the eternally perky instructor doing jumping jacks by your bed in the morning with a stopwatch, hollering, "Rise and shine, camper!" Your trainer oozes enthusiasm, and it begins to rub off. No, it's more like the trainer ties the treads onto your feet, carries you out the front door, and dumps you on the pavement, saying, "I'll beat you around the block."

And you're off and running—metaphorically speaking. You stretch your spiritual muscles, breathe the clean air of God's Word, sweat out the good prayers through your hardworking soul. Eventually, as with running (or so runners tell me), you begin to look forward to the way your heart pumps like a champ and the wind lifts the hair off your forehead and the day opens up like a flower while you're out there keeping spiritual stride.

Richard Foster wrote, "Prayer is like any other work; we may not feel like working, but once we have been at it for a bit, we begin to feel like working."[13] I can see how this is true. I love my job as a writer, but sometimes the prospect of facing yet another blank white page on the computer screen is not exactly my idea of a good time. And yet when I sit down and finally get into it, I discover that I really enjoy it after all and could continue writing all day, every day, if it weren't for the important interruption of Sabbath. And coffee.

In the same way, my enthusiasm for prayer grows with practice, and in the meantime, I can't imagine what I used to do before I got into the habit of it. But unfortunately, after a few months or years go by, and I revert back to slug-dom, I can't imagine why I ever thought spiritual disciplines were so great. I'm comfortable in my flab.

So the point is that if it weren't for the Holy Spirit as my personal trainer, I'd be a total loser.

Romans 8:26-28

Answers

Earlier in this Lenten season some friends and I decided to "turn our plates" and fast during lunch in order to pray through the list of our church prayer requests. The list included concerns for cancer victims, for families in difficult times, and even for a relative of mine who had been job-hunting for months but hadn't been hired anywhere yet (our prayer was that he would find a job by Easter). Over the past few weeks since then, we've been reminding each other to keep up those prayers, since it's easy to get discouraged and quit when nothing seems to be changing.

Well, this past week I found out that my relative got a job! After all these months of searching without any open doors, he finally found an employer who would take a chance on someone with a difficult past. After all these weeks my church family has been praying for him, he found a job *before* Easter.

Needless to say, this morning I couldn't wait to tell my congregation the news during the time for sharing joys and concerns. The funny thing was, every time I went to stand and speak, someone had already hopped to his or her feet with another joy to share. First was the young cancer survivor we'd been praying for who told us that, miraculously, her latest test results were clear after a scare that the cancer had possibly returned. Then came the announcement that a son-in-law we'd been praying for had received better-than-expected test results too. And here I thought I'd be the only one with good news!

Why are we so surprised when God answers prayer? Too often we act as though praying is like gambling: We throw a couple of prayers in the heavenly slot machine and wait to see if anything happens. We hope that if we do it enough times we'll get results eventually—but then when we do, we act completely flabbergasted, as if to say, "What are the odds?"

And yet our loving God is the same Jesus who healed the blind, the lame, the sick, and the world-weary. He's the same Jesus who gave his followers a lifelong vocation and purpose for living. He's the same Jesus who told us to pray to our heavenly Father and the mountains would move.

Have we forgotten the One we're praying to?

Psalm 120:1

When God Says No

In the reading for March 20, I told you about some prayers that were answered. I'm
still flying high from the joy of it all. And yet even as I celebrate these miracles (and of
course they are), I also recognize a problem with the way Christians generally talk about
prayer. We seem to think that the only time we get an answer from God is when he says
yes. What about when he says wait? What about those times he says no? Aren't those
answers too?

My suspicion is that we get more answers than we realize; they're just not always
what we want to hear.

Take my friend who is dying of cancer, for example. Years ago we prayed that she
would survive an incredibly risky procedure, and miraculously she did. To all appearances,
she was cured completely: God's answer was yes. Now she's sick again, and it doesn't look
good. For a time, when people asked her how she was doing, she'd say, "I'm blessed."
She had survived longer than anyone ever expected and lived life to the absolute fullest.
But I saw her recently after an absence of several months and was struck by how tired she
appeared, as if she was finally too exhausted to fight anymore. After all our years of prayer,
God's answer now seems to be no.

It's tempting to get angry at God when his answer isn't what I want to hear. In fact,
I *am* angry. At the same time, God can handle it when I'm mad at him. He knows that
anger is a natural stage in the grieving process, and he is willing to let me bluster and argue
and throw things—for now. But in time he will gently nudge me toward acceptance.

I don't have to like it, though, do I?

Psalm 28:1-2

When God Says Wait

We've been praying for months that my relative would find a job, and he finally did. But during those long months, everything seemed stacked against him; and as the days and weeks went by, we all became more and more discouraged. The more rejections he received and the longer he had to wait, the more he was tempted to give up. Those of us who were praying for him began to feel numb, like we were on autopilot, repeating the same phrases over and over again to a God who didn't seem to be listening.

But God *was* listening. And he *was* answering. It's just that his answer was wait.

One of my favorite songs by U2 is entitled "40," from their vintage album *War*. The lyrics are almost word-for-word from Psalm 40 and Psalm 13 and others. Back in the day, the band would finish their concerts with "40" and then slowly leave the stage as the audience sang the last line over and over again: "How long . . . to sing this song?" Who knows how many people in the crowd actually realized they were singing Scripture. But the point is, the band wasn't afraid to write a song based on an ancient psalm that wrestles with the struggle we all have when God's answer is wait.

How long must we pray the same prayer day after day? How long must we worry for our friends who are sick or in trouble? How long does God expect us to be faithful in prayer before we're granted permission to give up?

What if we wait our whole lives but never hear a yes?

Psalm 40 indicates that it's all worth it somehow. Through the process of waiting, God is still at work, giving us strength and transforming us into the people he wants us to be. We are never, ever, ever to give up.

Easier said than done; right?

Psalm 13; 40:1-5

"Go to Nineveh" or Whatever: Part 1

My friend Kate and I like to e-mail each other about spiritual issues, especially since we now live one thousand miles apart. Here's one of our recent conversations:

Kate: Last night, my husband had this "Go to Nineveh!" experience while I was away. Brad often prays fervently about our housing, but in this instance he got a clear message: Drive to Dyer Road. It's a road where there's a piece of property that he's always loved, but the property is on a seasonal road and we always wondered if it would work for us. Anyway, he drove out there, but he didn't know if Dyer Road is the point or if it's something along the way. So he saw a new piece of property and thought maybe he should look up the specs—but the new one is way too expensive. In the end, he feels muddled. What is God leading him to?

We rarely have those go-to-Nineveh moments, but when we do it's frustrating when we look on the map and there is no Nineveh after all—or no boats heading there or maybe we were supposed to meet someone on the way or maybe we're being waylaid on an important mission. Do you see what I mean? Last night I was reading the book of Matthew, and Joseph got all this direction from God (marry her, go here, no go back, okay now go to Nazareth) via dreams in which angels appear." Brad and I both fell asleep last night and dreamed, but sadly we had very unprovidential follow-up dreams.

Any ideas? Similar stories? I mean, your husband knew that God wanted all of him. Did Tom ever wonder what exactly that meant? Ministry? Missions?

Me: Hmm. Generally when someone gets the call to Nineveh or to ministry, it's something they'd rather *not* do instead of something they've been dreaming about for a while. Joseph really didn't want the mess of marrying an unwed mother, nor did he want to jeopardize their lives by leaving the country—in other words, the angels were constantly getting him to do things it never ever would have occurred to him to do. Regarding my husband's call to ministry: His call was quite specific, but it was the last thing he really wanted.

On a slightly different tack, when I met with the editor at the writer's conference in 2002, I was convinced that the meeting was providentially arranged so I could fulfill my dream of publishing the little fiction stories I pitched to her at the time. But of course that wasn't it at all—instead it was about a random nonfiction proposal that I submitted six months later, which eventually became a runaway best seller the next Christmas.[14] So the meeting *was* providentially arranged, but not according to any foresight I might have had at the time. Which means only God gets the credit. And I suppose that's the point.

Jonah 1:1-3

// See Matthew 1:18-20; 2:13-15, 19-23.

"Go to Nineveh" or Whatever: Part 2

Here's the continuation of the e-mail conversation with my friend Kate on the subject of hearing God's voice (see March 23). I should note parenthetically that Kate and I misspelled Nineveh throughout this entire correspondence: She called it "Nineva" and I called it "Ninevah." I still haven't figured out that whole spell-check thing for e-mail. . . .

Me: Perhaps your husband's "go-to-Ninevah" moment was God's way of acknowledging Brad's desire for that particular piece of property on Dyer Road—as in "Yes, Brad, I know this land you have in mind; and yes, it's mine and I can do with it what I will; but you need to trust me on this one." Or maybe an opportunity will open up; who knows? Whatever the case, my guess is it'll make sense retrospectively. Thankfully we're not the first disciples to experience this sense of confusion about what God is telling us to do. All throughout the Gospels we see those poor guys scratching their heads, saying "What the . . . ?" only to have their eyes opened after the Resurrection to everything Jesus said and did before it. Maybe that's why all the honest preachers don't recommend this faith thing for the faint of heart—because it gets so maddening!

Kate: Thanks for the ideas. Brad said it felt like he had God on the phone and then was put on hold for another call. "Go to . . . uh . . . er . . . could you hold on a minute?" Of course, I'm sure that's not what God did. Brad said he thinks it's like God is always speaking to us but there's all this white noise that we have to get past in order to hear God's voice.

Me: The ancient saints had another term for that sense of being on hold: They called it the "dark night of the soul." And I believe their term for "white noise" was (to keep it simple) *sin*. Our relationship with God is broken—or, as Paul says in 1 Corinthians 13:12, "Now we see things imperfectly as in a cloudy mirror." But the story doesn't end there. He adds, "But then we will see everything with perfect clarity. All that I know now is partial and incomplete, but then I will know everything completely." At least we have *some* visibility in the meantime, right?

Kate: Maybe the problem was that we didn't know how to spell *Nineveh*. We were going to "Nineva," hold the *h*.

Isaiah 59:1-2

Through a Glass Darkly

I've been thinking about prayer lately, particularly those murky moments when we're just not sure what God is saying, if he's saying anything at all. This is when Paul's words in 1 Corinthians 13:12 take on real poignancy. Maybe murkiness is the best we can hope for most of the time?

You call me to yourself
out of a mystery
for a mystery
for a reason that is beyond
what I can know.

I see only dimly.

My vision is like a mirror
in an old spare bedroom:
clouded, stained,
rippled with imperfections.
I squint into the glass
try to dust it off
first rubbing gently
then furiously
leaning forward and looking along
the plane to see the surface
instead of the reflection.
But the cloud and fog remain.

And so I try to content myself
with imperfect sight
knowing that someday

I shall see you

face to face.

1 Corinthians 13:12

Prayer. Life.

Here's another gem from my college journals:

> I've discovered that I can't go forward or have many "successes"
> spiritually, so to speak, until I start a serious life of prayer.
> Things have been leading up to this realization. Time and time
> again I've shied away from thinking about the topic. I wake up in
> the morning (having set my alarm the night before with the idea
> that I'll get up early to pray and have devotions) and lie in bed
> thinking about what I should be praying about or what I would be
> praying about if I weren't so tired or had any sort of drive to do it.
> It's ridiculous!
>
> Everything I hear lately, whether it's a chapel speaker
> talking about prayer and the mission field or Oswald Chambers in
> his devotional book *My Utmost for His Highest* or two different
> sermons at church or random readings or discussions—*all* of it ends
> up being about prayer eventually. I can't get past the truth that I
> won't make spiritual headway until I start praying.
>
> Oswald Chambers said, "Prayer does not fit us for the greater
> work; prayer *is* the greater work." And yet so often I crave
> "results," so I keep busy doing other things: organizing groups
> or volunteering for fund-raisers or signing up for Bible studies.
> But Chambers said the opposite: "You labour at prayer and results
> happen all the time from (God's) standpoint."[15]
>
> So I can't get around it: I must pray. I'm being driven to pray.
> It's hitting me on all sides and from all texts and mouths and songs
> and Scriptures. And I can no longer complain that I don't know how,
> because spiritual enlightenment doesn't come from an intellectual
> standpoint by intellectual means; it comes from obedience. We're
> constantly confronted with whatever God sets before us. We cannot
> go on until we've begun to obey whatever it is he's asking us to do,
> whether it's loving our neighbors or keeping the Sabbath or feeding
> the hungry or starting a life of prayer. For me, the biggest issue is
> connecting with my God more on a daily basis, seeking to know him.
> I can't ask how; I must simply dive in headfirst.

Funny how this same issue comes up again with every new season of my life. . . .

Ephesians 6:18-20

Three Words

One of my favorite authors, a twentieth-century British novelist by the name of Elizabeth Goudge, tells the story of a young woman named Mary who struggled with mental illness. Mary would go through seasons of depression and hospitalization, after which she felt raw and scared, wondering when the next bout would begin. After one of those bouts, when she had been feeling better for a while, her mother invited a group of people over for tea. One of the guests was a sweet elderly clergyman who seemed a bit out of place. He didn't have the same social graces as everyone else and was constantly spilling his tea or getting crumbs on his shirt. Eventually he and Mary ended up out in the garden, where Mary found herself telling him all about her struggles. He listened with kindness and promised to pray for her. Then, just before he left, he said:

> My dear, love, your God, is a trinity. There are three necessary prayers and they have three words each. They are these, "Lord have mercy. Thee I adore. Into Thy hands." Not difficult to remember. If in times of distress you hold to these you will do well.[16]

And then he was gone. Only later did Mary learn that the old gentleman, too, had been in and out of mental hospitals for most of his life.

Three simple prayers, three words each:
- *Lord have mercy*—a traditional prayer from the ancient church.
- *I adore you*—what one lover says to another, even when times are difficult.
- *Into your hands*—some of the last words of Jesus on the cross (see Luke 23:46).

Perhaps the next time you're overwhelmed with pain, anxiety, or fear—the next time words fail—these simple prayers can be a lifeline, like they are for me.

Psalm 9:9-14

Keeping a Prayer Journal

God gave us the gift of communication, but sometimes writing (even typing!) is easier than speaking. That's why I've found it helpful to keep a prayer journal over the years.

A prayer journal is a unique medium that offers the opportunity to express private prayers in written form. Because the act of writing demands a high level of concentration, it can help us stay focused during more extended times of prayer. Using a journal also provides a means for recording the insights or answers we might hear from God. Too often we forget what God has taught us or the ways he has answered prayer; a journal helps us look back and recognize his grace at work in our lives and the lives of those for whom we've prayed.

The history of written prayer goes back many thousands of years, even as far back as the court of King David, when psalms of request and praise were recorded for public use (see Psalms 88:1-2 and 89:1-2). In time, written prayers have also become part of the private devotional life of believers, often taking the form of journals or diaries. Today, a prayer journal might even take the form of a document typed and saved on the computer.

The intent of a journal is to enhance your communication with God—both in your desire to speak to him and his desire to speak to you. It can be as simple as making lists of joys and concerns or as complex as a letter complete with full sentences and paragraphs. My husband types his up on a computer, while I usually write mine by hand in a spiral-bound notebook. For most people, whatever the medium, it can be an opportunity to document the journey of prayer through various stages. By recording questions, requests, events, quotes, Scriptures, and experiences that impact one's faith, a person can look back at the ways God has given answers or brought insight through prayer.

That has certainly been true for me. I'm amazed as I look back through my prayer journals at how God has been at work in my life.

So what about you?

Psalm 9:1-2

ACTS: Part 1

Often what keeps me from writing in my prayer journal is the blank page. Sure, the empty space can be an invitation to encounter God in a unique way, but its very emptiness also can seem daunting. I don't always have coherent thoughts. I can't always imagine what I could say to God that would be worth putting on paper. Sometimes the only thing that works is to use a predetermined structure or "formula" just to get my thoughts flowing.

Here's one that I've found helpful. It's called ACTS, which stands for adoration, confession, thanksgiving, and supplication. I find that it works to write those headings down the left-hand side of a page, leaving space between each to write my thoughts. Ready to give it a try? Here's the first half of some exercises to get you started. (The second half is tomorrow's devotion.)

Adoration

Read Psalm 145. Make a list of the attributes you appreciate about God (holy, loving, creative, faithful, just), or write a love letter to God, expressing all the ways you adore and worship him. In other words, what makes God unique in the universe? Why does God have no equal or rival in your eyes? Write phrases you remember from Scripture, hymns, or praise choruses—maybe even listen to worship music as you write.

Confession

When we focus on the holy attributes of God, we quickly recognize how we have failed to serve him faithfully. We feel led to confess our sins to him. Thus, confession naturally follows adoration.

Read Psalm 51. Make a list of the ways you have failed to love God, others, and yourself. What have you done that is in direct contradiction to God's laws? What have you left undone? If you feel uncomfortable putting specifics on paper, write general headings and then pause to pray silently. First John 1:9 says, "If we confess our sins to him, he is faithful and just to forgive us our sins and to cleanse us from all wickedness."

Psalms 145; 51

ACTS: Part 2

On March 29, I introduced the concept of following a set pattern for keeping a prayer journal—otherwise the blank pages can seem rather daunting. The pattern I suggested was the ACTS "formula" (which I picked up somewhere during my youth ministry days, so I can't take credit for it). The letters stand for adoration, confession, thanksgiving, and supplication. Yesterday we looked at the first two; now let's look at the last two.

Thanksgiving

Jesus dealt with our sins by dying on the cross—we are forgiven people! This undeserved gift of grace is a reason to celebrate. Thus, after our prayers of confession, we offer God prayers of thanksgiving, not only for our salvation, but for all the ways God has blessed us.

Read Psalm 136 and notice the pattern used in this prayer. How can you use this pattern in your own prayers of thanksgiving? Consider writing letters to those who have shared God's grace with you; send the letters if you wish.

Supplication

Usually we're in such a hurry that we start with supplication (making requests) instead of taking the time to worship God, acknowledge our sins, and celebrate what God has done for us. But while these requests shouldn't be our only communication with God, he does desire for us to identify our concerns, much the same way a parent delights in having a child's honest communication about what the child needs. Even though "your Father knows exactly what you need even before you ask him" (Matthew 6:8), the very act of asking helps you identify your true needs and acknowledge your reliance on God.

Read Luke 11:9-13. Make a simple "grocery list" of requests for yourself and others. As the weeks and months go by, review that list and note any updates, breakthroughs, or responses. God is faithful!

Psalm 136; Luke 11:9-13

Greater than Our Hearts

How often do I begin my prayer time with negative self-talk rather than true confession, as if I must rehearse the litany of my human failings before God is able to hear me or act on my behalf? Grace, grace. To seek him, to bask in his presence, to allow him to gradually make me aware of my failures and faults, and then to let the Holy Spirit empower me for a change . . . That is true confession.

> As we come to the conclusion
> of this spring day, with the sun
> slanting across the walls,
> cozy restfulness descending
> like an afternoon nap,
> we confess that we
> are weary of our prayerless lives.
> We long
> for communion with you;
> we could break down and weep
> for lack of it. Why do we struggle
> so with prayer? Why
> do we ever long for what our
> wills cannot seem to produce,
> and then chide ourselves and walk around
> guilt-laden? We approach
> the rare times we do pray with
> a sense of grief, and spend the first
> portion of it reprimanding ourselves,
> a pale, twisted shadow of true confession,
> in our knowledge that—in this area
> of the spiritual life—we so miserably fail you.
> Lord, we pray that you would indeed
> be "greater than our hearts"
> when our hearts condemn us with false guilt,
> that our hearts would indeed be at rest
> in your presence, confident
> that even our faltering, shabby attempts
> are to you precious.

1 John 3:19-22 (NIV)

April's Fools

Lately I've decided that people are just plain weird. No doubt they think the same about me, especially when I'm standing in the bushes by the sidewalk, staring up into the trees trying to figure out what kind of bird just flew in front of me. Okay, so I guess that could be seen as a bit loopy, especially if they didn't happen to see the bird. But I have a perfectly good explanation for my behavior: I'm a bird-watcher, not a patient who forgot to take her meds.

Other people, however . . .

Exhibit A: My husband just came back from the grocery store with a story to tell. He was standing in the snack aisle, reaching for a box of my favorite crackers, when he heard a voice behind him. He turned around to see a strange woman chattering away in a thick foreign accent, who seemed to think she'd been deep in spiritual conversation with my husband for a while. She was earnestly rambling on about God, Muslims, Jews, Catholics, the number 666, the end of the world. For a moment, he wondered if this were a joke or if she were trying to evangelize him or something, but her tone was too conspiratorial. She told him she had a friend who didn't believe all that stuff. She was worried about this friend. She would be praying about it. Tom agreed that's important. He tried to get a word in edgewise. The woman kept rambling; he only understood roughly 20 percent of it. Then after a few minutes, she simply walked out of the store.

Now you could argue that she was crazy. Probably so. But isn't it weird that she picked probably the only guy in the whole store who actually believes in Jesus and doesn't mind spiritual conversations? In some ancient cultures, "crazy" people were thought to have a kind of sixth sense that allowed them to see truths that other people couldn't see. That's why Shakespeare's fools are often the only ones who tell the truth when everyone else is too afraid (I think of *King Lear*, for example). So when the apostle Paul told the Christians in Corinth, "The message of the cross is foolish to those who are headed for destruction" (1 Corinthians 1:18), he was bracing us for being looked at as lunatics, even when (or especially when?) we tell the truth.

People are weird, but Christians are *really* weird. It's good to remember, on this April Fools' Day, that we stand in solidarity with all the other fools out there.

1 Corinthians 1:26-29

National Poetry Month

So by now you've figured out that this isn't your usual devotional book, especially with the random poems thrown in here and there. Well, you're about to get a bunch more. That's because April is National Poetry Month, one of those rare seasons of sophistication in American culture that keep literary geeks like me from despairing of our society altogether. Tucked away in all my prayer journals from the past fifteen years are dozens and dozens of prose-poems that have become, in a way, psalms of my life. They record my reflections, insights, joys, heartbreaks, and awed thanksgivings. Not than I'm much of a poet, mind you, but sometimes poetry says what needs to be said more powerfully, succinctly, and memorably than straight prose.

God knows this, or the Bible wouldn't be full of poetry. The book of Psalms consists of one prayer-poem after another—not the sappy, rhyming Hallmark variety, obviously, but an ancient form of free-verse poetry that follows its own internal laws. For the people of the Old Testament, a poem wasn't something that rhymed at the end of each line; it was a series of parallelisms that echoed and reinforced one another. Here's a famous example:

> Shout with joy to the LORD, all the earth!
> Worship the LORD with gladness.
> Come before him, singing with joy.
>
> Psalm 100:1-2

Notice how all three lines say pretty much the same thing: Worship God with all you've got. The first line says to "shout," while the second says to worship "with gladness," and the third tells us to sing "with joy." Each line parallels the theme of the one before it, and yet each has a flavor of its own. So instead of just rhyming using sounds (such as "love" and "dove"), the ancient poets would rhyme using themes.

And that's a good thing, because Bible translation is difficult enough without having to find a corresponding rhyme in English for words that rhyme in Hebrew! C. S. Lewis wrote, "What an admirable thing it is in the divine economy that the sacred literature of the world [should]// have been entrusted to a people whose poetry, depending largely on parallelism, [should] remain poetry in any language you translate it into."[17]

I knew the Bible was important, but I didn't realize it was brilliant literature too. . . .

Psalm 100

// A fancy way of saying "was."

Spring Break

April has begun, which means it's the season for spring break. I've decided spring break is one of those overly hyped experiences that seems designed to disappoint, like prom. Especially when you're in college. You catch a ride home or hit the road for a warm destination, and by the end all you can think of is that you won't have to do it again for a long, long time—especially with *these people*. There's nothing that unravels or even destroys a friendship more quickly than a road trip. Everyone's annoying quirks become epic flaws, and by mile 263 you're thinking, *I swear, if she flips her ponytail like that one more time, I'm gonna cut it off.*

I remember one trip in particular in which I caught a ride home with an acquaintance and some of her friends, and by the end of it I didn't want to hear another word about Jake or Matt or whoever they obsessed about the whole time. I couldn't think of a bigger waste of time than seven hours talking about guys I had never met and would never meet. Plus, I was sick of all the cigarette ash everywhere. But lurking in the back of my mind was the small but persistent thought that Jesus wanted me to be there, if for no other reason than to listen to the people that he loved and had died for. It wasn't time wasted as far as he was concerned. So later I wrote:

> *Jesus, you encountered the cigarette smoke*
> *of your people's self-destruction*
> *and traveled long distances*
> *as they talked and talked*
> *about themselves and their boyfriends*
> *and their messed-up lives.*
> *You listened.*
> *You didn't filter their hearts*
> *through the tar*
> *or their words*
> *through the slang or crass language,*
> *but listened*
> *carefully—full of care—*
> *and through it all,*
> *you heard their hearts crying out*
> *for the grace to somehow stand*
> *in the presence of him who sees all*
> *and hears all*
> *and knows all*
>
> *and still loves.*

Romans 6:6-11

Traveling Companions

There's something about traveling among strangers that makes me feel like I'm stuck in a dream. Nothing seems real—not even my memories of home. And yet at the same time I begin to feel like the only reality is this train station or airport lounge. The only people I've ever known are these strangers whose faces have slowly become familiar. And it throws all my old life into a new light: I'm suddenly aware of how much I love my home and family, how much I take it for granted most of the time.

I was struck by this one spring break while leading a youth mission trip to Mexico. Sitting on the airplane, I wrote the following:

The successful departure amid loving parents left us without a safety net briefly, until the solid human reality of O'Hare Airport drifted its way into our consciousnesses again; and we were real. Real sights, real sounds, real smells, real conversations, real seats underneath us.

And these people who were so much strangers to us are now comfortable and known, our sometime traveling companions with their weaknesses and quirks. Even our fellow passengers feel more familiar than home—home that we seldom step back and really look at. More familiar than family—family whose faces we seldom really see, whose features and tones and mannerisms we have ceased to find remarkable. In the miracle of new people and new surroundings, we are restored to that and those which are our own.

Perhaps this is why Jesus made it his business to be constantly on the road. He was surrounded by nothing too familiar, only sunlight and wind and the rough faces of men and women who forever wondered at him, forever studied his expression and voice and hands, searching for signs of sameness with this fellow traveler. He was a familiar stranger, this Jesus. He had the air of rock-solid reality about him—more real than home or family or the tired, old life. And yet spending time with him put all those things in a new light, somehow. His companions suddenly sensed that life and home and loved ones were far more precious than they'd ever acknowledged before, and that the Lord is the giver of it all.

Luke 8:1-3

Jesus' Best Friend

When I think about Jesus and his itinerant band of followers, I'm especially intrigued by the disciple John, who is considered by many to have been Jesus' best friend. Usually when someone is your best friend, that person sees you in all your frailty and stupidity but loves you anyway. A best friend sees you in all your humanness, with a mixture of respect, bewilderment, loyalty, and even a small measure of contempt. But John's friendship with Jesus was different somehow.

We know that John was the "disciple [Jesus] loved" (John 19:26), the one closest to him, like a younger brother. And yet their closeness didn't blur John's vision, as so often happens in our friendships. From the beginning, Jesus was a wonderful mystery to John, but there never seemed to be doubt in his mind as to who Jesus really is: the Son of the Most High God, the Messiah, the Savior of the whole world.

What amazes me is that this knowledge didn't push John away from Jesus in fear or great reverence, but drew him in as a best friend, as someone who couldn't help but follow Jesus around like a puppy. He didn't put Jesus on a pedestal and keep him at a distance. He didn't force Jesus into some kind of prescribed role, like the other disciples often did, jockeying for positions of power in what they assumed would be his political coup. Rather, John treated him with love, respect, and loyalty; he treated him *as he was*, which meant that Jesus probably felt like he could be himself around John more than around any other person.

O Lord, you could be real around John, and you loved him. Perhaps you loved him because you could be real with him. It's hard to think of you as having needs, but if you got hungry, as we know you did, and if you were so tired you slept through a storm at sea, and if you wept over Lazarus and Jerusalem, then I must believe you needed human companionship like any other person, just as you needed to eat, to sleep, to grieve. And John was that loyal friend to you, that precious friendship of total trust and oneness of mind, so rare in this world. He was as much a gift to you as gold, frankincense, and myrrh.

Jesus, help me to learn from John how to be close to you, how to be your loyal friend, near to your heart. Amen.

John 1:16-18

Homeless

We talk about homelessness and about how Jesus can commiserate with the person who has no home or family to speak of. And it makes me wonder: Why throughout the Gospels is there so little about Christ's brothers and mother except when he is giving them up or giving them away? I can't help but think there must have been some kind of brokenness there. But surely not on Jesus' part . . . ! Perhaps a hardness of heart on their part? But surely not on the part of Mary . . . ! In the end, I'm bewildered by Christ's ideas of home and family.

> Lord Jesus,
> You had no place to live
> and yet you were at home
> wherever you went because
> the whole world was yours.
> You had no wealth or inheritance
> and yet you never lacked
> for your basic needs because
> the whole world was yours.
> You had no family, no domestic support,
> and yet you were knit to your disciples
> as brothers and friends. And even more—
> the whole world was yours.
> You had no earthly "responsibilities";
> you could roam where you wished;
> you were not bound by money or time;
> you had no family to take care of;
> and yet the weight and care of a whole world
> of grief was on your shoulders because
> it was yours.

Matthew 8:18-22

Priorities, Priorities

Well, as I write this entry Lent is winding down and Holy Week is right around the corner—that week in the church calendar running from Palm Sunday to Easter. It's one of my favorite times of the year.

Recently I was astounded to learn about a church somewhere that decided to move Easter to a different Sunday so it wouldn't interfere with spring break. Now I suppose you could argue that this was a noble thing to do, given our cultural situation. Families were missing one of the most important events in the Christian story because they were out of town, so the church attempted to accommodate their needs. And really, what difference does it make which Sunday you celebrate Easter on? Isn't every Sunday a mini-Easter, in a way?

Well, yes, I suppose. In ancient times Christian leaders moved the keeping of the Sabbath from Saturday (the traditional Jewish day of rest) to Sunday in recognition of Jesus' rising from the dead on a Sunday. So Sunday is not only the start of our week but a way to remember the beginning of our new lives in Christ as "Resurrection people." And yet Easter itself is unique because it's a part of the Jesus story that corresponds to an actual date on the calendar (whereas his birthday in December is simply a symbolic date, since we don't know exactly the time of year he was born).

We know Jesus celebrated the festival of Passover with his disciples—what we now call the Last Supper—during the week in which he was arrested, killed, and resurrected. According to Jewish tradition, the Passover is held on the fifteenth day of the month Nisan, the first month in the Jewish calendar, which roughly corresponds to our March/April time frame. So Easter isn't simply an arbitrary date pulled out of the air; it directly corresponds to Passover as Jesus knew it. It's still celebrated on the same day by Christians from almost every denomination, on every continent, in hundreds of languages, all around the world.

So the point is, Easter is there for a reason. To change the date is to cut oneself off from the ongoing story of the Christian year and from one's fellow Christians around the world who are all celebrating on the same day. But even more important, it shows just how messed up people's priorities are. If Easter is so crucial, then why not move *spring break* instead? (*Gasp!*) Or if that's not possible, why not stay in town rather than flying to Cancún? (*CHOKE, GASP!*)

No, really. I'm serious.

Luke 22:7-13

Palm Sunday

As a former church staff person, I can say that Palm Sunday and all the worship events of Easter week are utterly exhausting for the people in charge. Organizing a troop of kids to, say, parade around the sanctuary waving palm branches on cue is roughly the equivalent of herding cats. It makes me wonder how Jesus kept his sanity in the midst of all the original events that took place during those last days of his life. . . .

Lord, how did you do it?
With the watching, heckling,
scornful, crying, laughing crowds
and their pressing closeness,
their energy and heat and curiosity—
how did you remain yourself
and still keep your presence of mind?
How could you stand the noise
—all that noise—
without hollering,
"Shut UP! You're driving me insane!"?
Instead, your mind was clear and quiet,
like a still pool—unruffled.
Your will was hard and solid,
like a concrete slab—unchangeable.
Your heart was big, oh so deep,
like the ocean—infinite.
How did you have a patience so endless?
A kindness so honest?
A heart so outwardly turned
that it never burned with jealousy
or blurted out with pride or arrogance?
How did you have a tongue so subservient
that it never brought glory to its own wit in rudeness?

In fact, when asked if you would please
silence the crowds, thank you
(it was all rather embarrassing, really),
you merely grinned with joy and shouted to the sky,
"If they ever stopped this noise, this tumult,
this crowded hollering,
the stones themselves
would cry out!"

Luke 19:36-40

Holy Week

Lord, it is Holy Week,
and I'm astounded to think
that you knew what was coming
and yet you surrounded yourself
with hostile, skeptical crowds anyway;
you continued telling stories
to the ones you knew
would either betray you or desert you.
How did you do it, Jesus?
It's hard enough for me
to keep going when
I don't know what the future holds—
because I don't know what sort of Fridays
are around the corner—
and yet you, knowing
that you would suffer and die in a few short days,
kept going!
I will never understand.

All I know
is when the days grow difficult—
when it's the Monday of my own Jerusalem
and the crowds around me are testy
and the whole world seems
in a crucifying mood—
teach me how to put my hope
with rock-solid assurance
in Sunday.

What have been the Good Fridays in your life? When has a resurrection moment
turned around a situation that you thought was hopeless?

Luke 18:31-34; 19:41-48

You Gave Up All This: Part 1

I sit at the window
by the light of the moon
—not a mysterious moon tonight,
but a frankly honest sister.
All children are in bed
except myself,
wide awake
blinking at my sister-moon
and wondering in the still night air.
Lord, when I remember
That you gave up your life,
I rarely remember this is what you gave up.
Too often I think of the diseased crowds,
pressing close around you,
waiting for disaster.
This sick life I always think of,
and it seems not such a big loss.
But of course you gave up your
Life-purpose, in a way, which was
to bring Good News to the poor,
to put out your hand
and restore sight to a blind man,
to lift the evil spirit from a boy
writhing on the ground at your feet
—you gave that up too.
But you also gave up nighttime
and this very same moon
reflecting on the calm waters of Galilee.

And I wonder, how could you bear it?

How could I?

Psalm 24:1-2

You Gave Up All This: Part 2

You gave up swimming
and sprawling on hot rocks to dry off,
racing against the other boys
from this tree to that.
You gave up your family:
Mary smiling at the supper table,
sitting in the near-darkness
watching Joseph with his scarred hands
tell again the story of Jacob and Rachel,
David and Goliath. You gave up stories
and the way Peter phrased a question
and Joanna's way of laughing
and the evening comfort of a campfire
after a long day and a good meal.
You gave up all the things
that make life precious,
that make it good to be alive.
The fact that you are God
did not lessen the tearing you no doubt felt
at the knowledge that you must forsake
the only human life you'd ever known:
this world, this moon,
these people you love.
The fact that your death would reconcile
all the world
to yourself, to the living God,
did not make the separation
at that moment—that Gethsemane moment
with the moonlight
spilling on your shaking hands,
with the rock there
so real and cool and friendly and familiar
—that knowledge didn't make it somehow
bearable to leave it all.

Which is why they call you a Man of Sorrows,
well acquainted with grief.

He gave up all this. Could I? Could you?

John 16:16-24

Passover

A friend once invited me to a seder dinner—or Passover celebration—led by a Messianic Jew. This is someone with a Jewish background who has converted to Christianity but who still keeps some Jewish practices as expressions of Christian faith. One of those practices is the Passover supper, which rehearses the story of the Hebrews' exodus from slavery in Egypt. This supper is the meal Jesus was celebrating with his disciples on the night he was arrested, so it's common for Messianic Jews to reinterpret the ritual based on the things Jesus said and did at the time.

Our friend explained that in a Jewish seder, each item of food represents an element of the story, and you eat those items as the story is being told. But there's one part of the ritual in which the meaning is rather unclear. Three matzos—or pieces of unleavened bread, like large crackers—are stacked together, and the middle one is removed. This piece, known as the *afikomen*, is broken, and part of it is returned to the pile while the other is wrapped in a piece of linen and hidden somewhere for the children to find. Later, once the missing piece is found, it's passed around for everyone to break and eat.

In explaining this, our friend lifted up the three matzos and said, "On the night when he was betrayed, the Lord Jesus took some bread"—here he pulled out the middle matzo—"and gave thanks to God for it. Then he broke it in pieces and said, 'This is my body, which is given for you'" (1 Corinthians 11:23-24). Our friend broke the matzo, wrapped it in linen, and put it out of sight. The unexpected symbolism of the second person in the Trinity—the Son—being killed, wrapped in linen, and buried in a tomb was so powerful that we all sat there, speechless. Later, I wrote this prayer:

> *Lord, you took the middle matzo*
> *—the one that was yourself—*
> *and lifted it up*
> *as thousands had done before*
> *and you gave thanks for it and said,*
> *"This is my body,*
> *which is given for you,"*
> *and suddenly all of Passover*
> *burst open with meaning.*
> *This dry, unleavened cracker,*
> *this matzo, the middle matzo,*
> *whose meaning has always*
> *been rather unclear,*
> *suddenly represents*
> *Messiah himself,*
> *whose body we maim by our sin*
> *and whose blood we put*
> *on the doorposts of our hearts.*

Exodus 12:11-14; Luke 22:14-20

In the Garden

I'm continually awed by the parallels between the Old and New Testaments, particularly the Gospels. Jesus knew exactly what he was doing with each symbol, each phrase, each carefully chosen word—and the authors of the Gospels recognized those parallels too. Take the Garden of Gethsemane, for example. Outside of Jerusalem was a garden on the Mount of Olives that overlooked the city; and there Jesus prayed alone on his last night while his followers slept. The Passover meal was over; the soldiers were on their way with Judas to arrest Jesus and put him on trial in a midnight court. And meanwhile, Jesus could have run away. He could've fled the garden. He could've given in to the temptation to avoid doing what God wanted him to do. But he didn't. He obeyed.

Unlike Adam, the first human being, who also faced temptation in a garden once upon a time . . .

> *Lord, it wasn't during the Last Supper,*
> *surrounded by your beloved*
> *friends and followers,*
> *that you wept in sorrow.*
> *No, it was here in the garden,*
> *a place you gazed upon*
> *at the dawn of Creation*
> *and said, "It is good!"*
>
> *—a place where Adam*
> *faced temptation and failed.*
>
> *The first son of flesh*
> *took the cup of pleasure,*
> *which was not his to drink,*
> *so he lost Eden*
> *and all of heaven with it.*
>
> *And now here is another drink*
> *that you would refuse if possible*
>
> *but you cannot regain the Garden*
> *for the rest of us*
>
> *unless you drain the cup of suffering.*

Genesis 3:22-24; Luke 22:39-46

The Sin of the Whole World

I'm reading today from John 18 where Jesus is taken before Pilate for the final verdict before his execution. Verse 28 describes how the Jews of that day wouldn't come into Pilate's headquarters because they didn't want to risk defilement from interaction with a Gentile (non-Jew) and thus be unable to participate in the Passover feast. In other words, they had all kinds of laws about not becoming "contaminated" by people who were considered "unclean"; and if that ever happened, they had to go through intensive cleansing rituals supervised by the Temple priests. Until their cleanness was certified by the priests, which could take days or even weeks, they couldn't participate in worship or special feasts or any of the other religious rites.

So since the Passover was already underway, none of them dared to enter Pilate's quarters: Pilate had to come outside to speak to the crowd. And the fact that he did so just goes to show how eager he was to please the people; he didn't want a riot that would put a stain on his political reputation. But when it came to Jesus, nobody seemed to care whether the young rabbi became contaminated or not. He was a dead man anyway. So they sent Jesus inside to Pilate, though Jesus was a fellow Jew—and a good one, at that.

And so our Savior went alone into the place of defilement, technically losing his place among those "fit" to partake of the Passover. He entered the world of the Gentiles— he who was clean in every sense, our Passover sacrifice—and thus he took upon himself the uncleanness of the unbelievers, of the Roman world with all its cruelties, of Pilate with his belligerence and irreverence. He who had no sin took upon himself the sin of the whole world. Not just of his own people, but of every tribe and nation and race, including yours and mine.

John 18:28-40

Stations of the Cross

There's an ancient Christian tradition known as the Stations of the Cross, which often takes place during Holy Week, especially on Good Friday. A sanctuary is arranged with up to fourteen prayer stations, each one representing an episode from the last hours of Jesus' life. It starts with Jesus' midnight trial, after his arrest in the garden of Gethsemane, and then moves from his carrying the cross through the streets of Jerusalem all the way to his death and burial in the tomb. Worshippers walk from station to station, pausing at each one to remember that particular story and to pray. Sometimes there's a piece of visual art representing the episode from Jesus' life, such as a wood carving or a painting, and other times people simply pause to read the story from the Bible. Whatever the case, by the time they're finished, they've relived the essential moments of the Passion narrative and prepared their hearts for the silence of Holy Saturday and for the promise of Easter.

One year my church decided to do something like that, except instead of creating a dozen or so different stations, we made a large cross from the trunk and branches of the Christmas tree that had stood in the hallway during Advent—and it was the *cross* that moved from station to station during the six weeks of Lent. First it started out near the entrance of the sanctuary; the following week it had progressed a few steps down the aisle toward the altar; and the following week it had moved even farther. The plan was that by Good Friday the cross would be on the stage in front of the altar.

But some people weren't very happy with this arrangement, particularly while the cross was still in the aisle. Its arms were just high enough that they could clothesline you if you weren't paying attention, and they were just long enough that you couldn't simply walk around the cross to reach your seat. The only way to make it down the aisle was to duck under those arms.

Which was the point, of course. The only way to progress in the spiritual life is through the Cross of Jesus Christ. There is no Easter without Good Friday. As Oswald Chambers said, "We are too much given to thinking of the Cross as something we have to get through; we get *through* it in order to get into it."[18]

Luke 23:26-46

A Deeper Reality

The poet in Psalm 22:1 cried out, "My God, my God, why have you abandoned me?"—one of the most honest prayers in the world. The psalmist wasn't trying to gloss over his miserable circumstances by saying, "It's not that bad" or "It must be God's will"; he was desperately begging for answers. When I'm in pain, I can hardly string three words together, let alone articulate a coherent prayer to God! But I can relate to what the psalmist was feeling. Lurking behind the blankness and terror of pain or fear is the horrible sense that God is far, far away.

Jesus knew that psalm by heart, and he quoted it while he was dying on the cross (see Matthew 27:46). Somehow through the haze of pain he summoned ancient words to express his spiritual agony. The interesting thing is what Jesus *didn't* say: He didn't say, "Make it go away" like many of us would. Instead, he quoted a beloved Scripture that he had studied and memorized long before this time of trial had come along.

It's an important lesson for the rest of us. Whenever we get irritated by our pastor's or mentor's insistence that we take the time to memorize verses of Scripture, we need to remember that they aren't saying this to make us feel bad. They're not simply being annoying. They're actually trying to help us get in touch with the deeper reality that God's Word is a lifeline when all other words fail. If we become familiar with the words of Scripture during the good times, then when times are bad—when pain or fear feels like the only reality—we can dredge up those words out of the depths of our souls and cling to them. This goes for both the hopeful promises (such as Joshua 1:5: "I will not fail you or abandon you") and the honest questions, like in this psalm.

There's no doubt Jesus knew the rest of Psalm 22. He knew that God had not "turned his back" (verse 24), and that "his righteous acts will be told to those not yet born" (verse 31).

And perhaps Jesus left the rest of the psalm unsaid because he expects us to know God's Word by heart too.

Psalm 22

Praying the Psalms

The twentieth-century theologian and martyr Dietrich Bonhoeffer wrote, "The Psalter is the prayer book of Jesus Christ."[19] In other words, we are to read the psalms as if we're over-hearing Jesus pray—even pray for us—through those ancient words.

So what do we hear Jesus praying in Psalm 31? Tucked away in these desperate verses are the words "I entrust my spirit into your hand" (verse 5), also known as the last words of Jesus as he was dying (see Luke 23:46). I remember one of my undergraduate professors saying that it's likely Jesus actually repeated the *entire* psalm by memory while hanging on the cross. This seems plausible. If so, what heartbreak and yet what triumph are wrapped up in Psalm 31!

"Rescue me," the psalmist prays in verse 5, "for you are a faithful God." And yet Jesus wasn't rescued from death—not until he had passed through it to the other side.

"But I am trusting you, O LORD," says verse 14. "My future is in your hands" (verse 15). This would have given Jesus an anchor of reality to cling to amid the fog of pain—not to mention a pep talk to any of his followers who stood within the sound of his voice. They also might have heard:

> Love the LORD, all you godly ones!
> For the LORD protects those who are loyal to him,
> but he harshly punishes the arrogant.
> So be strong and courageous,
> all you who put your hope in the LORD!
>
> Psalm 31:23-24

I'd guess this psalm would have incensed the religious leaders who had put Jesus on trial the night before. "Silence their lying lips—those proud and arrogant lips that accuse the godly" (verse 18).

What other verses in this psalm provide insight into Jesus' last moments?

Psalm 31

"Tell It Again"

If I've told this story once, I've told it a thousand times; but I'll tell it again because I love it so much!

While I was in college, I volunteered with an inner-city ministry for children in the housing projects on the south side of Chicago. Every spring we had an Easter banquet, and the kids would get all dressed up and behave like saints for five minutes or so. This particular year I had a little girl named Kiki on my lap—she looked so cute in her Sunday best and was acting prim and proper for once. I knew my time was limited, so while I had her attention, I said, "Kiki, do you know why we're having this party? Have you ever heard the Easter story?" She shook her head.

So I said, "There once was a man named Jesus, . . ." and went ahead and told what happened to him in words she could understand. "A long time ago God sent his only Son, Jesus, to live here on earth with us. He was the best man who ever lived. He healed the sick, loved everybody, and taught the truth about God to anyone who would listen. But people didn't always want to hear what he had to say. Some of them got very angry and figured out a way to get him arrested. So they put him on trial and found him guilty—even though he hadn't done anything wrong—and decided he should be put to death. The next day they hung him on a cross, where he died. His best friends buried him in a tomb. But do you know what happened? Death can't keep the Son of God down! Three days later, early on a Sunday morning, he was alive again—he passed through death and came out on the other side, alive again! And someday, he promises, we'll be with him again. That's what Easter is all about."

The whole time I was speaking, Kiki was perfectly still, like a child enchanted. It was as if I were weaving a magic spell, reciting a string of words that had the power to change the fate of mortals. When I was done, there was a pause, and then she said, "Tell it again."

So I did. And when I was done telling it a second time, she pointed to her friend who was sitting next to us and said, "Tell her." So I said, "You help me tell her," and together we shared the Easter story.

It's so easy for those of us who've heard the story all our lives to forget the power of that tale, how it grips the imagination like a spell of enchantment. But did you know that's where the word *gospel* comes from? It comes from the Old English for "good spell," or "good story." The story of Jesus is indeed the "Good Spell," the good magic, the best kind of enchantment that can transform lives. How could we ever forget?

Romans 1:16-17

Fish for Breakfast

After his resurrection, Jesus served his disciples fish for breakfast, which has always made me wonder: Who cleaned the fish?

I'm guessing Jesus himself did. With his resurrected hands, scarred from the cross, maybe he picked up a flat, sharp stone and skinned and gutted the freshly caught creatures—which, if you've ever cleaned a fish, you know is a messy and smelly business. Especially in the damp chill of a lakeside morning. But I'm guessing he did so with a reverent kind of joy on his face, praising God not only for the gift of fish but also for the gift of a new day after his dark journey through death and beyond. The resurrected Jesus was no ghost. He was real and warm and alive. And he wanted some breakfast.

It's easy to think of the spiritual life as that which raises us above the everyday world to a higher, more enlightened level or something. We want to reach a state in which we're beyond messy chores and ordinary tasks. And yet recently I was chastened by the words of a professor who reminded us that as Christians we believe in the resurrection of the body, not just the spirit. This means we throw off all those pagan tendencies toward calling the body bad and the spirit good and instead embrace Genesis 1:31, in which God "looked over all he had made, and he saw that it was very good!"—our human bodies included.

So there's no such thing as a more "spiritual" or "enlightened" plane of existence, as if God weren't really interested in our physical selves. Because of Christ's bodily resurrection after death, we claim the hope that one day our bodies, too, will be "raised in glory" (1 Corinthians 15:43). None of this business about becoming disembodied spirits or ghosts or angels after we die. We will be our own bodily selves, eating and talking and walking and laughing, just as Jesus did after his resurrection. Except, like Jesus, our bodies will no longer be subject to decay like they were before; they will be renewed, heavenly bodies, never to die again. This is good news!

John 21:1-14; 1 Corinthians 15:35-44

Fully Human

Jesus, so often I lose sight of you as a real human being. I fail to think of you personally and specifically, with a face and hands and feet, a voice, a smile, a laugh, a manner of speech particular to you. "Out of sight, out of mind," the saying goes—what a painful reality! I can't see you, so it's easy to forget you. I imagine your disciples experienced the same thing, in time, after you were gone . . . the failure to recall your face, a strange sense of panic at their inability to remember your voice or the way you phrased certain thoughts, even the way you said their names. Just as the rest of us lose friends or relatives and begin to forget what their physical presence was like, the disciples must have struggled to remember you— except they didn't have the blessing of photography to help.

The New Testament offers no descriptions of your physical appearance, unlike your ancestor David, who was described as "dark and handsome, with beautiful eyes" (1 Samuel 16:12); which leads me to believe that you were rather ordinary in appearance, maybe even forgettable. And yet you were recognized by hundreds and followed by thousands, and eventually you could go nowhere openly. I wonder how many of your disciples later attempted to describe you to those who had never seen you, or sketched your image in the sand out of nostalgia? I wonder if any of your half brothers looked like you,// with Mary's eyes, and thus became precious echoes of your face to those who had known you well?

I don't wish to set up an idol or a false image of you to worship. But picturing you as a real person keeps me from thinking you're just a metaphor or merely an example of God's love—an illustration that could easily be replaced by something else. You are yourself, and no other. There never was anyone like you, and there never will be again. Picturing your face, imagining your voice, helps me experience grace as a tangible person who sits down at the table and looks me in the eye. I don't ever want to forget you. Amen.

Hebrews 2:14-15

// See Matthew 13:55.

These Are Written

> The disciples saw Jesus do many other miraculous signs in addition to the ones recorded in this book. But these are written so that you may continue to believe that Jesus is the Messiah, the Son of God, and that by believing in him you will have life by the power of his name.
>
> John 20:30-31

Notice that the above passage comes just after the Resurrection story in John's Gospel. As a writer, I instinctively wonder why it was so important for John to offer this explanation. Perhaps there were as many stories about the resurrected Jesus as there were people to witness him walking around—and we're assured there were hundreds of witnesses who saw him alive and in person after Easter Sunday (see 1 Corinthians 15:3-7). John probably could've spent the rest of his life collecting those stories and writing them down. But he didn't. He chose to record just a few, and that's what ended up in his Gospel.

So how did he decide what to include and what to edit out? Especially when he loved Jesus so much that he probably could've talked about him all day long, to anybody who would listen, for the rest of his life . . . ?

John told us exactly what he had to do. He chose only those stories that accomplished his purpose. And what was his purpose? What was his driving theme? That his readers "may continue to believe that Jesus is the Messiah, the Son of God." Any story that didn't accomplish this purpose just didn't make the cut.

So what about my own life? What if I'm a book that others are reading? If my theme is Jesus, what do I include and what must be edited out?

John 20:30-31

Your Life Is a Book

Whether we like it or not, our lives are stories that other people are reading. Each of us is a book, with a beginning, a middle, and an end. When people read that book, what do they learn? What would they say is the purpose of that book? What is the defining theme?

Well, if the title of my life is *Christian*—if that's the identity I've chosen as a follower of Jesus—then the purpose or theme of my story is the same as John's in his Gospel (see April 21). It's to show people who Jesus is. It's to point others to God. This goes for my words, actions, goals, obligations, spending habits, relationships, and everything in between. If none of those things match my title, the people reading the book of my life will complain that my inner chapters don't live up to the promise of Christian. Instead, they'll say I should be titled Bookworm or Shopaholic or Whiner. Catch those readers in a bad mood and they'll simply settle for Hypocrite and call it a day.

When other people read the story of your life—when they observe you going about your day, a living and breathing book—what are they learning? How can you craft and shape the manuscript of who you are so that it accomplishes the purpose you've stated in the title, in the opening sentence? Because your title is a promise; it means your inner material matches what you say up front about yourself. And if it doesn't, take it from a writer: Your readers have every reason to blow you off.

1 Peter 1:23–2:3

The Deletion Business

People often ask me what it's like to be a writer. I haven't come up with a good answer yet. Sometimes it feels like being a gardener or a farmer: You throw a bunch of stuff out there and see what grows and what doesn't, and then you spend the rest of the time yanking up weeds and pruning everything back. It's an organic process that takes a good deal of hard work, including cutting out stuff that really shouldn't be there (such as annoying adverbs) and thinning good growth that you'd rather not get rid of (such as interesting little tangents).

With most of my manuscripts, if I were to include everything I could think of about the topic I'm working on, I suppose my laptop itself could not contain the words that would be written. Especially if I think every word is pure brilliance. But a book that size would be unbearable. It would ramble terribly. It would be downright awful in spots. Critics would rant about how the author couldn't keep to the point. For any book to be successful, it must have a clear sense of its purpose and direction; everything extra must be cut.

So while writers are in the writing business, they're also in the deletion business—rather like Christians, come to think of it. Our main vocation is to tell the story of Jesus to the world by our actions and words (see April 21–22). This includes deleting those things that hinder "readers" of our lives from discerning our main theme—stuff like *sin*, to use an obvious example.

What have you cut out lately?

Matthew 13:3-9

The Rejection Business

I'm daunted when I walk into a bookstore. Who am I to think I could make a worthwhile contribution to the piles and piles of books in there? Why do I believe there's something new to say that hasn't already been said in the history of the English language, using just twenty-six little letters of the alphabet, arranged in some brand-new way? It seems impossible.

There's a saying in the publishing world that while editors are in the publishing business, they're also in the rejection business. For every book that sees the light of day, there are hundreds and hundreds of manuscripts that end up in the circular file (read: *recycle bin*). Many of them for good reasons, but some just because the market wasn't right or because the editor had something nasty for lunch and was feeling crabby. Whatever the case, there are a lot of good stories that never make it into the hands of readers. If all the stories that could be told were actually published, I suppose all the bookstores of the world could not contain the stuff that would be written.

I picture the disciple John, working hard on his Gospel. Along comes another disciple who says, "Don't forget about the fish. Remember the fish?" And John says, "I've got the fish." The other one says, "Okay, so is Peter's denial in there? That's a good one." And John says, "Yeah, I got it. Thanks." The disciple sits down, squints at the parchment, and then says, "Hey, what about the wise men? You forgot about the wise men." John tucks the quill behind his ear and sighs. "Look," he says. "That story is good too. *All* the stories about Jesus are good. But I can't tell everything."

We Christians may be in the publishing business—that is, telling stories about Jesus to the world—but we're also in the rejection business. Sure, we need to cut out the sin that thwarts our ultimate theme and purpose. But what about those *good* things that might crowd out the image of Christ in us if we're not careful? Volunteer commitments, social obligations, extracurricular activities . . . all good things, but not perhaps the *best*.

What healthy growth needs to be pruned back so we can stick to the point?

John 21:25

Time Is Short

We're talking about the Gospel of John and the storytelling tactics he used to convey his message. Why did he tell some stories and not others?

In addition to developing his theme in the most effective way possible, John knew his time was short. The early disciples didn't exactly live a life of leisure, casually spreading the Good News to the next town whenever it struck their fancy. Instead, they fled persecution from city to city for most of their brief lives. Many of them were hunted down and imprisoned or killed within a few years after Jesus' resurrection. John was one of the few who lived to old age, or so tradition holds. Some scholars believe that by the time he wrote the book of Revelation toward the end of his life, he had been imprisoned on the island of Patmos in the Mediterranean Sea for years—possibly even sentenced to hard labor. He knew that all over the Roman world, Christian converts were dying and in prison for their beliefs. If they had the chance to read his Gospel at all, it wasn't a leisurely stroll through an eight-hundred-page Harry Potter novel during a semester of study halls; it was a hasty chapter here and there by candlelight, snatched between night watches in a prison cell somewhere. Some of John's readers wouldn't have reached the final chapter before their time in this world was up.

So if he was going to accomplish what he stated as his main theme, he couldn't go down every tangent he would have liked, or his readers would never hear the really important stuff.

Like John, we have tangents we'd love to go down, endless appendixes that could derail us from fully developing the theme God has given us. But time is short. Our audience is here today and gone tomorrow. We ourselves only have so much time in our overly crowded schedules. Why waste it on nonessentials?

Take it from a writer. You don't get to follow every tangent (hobby, mission, theological rabbit trail). Life is just too short.

2 Peter 1:12-15

Know Your Audience

John's second storytelling tactic, besides keeping it to the point (see April 24–25), was that he knew his audience. He knew that people were desperate for the Good News. He had to cut out what didn't belong, including details about Jesus' appearance, age, mannerisms, and favorite food. I'm sure many biblical scholars since then have wished he hadn't, but John knew his purpose. He wasn't writing for them. He was writing for the lost and the broken and the desperate. His intended readers needed the stories that would lead to their salvation, not to another PhD. If he dropped that focus, if he forgot his audience, then he could easily lead them astray into trivialities, where they'd lose interest or lose their trust in him and go off searching for some other story that would give them a straight answer.

The same is true for us. Who are the people we sit down with at lunch every day? Who observes our actions, words, mannerisms, facial expressions, and habits at work or school? Who serves us coffee, scans our groceries, hauls our garbage? These people are our audience. They are the ones who're reading the books of our lives. We're not "writing" for other Christians. In fact (like Paul at times), we may not particularly *care* what other believers have to say about us (see Galatians 1:10). Instead, we're writing for the hurting, the lonely, the desperate, the bored. If we have any sense of them as real human beings—if we actually look them in the eyes and listen to what they say—then we begin to have a good handle on what aspect of the story they need to hear. We know our audience.

1 John 1:1-4

It's Not about You

One thing I notice about the disciple John is that even though he was one of the main characters in his own Gospel, he didn't let himself get in the way. In fact, you'll notice that the Gospel of John is almost never, ever about John (unless it's referring to the other John, John the Baptist). It's about Jesus. Even when the chapter he was writing involved himself as a character, John didn't mention himself by name; he refers to "the disciple Jesus loved" (John 13:23) or "that other disciple" (John 18:15). Only by a close reading do we conclude he must be referring to himself.

Talk about modesty! Unlike today's celebrities, whose autobiographies feature their names in large type and their faces (or bodies) even larger, John intended to be almost invisible. So even though he's the author, as well as one of the main characters of this particular story, he doesn't get the glory.

In the same way, our story is *not* about us. Even though my life might be the Gospel according to Sarah, that doesn't mean it's the Gospel *about* Sarah. I'm not the most important person in this story. And neither are you the hero or the star of the book of your life—not if your title is *Christian* (which originally meant "little Christ"). This is a counterintuitive idea in our culture. It's not fun or ego stroking to hear that we don't get to take center stage even in our own story. But if we take our cue from John, it's the only way to accomplish our stated purpose, which is to glorify Jesus, not ourselves.

To say that my life is a book doesn't mean it's an autobiography.

John 21:20-24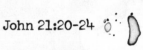

Sharing the Story

Of course, if you've been paying attention to everything I've said over the past few days (see April 21–27), you realize what I'm *really* talking about is evangelism: the process of sharing your faith. Sure, many people are uncomfortable with that term. They associate it with forcing others to listen to something they really don't want to hear or standing on street corners holding signs announcing, "Vengeance is mine, saith the Lord." Those are really lousy depictions of what it means to be an evangelist. We'll explore this topic further next month, but suffice it to say that evangelism means sharing the Good News about Jesus. If you call yourself a Christian, the book of your life is evangelistic by definition—the title of your book states it openly, and your words and behavior conform to that stated purpose.

Most of the time this means we aren't verbally telling the story of Jesus so much as living it. But part of living the story also means telling it sometimes. The call to articulate the Good News isn't just for the preachers or teachers or Lauren Winners// who stand in pulpits or teach Sunday school or write memoirs charting their conversion stories. It's something we're *all* called to do, on a regular basis, such as when the audience in our lives asks us point-blank why we go to church or what we believe or what we think about the AIDS pandemic or any of the various conversations we find ourselves in from day to day. We have a responsibility to match our verbal communication with our stated purpose, which is to glorify God.

So what's *your* story?

1 Peter 3:13-16

// Author of the memoir *Girl Meets God*, which describes her conversion from Judaism to Christianity.

Pruning Required

I step outside of my grandparents' house in this warm spring weather, and there, to my astonishment, are green shoots pushing up from the remains of the hydrangea bush I thought we killed last fall. It was an enormous bush with huge bluish-purple flowers, and my instinct was to leave it alone, but my grandfather insisted we chop it back to just six inches above the ground. I stood there, protesting, as my father took out large clippers and cut away. Soon there was nothing left but dead-looking stalks. I thought for sure we'd killed it.

But no, here are the green shoots, and the bush most likely will be even taller and bloom even better this year than last. Which brings up a spiritual point, of course. Urban T. Holmes III wrote:

> Any good gardener knows that beautiful roses require careful pruning. Pieces of living plant have to die. . . . We seem to have lost the insight that growth in Christ requires careful pruning. Pieces of us by our intentional action need to die if we are to become the person that is God's vision.[20]

In his context he's speaking about giving up certain behaviors or habits for Lent. He's troubled by how people find the idea of "giving up" anything so silly that they speak of "taking on" something new instead (which I've done too—and certainly it's appropriate at times). But he challenges this as the only attitude:

> What we failed to understand was that a life incapable of significant sacrifice is also incapable of courageous action.[21]

This isn't the first time I've wrestled with this quote. Beyond its Lenten connotations, I find it has something profound to say about American culture in general. Considering our present self-absorption and moral adrift-ness, is it possible that our decisions to take no risks and make no sacrifices in our personal lives have made us a people incapable of meaningful (i.e., "courageous") action? Or if we do act, don't we often act too late, when crisis has forced the inevitable upon us?

In my own life, what am I not willing to give up? What must I prune in order to become healthier and more effective? What must be taken from me before I'm able to courageously give of myself to others?

John 15:1-4

Gone to the Birds

Today it's so warm the birds are confused and think it's full-on summer. They're singing away and nesting like crazy, which reminds me of the robins that built a nest over our back door last year.

At first I was *not* happy. The last thing I wanted were "neighbors" that pooped on my head and dive-bombed me every time I exited my own house. In fact, in the past when they'd tried to build there, I had successfully stopped them by knocking down the unfinished construction project with a broom. This would happen several times in a row before they'd finally take the hint and go somewhere else. But last summer a pair of robins managed to finish before I knew what was happening, and in no time there were three little blue eggs in the nest—and then three fluffy chicks with scrawny necks and enormous beaks. Their parents chirped loudly at us whenever we tried to leave the house, as if it were *their* property. And of course they pooped all over the deck and even on the car. It was all very annoying and amusing at the same time.

When I read today's psalm, I'm tickled by the idea that there would have been birds flying in and out of the ancient Temple in Jerusalem all year round. That's because it had no glass on the windows. While the people knelt solemnly in prayer and the priests offered sacrifices, the birds cheerfully chirped and flew around and built their nests in the high corners at the top of pillars, where the priests couldn't reach. What a mess the swallows must have made! And they would've had no concept that some parts of the temple were considered holier than others—such as the Most Holy Place,// where not even the priests dared to go except one who was selected once a year. But did the birds care? Nope, they built their nests wherever they pleased, even right over the high altar behind the curtain that hid the Most Holy Place from the rest of the sanctuary.

I can just picture the psalmist kneeling on the floor, glancing up in amusement as he watched the birds coming and going. All he desired was to get close to God, to make his spiritual home as close to God's holiness as possible, no matter what kind of fuss everybody made about it. So he was jealous that the birds could make their home in the very heart of the sanctuary, where humans dared not go. He wished he could be like them, going fearlessly every day where angels fear to tread.

What if we wanted that too?

Psalm 84:1-4

// See Leviticus 16.

Solid Things

People often question how Christians can believe in a God whose existence remains a scientific uncertainty, an invisible, immaterial mystery. And I ask, Can you prove a loving relationship? Is my marriage still tangible, say, when my husband and I are on opposite sides of the planet? Is a friend still a friend when I can't see her face-to-face? There are some immaterial things beyond the reach of scientific certainty that, if they were solid objects, would shake the very earth.

In the high, clear blue
of this bright day,
I praise you, Lord.
For you created this infinite sky,
the feather-clouds, stately,
that glide across the sun, so high.
The obnoxious green of new life sprawls
with mad delight
over lawn and garden,
fence and field.
The flowers jump out
to see what's going on;
blossoms hold nothing back
with their heady, thick perfume
—like old ladies in church
convinced the winter-world's senses
have dulled and grown rusty,
and therefore people should shout more,
should laugh as if they could
fill space with sound.
Every impression
attempts to be tangible somehow,
as if the aroma of the apricot tree
were a truck plowing us over,
the brilliant sky a freight train,
my friend's laughter or music
like brick walls, impenetrable.

Solid, material,
the sunlight spills onto this page

and I jump into the arms
of the One who made it all.

Psalm 104:1-5

Beginnings and Endings

May is underway, that strange month of beginnings and endings. As the earth in this hemisphere shifts into a new season of summer, with new life springing up everywhere, the school year careens to a close. Here in our college town, folks are cramming for finals, packing up dorms and offices, and shuttling moving vans from one end of the city to the other. The post office is jammed. Seniors stand in clumps in the quad, crying, hugging, promising all kinds of things they'll never be able to deliver. And meanwhile a baby bunny peeks out from a hedge, blinking in astonishment at this marvelous new world, at the beginning of a lifetime that stretches before him on the grass.

Beginnings, endings. Such is May in the shifting of seasons. Such is May in the secular calendar. And such is May in the liturgical year, in the way the church structures its own schedule. After Easter we remember the forty days our resurrected Lord hung out with his disciples before he returned to heaven (see Acts 1:3). This is when we retell the story of how his earthly ministry came to an unexpected close. But then a new era begins: After the Ascension the disciples waited in Jerusalem, as Jesus had commanded, until the Holy Spirit fell upon them in the power of Pentecost. We remember their empowerment, their sudden boldness to spread the Good News, in what we call the birthday of the church.

All this is recounted during the month of May," and after that comes the longest season in the church year: the season of Pentecost, sometimes known as the second stretch of Ordinary Time. It goes from late May to late November, culminating with "Christ the King Sunday," when we look toward his promised return in glory and the end of our world as we know it.

Endings, beginnings; old life, new life. What's ending in your life these days? What's just getting started? Where is God in the midst of it all?

Isaiah 44:6-8

// See May 10.

Grown Up

When I was a junior in college, I lived in a house with seven other women, including several seniors I grew quite close to. Toward the end of the school year, I became extra-conscious of the fact that our time together was short, that we were growing up faster than we knew. Here are my reflections from that time:

Suddenly
there are only a few more weeks
of this school year—
less than a month
with this community
I've grown to love.
I won't miss the schedules,
the stress of deadlines.
(How long has it been since
I didn't have either of those?
Two years? Fifteen?)
But I will miss the playfulness
of pretending to be grown-ups,
the sisterhood of silliness.

Now, I am *grown up.*
I'm twenty and I march
down the sidewalk thinking,

I'm twenty and I'm awake,
and all this grown-up life is
no longer a game.
Back when I was a child,
I spoke and thought and reasoned
like a child. But now
that I'm grown up

I'm scared.

1 Corinthians 13:11

This Is Your Body

I wrote this prayer during my junior year of college, the week before my housemates graduated (see May 3). Somehow I knew life would send us in many different directions, never to live in the same town—let alone the same house—again.

I praise you for community,
for the sobbing joy
that brims up in me
when I think of the women here.
Is this what it means
to be your body, the church,
we seven, who, giggling,
sing "Happy Birthday"
or rake the yard together
or sit around the Sunday table
eating homemade pizza?
We sit banqueting now,
but then Sunday—Graduation Day—
empties the table,
wine glasses half full,
bread crumbs on the cloth.
Sunday sends us spinning
to the four corners of the earth,
promising to write
when we have time,
when we remember.
We don't want this to happen,
this uprooting, this permanent severing.
No. No.

But Lord, we are your body

broken again
and again
and again.

Acts 20:16-27, 36-38

Homeward

Well, my husband and I are moving once more. After relocating last fall to North Carolina for graduate school, we're headed to Virginia for the summer so he can complete a required internship. And even as we load the car, my heart aches for the familiar things of what I consider my true hometown in Michigan: the usual routine, the voices of friends and neighbors, even the bank teller who was there at the local branch every Tuesday. The old familiar life was steady and comfortable; this new life is unsettling and at times scary. Even when I'm busy, in the background of my mind is a restlessness that seems to say, *Hadn't you better get going now?* But where would I go? Each new place is where I live.

Meanwhile, my grandma's mind wanders these days. She doesn't always recognize my grandpa. And even though they live in the same house they built more than fifty years ago, she thinks she's somewhere else—visiting friends or at a hotel somewhere far away. She pesters Grandpa every evening, in her dear way, that she'd better start packing, or her husband will start to wonder where she is. And what will he eat for dinner if she's not there? Hadn't they better get going?

Grandpa tries to be patient. He explains things over and over again. She looks at him with deep skepticism and shakes her head. She occasionally pleads. This is *not* home. She wants to go back *now*.

My sister and I have discussed this, wondering if perhaps Grandma is onto something. Spiritually speaking, none of us are home. Not really.

Every morning as I come to consciousness in a new place, I find myself repeating the words of one of the most ancient of all psalms, older even than David's psalms, coined by a displaced wanderer named Moses: "Lord, through all the generations you have been our home!" (Psalm 90:1). Psalm 91, which follows it, carries on the same theme: "Those who live in the shelter of the Most High will find rest in the shadow of the Almighty" (verse 1). God is our dwelling place. Home is not the place where we came from. Not where we're headed. Not even where we are now. Until we're with him forever, we will always be strangers in a strange land.

Which explains the homeward ache . . .

Psalm 91

A Pattern of Threes

> He will again send you Jesus, your appointed Messiah. For he must remain in heaven
> until the time for the final restoration of all things.   Acts 3:20-21

The exact date varies each year, but May is when we remember the ascension of Jesus,
in which he was lifted up to heaven forty days after his crucifixion. And as I read Peter's
defense of the gospel in Acts 3, I'm struck by the phrase, "He must remain in heaven."
Why must he? If what Jesus accomplished was truly "once for all" (see Hebrews 7:27),
why wasn't his resurrection the end of the story? Why couldn't he just stay with us
forever? Why did he have to go away again and leave us behind?

Too often we gloss over the Ascension because we don't understand it and can't
really explain it. It seems too convenient somehow, like the Mormon story of Joseph
Smith's tablets being discovered, interpreted, and written down but then whisked away
by angels before the general population had time to see them. Why remove the original
evidence? Peter's explanation of Christ's physical absence would seem suspect to me
except for the unutterable faith he and the early apostles had. They didn't think it was
weird that the risen Savior simply left them on their own. They also didn't act like they
were making the whole thing up. According to Luke 24:50-53, Jesus appeared, spent some
time with them, and then ascended into the sky amid a bunch of witnesses. So if it were
a collective lie made up by a large group of followers, wouldn't the whole fabric of the lie
fall apart at some point, on somebody's deathbed, when the agony of guilt or the burning flesh of martyrdom was so overwhelming that one of them confessed to the corporate
conspiracy?

I'm looking for a pattern here, maybe of threes. Maybe the theological point is that
we're simply not humanly capable of comprehending more than one aspect of the Trinity
at a time, even when it's right in front of our noses (as when the Spirit descended on Jesus
during his baptism and the Father's voice resounded from heaven—Father, Son, and Holy
Spirit—and those who saw it didn't have a clue what was happening at the time). In the
long unfolding of human history, first we encounter the God of the Hebrew Scriptures;
then we encounter the Word made flesh, dwelling among us; and now we've been given
the Holy Spirit, our comforter and guide. This is our limitation for now, at least—until all
things in God's plan are fulfilled and Jesus returns, when we're finally healed enough to see
that it has been *one* God working in power and unity all the time. Meanwhile, it's my own
sin and brokenness that keep me from seeing him.

Knowing this makes Christ's physical absence a little more bearable somehow. But
I still miss him.

Acts 1:6-11; 3:17-21

Marching Orders

Before his ascension (see May 6), Jesus' last words to his disciples were about their evangelistic mission: "[Tell] people about me everywhere—in Jerusalem, throughout Judea, in Samaria, and to the ends of the earth" (Acts 1:8). In Matthew's Gospel, Jesus gives specifics about how they are to accomplish this mission: "Go and make disciples of all the nations, baptizing them in the name of the Father and the Son and the Holy Spirit. Teach these new disciples to obey all the commands I have given you" (28:19-20). Biblical scholars call this the great commission: Jesus is commissioning his followers to go into all the world and spread the news.

Note the tone of his language. Go. Make disciples. Baptize. Teach. These are not mere suggestions; they're commandments. He's not offering a few helpful ideas for the occasional community service project; he's issuing marching orders. Hence the term *apostles*, or "sent ones"—you might as well call them soldiers. Jesus the Major General sends them from the mountaintop of his ascension back down into the valley of the lost, the broken, the oppressed, and the seeking, which means the apostles from now on are to be full-time evangelists—those who share the *euangelion*, the Good News, about Jesus Christ with the world.

But Jesus' last words aren't just for the disciples. They're for us, too. We are the heirs of his last will and testament, the keepers of the commandment he issued from the mountaintop before he left. We walk around with our commissioning papers tucked in our spiritual pockets, soldiers on deployment to a foreign land, with the words of our commanding officer ringing in our ears. The trouble is, we act like we have no idea what God wants from us. "Please, please tell me," we earnestly pray, "what is your plan for my life? What do you want me to do?"

What, are we deaf?

Matthew 28:16-20

No Shame

Okay, so the final thought in the May 7 devo was a bit harsh. Obviously not everyone is comfortable with the idea that Christ commands *all* of us to be evangelists—I can't say I'm terribly excited about it myself. As I mentioned in the April devotions, most of our hang-ups have to do with misconceptions about what evangelism really is. We think of evangelists as those red-faced preachers yelling on TV or those guys in black suits who go from door to door asking desperate housewives if they're happy with life. And my guess is that the apostle Paul—perhaps the most influential evangelist of all time—wouldn't have found either example all that troubling—at least not their boldness to talk about spiritual matters to anyone who would listen. I mean, this is the same guy who said, "I am not ashamed of this Good News about Christ" (Romans 1:16). So we won't get any sympathy there.

At the same time, I doubt Paul would have said that TV evangelism is the *only* way to go or that the guys in black suits have a corner on conversion. More likely he would have agreed with Saint Francis, to whom the following quote is attributed: "Preach the Gospel at all times; if necessary, use words." Which is to say, point people to Jesus by your actions first, not your talk. This is nothing new.

But I'm a babbler. I've always had this impulse to explain things—which can be good when I'm exercising the spiritual gift of teaching; otherwise it gets me in trouble. Later I feel lousy about it, mortified that I didn't have the self-control to hold my tongue. *Shame, shame*, whispers a voice in the back of my mind. *How embarrassing. You can't make a convincing explanation of faith even to the people who ask you. So why bother?* I learn to keep to safe topics, like fashion or movies, rather than the Good News about Christ.

No doubt many of the early Christians experienced the same struggle, or Paul wouldn't have encouraged them so often not to be ashamed. "Be a good worker," he wrote to a young pastor named Timothy, "one who does not need to be ashamed and who correctly explains the word of truth" (2 Timothy 2:15). Earlier he said, "God has not given us a spirit of fear and timidity, but of power, love, and self-discipline" (1:7).

So in the end I'm not the one who is the evangelist; it's the Holy Spirit working *through* me. What a relief!

Psalm 119:41-48

Forget Eloquence

> Christ didn't send me to baptize, but to preach the Good News—and not with
> clever speech, for fear that the cross of Christ would lose its power.
>
> I Corinthians 1:17

This is an odd idea of Paul's, that he would feel led to proclaim the gospel to the Greeks *without* eloquence. From all we know of him, Paul was one of the most brilliant men of his time: quite likely trained in classical debate and able to converse with the best minds in the marketplaces and synagogues of the ancient world. He wowed the Greeks of Athens in Acts 17 by quoting their own poets; he stunned governors and kings with his wit, even prompting one of them to exclaim, "Do you think you can persuade me to become a Christian so quickly?" (Acts 26:28). For all intents and purposes, this might have been exactly why God chose Paul in the first place: to pack a polemical punch. If anything impressed the ancient world, it was eloquence.

But for some reason—perhaps because his audience was impressed by it—Paul felt that to speak with his usual power would water down the potency of the gospel. It would put the focus on Paul rather than on the Cross. The Good News would've become merely one among many finely crafted arguments, promoting yet another trendy school of thought, whereas a simple presentation of the gospel, without frills, would've highlighted the truth in such a way that the Greeks would have been both repelled by its seeming "foolishness" and compelled by its bare-bones grace.

Paul wrote to the converted Greeks and Jews in Corinth, "When I first came to you, dear brothers and sisters, I didn't use lofty words and impressive wisdom to tell you God's secret plan" (I Corinthians 2:1). For an inveterate babbler like me, who stumbles over her words in an attempt to sound brilliant, this is good news. Keep it simple, stupid!

1 Corinthians 1:17-25

The Expected Unexpected

In the absence of a specific date that stays the same each year, it seems appropriate to tackle Pentecost at this point in our liturgical story. Not that I advocate switching the church calendar around!// The book of Acts is quite clear about dates and times for this particular event. The Holy Spirit came upon the disciples during the festival of Pentecost, which in those days came fifty days after the celebration of Passover (see today's Scripture). So these events happened roughly six weeks after Jesus' resurrection and shortly after his ascension. But for literary purposes I will overthrow two thousand years of tradition(!) and speak in generalities. Pentecost is generally celebrated in the month of May. Good enough.

Anyway, before his ascension, Jesus told his disciples, "Do not leave Jerusalem until the Father sends you the gift he promised. . . . John baptized with water, but in just a few days you will be baptized with the Holy Spirit" (Acts 1:4-5)—one of many cryptic statements that only became clear after the fact, I imagine. Shortly thereafter, Jesus rose into heaven, leaving his disciples behind, and they dutifully made their way back to the house in Jerusalem where they were staying.

It must have felt like a sad, empty place. Their leader was gone—again. They probably felt restless, wondering just what Jesus meant by the Father's promise. Some of them probably began turning their thoughts toward home and family, which they had left behind long ago in their decision to follow Jesus. But they stayed in Jerusalem anyway, where they "met together and were constantly united in prayer, along with Mary the mother of Jesus, several other women, and the brothers of Jesus" (Acts 1:14).

And it was while they were meeting that the expected unexpectedly happened. Suddenly they were caught in a supernatural hurricane, a spiritual volcano, a cosmic flood. The Holy Spirit descended upon them, even as he rose up within them, and they were engulfed by the power and the presence of God like never before. They became like the prophets of old, empowered to speak the truth—but bolder. No longer would they pine after their distant and departed teacher; the Spirit of Jesus was now the air in their lungs, the fire in their eyes, the words on their lips. Emboldened, empowered, they left the upper room and went out to change the world.

O Holy Spirit, I can't help wondering, *where are you now?*

Acts 2:1-21

// See my rant on April 7 about the church that decided to move Easter to a different date because it interfered with spring break. Of course, it's impossible to stick with specific dates in this devotional, since it's not geared for any one particular year, but I'm trying to keep as close to the general calendar as possible.

Where Are You Now?

I hate to say it, but there seems to be a mighty disconnect between the story of Pentecost in the second chapter of Acts and the spiritual life of many mainstream Christians today. I don't mean to sound dismissive of all the heroic things churches are doing—missions and medical clinics and food pantries and such. And I don't mean to discount the experiences of many denominations worldwide for whom the Holy Spirit is a vital expression of faith and worship. I'm just being honest here. The spiritual life of the average Christian I know is pretty quiet.

Which leads to several interesting questions. First, does this mean the disciples were *above* average? Are certain people hardwired for Spirit-empowered preaching and evangelism, while the rest of us are not? Or does the Spirit override our natural tendencies and use us to the glory of God anyway?

Second, if the Spirit could do that for Peter and the disciples, why not for *every* Christian? Why not for me right now? Why can't I simply walk out of this house, drive to the mall, stand up in the food court, and preach the gospel?

Third, if the Holy Spirit could empower the believers in that Pentecost moment, why not *every* moment? Why aren't tongues or flames of fire visibly resting on Christians all the time, as they did for the disciples in Acts 2? Has the Spirit finished with us, or is there more to come?

I could go on and on. If you've ever studied theology, you know I'm wandering into very tricky territory indeed. In the end, what it boils down to is whether the Spirit's activity has anything to do with us—with our openness or desire or earnest prayer—or whether it's purely a gift. I won't pretend to have all the answers. Certainly we shouldn't try to manipulate the Spirit like some sort of genie who comes and goes as we please. But on the other hand, have we ever *really* asked God to empower us?

Or are we too afraid of what might happen if we did?

Acts 4:23-31

The Seal

In my days as a youth director, the occasional student would come to me in a panic, wondering if he or she was truly saved. I'd ask, "Do you believe in Jesus Christ as Lord and Savior of your life?" and generally they'd say yes. So we'd read Paul's words of assurance in Romans 10:9: "If you confess with your mouth that Jesus is Lord and believe in your heart that God raised him from the dead, you will be saved." The trouble was, this didn't always satisfy their anxiety. "But how do I know for *sure*?" they'd wail. I'd prayerfully look them in the eye and say, "I see the Holy Spirit at work in you. That is proof you belong to God."

O Holy Spirit, where are you now? I've been asking. The answer is, the Holy Spirit is here. The third person in the Trinity is living and active in my life and yours if we trust Christ. I believe that to be true just as I believe the sun is behind the clouds on this gray, rainy day. I believe the Spirit is at work not only because I've witnessed his mysterious activity in my life and others' (albeit in mostly quiet ways) but also because I believe what Paul said in Ephesians 1:13:

> When you believed in Christ, he identified you as his own by giving you the Holy Spirit, whom he promised long ago.

The NIV says it this way: that we were "marked . . . with a seal, the promised Holy Spirit." I like that word *seal*. In ancient times, the great lords and kings would write an important document, roll or fold it up, pour a small amount of melted wax on the edges, and then press an insignia (such as a ring) onto the wax. Once the wax hardened, the document was officially sealed. Often the insignia included the lord's initials or his family crest, which identified the document as created by him—his property.

If I'm a Christian—if I am "in Christ" (which in the New Testament is code for believing and having been baptized), then it's not a question of whether or not I have received the Holy Spirit or been given some sort of unique blessing that other Christians don't have. *All* those who believe in Christ belong to him, and the proof of that belonging is the seal of the Holy Spirit upon us—manifested in different ways, certainly, through different gifts and expressions, but present nonetheless.

O Holy Spirit, where are you now? we may wonder sometimes.

Here, Christ reassures us. *Don't you see my seal?*

Ephesians 1:9-14

Not Only with Words

> When we brought you the Good News, it was not only with words but also with
> power, for the Holy Spirit gave you full assurance that what we said was true.
>
> I Thessalonians 1:5

That phrase "not only with words" touches on an issue that continues to fascinate me as I read the Scriptures and witness my own and others' spiritual growth. Something is going on in the Bible that's greater than the sum of its parts. You can string all kinds of words together into sentences, and they can even be meaningful, but they don't transform lives the way Scripture does. You can write a Pulitzer prize–winning novel that might "touch" readers, but it won't have the same startling grip on the soul that the Bible can.

"The word of God is alive and powerful," wrote the author of Hebrews. "It is sharper than the sharpest two-edged sword, cutting between soul and spirit. . . . It exposes our innermost thoughts and desires" (4:12). To which I reply, "You're not kidding." I've experienced this in my own life, and I've watched it happen to countless others in the church. One moment we're just average pew-sitters: mired in apathy, happily biblically illiterate (after all, ignorance is bliss), without the merest glimmer of interest in applying the truths of Scripture to everyday life—and the next moment we're driven, as a friend once put it, with "an insatiable thirst for all things Christian, for Christ." We can't get enough of God's Word. We devour every spiritual book we're given. We're constantly asking, "What's next?" We can't be called off this unstinting quest for more of God, for more of the Bible.

So what made the difference? The presence and power of the Holy Spirit—that's the only way I can account for what's going on. One moment the world and all it contains is utterly ordinary, and the next . . .

> Earth's crammed with heaven,
>   And every common bush afire with God:
> But only he who sees, takes off his shoes,
>   The rest sit round it, and pluck blackberries."

1 Thessalonians 1:4-9

// From the poem "Aurora Leigh," by Elizabeth Barrett Browning (1806–1861).

Eyes Wide Open

I vividly remember the moment.

I was sitting alone in the kitchen of my parents' house, reading the Bible. Just a few days earlier, my parents had helped me move back home after a difficult freshman year at college, and I was feeling the odd disconnect that happens when a place that was once familiar now feels strange. So there I was in the unfamiliar kitchen of my former home, sunlight streaming onto the pages of Romans, when suddenly I *got* it. The words I was reading leaped to life for the first time. It was as if someone had finally given me an English translation after years of my trying to decipher a foreign language edition.

> Even though the Gentiles were not trying to follow God's standards, they were made right with God. And it was by faith that this took place. But the people of Israel, who tried so hard to get right with God by keeping the law, never succeeded. Why not? Because they were trying to get right with God by keeping the law instead of by trusting in him. They stumbled over the great rock in their path.   Romans 9:30-32

Suddenly it hit me. For the past year, I'd been like the ancient Jews, trying and trying to make God happy by following the rules. Get up early, read the Bible, pray, go to church, volunteer in missions, give money, act happy, do well in school, look perfect, blah, blah, blah. And I was stumbling every time I turned around. I was tripping and falling over my own pride, feeling so full of shame and failure most of the time that I was just plain miserable.

I'm sure that at some point in my past, a wise parent or mentor had told me I can't do it on my own, that my righteousness comes from Christ alone rather than any effort of mine. But in that moment I finally understood. No longer did I need to work so hard to be a Christian superhero, able to leap tall expectations in a single bound. *Faith alone* made me right with God, through the power of Jesus Christ (see today's text). The Word in that moment was so freeing—and so obvious—I began to laugh aloud.

It wasn't until later I learned that a similar thing had happened to a young monk named Martin Luther, almost five hundred years ago. But that's another story. . . .

Romans 7:4-6

The Wind in My Sails

A few weeks after my watershed moment reading Romans (see May 14), I went to work at a Christian camp for the summer. For staff training, we broke into small groups of fifteen and left for several days to "bond." Some groups went biking, hiking, or rock climbing; ours loaded up a thirty-foot boat called a Voyageur canoe and headed to the Lake Michigan coast. On a gorgeous sunny day in early summer, we launched that long skinny boat into the freezing water and climbed aboard like Vikings, fourteen of us seated in pairs from bow to stern with our skipper in the rear to man the rudder. At his word we began paddling in unison, counting aloud the strokes: "One—two—three—four," all the way to one hundred; and then we started over again. During each set of one-hundred strokes, a pair of paddlers got to rest—a system we quickly learned to appreciate.

That's because paddling a Voyageur canoe is *work*. First your arms ache; then your back; then your butt. And if the waves are coming at you in breakers off the open water, it feels like you're not going anywhere. By midday we were all exhausted. But our skipper was a wise man. He knew that around midday a strong breeze would rise. So he let us drift while the pair in front raised a tall pole, locked it upright in the bow, and added a crosspiece with a large square of canvas attached. As the wind caught the canvas, the boat began plowing effortlessly through the waves. So we rested our paddles and turned our tired faces to the sun, because our canoe was also a square-rigger—a sailboat.

Later I wrote:

> I want to sail rather than row. I want to move forward in life and
> ministry by the power of the Holy Spirit, rather than by my own
> tiny will. Sure, sailing isn't always predictable: If the wind falls
> or a storm rises, so be it! I will drift again or ride it out or seek a
> harbor somewhere. But to spend my life rowing, without a moment's
> relief—exhausted; blistered; aching all over; numb in body, mind,
> and spirit; more slave than crew. . . . It's my own doing if I fail to
> raise the sails and let the Holy Spirit do the work; and it's my own
> doing if I never arrive at the destination God has for me.

There's a reason the word *spirit* in Hebrew is also translated as *breath* and *wind*. . . .

John 6:61-65

Old Friends

Yet another flashback from my college journals demonstrates my lifelong queasiness with the concept of sharing my faith. Why is it so tough to talk about Jesus with those old friends who've known us the longest, who've seen us at our worst and wouldn't hesitate calling our bluff?

When I think about going back home to work for the summer, I just don't feel like dealing with all the same people I went to high school with. I get rebellious and ornery just thinking about it, and I give myself an ultimatum like, "Save them or join them"—as if I can't befriend them unless they're all hot-blooded Christians. Is everything and everybody a "mission" or a "project"? I tend to think, *Oh, if only this person were a Christian, I could be so much more myself around them.* And yet the apostle Paul reminded us that Jesus died for us "while we were still sinners" (Romans 5:8). Jesus meets people where they are. Why can't I?

I know now that my attitude about my old friends has been wrong. How can I sincerely love them if I've taken no interest in each individual as he or she is—as a member of the human race, created and loved by God, someone Jesus died for? Why am I not humbly praying that God would allow me the chance, just once, to bring Jesus into the conversation naturally, relevantly, *because I love the listener*—not forcibly or because I think I must or because all other topics feel shallow and worthless?

I'm especially ashamed to look back on how I treated the guys I dated as "projects"—and my closest friends, too—without ever considering them as *people*. And here I've been reading 1 Corinthians 13, all about love. I could talk my friends' ears off twenty-four hours a day, and it would probably do more harm than good. Noise, noise, noise. But if I went alone into my room, closed the door, and prayed for them even *once*—! That's when I'd show true compassion and love for the person as an individual. That's when the great ship might start to turn around.

1 Corinthians 13:1-3

I'll Pray for You

Lately I've noticed how slow we are to ask our non-Christian friends, "How can I pray for you?" Sure, we ask our *Christian* friends that question all the time; intercessory prayer is one of the important roles we play in each other's lives. But what about everyone else? In my experience, this seems to be the one question that opens doors. For some reason there's still a general openness on the part of nonbelievers to the concept of prayer, even if they disagree with our basic beliefs about whom we're praying to. Only a bitter, angry old sinner resents such a question. Most everyone else says, "Well, it can't hurt; it might help." And when we honor their requests and then return later with, "I've been praying for you. How are things going?"—it's amazing how God opens doors for further conversation about faith.

If this is so, why are we so slow, so reticent, to ask? Maybe because it doesn't even occur to us. Or maybe, if we're honest, we just don't care enough about people to bother.

The flip side of this is my own experience of being prayed for. I feel like crying whenever people tell me they're praying for me. It's like I've been chosen for the Nobel Prize or something. Somehow they love me enough to remember me to God; they feel my life is worth the effort of praying about—out of all their personal struggles and problems, and out of all the hundreds of people they know, they bother to remember *me*. I find this astounding. They bother to remember this unworthy little person, this self-obsessed materialist, someone so intensely selfish that when she prays she can only whine to God about how she can't pray. What's wrong with this picture?

Matthew 5:43-48

If My People

Christians like to gripe that the United States is going down the toilet and that usually there's some person or group to blame: politicians, celebrities, you name it. But what if the problem is *us*?

If my people who are called by my name

"You know what's wrong
with this country?" said the
preacher to the talk-show host.

will humble themselves

"It's all those drug dealers
and hookers and porn stars out there

and pray

those pimps and
gangsters and devil worshippers

and seek my face

those pagans, they're the ones
messing up this country

and turn from their wicked ways,

it's because of them
that all this bad stuff happens

I will hear from heaven

the bombs and wars
and natural disasters

and will forgive their sins

it's all the wrath of God
against the unbelievers, you know."

and restore their land.

2 Chronicles 7:11-16

The More Enduring Story

> I felt the Gospel to be eternal; I felt politics and culture, including Christian culture, to be in time. I was made always to go beyond time. —— Carlo Carretto[//]

When I was a full-time youth minister, I had a mailbox at the church where people could drop things off for me. Now and then I'd find some article or curriculum stuffed in there by a well-meaning parent who was concerned about the "teen scene"—parties, drugs, sex, binge drinking, etc. "Did you read the article?" they'd ask later, an anxious expression on their face. "Yes," I'd reply. "Well, are we going to do anything about it?" they'd press me. "Are we going to teach against this stuff?" And I'd hem and haw and shuffle my feet and mumble, "Um, sometime, maybe." Not the answer they were looking for, no doubt.

But how was I to explain that I cared too much about their kids to teach anything but the gospel?

You see, I believe the story of Jesus is eternal. It's the only news worth hearing. Once you step inside that story, the world begins to lose its grip on your soul. Sure, you may still struggle in your friendships, wrestle with unhealthy behaviors, and make poor decisions. But the longer you live inside that story—the longer you marinate in the flavor of the character of Christ—the more it becomes part of who you are. In time, it doesn't matter what temporary cultural "scene" you find yourself in: Christ is all in all.

"Since all the world is but a story," Saint Columba of Scotland is credited as saying, "it were well for thee to buy the more enduring story, rather than the story that is less enduring." Instead of continually harping on how our youth must plug their ears to the stories of this world, I want to give them "the more enduring story" that is Jesus Christ. I want them to listen to the eternal so often and so long that eventually they will hear what God wants them to do within their own culture, in their own time, right now.

1 Corinthians 2:1-5

[//] Carlo Carretto (1910–1988) was an Italian Catholic activist who abruptly dropped everything in midlife to join a monastic community in the desert. His writings touched many lives, particularly his book *I, Francis* (the source of this quote), in which he wrote from the perspective of the medieval monk Saint Francis of Assisi.

Choosing What's Best

If you did a random survey of a handful of people and asked them the number one problem facing youth in our culture, you'd likely get answers like alcohol or drugs or promiscuity or peer pressure. But maybe there's something deeper, more foundational than these issues. Maybe the heart of the problem for Christians of any age is the inability to practice discernment.

Discernment is how we determine what is the best course of action—it's how we determine God's will or plan for us. If I were to put on my youth minister hat again and give a "youth talk" on the subject, here's what I would say:

Does the Christian life boil down to deciding what is good and what is bad? No. Those things are already decided for you. In fact, *all* people have access to knowledge of God's will when it comes to deciding between good and bad. When Adam and Eve ate the forbidden fruit, God said, "The human beings have become like us, knowing both good and evil" (Genesis 3:22). Lying, cheating, stealing, pornography (which is at heart idolatry), anger, verbal abuse, messing around sexually—no one needs to tell you those are wrong. You *know* they're wrong." It doesn't take some kind of special discernment to figure these things out. But it does take the power of the Holy Spirit to help you resist them.

Meanwhile, some of you have probably discovered that the longer you walk with Jesus, the easier it becomes to avoid deliberately doing evil. You just don't care to do as many of those things. Perhaps you've begun to find Christian friends who hold you accountable and keep you from messing around. And even if you *do* mess up, you're not as fearful of asking for forgiveness and starting over because you've experienced the grace and love of Jesus. It doesn't mean you're never going to sin, but it does mean sin doesn't cling the way it once did.

So the ultimate quest in the Christian life is not about choosing good over evil—that ability comes with time, through the power of the Holy Spirit. Instead, our ultimate quest is to discern what's good versus what's *best*. How do we decide which college to go to, which career path to take, which person to marry? How do we know when God wants us to start a new ministry or respond to one of many needs in this hurting world? Out of a plethora of good things, somehow we must discern what is God's best for us. And it may not be the same as what God desires for someone else. Only God knows which choices you need to make. Tuning in to him through prayer, Scripture, reflection, and talking with Christian mentors is how you discover what those are. Choosing God's best is what we mean by discernment, and that's the task of the Christian life.

Philippians 1:9-11

// See Romans 1:18-20.

You Will Surrender

Let's say I'm wearing my youth ministry hat, and from under its brim I see plenty of students who are teetering on the fence between life-altering good choices and life-altering bad ones. And if I were to give a "youth talk" on the subject, here's what I would say:

If you will not surrender your life to Jesus, then you will surrender your life to *some-thing*. There is no third option labeled "perfect independence." If you don't choose Christ, you will lose yourself to one thing or another, and it will very likely be an unconscious losing. In fact, the thing you are losing yourself to is very likely at this moment remaking you in its own image. Your whole self is being redefined and recrafted to suit the master you serve.

So who is your master? Is it your job? your family? exercise? possessions? food? a consuming hobby? None of these are bad in and of themselves. But have you allowed them to become obstacles to your relationship with Jesus Christ? And meanwhile there are plenty of negative things that all of us, at one time or another, have allowed ourselves to become slaves to: addictions, unhealthy relationships, consumer debt, lying, gossip, a bad temper, sneering sarcasm, sexual fantasies. If you've ever been trapped by any of these, you know exactly what Jesus meant when he said, "I tell you the truth, everyone who sins is a slave of sin" (John 8:34). By contrast, if you've surrendered your life to Jesus, you know precisely what he means when he says, "If the Son sets you free, you are truly free" (John 8:36).

Listen for a moment. It's as if Jesus is saying, *When I am Lord of your life, I will give you back yourself, the self that you lost to all these other unworthy masters. I will show you who you were created to be, and we will begin the process of cutting out anything that is not of me and cultivating and nurturing the things that are truly me in you. But be prepared. This will require death—death of the old life, the old masters, the old loves. It will not be pretty.*

Dare we surrender?

Romans 6:12-18

Every Knee Will Bow

If you hear echoes of C. S. Lewis in what I'm saying, that's because he has been one of the most influential authors—as well as one of the most significant Christians and teachers—in my life (though he died ten years before I was born). This is not the first time I've mentioned him, and it won't be the last. Sometime in high school, I picked up his startling little book *Mere Christianity*, and I felt like a sane person for the first time in my life. For years the surrounding culture had made me feel like an idiot for believing in God and Jesus. This was the eighties, remember, before spirituality was "cool," and I spent much of that decade in the Northeast, where Christianity had ceased to be an acceptable worldview around the time of Darwin. Most of my friends would've agreed with Lucifer's boast in *Paradise Lost*, "Better to reign in Hell than serve in Heaven"—though they would've added, "Not that I believe in either."

So I was more than just a fish out of water; I was a fish who had been dragged out of the pond and now lay on the grass, gasping up at the crowd of people who stood sneering over me, who poked me now and then, waiting for me to die. Or at least, that's how it felt.

Then along came C. S. Lewis, who calmly picked me up by the tail and threw me back into the water. And I realized I wasn't crazy. In fact, I was saner than most. Here's one of his statements that made sense the instant I read it: "Fallen man is not simply an imperfect creature who needs improvement: he is a rebel who must lay down his arms."[22]

So we're back to the issue of surrender again. Yes, we *will* surrender in the end. One of the earliest Christian confessions went like this: "At the name of Jesus every knee should bow, in heaven and on earth and under the earth, and every tongue confess that Jesus Christ is Lord, to the glory of God the Father" (Philippians 2:10-11). The question is whether we'll lay down our arms willingly *now*, or if one day we'll find ourselves on the wrong side of the final battlefield, the hosts of heaven arrayed before us as an army with banners.

Philippians 2:5-11

Whose Will Be Done?

If you haven't yet, I'd encourage you to read Thomas Merton's autobiography, *The Seven Storey Mountain*. He's like a Catholic version of C. S. Lewis, except instead of converting from atheism to the Church of England, he converted from hedonism to monasticism. Yep, he went from being an intellectual party boy from Columbia University to being a Trappist monk in the wooded valleys of Kentucky. Not the usual career path for a bright young man in our success-oriented society, that's for sure.

Although his autobiography speaks powerfully to his Catholic faith (as it should), it is accessible to everyone, much like C. S. Lewis's *Surprised by Joy*—another good read. In fact, what I notice about both Merton and Lewis is their similar understanding of sin and hell. To them, hell is not a place God arbitrarily sends people as punishment for their sins—hell is a place people *choose*. Merton wrote:

> Why should anyone be shattered by the thought of hell? It is not compulsory for anyone to go there. Those who do, do so by their own choice, and against the will of God, and they can only get into hell by defying and resisting all the work of Providence and grace. It is their own will that takes them there, not God's.[23]

Merton and Lewis believed strongly in free will. They knew that before their conversions, it wasn't their intellectual hang-ups or theological objections that kept them from submitting to Jesus—those were just excuses. It was their own obstinate desire to be left alone and do as they pleased. Merton said, "I was to be punished for my sins by my sins themselves."[24] God doesn't sit up there in heaven, blasting us whenever we mess up. We reap the consequences of our own behavior.

Likewise, according to these men, God doesn't choose hell for some people and heaven for others. We won't stand before Christ on Judgment Day like a batch of mute vegetables at the grocery store and hear, "Keep this one, it seems fine; but that one is rotten, no good—throw it out." Rather, I imagine he will ask each one of us, "Do you love me?" and the only thing compulsory about our answer will be honesty.

John 21:15-19

Come, Lord Jesus

Something else I read in high school that kind of turned my world upside down, in addition to C. S. Lewis's *Mere Christianity* and *The Screwtape Letters*, was Matthew 24. For some reason you don't hear a lot of sermons on Jesus' prophecies about the end times—or maybe it was just the churches I attended—but his words seemed suitably freaky to a fifteen-year-old, once I discovered them. If I wanted to convince my friends that there really was bizarre stuff in the Bible, I told them to read Matthew 24. "It'll give you nightmares," I'd say cryptically. "Really?" they'd reply. "That's cool."

Anyway, I suppose that chapter has added plenty of fuel to the fire of end-times prophecy and literature over the years. But what fascinated me most was Christ's assumption that his listeners would experience all the final events firsthand. "I tell you the truth," he told them, "this generation will not pass from the scene until all these things take place" (verse 34). And I thought, *Well, it didn't happen to that generation, so what if he's talking to us, right now? What if he means my generation?* And I'd walk down the hallways of school thinking, *What if he returns today? I'd better be ready.*

Theologians would say I had a strong eschatological worldview. Psychologists would say I was just projecting my adolescent angst about puberty and change onto the Apocalypse out of some wish to make all my problems go away. Perhaps that's true—now that I'm a happily married woman in my mid-thirties, I certainly don't wake up every morning thinking, *I wish Jesus would come back today.* In many respects, the more comfortable and secure we feel in life and with ourselves, the less interested we are in Christ's return. In fact, we'd rather he didn't show up and spoil our fun.

But when you're fifteen and most of the world seems to be conspiring to make you miserable—or when you're poor, oppressed, or abused; when you're daily persecuted for your faith, as were the early Christians—then Christ's promises in Matthew 24 become light in the darkness. They are the life preserver you cling to. The sooner Jesus returns, the better.

Which is why some of the last words in the Bible are, "He who is the faithful witness to all these things says, 'Yes, I am coming soon!'"—to which the author adds, "Amen! Come, Lord Jesus!" (Revelation 22:20).

Can we honestly pray this too?

Matthew 24:4-14

When the Tree Blooms

Standing in the checkout lane at the grocery store, I'm not surprised to see yet another tabloid predicting the end is near. Some prophet has read the signs, studied the Scriptures, and solved the cryptic message behind Jesus' words in Matthew 24, for example. But is Christ's message all that cryptic? What if his point is not "look for the signs" but "look for me"? Are we paying attention?

In this blooming
bountiful spring,
I think of the fig tree
with its buds, hints
of inevitable summer
at the tip of every twig.
You said the signs would come
in just that way,
the signs of the end of the age.
Yet they seem so ordinary somehow,
like predictions in the astrology section
of the daily paper.
How normal those prophecies
in this crazy, hideous century!
On the heels of El Niño,
hurricane, flood, tsunami,
I wonder if the world
can progress much longer
without spontaneously combusting.
Are we being given hints
of the inevitable
approaching?
I used to feel—to know—
that mine was somehow the last
generation on this earth,
that the Second Coming
would happen in my lifetime.
I don't now. Maybe I should.
Was that merely the inability
of youth to comprehend finitude? Mortality? Death?
What are you saying? What deep
yearning are you speaking to?
What great reality are you unfolding?

Yourself.

Matthew 24:32-35

The End of the Age

Earlier this month we talked about Christ's ascension, when he was lifted up to heaven in the presence of his disciples forty days after his resurrection. He remains in heaven, Peter told the crowds in Acts 3:21, until "the final restoration of all things." We then explored the significance of Pentecost, which happened shortly after the Ascension (see Acts 2), and the role of the Holy Spirit in our lives today. It seems natural to follow these celebrations with some musings on the second coming of Christ—or the promise we have from Scripture that one day Jesus will return to reign forever, and all things will be renewed.

The presence of the Holy Spirit, Paul said, is something like a down payment until that happens (see 2 Corinthians 5:4-5). The Spirit of Jesus is with us until we see him face-to-face. This is why, at the end of Matthew's Gospel, Christ tells his disciples, "Be sure of this: I am with you always, even to the end of the age" (28:20). Even though they'd soon be deprived of his physical presence, he would be with them "in spirit"—and this was more than just a cheesy euphemism for "I'll be thinking of you." He was saying, in essence, "My life, my breath, my spirit *will be in you* until I return."

I'm glad I discovered that verse during my senior year of high school. Up to that point I'd read all the alarming prophecies in Matthew 24 and gotten myself "properly scared," to quote Flannery O'Connor. But then I found Matthew 28:20, and it was not only Jesus' promise to be with me that I found comforting but also the phrase "to the end of the age." Besides being epic in scope, it had a poetic ring to it.

Later I learned that the ancient peoples of the Mediterranean world thought of human history as happening in a series of ages, or eras. This is different than our modern approach, which carves up the time line according to various advances in human progress (the Stone Age, the Iron Age, etc.). For the ancients, each age was determined by how it would end—the first with water (Noah's flood, anyone?) and someday, at the end of all things, with fire."

Whatever the case, Jesus will be with us through it all. Amen, and amen!

Matthew 28:20; 2 Corinthians 5:6-10

// See 2 Peter 3, which is the text for May 27.

A Foot in Both Kingdoms

I no longer think of time
as linear marks
on a line, but circles, cycles,
theater in the round.
Time is cyclical—painfully,
since we never seem
to learn from one generation to the next.
We can't seem to grasp how
to stay unburdened from
the cares of this world
and instead live ever-ready
for the coming of the Kingdom.

It is near.
Christ's return is forever
sealed as the fate
of this lonely, precious planet.

I think of the nagging
impatience I feel
toward any faith community
I happen to be part of. Why?
Perhaps I'm an idealist
with a low tolerance for dithering.
I want the promised Kingdom
without the present one.
I want to be with God's people
and their heavenly selves
more than they want heaven.

But in the meantime
I must learn to dance

with a foot in both kingdoms.

Which kingdom do you find it easier to keep a foot in?

2 Peter 3:1-14

Finals

Let's say it's finals week and you're feeling pretty good about things. You face two tests today and two tomorrow, followed by Kickboxing 301 on Thursday—and then you're done. By paying close attention last Friday, you deduced that your teachers' grim advice to study, study, study was in fact a ploy to spoil your weekend (like anyone with brains would fall for that!), and besides, you've been breezing along in most of your classes without so much as cracking open a textbook. So after a very busy weekend in which you—not once, but twice—trounced some guy from Hong Kong in an online game of Risk, you skim your notes during breakfast and now arrive for the first exam.

Your teacher writes three questions on the board: What is your name? (1 point); What is your favorite color? (1 point); and What is the benignant rapprochement between ekistics and architectonics in the antediluvian period? (98 points).

Your brain freezes. *Ekistics*? Is that even English? You glance around. With a growing sense of panic, you realize your classmates are dutifully scribbling their answers with perfect nonchalance. No frowns, no pauses, no nervous throat-clearing. They keep scribbling, sentence after sentence, paragraph after paragraph, while damp patches of sweat form under your armpits.

Okay, wake up. It's just a dream. From somewhere deep in the well of your psyche you've dredged up stressful school memories (with a little Monty Python thrown in too). But take a deep breath. Unless you're currently enrolled in some variety of summer school, those dreadful days of finals are over.

Well, until Christ returns, of course. Today's parable gives us a taste of what Jesus expects of us in preparation. Feed the hungry. Show hospitality to strangers. Clothe the poor. Care for the sick. Visit prisoners.

Rather hard to cram for that final, eh?

Matthew 25:31-46

Wedding Season

My husband and I were on a long walk one afternoon when we decided to stop for ice cream on campus and then head to the chapel cloister, where there is a bench to sit on. We'd been there no more than two minutes when we glanced up to see a gorgeous bride waiting at the side door of the chapel for her cue to enter. She was alone—I have no idea where her father was—and she was pacing. Then suddenly she noticed us, two goons in shorts and T-shirts, sweaty and gross, snarfing sticky ice cream out of a paper cup. We waved sheepishly. She smiled. It was the biggest moment of her life, but no matter what happened, the world of goons and ice cream would go on. Thanks be to God.

It seems appropriate to be discussing the Second Coming smack in the middle of America's biggest wedding season. This is the time of year when love-struck couples gaze into each other's eyes and make promises they wouldn't dare make to their parents, to their best friends, or even to God. Florists are frantic. Mothers and fathers run hither and yon, spending gobs of money so their reputations are preserved and their grown children are satisfied. Churches are booked every Saturday for weeks on end. And in the midst of it all whispers a voice from Revelation, saying, "The Spirit and the bride say, 'Come'" (22:17).

Come, you who are frantic.

Come, you who pace the cloister, fatherless.

Come, you who think earthly marriage will satisfy your every longing and desire.

Jesus will return like a groom for the church, his bride, and then all the florists and parents, graduates and goons of the world will cease their striving, and the great wedding banquet will begin.

Matthew 25:1-13

The Mysterious Marriage

Lord, I'm having trouble with the idea of your people (Israel; the church) as your bride. Carlo Carretto wrote, "It is difficult to make a marriage between two persons who are in such different circumstances. He brings you his all, while you can only bring him your nothing."[25] *That image of marriage unsettles me. My husband and I strive to find balance, to shoulder responsibilities based on strengths and gifts, to build an egalitarian model of marriage in which neither is in charge but both "submit to one another out of reverence for Christ" (Ephesians 5:21). But between you, Lord, and the church, there is definitely an imbalance.*

She could never be a worthy bride for you, and yet you call her so. She owes you a debt she could never hope to repay—one that should rightfully make her your slave—and yet you waive it all to have her beside you, free and freely loving you. Her love for you will never be as great as yours for her, yet still you would have her. Somehow her flaws and failures don't push you away, though at times she makes you angry. In the end, her home is by your side for all eternity—though she is there by grace and grace alone.

What prompted this betrothal in the first place? What prompted your desire to be more than just our Father but our Bridegroom, too? Were you lonely, God? Like Adam, was it not good for you to be alone? Did you long for conversation? Did you yearn for human companionship?

I'm sorry your bride is poor at these things. Prayer doesn't come easily most of the time. She doesn't yet understand how to love you, but if all you've said is true, one day she will.

Amen.

Isaiah 62:1-5; Revelation 21:2-3

Gut Instinct

I will tell you a slightly embarrassing story. Before I was married I lived alone for several years, and like most young women in today's hypervigilant culture, I learned to be careful about locking my doors and listening for odd noises at night. My undergraduate self-defense class had taught me just enough to feel paranoid but not enough to feel confident about being a lone female out there in the world, so I breathed a sigh of relief when my new husband finally joined me in the apartment.

Then one night as I was falling asleep, a sound jolted me wide awake. Fear flooded my body. I felt frozen to the sheets. Someone was in the apartment. In fact, someone was in *this very room*. I'd heard it, the unmistakable sound of a man clearing his throat. Where to run? Where to hide?

The sound came again, *this time from right next to me*, but just as I was leaping up to grab something heavy, it occurred to me that my new husband should handle this situation. And then I laughed out loud because my new husband *was* the situation. The man clearing his throat was none other than my very own spouse, of course, but I in my half-asleep daze had forgotten I was married.

Forgotten? Such an important, life-altering fact? It's like forgetting your last name or your mailing address. It's like forgetting your face in the mirror. Who forgets such things?

Humans do. We are imperfect creatures. While our minds may grasp a vital fact, such as the basic physics of a plane in flight (air holds us up), our bodies operate on instinct (gravity should pull us down). We may even comprehend a spiritual or moral truth and yet still do the opposite, because our bodies and wills insist on it. For example: I may know it's wrong to turn away from a person in need, but I'd really like to keep that twenty in my pocket. But the longer we're on this Christian journey, said the apostle James (see today's text), the less we're to operate on gut instinct and the more we're to live by the truth. And then in time, the truth will *be* our gut instinct.

I'm happy to say I no longer freak out when I hear a man cough or clear his throat in my room in the middle of the night. After ten years—as of today, our anniversary—my mind and body are in harmony on this point. If anything, now I have a hard time falling asleep without my husband in the room. Perhaps this is what my spiritual instincts will be like someday, the longer I stay on this Christian journey?

James 1:22-25

June Is Busting Out All Over

It's June, it's June, and I'm in Virginia for the most beautiful month of the summer. June is "busting out all over," as the old musical goes—everything is blooming and growing like mad, and I wake up wondering how I migrated down here to the jungle from the tundra. Where I come from in northern Michigan, the growing season is roughly twelve weeks long (no joke), so most of the plants are shy, tentative creatures, sticking out a toe or a tendril into the chilly mornings only to pull back at night. The leaves are small; the flowers dare not grow large and showy, or the whole plant might be killed off by frost. Frost in June? Why yes—I've seen *snow* in June. But the plants down here have little to fear; they sprawl luxuriously, big and bold.

I'm living in Virginia for the first summer in my life, so I sit outside on the deck of our borrowed home in shorts and a tank top, soaking up the wild and glorious green of God's creation. And this is my theme. This is my story, this is my song, praising my Creator all the day long. I pick up my Bible under the tall, whispering trees and turn from Revelation, which was a theme in the May devotions, back to Genesis: from endings to beginnings. I read that God created the heavens and the earth and all the green, growing things that sprawl in the alley and all the creatures that chirp and bark and rustle in the undergrowth. He created June and Virginia and the thunderstorms that roll across the James River at night; he created all this and called it good. And then he created you and me and called it *very* good (see Genesis 1:31).

I look around and see the mark of the Maker on all he has created, the signature beauty that reveals the work of his hands. And I want to improvise on this theme for a while. I want to consider how God reveals himself to us through nature, in the artistic design of his creative genius all around us, in the creativity of us human creatures who are made in his image.

Because if we're not listening to how God speaks to us through these created things, why should we be surprised if we can't hear him through anything else?

Psalm 104:24-31

The Ultimate Creative Kid

In the evening my husband and I like to go on walks around the neighborhood. Yesterday as we were ambling along we came across several sections of sidewalk that had been elaborately decorated in neon-colored chalk by an ambitious young artist. There were flowers and cats and swirls and patterns of every hue, an extravagant showcase of creativity that made me grin with delight. I wanted to pick up some chalk and add my own artistic flair to the next section of sidewalk. And isn't our planet like that? We turn a corner and find ourselves grinning at some new vision of creation; God the ambitious Artist has been very, very busy. Have we noticed?

Praise the Lord!

He is the ultimate Creative Kid.
He paints and sketches
and weaves and sews;
he dabbles for fun
and yet puts in painstaking detail.
He is proud of his work.
He shows it off.
The whole earth is laced with his glory!
He is rich in the best materials
and shares them freely;
he uses them generously.
He double-paints the sky;
he wraps the oceans in hue after hue.
His people, his design,
he molds from the earth
out of the richest clay,
their colors extravagant
and gorgeous.
His human creatures are never
meant to harden
into twisted, untouchable shapes,
but to be usable, moldable,
shaped as he designs—
and then reshaped.

Praise the Lord!

Isaiah 45:9-12

There Was Evening, and There Was Morning

I'm improvising on the theme of Creation, exploring the unexplored in the first chapter of Genesis. And I notice a curious little phrase at the end of each section, which gets lost in some translations, that goes something like this: "There was evening and there was morning—the second day" (the third day, the fourth day, etc.). Some believe this indicates how the Jews mark time: Each twenty-four-hour period begins at sundown and ends at the next sundown. So now I wonder: Instead of starting a new creative spurt as the sun rose, what if God began at *sunset* and worked all night long, hammering away at the planet until something new and astonishing appeared with the rising of the sun?

It reminds me of those massive thunderstorms that roll across the James River at night when I'm trying to sleep. First I hear the wind rising in the trees, slapping branches against the side of the house. Then thunder rumbles in the distance. Soon I hunker down as lightning dances in the sky like a strobe and thunder shakes the ground. I cover my ears and hide my face as the wind roars through the trees, hoping nothing really bad happens to the house or the car. The electricity goes out.

In time the storm passes and I eventually fall asleep again, only to wake to a new world. Lines and trees are down. The neighbor's lawn furniture is in our yard, tumbled like clothes in a washer. Shingles from somebody's roof are scattered all over the street. I spend half the morning cleaning up, wondering if yet another storm will jumble everything again tonight. In the end, I breathe a sigh of relief when the season of summer storms passes and I can sleep again.

So when the six days of creation were over, maybe it wasn't just God who needed the rest, but the exhausted earth itself. Shocked and raw and trembling, the planet needed a break from the fire and bellows, from the continual smash of God's creative power on the anvil. Perhaps the seventh day was the first foreshadowing of grace.

Genesis 1:31–2:3 (NIV)

The Sky Is Talking

During my first week in Kenya as an exchange student, I had a sudden urge to climb up to the open rooftop of our dorm and look at the night sky. Stargazing is something I've always been fascinated with ever since my first trip to the planetarium in elementary school. Living as far north as I have for most of my life—where the air is clear and the big-city lights are far, far away—I've developed the knack for picking out constellations and planets with relative ease. But as I climbed onto the rooftop of my African dorm, two degrees south of the equator in another hemisphere, I felt like I'd landed on Mars.

Nothing I saw in the sky looked familiar. My eyes roamed frantically for some kind of bearing, a marker that would point to, say, the North Star or the Corona constellation. Nothing. It was a jumble of lights without any coherent pattern. But my African friends knew better. They could pick out their own stars and constellations without a problem. They knew the night sky in their own hemisphere, and to them it was an eloquent and timeless pattern that was mysterious and beautiful, just as the sky is in my hometown. Once my eyes adjusted, I began to trace those new patterns too.

When I look to the earth itself, I can see that each corner of the planet has been given little pieces of the big picture. In Africa there's the wide-open savanna; in Colorado there are mountains upon mountains; and each location gives a slightly different spin on this God we know as Creator. The sky, however—no matter where you live or what language you speak—is inescapable, omnipresent. The stars, the moon, and the sun are visible to every human being in the world; even the blind can feel the sun's warmth.

And so, wrote the psalmist, "The heavens proclaim the glory of God. . . . Their message has gone throughout the earth, and their words to all the world" (Psalm 19:1, 4). In Theology 101 we call this "general revelation," or the knowledge about God that's available to all people, anywhere on the planet, if they'd only step outside their front door and look around. But just in case they miss it, all they need to do is to read Psalm 19. Look up, the psalmist says. No matter where you live, the sky is trying to tell you something.

Psalm 19:1-6

Dawn of Creation

In reading the first chapter of Genesis more closely, I find it interesting that God creates day and night many verses before creating the sun and moon. What gave the light during the day? What made the darkness dark? And odder still is the fact that vegetation is created before the sun too! It seems ridiculous from a scientific standpoint, and yet it leads me to think about night and day, darkness and light differently. Christians speak of them in spiritual terms all the time, and we generally mean spiritual warfare, the battle for souls: Light against Darkness (capital *L*, capital *D*). But if both day and night were there at the beginning of creation, at God's bidding, were they necessarily in conflict? Probably not . . . yet. In the beginning there was night, one of the firstborn of all creation, and somehow it was good.

Anyway, until the sun came along, what or who provided the light so the vegetation could grow and flourish? Perhaps, as in J. R. R. Tolkien's imaginary account of the creation of Middle-earth,[26] the trees themselves gave off light. More likely it was God himself. As the book of Revelation suggests, someday at the end of all things, God himself will be our light (see Revelation 21:23). Perhaps that's what the world was like before he made the sun and moon: lit by his presence. After all, Jesus says he is the Light of the World (see John 8:12), and who's to say he's speaking figuratively?

Meanwhile, I wonder if the darkness in the Creation story was generated by God too, not just by the absence of light. I mean, darkness can be comfy sometimes. When I'm ill with a migraine, that's all I want. But as a child I was terrified of the dark. Nighttime is when scary things happen. So what did the night at the first wave of Creation feel like without the presence of evil? We can hardly imagine. The closest I can come to it is a warm summer evening with crickets chirping in the tall grass and stars glowing softly overhead—no terror to steal the peace from the world.

O, for a night like that, Lord God! Restore night to your dominion and once again call it good, that the children of this world might sit on their front porches in the warmth of a summer evening or nestle in their beds under the glimmer of stars and dream deep dreams without fear. Amen.

Genesis 1:1-5, 11-19

General Revelation

My theme right now is Creation, so I'll interject a little Theology 101. Nature is where the study of God starts (*theo* is Greek for God; *logy* means "the study of"). This is where we begin to grasp just who this Being is whom we call "Lord"—because without God revealing himself to us in some way, the veil is forever drawn over our minds. We can't pull back the curtain to glimpse his character on our own power, so God must unveil himself, reveal himself, offer some kind of revelation. He does so first through nature.

The apostle Paul wrote, "Ever since the world was created, people have seen the earth and sky. Through everything God made, they can clearly see his invisible qualities— his eternal power and divine nature" (Romans 1:20). In other words, all human beings can look around at this gorgeous and terrifying planet and learn three important things about the One who created it. First, the Creator is powerful. None of us are strong enough to make a Mount Everest, so someone incredibly big and mighty must have done it. Second, if a Mount Everest can outlast any of us humans, then the Creator must outlast *it*; he must be older even than the mountains, the earth, and the sky. In fact, he must be eternal. Third, if the Creator can make an Everest, and if the Creator can outlast the earth itself, then he is not like us—he must be a different Being entirely. In short, he must be divine.

This, Paul said, is what we can learn about God from creation: his eternal power and divine nature. Theologians call this knowledge *general revelation*. That's because everyone on the planet has access to the information about God that can be gleaned from the world around us. Which is why, Paul said, we have "no excuse for not knowing God" (Romans 1:20).

So the next time I'm tempted to whine and complain about how God is silent and invisible—that he never speaks to me—I'd better pause and study the nearest tree.

Romans 1:18-20

Special Revelation: Part 1

I'm exploring in these early June devotions how God reveals himself to us through his beautiful, alarming creation. And already I've run into a snag. As marvelous as creation is, it can only take us so far. General revelation (see June 6) only gives us a small part of the total picture of who God is.

Most of the world's religions believe in a god or gods who have eternal power and divine nature; there's nothing unusual in what Paul is saying in Romans 1:20. What's unusual is that Paul doesn't look around at the terrible beauty of creation and assume that its creator must somehow be terrible too, as many other religions do. He doesn't look at things like natural disasters or sudden infant death syndrome and decide that God must be (a) cruel, (b) fickle, (c) forgetful, (d) absent, or (e) asleep. That's because Paul is privy to information that's not available in nature. He has been given access to exclusive knowledge that comes from a very special source: what theologians call *special revelation*, or God's Word.

God has spoken. That's what we mean when we say "the Word of God." We mean that God hasn't left us to our own devices, bumbling along as best we can with our partial understandings that lead to misconceptions about his character. God has spoken to and through his people, revealing things that we never would have known otherwise. Through his Word we learn that he is compassionate, gracious, loyal, patient, ever-present, a Father, a Lover, a Servant-King. Above all, we learn that God is love (see 1 John 4:7-8). This information, born out of human encounters with his divine character, has been collected from generation to generation and written down in a unique and unsurpassed book we call the Bible. This is what we mean when we say "God's Word."

The Bible is special revelation—not because the people who read it are somehow more special than others, but because God has spoken uniquely and definitively through it—to a particular people, at a particular time, for a particular purpose. Now it's our job to share that Word with others.

Psalm 119:105-112

Special Revelation: Part 2

Theology 101 is still in session, and right now we're exploring the concept of "special revelation," or the knowledge about God's character that he reveals to us through his Word. And of course when we say "God's Word," we usually mean the Bible. But the disciple John added a deeper definition. Here's what he said in the opening chapter of his Gospel: "In the beginning the Word already existed. The Word was with God, and the Word was God. He existed in the beginning with God. God created everything through him, and nothing was created except through him" (John 1:1-3). So apparently the Word isn't just a book, it's a person. And of course John is talking about Jesus.

This would have been a radical concept in John's day. Up to that point, the Jewish people considered the Law and the Prophets (the bulk of the books in the Old Testament) as the sum total of God's Word. This law told them more about God than anything else in the universe, including all of creation. But then along came Jesus, who claimed not only to speak the words of God but to *be* God. "Heaven and earth will disappear," he had the boldness to say, "but my words will never disappear" (Matthew 24:35).

Jesus is the *ultimate* Word of God. His life and his words fulfilled everything God had already said about himself throughout the history of God's people. The author of Hebrews wrote, "Long ago God spoke many times and in many ways to our ancestors through the prophets. And now in these final days, he has spoken to us through his Son" (1:1-2). Jesus is the fulfillment of everything in the Scriptures, the fullest expression of God's character, the most special revelation of God to the world.

So while the rest of us babble on and on trying to explain the faith using all kinds of words, God spoke once and for all, with just one Word.

Hebrews 1:1-3

Four-Act Play

I've always felt like each part of the day has its own mood, as if the curtain falls between acts and then opens to a completely new scene. Perhaps this is why some Christian traditions mark each section of the day with prayer and Scripture reading, sometimes called the canonical hours or the "liturgy of the hours." What would happen if we intentionally invited God into the drama of our lives every morning, afternoon, evening, and nighttime?

Praise the Lord!

Praise the Lord in the morning
when the earth remembers Creation day
and the sun comes up sparkling
and the sky laughs for joy
at the birth of the Morning Star.

Praise the Lord in the afternoon
when the earth remembers hard work
and Jesus
and hot sun
and crowds
and tired, dusty feet.

Praise the Lord in the evening
when the earth remembers THE END
and marches glory and victory
across the sky in red and gold—
or in wind
or stillness
or long, sleepy shadows.

Praise the Lord in the nighttime
when the earth remembers the tomb
and the cold waiting,
silent sleeping,
holding its breath
before it sighs and yawns
and stretches and sits up again—

Praise the Lord!

Psalm 111

Words Have Power

We humans are made in the image of God, which means we're created to create things, just as our Creator does. We're made to play.

Many of us have some kind of hobby or creative medium, such as playing the guitar or dancing or oil painting. My hobby also happens to be my vocation: creative writing. Unlike many hobbies, which are expensive, the great thing about creative writing is that *words are cheap*. In fact, most of the time, they're free. If you can speak, read, and write, then you can do this hobby anytime, anywhere, without having to purchase, say, 250 pounds of words the way my friend Catherine, a potter, has to purchase 250 pounds of clay. Words are cheap, which is why it's so easy to treat them casually. It's easy to write e-mails and text-message each other without really paying attention to the words we're using.

But we must never forget that *words also have power*. In ancient times, to know the name of something was to have power over it, which is why Adam could name the animals in Genesis 2:19-20 but Jacob was not told the name of the angel who wrestled with him in Genesis 32:22-30.[27]

One of the ways we try to have power over things is by labeling them with adjectives: poor, rich, smart, slow, geeky, hot, black, white—including the word *Christian*. For some reason, we think that if we can discern whether or not something is "Christian," then we've got it figured out, then we know whether or not it's "safe." This is true for things like "Christian" music, "Christian" clothing, and yes, even "Christian" books. But take it from a word-geek:

The word *Christian* is not meant to be an adjective. It's a noun.

So, inanimate objects aren't Christian. *We* are.

How does this change the way we use that word?

Genesis 1:26-27; 2:19-20

Christian or Not?

One of my favorite poems is titled "Filling Station," by the American poet Elizabeth Bishop." Here's the scene: The narrator has just pulled up to a dumpy little full-service gas station in the middle of nowhere. She begins to observe her surroundings: she notices the dirt, the uncivilized-ness, the general grunge. And yet in the midst of it all there seems to be evidence that someone in that place must care about beauty and creativity. On the porch is a wicker sofa. Next to it is a *taboret*, or fancy little end table. On the *taboret* is a hirsute begonia, one of those flowering plants with fuzzy leaves. The poet begins to realize that somebody cares enough to make this a homely kind of place in the midst of the grime and grease. "Somebody," she writes in the closing line, "loves us all."

But who is this Somebody with a capital *S*?

As a Christian, I have my own ideas about this Somebody. To me the poem can lead us to think about our world—about the mess that it's in and yet how it still shows evidence of God's beauty and even love. In this sense, the poem speaks to me as a Christian, though that may not be what the poet intended. It even could possibly speak to someone who is spiritually asking the same questions as the poet but isn't sure who the Somebody is. But I'm cautious about labeling it a "Christian" poem.

That's because, as I said on June 10, *Christian* is not intended to be an adjective. It's a noun. It describes a person, not a thing. You are a Christian, I am a Christian; but this laptop isn't a "Christian" laptop. The same is true with art. We must be careful, as one of my college professors once said, not to "baptize" the books or music or poems or artwork that we love by insisting they have some kind of inherent Christian meaning.

At the same time, God is out there, infusing inanimate objects with the meaning he wants us to discover. And sometimes he'll even use the "secular" things of this world—including a poem by someone who may or may not be a Christian—to show us something new about himself.

And why not? That's what he did with two beams of Roman wood formed in the shape of a cross.

Acts 17:22-28

// To read the complete poem, posted with permission on the Web site of the Academy of American Poets, go to http://www.poets.org/viewmedia.php/prmMID/15215.

Art as Worship

It's easy to use the word *Christian* as an adjective rather than a noun. We talk of Christian music, Christian movies, and Christian books, as if this somehow helps us claim them or label them as "safe." For example, people often ask me if *The Lord of the Rings* is a Christian story. Well, we can say that J. R. R. Tolkien was a Christian.[28] And we can also say that the more he marinated in the flavor of his Christian faith, the more that flavor came out in his writing.[29] In fact, we can even say that Tolkien saw his creativity as a form of worship to the Creator God—as Tolkien said, a "Sub-creative Art."[//] He saw God as the original Creator and we human beings, made in his image, as "sub-creators." We engage in the activity of creation because that's what we were made to do.

On the one hand I believe reading Tolkien's tale can be a means of worshipping God; I know several people who were drawn to Jesus after reading *The Lord of the Rings*. But we must be very cautious about saying Tolkien's story is "Christian" or "not Christian." Tolkien was a Christian. That's about as far as we can go.

Even so, as Christians we can learn a lot from that master storyteller. We can experience the arts as a way to commune with God, connect with God, and experience God speaking to us. Art can speak to us of God's glory whether or not the poet or author or painter intended it. So perhaps a better adjective than *Christian* would be *sacred*—art that speaks of the holy and divine.

Meanwhile, just because someone is a Christian does not mean his or her art must be filled with crosses or mention God and Jesus directly. A work of art may do those things, but it may not. And yet the more an artist marinates in the flavor of his or her faith, the more that flavor will most likely come out in all he or she does.

How is your life a work of art, a piece of music, a poem to God's glory?

Exodus 35:20–36:1

[//] See Tolkien's wonderful essay "On Fairy-Stories," published in *The Tolkien Reader* (New York: Del Rey, 1986). Have you ever noticed how all the really interesting stuff can be found in a book's footnotes?

True Glory

Glory has always been an elusive term for me. I tend to cringe at its use, especially in revivalist worship services—mostly because I'm not sure what it means.

For instance, in high school choir I learned a choral piece from Handel's *Messiah* in which we sang the same line over and over again: "And the glory, the glory of the Lord shall be reveal-ed." By the end, we must have sung *glory* a thousand times, but I still wasn't sure what we were hoping would be reveal-ed.

And then there's the Westminster Shorter Catechism, which is what many Presbyterian and Reformed youth learn during their confirmation training. The pastor asks, "What is the chief end of man?" and the students respond, "To glorify God, and to enjoy him forever." But what does it mean to *glorify*?

Does God naturally have his own glory, or do we give it to him?

Perhaps the second-century bishop Irenaeus was asked the same questions. He said, "The glory of God is a human being fully alive." I find this to be a powerful answer to my bewilderment. Glory means that if a human being is doing what he or she was created to do, then God is honored. Other people take notice. The world wakes up a little bit, sees things in a clearer, holier light, and seeks the source of that light.

It also explains the thrill I get whenever I experience a particularly well-performed piece of music or drama. When my husband took me to see the live stage performance of *Riverdance*, the mere sight of all those step-dancers effortlessly executing an incredibly complicated set of moves—in unison—caused me to burst into tears. All I could think was "glory to God!—*glory!*" And the show wasn't necessarily about God at all. Something about how those performers used their talents to their utmost, to their fullest potential, was glorifying to God. They were up there, fully alive, because he was the one who created them to do what they were doing. He gave them their gifts and abilities, and in using them they were more fully alive than most of us who call ourselves Christians are on a Sunday morning—half awake, dozing over our Starbucks.

Am I fully alive today? Is my life glorifying to God?

John 17:1-5, 20-24

Grandpa: Part 1

If "the glory of God is a human being fully alive," as the second-century bishop Irenaeus said, then let me tell you about one such human being. He is my ninety-something-year-old grandfather, and he has lived his life to the glory of God for almost a century. For years, whenever I was there for a visit and we had the chance, I'd pull out an old cassette recorder, pop in a blank tape (old school, I know), and then ask Grandpa a question: What was your school like? How did you meet Grandma? What was your first job? When did you first take faith seriously? And patiently he would tell me stories.

One evening, after we had run out of tape and everyone had gone to bed, I sat alone in the guest room and reflected on what a privilege it is to be the keeper of these tales. They have been entrusted to my generation, and we'd better not waste them or lose them. So I wrote:

> A century.
> How many people he has known!
> How many faces
> his pale blue eyes have gazed upon,
> long before the wrinkles set in
> and the crown of hair thinned away
> like a dandelion stalk.
>
> He is old, my grandfather,
> and I sit with him
> in the hollow of lamplight
> at our family table,
> just us two.
> He is talking of all
> his eyes have seen
>
> and I am in awe
> that in this hour
> he should choose
> such a small person
>
> to cast his pearls upon.//

Psalm 71:7-9

// Reference to Matthew 7:6: "Don't waste what is holy on people who are unholy. Don't throw your pearls to pigs!"

Grandpa: Part 2

Today is my grandparents' sixty-somethingth anniversary, and I marvel at their love for God, for each other, and for my family and me. Here's the second part of June 14's poem about my grandfather:

> *"I can remember*
> *the first time I held you*
> *in my arms," he tells me,*
> *his voice choked with emotion.*
> *Our eyes are blurred, burning*
> *as we hug good-night.*
> *These same arms held me*
> *when I was just a few hours old*
> *and have held me since,*
> *one of his beloved grandchildren.*
> *I'm still amazed*
> *that somehow amid*
> *a century of memories*
> *he remembers my birth. Amid*
> *the Hitlers and atomic bombs,*
> *assassinations and Vietcongs,*
> *he remembers a tiny, squalling,*
> *obscure infant's arrival into the world.*
> *How? Why?*
> *In all the tales he has told by lamplight—*
> *of two World Wars, the Great Depression,*
> *the loss of a son—it's the birth*
> *of a grandchild that makes his voice*
> *wobble and break down for love.*
> *And I can't grasp the thought*
> *that—like Grandpa—*
> *my heavenly Father*
> *looks down through the centuries*
> *of human history,*
> *through the mighty heave*
> *and crush of time,*
>
> *and yet holds out his arms*
>
> *to me.*

Psalm 102:25-28

Treasure

In all this talk about creation and creativity and living life to the glory of God, I'm on a poetry kick. (I suppose it's understandable—so were the psalmists.) Here's a reflection on how—of all the created things in this world that we treasure—people are the most important. Why is this so easy to forget?

Yesterday,
my husband accidentally broke
all but two in a set of matching dishes.
They crashed from the cupboard
while he in slow motion tried
to stop them; within seconds
a treasured wedding gift
was in pieces on the floor—
me standing in the doorway, frozen.
First, a flash of anger, a moment of loss,
and then Midwestern pragmatism
as we moved to clean them up.
It won't be long before there's only one
left in the original set,
the sort of thing you see in antique stores
among the lone cups, saucers,
gravy boats, and platters.
In fifty years someone will pick it up
and wonder who owned it and when
and if the owners are still married
or lonely in some nursing home
with no one to visit them.

When I am old and dying,
will I look back with regret
on the untold things I've broken
or lost, and wish I had them with me,
lined up along the windowsill
like so many flower arrangements,
like so many mourning relatives?

Matthew 6:19-21

At the Nursing Home

During my sophomore year of college, my roommates and I participated in a weekly ministry leading worship at a local nursing home. While I banged out hymns on the old piano in the dining room, the other students cheerfully stumbled through the lyrics as the elderly residents sang along, and then we'd wheel folks back to their rooms for a brief chat before bedtime. I remember thinking, *This will be me someday.* I hoped then (and still hope now) that someone will visit with the love of Jesus, so I'll know I'm not forgotten.

The old ladies line up
along the wall, frail
as porcelain, fine
as bone china,
the last remaining
items from twelve-piece
family heirloom sets—
flowered, with swirls
of gold filigree on the rims,
the occasional crack and chip
marring their features.
Lined up along the shelves
like dusty antiques,
price tags dangling
from their handles,
who will have this one,
or that, to treasure?
Who will own and love
the last of that original wedding set
before it finally breaks to bits?
They have outlived
their spouses and their children,
the last
of their pattern and design,
mere collections now
of mismatched cups and saucers
that no one uses anymore,
only looks at.

Which is why
I like to think of God

as the Great Bargain Hunter.   Psalm 31:9-16

Be Our Guest

When I picture my beloved family—my dad and mom, my sister, my grandparents—it is dinnertime during my childhood. We grasp hands while the food cools, while Dad or Grandpa says a careful, thankful prayer or leads us together in "Come, Lord Jesus, be our guest; let thy gifts to us be blessed. Amen."

And I picture Jesus there. We extend the invitation, and he accepts. He sits down with us, takes my grubby, squirming hand in his. He listens carefully as the conversation flows, as Abbie and I giggle or bicker or dance off into some imaginary world, the two of us returning to earth just long enough to pass the salt. He watches Abbie watch me, watches me show off for this sister whose hero I want so much to be, watches me fail her, watches the both of us build a friendship out of the chaos of school life. He smiles.

He calms my father's heart, helps Dad place the overwhelming burden of ministry at the foot of the cross—while Abbie and I watch (Dad doesn't know we're watching). The wrinkle in my father's forehead relaxes; he says a goofy pun while we roll our eyes and love him for being ours.

My mother props her feet up onto Dad's chair as she fills out her daily journal, recording God's faithfulness into the lines of our lives. Every entry is an answered prayer or a new arena for God to do his work. She sighs a mom-sigh, rubs her neck, and I love her for being mine.

Jesus sits with us. He gazes at my grandparents, their love for each other the very expression of his heart, the mirror of a lifetime spent walking with him. He leans forward and whispers to me, *See—I keep my promises. I am faithful from generation to generation.* And even as a child, I realize this is true.

So now I sit down with my new family, my husband. It's no wonder we love to grocery shop, to create a meal together, to open our home to our families, to our community. Because Jesus is here. He sits with us, passes the salt, whispers how he keeps his promises, records his faithfulness into the lines of our lives. In Christ we embark on a lifetime of meals together . . . with family, friend, and stranger . . . every supper the first and the last."

Luke 24:28-31; Revelation 3:20

// I first prepared this piece of writing to read aloud at my wedding.

Spiritual Godparents: Part 1

Mark Twain once joked, "When I was a boy of fourteen, my father was so ignorant I could hardly stand to have the old man around. But when I got to be twenty-one, I was astonished at how much the old man had learned in seven years." Hilarious and all too true! Unfortunately, this is how many of us treat our elders (especially our fathers) until we grow old enough to realize just how important their wisdom and experience are.

Of course, not every father-child relationship is a good one. For some, a relationship with a father may not even be possible. That's when we turn to father figures, those adopted "godparents" who take an interest in our spiritual development. One such relationship in Scripture is that of young Timothy and the older apostle Paul. As I've said before, Paul was the first Christian missionary who traveled around the Mediterranean preaching the Good News about Jesus and setting up churches in key cities of the ancient world. Timothy, meanwhile, was a young man whom Paul met on one of his early journeys.

By piecing together information from the book of Acts and from Paul's letters to Timothy, we can glean something about who this young man was. We know his father was Greek and his mother was Jewish (see Acts 16:1), but for whatever reason he was not circumcised as a baby (a vital Jewish custom). He learned the Hebrew Scriptures from his mother and grandmother (see 2 Timothy 1:5; 3:14-15), but we know nothing about his father's faith—quite likely it wasn't worth mentioning. And although Paul first met Timothy on one of his early missionary journeys, perhaps when Timothy was still a boy in Lystra, it was on a later trip that Timothy became one of Paul's traveling companions. Eventually Paul installed him as one of the first pastors of the church in Ephesus (see 1 Timothy 1:3).

The last known letter of Paul is 2 Timothy, in which he urged Timothy to come visit him before winter when he was imprisoned in Rome. We don't know if Timothy made it to Rome before Paul's execution. But we do know that Paul—who quite possibly had no children or family of his own—deeply loved Timothy as his spiritual "son." Obviously Timothy was an important support to his mentor. So the relationship went both ways.

Sometimes I feel like the older Christians are constantly pouring their time and energy into the lives of younger ones without receiving much in return. Paul and Timothy's relationship makes me wonder: How can we be more diligent about praying for our spiritual mentors and godparents? How can we be a support to them when they face the winters of their own lives while we're still in summer?

2 Timothy 4:6-13, 21-22

Spiritual Godparents: Part 2

On June 19 we talked about the New Testament friendship between a young man named Timothy and his mentor, Paul. Paul essentially adopted Timothy as his spiritual "son," and meanwhile Timothy provided support to Paul when times were rough. It sounds like the kind of relationship I'd like to have. So how do we spot our spiritual godparents? Here are some thoughts, gleaned from Paul's letters:

1. *Relationship*. In both letters, Paul greets Timothy with an affirmation of who he is in Paul's eyes, a beloved "son" (see 1 Timothy 1:2 and 2 Timothy 1:2). Consider: Who has claimed you and loved you as a spiritual "daughter or son," even if the two of you are not technically related?

2. *Legacy*. Paul reminds Timothy of the stories that have shaped Timothy's identity as a child of God: both Paul's personal story (see 1 Timothy 1:12-17 and 2 Timothy 1:8-14; 3:10-11) and the legacy of faith that Timothy received from his mother and grandmother (see 2 Timothy 1:5-6; 3:14-15). Consider: What are the stories your spiritual godparents have shared with you? What spiritual legacy have you been given?

3. *Affirmation*. Paul encourages Timothy to utilize his spiritual gift of teaching for the strengthening of God's people. It's obvious that Paul was instrumental in identifying this gift through prayer and the laying on of hands (2 Timothy 1:6), thereby assuring Timothy of his role in the church. Consider: What spiritual gifts have others identified in you? (See Romans 12:6-8 for some ideas.)

4. *Advice and Instructions*. Paul's letters are full of instructions and advice, mostly on how Timothy can best guide the congregations he pastors. This is a crucial part of Paul's mentoring relationship with Timothy—and we can be fairly certain that Timothy didn't fold his arms, roll his eyes, and say, "Here we go again. . . ." Consider: To whom do you go to for advice? How do you respond when your mentors spontaneously offer their insights and instructions?

5. *Prayer*. Paul tells Timothy, "Night and day I constantly remember you in my prayers" (2 Timothy 1:3). He doesn't say this simply to make Timothy feel good. Paul really and truly means it. Throughout both letters, we catch glimpses of Paul's dreams and hopes for Timothy, echoes of the content of his prayers. Consider: Who prays for you—and what do they pray? What do they share about their vision for your life?

And if no one currently fits the bill of spiritual godparent in your life, how might you intentionally seek the friendship of an older role model in your church? Okay, clubbing and barhopping are out, so what about taking an older person out for Saturday brunch?

1 Timothy 6:11-16

Ancient of Days

In the small front yard of our summer bungalow is a simply enormous tree—one of those giant loblolly pines that grow straight up for several stories before branching out into various apartment complexes for birds. If I lie on my back on the couch in the living room, under the picture window, I can look directly up into the tree. And that's what I was doing a few moments ago as the sun was setting on this, the longest day of the year. The bark glowed red in splotches where the sun filtered through the other trees, and something about the whole scene made me wonder how many years that pine has been standing there, watching sunsets, and how many young women like me it has watched grow old, like the dear lady who owns this house.

I wonder how many kids have walked past that tree on their way to school, kids who are now grown-ups with their own kids and who look at the tree and think, *Man, some things never change.* We grow up, we gather scars like badges of honor, we change so much over the years that our friends back home don't even recognize us, and still that tree stands there like a sentinel on the edge of twilight, facing the forces of darkness without flinching. It's not afraid of growing old like we are. It knows age means strength. It glories in its scars and wrinkles. It sheds its needles without grieving the loss and some-how even looks dignified. I find it heartening, in this wacky year of so much change in my life, to gaze at a pine tree that isn't going anywhere anytime soon.

"All changing unchanged Ancient of days,"[30] wrote the seventeenth-century poet and priest John Donne. He wasn't speaking of a tree; he was speaking of God, the most Ancient of all ancients, who has seen more days and sunsets and solstices than the weari-est tree on this tired, dusty planet. And yet even though I can count on God to stand immovable in steadfast dignity like my loblolly pine, he is also as fresh and alive and unpre-dictable as a puppy, as surprising as the clouds at sunset. He is somehow all-changing and yet unchanged at the same time. He is the Ancient Youth, the oldest living being ever to cry in a cradle.

There are times when I need him to startle me with his unpredictability, to shock me out of my comfortable rut of spiritual laziness; but there are other times, like this long evening, when I need him to be my Ancient of Days. And he is.

Ezekiel 17:22-24

Further In

The house I'm living in for the summer belongs to a delightful old professor, which means it's full of books—hurrah! But just as thrilling, the church where my husband is an intern has a separate room *just for the library* (there's even a children's library across the hall). It contains floor-to-ceiling bookshelves on every wall, comfy leather chairs, and an elderly librarian who stamps the cards when you check out. No computer, no scanner, no electronic buzz when you enter the room, just shelf upon shelf of delights.

Okay, so I'm a geek. I'll admit it. Each week I pull old and new treats from the shelves of our temporary home and devour them: Shakespeare's *Hamlet*, C. S. Lewis's *Letters to an American Lady*, Kathleen Norris's *The Cloister Walk*. I gobble up the poems of John Donne, T. S. Eliot, Annie Dillard. Each day I step "further in" to magical worlds beyond the spare room of this old professor's house, and I feel my imagination and spirit expanding. It's like I've come home.

On June 21 I mentioned the seventeenth-century poet John Donne (whose spelling, by the way, gives my laptop fits—red squiggly lines all over the place). Though his words and expressions may seem quaint to us at first, rusted over with the passing of centuries, they are some of the most powerful poems ever written by a Christian in the English language. If we do not feel both convicted and cleansed after reading them, as from a good scrubbing with an abrasive soap, then we must not have been listening. Here are two lines that particularly skewer me as I attempt to write a year's worth of profound, articulate, witty, and wise devotions:

> When wee are mov'd to seeme religious
> Only to vent wit, Lord deliver us.[31]

Amen and amen. How many pastors need to tape those lines to their bathroom mirrors on Sunday morning?

(Perhaps they would if their parishioners thought it was both sensible and necessary for a pastor to read great literature. But that's another soapbox. . . .)

Ecclesiastes 12:9-14

The Power of Stories

Once, as a child, I looked up from a book I'd been engrossed in for hours, and there was my mother standing over me, hand on one hip. "Sarah, I've called you *three times*!" she said in exasperation. I sat with my mouth hanging open. "Y-you did?" I managed to say. I was being honest. I hadn't heard a thing. I'd been lost in the enchanted world of my imagination, out of earshot from the ordinary.

And it wasn't the first time. My grandfather once attempted to join my sister and me as we were deep in the throes of some make-believe (Hansel and Gretel running from the witch, perhaps), and one of us turned to him and said, "Grandpa, you are not *of* this world." He laughed uproariously then and continues to laugh about it now. Thank goodness our family didn't think we were deeply disturbed or something! They knew healthy, creative play when they saw it. Sure, they were frustrated when our imaginations took us a little too deep into la-la land, but they knew the power of good stories could shape a person's character from the inside out.

"We are all, in fact, the products of our stories," wrote Daniel Taylor, "including the stories from literature. I believe, for instance, that my life took a slight but perceptible change in direction in my late teens from reading J. R. R. Tolkien's *The Lord of the Rings*."[32] He's not the first person to indicate the power of story to shape a person's life. In this case, he was speaking of a tale whose foundation is essentially Christian, as Tolkien himself indicated (see June 12). As with Jesus' parables, a story like *The Lord of the Rings* sinks into the imagination and stays, slowly growing in significance over time. It lifts us out of the everyday world and shows us a higher, holier way of being. It challenges us to live those truths in the real world just as we lived in them in the story, and thus we are changed.

That's the power of story. That's the power of parable, and of Scripture. That's what shaped my imagination and faith as a child, to make me the person I am today.

What formative stories can I offer others, so they, too, can make those "slight but perceptible change[s]"?

Matthew 13:34-35

The Play's the Thing

The play's the thing
Wherein I'll catch the conscience of the King.

Hamlet

Ah, Hamlet. I sit here in the sunny living room of our summer bungalow reading Shakespeare, the street outside sizzling in the Southern heat. But in my mind I'm standing on a medieval battlement with the Prince of Denmark as a frigid wind tears at our cloaks. "To be or not to be?" he wonders aloud, and the wind snatches his words away. His uncle murdered his father and is now married to his mother, and Hamlet must somehow confront them both and right the wrong—or his life isn't worth living. But how? If he does so directly, they will convince everyone he's crazy and whisk him off to prison—or worse. In the midst of these musings, along comes a traveling drama troupe, which gives Hamlet an idea. He'll write a play that mirrors the events of his father's death, and the players will present it to the imposter king and his new wife. Thus the "truth will out" before the monarchs know what hit them.

Hmm . . . it all sounds vaguely familiar, like another, older story that we find in today's Scripture reading. The prophet Nathan, rather than confronting the powerful King David directly about his adultery with Bathsheba and the murder of her husband, tells him a simple parable. The truth comes out, and David repents. It's the same tactic Jesus used too, in telling stories about the Kingdom. Eugene Peterson wrote, "As people heard Jesus tell these stories, they saw at once that they weren't about God, so there was nothing in them threatening their own sovereignty. They relaxed their defenses." Then later, "the stories lodged in their imagination. And then, like a time bomb, they would explode in their unprotected hearts. An abyss opened at their very feet. He *was* talking about God; they had been invaded."[33]

Story is subversive—its truths lie below the surface, like a tidal current, rather than blatant and obvious for all to see. (Or at least, the best stories are that way.) Rather than confronting a listener with bald statements of fact, which the listener might quickly reject out of pride or impatience or downright rebellion, story slips through the back door of imagination, sits down in the kitchen of the soul, and slowly makes its truths evident over a cup of coffee. The listener's defenses are down; he or she doesn't realize the whole house is under siege until it's too late. The listener can no longer avoid the truth; it's sitting at the kitchen table, and he or she invited it in unawares.

So, to subvert or not to subvert? That is the question.

2 Samuel 12:1-13

Missing the Forest

Considering the power of subversion (see June 24), it's amazing how few preachers and Christian leaders utilize it. If the church wishes to reach a generation like mine full of hard-boiled skeptics—who've heard it all before—then head-on confrontation won't get very far. All our walls are up and manned with archers, arrows at the ready. The church will be turned back at the gate before it has even learned our names.

For some reason many Christians don't seem to understand this. I can only conclude it's because they don't read enough great literature. I mean, when was the last time you found a church small group that was reading Dostoyevsky's *Crime and Punishment*? And yet wouldn't it be interesting to hear a discussion or sermon flavored with the powerful redemption of a murderer like Raskolnikov and his prostitute girlfriend? I offhandedly recommended that book to two high school students who were tired of hearing the same old, same old rhetoric from their parents and from the pulpit. Later they said, "That story was awesome! Why haven't we heard of it before?" Maybe it's time Christian bookstores started carrying the classics. Maybe it's time Christians started reading them.

Anyway, the other problem I see is that many Christians don't read their own book, the Bible, through literary eyes. They don't recognize how important it is to engage with character, plot, setting, and tone, and they instead look for lessons, principles, platitudes, or subpoints. Thus the Sermon on the Mount, for example, gets boiled down to a handy acronyms like FROG ("fully rely on God"), when what we really should be concerned about is who Jesus is speaking to, and where and why. If we actually paid attention to these concerns, we might find ourselves blinking in bewilderment, as those early disciples must have done, wondering *how exactly* Jesus expects us to enter the Kingdom he keeps talking about. And we'd thirst for more.

Writes Kurt Bruner:

> It's much easier to hold the attention of a culture with "Once upon a time" than it is with "Open your Bibles to." The irony is that the Bible is the ultimate "Once upon a time." . . . The twists and turns reflected in the gospel are far more compelling than any novel ever to appear on The New York Times bestseller list. Somewhere along the way, we as Christians have become so focused on the lessons that we have lost the story—missing the forest for the trees.[34]

I want to step back and look at the forest again.

Mark 4:10-13

Take from Me Books

Sometimes I wonder if I love books too much. Whenever I enter a bookstore, I'm like a kid on Christmas morning, eyes big and round, mouth hanging slightly open. I want everything. I find each section mesmerizing, especially the children's corner. I could curl up on those comfy beanbag chairs and read the great classics all day long—youth fiction such as *The Westing Game* or *The Borrowers* or *From the Mixed-Up Files of Mrs. Basil E. Frankweiler*. Now *that's* great literature.

But then lurking in the back of my mind are the tremendous needs of this sad, hurting planet. Couldn't I better spend my time helping at the literacy center? Shouldn't I volunteer at the soup kitchen instead of reading fiction on the porch swing in the lazy summer heat? Yes—and no.

As Christians, we must respond to the needs of this world, but only those needs to which Christ specifically calls us. Otherwise we might easily become overwhelmed or think of ourselves as spiritual superheroes. When he presses upon our hearts a certain need at a certain time, that is our task. But he also calls us to marinate in the things that flavor our souls and vocations, and for me that happens to be literature. How can I write anything if I'm reading nothing? Writers begin by reading. Artists begin by studying the masters and then mimicking their styles. And meanwhile the world is enriched by their work, but most especially when that work is done to the glory of God.

I've learned that the more I try to turn my back on books and do the "spiritual" tasks I think God wants, the more "the author and perfecter of our faith"[/] throws books in my way—both to read and to write. And thus I pray with one of my favorite poets:

> Take from me leisure, all familiar places;
> Take all the lovely things of earth and air
> Take from me books; take all my precious faces;
> Take words melodious, and their songful linking;
> Take scents, and sounds, and all thy outsides fair;
> Draw nearer, taking, and, to my sober thinking,
> Thou bring'st them nearer all, and ready to my prayer.
>
> From *The Diary of an Old Soul*, by George MacDonald[35]

Psalm 78:1-8

// Hebrews 12:2 (NIV).

Worth Being Concerned About

You will hear me say this many times: I do not cook. Though I love to host people in my home, it's at my husband's discretion because *he* will be the one cooking for everybody—which, providentially, he enjoys and is very gifted at. Sure, I'll clean the bathroom and set the table and wash the dishes, but otherwise I'm about as undomestic as they come. For example, I panic when invited to a potluck. It's probably what nonmusical people feel like when invited to an open mike night where everyone is expected to perform a song or poem or whatever. "Oh, just prepare a little something," the hostess says soothingly, "nothing too involved." Yeah, right.

My lack of skills in the kitchen is difficult for people to understand, especially other women. It's simply expected that *we* do most of the cooking and that men . . . um . . . bring home the bacon, I guess. In my marriage those roles are reversed. Generally *I'm* the one bringing home the bacon, and Tom is the one who wraps it around some venison backstrap, bastes it with a glaze, and serves it with cherry chutney sauce and rosemary redskin potatoes. And meanwhile he still manages to look manly.

Anyway, I've always found the story of Mary and Martha fascinating (see today's text)—not because I'm one of those Marthas in our culture who try to make their entrées look like something out of *Good Housekeeping*, but because I'm more like Mary. I'd rather hang out with the guys in the living room, soaking up the wisdom of a visiting scholar, than mess around in the kitchen. I'd rather talk about postliberal theology and Neoplatonism with my friends than the latest *Martha Stewart Living*. And it's heartening to know that Jesus doesn't think this is odd. In fact, he encourages it.

At the same time, the world needs to be fed. People are hungry. *I'm* hungry. Christians are called to practice hospitality, to welcome others into their homes as the biblical Martha did. The needs of the world press in upon us, no matter how much we prefer sitting quietly with a good book or even the Good Book. Somehow women and men alike must find a holy balance between the "one thing worth being concerned about" (Luke 10:42) and the concerns of the world Jesus died for.

Luke 10:38-42

Not Needed

I know I'm not the first person to feel the tension between the life of contemplation and the life of outreach, between solitude and service. And this goes beyond extrovert-introvert personality differences. According to the accepted model of evangelicalism, we're to go out and change the world for Jesus—that's our primary job, extroverts and introverts alike (though extroverts definitely have the edge). We can understand if people take a five-minute "quiet time" to kick-start the day, but if this stretches to five hours we begin to think they're being irresponsible. We're leery of monastic solitude or silence; we're not sure about contemplative reading or even writing, much less poetry—unless it's somehow directly linked to evangelism. After all, the world needs us.

But that's just the attitude I find troubling. *The world needs us*—as if all creation and human existence would come to a screeching halt if Christians stopped doing, doing, doing. What if we humbly recognized for once that we are ultimately *unnecessary* in the grand scheme of things? that we're only as useful as God chooses to make us—and the rest of the time we're just in the way? What if we, like the early Christians, took not just forty minutes alone with God, but forty hours? forty days? forty months?

If we're honest, I think many of us are scared of the contemplative life. We're scared because it proves what we've always feared: *We're not needed.* As much as the devil would like to convince us otherwise (if you turn these stones to bread, you could feed the hungry, for example), God doesn't need us. In fact the reverse is true: *We need God.* Desperately. Jonathan Wilson-Hartgrove wrote, "Contemplation is not about a 'quiet time' when we can feel safe with God. In contemplation we learn to trust God precisely because we need him."[36]

(Incidentally, he wrote this from the Walltown ghetto of Durham, North Carolina, where he and his Christian friends have deliberately chosen to live in solidarity with the poor. . . .)

Luke 4:1-13

Recording God's Faithfulness

I have, since earlier this month, read much and prayed much—I simply haven't written a whole lot in my prayer journal. I must remember to write, for it chronicles God's work in my life. It adds an extra layer of awareness to my days. I'm not sure why this is, but unrecorded days seem to not exist somehow. During the years I went without journaling, such as my courtship, engagement, and first two years of marriage, which included various vocational decisions and personal losses . . . what was I thinking about in those turbulent times? I was unsettled, I recall. I was unsure, chaotic, and spontaneous. But there were also beauties and delights that I've since forgotten, all because I failed to document them.

Even so, perhaps it's a blessing I didn't inflict my written agonies on the world at the time. Someone once said, "Ninety percent of what we write is garbage. Concentrate on the 10 percent." This goes for prayer journals too. Certainly our God is gracious, patient, and compassionate. But even he must reach a point where he says, *Enough of this nonsense. Please, please put down your pen. Let me write instead.* Eventually we recognize that our "personal" journals should in some fashion acknowledge God's sovereignty; otherwise we'd better give up the whole enterprise. Perhaps, during those self-centered (and thus unrecorded) years, I was just being honest.

> O Lord, I commit the rest of this year to you. I commit my hands to recording your presence within the lines of my life, to documenting my journey and your sure, steady transformation of me into the likeness of your Son, Jesus. I'm still unsure about the future, still unsettled about my vocation at times, but I pray for the fruit of your Holy Spirit to be evident in my life—your peace, particularly. When people spend time with me, may they come away feeling settled and sure, having been with someone who knows something about your faithfulness and remembered to write it down. Amen.

Ecclesiastes 12:1-7

There Is None like Him

Let us sing,
sing a new song

a song of praise
to our God:

"He is faithful"
— we were the ones to let go of his hand.

"He is merciful"
— like a good Father, he didn't let us stray very far.

"He is just"
— our hands still smart from his reprimand.

"He is loving"
— he pulled out the Band-Aids while we cried.

"He is creative"
— they had cool cartoons all over them.

"He is powerful"
— while he put them on, we felt the might of his huge hands encompassing our
*   tiny, grubby ones.*

"He is patient"
— while we "ow!"ed and complained and asked billions of questions.

"He is able"
— he quickly bandaged us; he answered our every urgent question.

"He is holy"
— we looked up in teary-eyed amazement at such a loving Parent, such a
*   fathomless mind, such a persevering and comforting Spirit, such uncontested*
*   strength—and realized he is wholly Other.*

There is none like him.

Jeremiah 10:6-7

The Usual

Well, I'm halfway through writing this *Daily Grind*, and so far the most grinding thing about it is its sheer dailiness. I suppose that's what the coffeehouse employees at the nearby shopping center feel like when they trudge to work at four in the morning. They roast and grind yet *another* batch of beans, just like they did yesterday, and the same crowd of caffeine junkies stumbles in bleary eyed, just like they did yesterday. The barista behind the counter says to the man in the crumpled suit, "The usual?" and he nods, wordless. (Incidentally, baristas must be the unsung heroes of corporate America, now that I think about it. Tell me what executive office could possibly function without them—at least before 10 a.m.?)

Anyway, this reminds me of the story Annie Dillard tells about the church she attended for a while, where the same prayer requests were repeated Sunday after Sunday. One morning while leading his congregation in prayer, the pastor suddenly blurted out, "Lord, we bring you these same petitions every week." Annie writes, "After a shocked pause, he continued reading the prayer. Because of this, I like him very much."[37] I think I'd like him too. Honesty in prayer is not always easy, especially when we grow weary of repeating ourselves day after day. But it's especially difficult when you're the one up front, leading a group of Christians through the same list of requests that you said yesterday or last week or last month or even last year.

And yet I believe God understands the dailiness of our prayers. I can almost picture him behind the heavenly counter, saying, "The usual?" as we nod wordlessly and hold out our cups. Yes, please: the usual. The usual requests. The usual concerns. The usual everything, world without end, amen.

Perhaps this is why Jesus instructed us to pray for our *daily* bread. Not because God is somehow unreliable, letting us starve one day and filling us the next, but because God is like our coffeehouse barista: He's there every day, if only we bother to show up and ask.

Luke 11:1-10

Summer Break

Maybe it's a hangover from my school days, but summer seems like the proper time for a break from all this dailiness. It'd be nice to put off writing these daily devotions until September, for instance. I'm sure the barista at the coffeehouse down the street would like a break from roasting beans. When life is particularly a grind, I think about how I'd like to be a kid on summer break again and go off to camp or vacation Bible school or just swing under the tree in the backyard for hours on end. Somehow my days seemed less *daily* when I was a kid. But for those of us who call ourselves contributing members of society (or more important, *Christians*), work doesn't stop just because school does.

The closest I can come to a break from the daily grind is to participate in camps and mission trips with kids who are on vacation. Something about getting out of your normal routine—especially breaking out of your comfort zone in a cross-cultural setting—charges the everyday world with new meaning once you return. I remember one mom telling me after her son had come home from camp, "He's a different kid. He's actually *nice!*" I'm guessing that's because camp interrupted his usual pattern of behavior and made him realize how much easier life is when you actually attempt to get along with everybody. You learn very quickly at camp that nobody wants to hang out with a grouch—besides, your leaders won't let you get away with that attitude for long. So you learn a new pattern of behavior, *Christian* behavior, and hopefully this translates to your everyday world when you return home.

There can be something spiritually formative about time away from home in the sense that it can help us break old habits and establish new, healthy patterns of Christian living. But the real trick comes in maintaining those new patterns when we're back home and the usual routine starts up again. We can't stay in a perpetual state of summer break, even spiritually, or we'll never learn to find God in the daily grind.

Hebrews 10:23-25

Who Can Be against Us?

Here's what I wrote on the last morning of a summer camp I worked at recently. (To give you some background, this particular camp was a multiweek theological academy for Christian youth, held on the campus of a major university.)

It's our last morning of camp before parents arrive and shuttles start leaving in shifts for the airport. Everyone looks frantic and bleary eyed. Luggage is piled all over the sidewalk. There are sad hugs, muffled good-byes, hand-squeezing, backslapping. No one really wants this to be over, yet we know it's time. And now our chaplain calls us together for one last worship service, one last ritual of morning prayer like we've been doing every day for two straight weeks.

Except this time, instead of having us process into the main chapel, where it's quiet and worshipful, he gathers us in the center of the quad, right in the heart of campus. At first it's decently quiet—not many other folks from volleyball camp or soccer camp or whatever are around at this hour. But then as our worship service continues, the quad becomes more and more crowded. People spill out of the great hall after breakfast. Frisbees fly. People gawk. Someone even heckles us to sing louder.

We hunker down, pray quietly, sing even more quietly. "God is for us," we nearly whisper—when just yesterday we bellowed it boldly in the sanctuary—"who can be against us?" It's one thing to belt out what we believe while in a house of worship; it's quite another to live it in the real world. Some of us look downright mortified. This faith thing, which seemed so easy when we were all alone together, suddenly comes with a price. It costs us our pride, for one. And our sense of cool. It will most likely cost us our future "success" in the eyes of the world too. People might even heckle.

But are we listening to our own words? If God is for us, what difference does it make whether we sing in the sanctuary or carol in the quad? Who can be against us, except our own embarrassed selves?

Romans 8:31-34

Interdependence Day

It's July 4, and my husband and I are visiting the colonial village of Yorktown, Virginia, for the navy band and fireworks—along with about 236,857 other people. I'm not kidding. There are *hordes* of tourists here, milling about the historic streets, parading down the boardwalk along the river, slurping ice cream, playing in the sand, getting sand in their ice cream, getting ice cream and sand in their hair—you get the picture. It's a mess. Yet apparently this is the way we Americans like to celebrate our independence, our freedom, our Lone Ranger frontier spirit—by cramming ourselves into the smallest possible space with thousands of other people and doing exactly what they're doing.

Which is poetic, in a way. As much as we like to celebrate our individual autonomy, very few of us have opted for life in a hermitage, cut off from the rest of the world. We like to *think* we're independent, but in truth we need each other. We are *inter*dependent—vitally connected to one another, unable to function without the help, hospitality, and enduring patience of our neighbors. And as far as we as a nation are concerned, this includes our international neighbors. Yorktown, for example, reminds us of the debt we owe to the French for our success in the Revolutionary War. So even though America may celebrate its independence, we are part of a global community which we are dependent on and accountable to. In truth, this is our *Inter*dependence Day.

If this is true for America and for every other nation on the planet, it's true for you and me as individuals—but most especially if we call ourselves Christians. Yes, God made us with unique gifts and callings . But he also placed us within a body of believers we are dependent on and accountable to. There should be none of this business about "taking a break from church for a while" or "I prefer to worship God without the distraction of other people." No matter what our temperament, the Christian life is one of interdependence, not independence. There are no Lone Ranger Christians.

Ephesians 2:11-18

Blue Heaven

The first of many crazy ideas I had as a youth director was to take a bunch of kids from our small town in Michigan to inner-city Chicago. The main objective was for them to experience worship and ministry alongside Christians who didn't look anything like them and thus to be startled out of their adolescent complacency for once.

So I took them to Jesus People USA, a Christian community on the North Side that opens its doors to people of every ethnicity and background, including the homeless, the mentally ill, the prostitutes, and the tax col—um, I mean, sinners. And at first I thought the shock would be too much for our kids. As I looked at their faces, it seemed like they were totally distracted from the real point of being there, which was to experience God's Kingdom in a new way, as something far bigger than they had ever imagined. I almost despaired of this happening until later that evening, when one of them wrote in the group journal, "At church I was surprised to see a guy with blue hair. But then I realized, God loves everybody, even people with blue hair." Houston, we have contact.

A few years later I took our youth group to visit that same church, and sitting behind us was a guy in dreadlocks with a bone through his nose—yes, I said a *bone*. Needless to say, our kids were staring. I'm sure some of them were thinking, *Wow, there are some wacky visitors here today.* But then came the commissioning service for a new batch of elected elders, in which former elders were invited to come down and pray. And down went Bone-in-Nose Man. No, he wasn't being commissioned as an elder, *he had already served as one.* Astonished, a kid turned to me and said, "He's an *elder*?" And I said, "Welcome to the family!"

God's heaven is not homogenous. When we get there, very few of us will be singing in English or even *know* English. We may see more blue hair and bones in noses than we ever wanted to see. Yet even now our little individual lives are just a narrow slice of God's big picture, and our home cultures are just a tiny window into the wide world of his grace.

1 Chronicles 16:23-30

Every Tribe and Nation

I haven't always grasped this global view of the Kingdom, particularly the interdependent relationships we as individuals and cultures have with one another in the body of Christ. I suppose all people are guilty of an ethnocentric view of the world, but Anglo-American society seems especially guilty of this. And the Church isn't exempt, as much as we'd like to claim we have a "heart for the nations" and promote things like missions and evangelism. Unfortunately, this impulse is often eclipsed by our desire to feel comfortable on this planet by making everyone else look and sound just like us (as if Jesus spoke English).

For example, talk to any older Native American Christian, and most will tell you that when they were children, drumming and other expressions of their culture were equated with worship of pagan gods. They were told this by generations of Christian elders, who had heard it from white missionaries, and so they learned to give up all such practices if they wished to follow Jesus. Yet some younger Natives are now asking the question: What if we praised God with the language and instruments and musical tones he gave us? What if we reclaimed all those things for the Kingdom so the world can see just how big and awesome Jesus is?

I had several experiences during my undergraduate years that blew open my ethnocentric worldview by showing me just how diverse and glorious God's Kingdom is. It started with a weekly student-led ministry in inner-city Chicago, tutoring children in housing projects, and then continued with several summer day camps on Native reservations in the Georgian Bay area of Ontario. I encountered children who weren't afraid to be themselves before God—even if their elders were wary of these white Christians and the foreign culture they represented. I was invited to sing gospel songs in the urban ghetto and drum psalms on the shores of Lake Huron, and in each region, the name of Jesus was lifted up. I experienced a little glimpse of John's vision in Revelation, where he saw "a vast crowd, too great to count, from every nation and tribe and people and language, standing in front of the throne and before the Lamb" (7:9).

So here's my question: If this is what the heavenly Kingdom looks like, why don't our churches reflect this on Sunday morning?

Revelation 7:9-12

Everything That Has Breath

Whenever I'm thrust into another cultural setting (see July 6). I'm struck by the unique and beautiful way Christians in those places worship God. What if I stopped thinking the whole world has to conform to my American sensibilities and instead embraced the wild diversity of God's nonconformist Kingdom?

Let the peoples praise him;
let all the peoples praise him!

Let the warm rhythm
of hip-hop girls and boys,
tussling and tumbling and
dancing and shouting
on the hot, cracked concrete
sprinkled with glass like diamonds
—let them stand up and holler hallelujah:
"Bless the Lord, O my soul,
and all that is within me—
all my rhythm, my voice,
my jump and dance—
bless his holy name!"

Let the peoples praise him;
let all the peoples praise him!

Let the strong, silent Native
swimming in Canadian summer,
half-smiling on the high rocks
over French River,
hurdle himself into the deeps
of almighty God,
mount up on wings like eagles,
run and not grow weary,
walk and not faint.

Let everything that has breath
Praise the Lord!

Psalm 113

Sheer Exhaustion

I'm exhausted. I've had weeks to catch up on sleep since I returned home from youth camp, but I'm still dead on my feet. Every day we went to bed around midnight, got up by 7 a.m., and didn't stop running crazy until we dropped into bed again seventeen hours later. I used to live at that pace all the time, especially during my college years (and I always wondered why I felt so crummy in the mornings too!). The truth is, after a while that kind of lifestyle takes its toll—which means we pay for it later.

Exhibit A: Ever since camp, my days have gone as follows: I crawl out of bed in the mornings long after normal people have already left for work. My routine includes a shower, breakfast, coffee, and then a prolonged period of moping in between checking e-mail and attempting to read a book. Generally I don't get much farther than a few pages before I fall asleep. So I rally and attempt to do something productive, like wash all three dishes in the sink. Then I check e-mail again. Then I read some more. And fall asleep. I just can't seem to summon the energy for anything else.

I think about that story of the disciples in the boat, with Jesus crashed in the stern. We wonder how he possibly could have slept through a storm so violent that the boat was getting swamped, waves pouring over the sides, and the disciples unable to bail fast enough. The wind must have been horrific too—ripping at the sails, tangling the lines, snatching words so the disciples had to shout to be heard. And still Jesus slept.

All I can think is how tired he must have been. Not just from two weeks of intense ministry, like my camp, but from *two years*, at least—if not more. All day long he poured himself into the needy, the hurting, the diseased, the lonely. He counseled late-night visitors such as Nicodemus. He got up early to go off by himself and pray. When did he sleep? Not very often. On boats, apparently, when the rocking of the waves gradually lulled his tired eyes closed. Sheer exhaustion occasionally took over.

And yet the world needed him. The disciples shook him awake, and instead of moping and complaining and falling asleep again, he summoned the energy to halt the wind and the waves.

What kind of man was this, that even his own *body* obeyed him?

Luke 8:22-25

Calming the Storm

Where I come from, storms are serious business. My former hometown sits on a series of terraced hills overlooking a large bay on Lake Michigan. The bay is oriented northwest, which means it's wide open to massive fronts coming across the lake from Canada. Weather systems have plenty of time and distance to gather momentum, so by the time they slam into our downtown waterfront, they can inflict some serious damage. Just last winter the massive concrete pier that guards the city harbor was breached by a series of breakers so large they looked like houses. Needless to say, it takes hours—even days—for the water to calm down after a storm, even when the wind has long since died and it has become perfectly quiet inland.

That's why I'm so intrigued by the story of Jesus calming the storm. It's one thing for the wind to die to a whisper mere seconds after it's been howling like a beast; most of us have experienced the mysterious capriciousness of air currents, especially if you've spent any time on a body of water. But for the waves to suddenly be still? All you have to do is start a ripple effect in your bathtub to realize just how long it takes for water to calm down after it's been disturbed. For this to happen instantaneously would take a miracle.

Perhaps that's why, according to today's story in Mark, Jesus spoke to the wind and the waves *separately*. To the wind he said something rather like "shame on you," but to the waves he issued a command: "Quiet down!" or in some translations, "Peace, be still." His first reaction upon waking was to tackle the immediate problems facing his followers, which in this case were twofold: wind, which created the waves; and waves, which would not cease just because the wind had died.

As the boat was sinking, Jesus didn't philosophize with the disciples about their lack of faith; he calmed the storm first. Only then did he discuss their spiritual condition. I need to keep this in mind when interacting with people who are "perishing" in any number of ways. Address the threat, then deal with their spiritual condition. But in the meantime I must be sure not to overlook other issues just because we've dealt with the obvious problem. Just because a young woman has gotten out of a bad dating relationship, for example, doesn't mean her eating disorder will also go away. I must be on the watch for what may swamp the boat.

Psalm 107:23-32; Mark 4:35-41

Gotcha

If you haven't figured it out yet, I'm a Great Lakes girl. Most of my summer memories involve water in some form or another. In fact, one of my earliest memories is of running down a red dock on a crystal clear lake in northern Michigan and suddenly finding myself toppled head over heels into the shallows. I landed underwater on the sunny lake floor with my eyes still open, sand billowing and little minnows darting away in every direction. But just as my arms started flailing, I felt a strong hand on the back of my shirt, and someone pulled me out—probably my dad or maybe an uncle. Whoever it was, he was laughing. "Gotcha," he said, like I was the fish that almost got away. I had been underwater just long enough to be surprised but not long enough to be scared—though I learned my lesson about running on docks.

Gotcha. How many times has God said that to us? We hear him say, *Don't run on the dock* a hundred times, but what do we do? Of course we run, giggling, until our feet land on nothing but air, and we go down, down, down into the water of our own foolishness. And he is gracious enough to grab the backs of our shirts and pull us out again. For now. While we're spiritual toddlers, we experience the grace of God as Superdad, bailing us out of trouble when we've deliberately done what we knew we shouldn't. But what would we think of a grown person who insisted on running on docks, willy-nilly, and still fell in? We'd help them out of the water when we could, but we wouldn't trust them with other responsibilities. God expects us to mature spiritually too. We will not run on docks forever and get away with it.

What docks do I keep running down? How about you?

Jeremiah 5:20-25

Just Trust Me

I was regularly aboard sailboats before I could even walk. As a child I'd sit on my dad's lap with my hand on his hand, steering the tiller, while he taught me how to watch for the sail to "luff," or flutter, which meant I was too high up into the wind. I wasn't exactly sure why this was important, but I'd push the tiller when he did, and the sail would fill with wind again, and the boat would dart forward through the waves. I learned to listen for that particular hum a sailboat makes when it's happy, when all the lines and sheets are properly adjusted to the wind angle.

I grew up sailing, but I wouldn't say this made me a sailor. I can tell by instinct what needs to happen, but I couldn't tell you why. Somehow in all our sailing trips I didn't bother to learn the essential theories behind the art. I simply knew that if you pulled a certain line, the sail would come in, and if it was really windy, you wrapped the line around a knobby thingy on the rail and used a funky tool called a winch handle to do the work of bringing in the sail for you. (I also learned the hard way that winch handles don't float.)

So when my future husband came along and I attempted to teach him the basics of sailing, it was more than just fruitless; it was embarrassing. "Pull in that line!" I'd yell, and he'd yell, "Why?" and I'd scream, "Just trust me!" as we careened into another boat. It took several afternoons out on the water with my father—and several summers working at a camp with sailboats—before my husband got the hang of things, and now he's a better sailor than I am. That's because, unlike me, he bothered to ask why.

The spiritual life is an awful lot like this, I've found. It's tempting for those of us who've grown up in the Christian faith to simply rely on our elders (leaders, pastors) to comprehend and articulate all the reasons we do what we do. We may know by instinct what needs to happen, but we couldn't explain it to a newcomer if our lives depended on it. And sometimes lives *do* depend on it. When we're sitting in the emergency room with a friend who has lost a loved one and our friend looks at us through tear-filled eyes and asks, "Why?" will we say, "Just trust me"?

Will that be enough?

Proverbs 3:1-8

I Trust You 18.3 Percent

One summer afternoon I took a group of middle school campers to a lakefront resort so they could learn the basics of sailing. We were split into small groups, and since I am an experienced sailor(!) I ended up with three guys who had never stepped foot on a boat in their lives. This included a boy with mild autism whom we'll call Bobby. He didn't like water. In fact, Bobby found the whole wide world generally alarming. But he trusted me. Tons. In fact, he probably would've jumped out of an airplane if I said it was okay. So we all climbed aboard, and off we sailed.

At first everything went fine. I explained how the boat worked as we sailed in easy circles around the skinny arm of the lake. But then the wind began to pick up, and it was all I could do to keep us headed in one direction without running into the other boats. I could tell Bobby had a death grip on the railing. Periodically he would turn around and say, "Sarah, I trust you 82 percent" or "I trust you 74 percent"—and pretty soon it was clear my ratings were going down. By the time Bobby reached 18.3 percent, I flagged down the nearest sailing instructor who was monitoring the fleet from his Boston whaler. He motored up. "What's wrong?" he yelled. I yelled back, "This kid needs to get off the water." So we carefully maneuvered alongside each other, Bobby clambered into the whaler, and he was taken back to shore.

How many times have I turned to God when things were rough and said, "I trust you 18.3 percent"? Back on shore, when everything's great, we feel like we can trust God with anything. But when reality sets in, when this spiritual life really gets underway, it's tempting to bail on him. We're like Peter in today's story, so focused on the wind and the waves that we lose our faith in the One in charge. "I trust you 18.3 percent," Peter might as well have been saying as the water closed over his head. And Jesus reached out a hand anyway.

Matthew 14:22-33

Spiritual Radar

A few years ago my husband and I joined the crew of a sailboat that was being transported from the top of Lake Michigan to the farthest eastern shore of Lake Ontario—a two-week trip of over 650 miles on four of the Great Lakes. Due to lousy winds and a series of thunderstorms, we were often running late from port to port, so we'd make up time by sailing all night, taking turns by pairs in four-hour shifts. Yes, I said *all night. In the dark*.

Obviously there's no way we could have sailed in the dark without various modern navigational instruments, such as a compass, sonar, radar, and Global Positioning System (GPS), which tells you where you are on the planet, more or less accurately. At first it seemed crazy to plunge into the dark without headlights. On moonless or foggy nights it was like driving blind, so I learned to keep my eyes fixed on the glowing panels next to the wheel instead of on the total blackness ahead. The compass told us our direction so we knew which way to go, while the sonar told us our depth so we wouldn't run aground. And the radar showed if anything was in the water ahead of us or around us so we wouldn't run into anything. *Good enough,* I thought.

One foggy night it was my turn at the wheel. It was a quiet night. There wasn't a boat to be seen on the radar for miles and miles. No lighthouses, not even the shoreline. And after a couple of hours, it occurred to me that I *should* be seeing the shore by now; in fact, my GPS unit was telling me I was just a few miles from our destination. But nothing was showing up on the radar. So I called the captain, who came up on deck to check things out. He took one look at the radar screen and said, "Oh, you should probably turn up the gain." He reached down and turned some knob, and all of sudden the screen sprang to life with dots and ripples representing hundreds of solid objects in every direction, including a long jagged line of shore off our port side. "Yikes," he said calmly, and he went back down below.

I sat there with my hands frozen to the wheel. All I could think of was the countless hours I had sat there with the gain on low—without enough voltage to pick up even the largest vessels—thinking everything was fine. But turn the gain up and suddenly the water was alive with dangers on every side. We made it safely to harbor that night, but only after I'd learned an important navigational lesson.

There's a spiritual truth in all this. The longer we live this spiritual life, the more fine-tuned our sensitivity to sin becomes. That's because the Holy Spirit is like a sounding device. The more we live in tune with the Spirit, the greater the gain on our spiritual radar and the more we pick up on the sin in our lives and the lives of others. We suddenly realize just how dangerous our path has been all this time. Our only response is gratitude and a willingness to navigate more carefully from now on.

1 Corinthians 2:10-16

Prince of Peace

In today's Scripture Jesus promises to give a peace that's different from anything the world can offer. Elsewhere in the Bible he's referred to as the "Prince of Peace" (Isaiah 9:6), which gives us the sense that there's a Kingdom somewhere in which his peace is the norm. Of course my imagination wanders. . . . What if the inner peace of Christ were reflected in the exterior world too? Would I feel at home there, or would my own restlessness make me a stranger?

> Dusk on the shore.
> Long shadows melt
> into gathering darkness,
> a warm, cozy gray
> that smells of sweetgrass
> and sand and campfire.
> The lights across the lake
> glitter strong and safe;
> crickets' rhythm steady
> by the white birch and the tall pine.
> Water curls against the sand,
> whispering against the red dock,
> while a sailboat, pale and slender,
> bobs gently, turning in a slow dance.
> The world is still, sleepy.
>
> A man walks there
> at the end of the road,
> past the birch and the red dock
> along the sand.
> His bare feet gently
> move amid the ebbing ripples.
> He is young, and terribly old,
> stepping out from the sand he rolled into being
> with his fingertips.
> He walks on the water
> that he made.
> He is the very Prince of this night,
> the Prince of all the peace
> that now settles on the water
> in the air and along the sand.

All nights in his Kingdom are so.   John 14:27-29

The Gift Giver

One glorious afternoon my husband and I biked down to the Lake Michigan waterfront and sat at the end of the pier for awhile. The wind was ferocious in a cloud-scuttled sky; sailboats raced in the bay. We turned and noticed that a friend of ours had just pulled his boat into the nearest slip and was wrapping up the mainsail. We shouted and waved, and with excitement he asked if we'd like to join him for another sail.

Such joy at being alive, out there in the power of God's wind and water! Such a big, beautiful planet we've been given, and such fun ways to enjoy it! The hull slammed down from the crests of whitecaps that rolled along in great boiling swells, while the wind roared in the rigging, flags flapping. Our ears rang for hours afterward. Later I wrote:

> *You are the great Gift Giver;*
> *you delight in our smiles of joy,*
> *in the laughter*
> *that wells up from the human soul*
> *when news that is too good to be true*
> *turns out to be true anyway.*
> *You are pure: you give*
> *without any underlying motive,*
> *out of the fullness of yourself.*
> *You stand at the threshold of our lives*
> *with your arms full of presents,*
> *waiting for us to speak our need*
> *and answer the door.*
> *The beauty of this day*
> *I accept as a free gift,*
> *delighting in your deep understanding*
> *of our need for sunlight and play.*
> *O God, for your faithfulness*
> *and steadfast love,*
> *I praise you!*

Matthew 7:7-11

Surprise Island

Besides sailing, another summer activity that has been a regular part of my more recent adulthood is backpacking. One year our church's summer youth intern planned a hiking trip and invited me along as a chaperone. This was a nice change of pace, since as youth director, planning such things usually fell to me. (Nobody's fault but mine: I'm horrible at delegating.)

So it was great to have someone else in charge for once . . . only there were several problems. First, on the morning we were supposed to leave, it was raining. Hard. Second, our intern was delightful but somewhat disorganized, so when I arrived, her gear and supplies were all over the youth room floor. Clearly we wouldn't be leaving anytime soon. Third, the ferry we thought would take us to our destination (an island in Lake Michigan) ran only every other day, so we needed to think of a Plan B rather quickly. Needless to say, I wasn't a very happy camper—and we weren't even camping yet.

Eventually we loaded up the van and headed north to the Pictured Rocks area of Lake Superior, thinking that if nothing else, we could hike along the shore and then camp. The farther north we drove, the clearer the skies became until we arrived at the lake amid blazing sunshine and a warm breeze. Cheerfully we drove to the ranger station to find some maps and establish our itinerary. That's when we saw it. Framed on the wall was the map of an island just offshore, a backcountry zone complete with brand-new group campsites, miles of coastal trails, and—the icing on the cake—a ferry leaving in just a few hours. By midafternoon we were standing on a sandy island track overlooking Lake Superior, marveling at the aqua-blue water and the cloudless sky.

But still I held back my gratitude, waiting for a sudden storm to sweep us away or for the ferry to sink or for bears to steal our food.

None of that happened, of course. It wasn't until the following morning—after a spectacular evening swim in the surf and then wandering alone to a sunny glade on a bluff overlooking the lake—that it hit me. There I was, expecting the worst because we hadn't planned every detail of this trip, and God was saying, *Would you relax for a moment and let me bless you?*

Would I? Would you?

Ephesians 3:14-21

Tumbled in Grace

It's easy to get so wrapped up in the crazy details of special events, such as vacations or hiking trips or weddings, that we miss God's whispers of grace. Here are some reflections on that theme from the backpacking adventure I mentioned on July 16:

> Lord God,
> It's an undeserved gift
> to be here on this surprise island
> with its bluffs and cliffs,
> rocky headlands and
> blue emptiness of waves.
> Yesterday, while shafts of light
> broke through the evening clouds,
> we tumbled in iridescent waves,
> thrown like pebbles
> into the untamed power
> of your love for us.
> We washed in your cleansing might
> like stones worn smooth by grace,
> rounded by surf and suffering,
> pummeled to a holy sheen.
> Swimming in the tempest,
> we were upheld by the safest
> power I have ever known,
> drawn and pulled into
> crashing torrents of beauty,
> only to be brought to shore again whole.
> Even now in this hot morning sun,
> in this gorgeous glade
> with the distant headlands,
> beckoning and mysterious
> to these gaping travelers,
> surrounded by aspens and seagulls,
> raspberries and Narnian freshness—
> even now the waves roar
> with a strength more holy than thought,
>
> and I am in awe
>
> of You.

Psalm 33:1-5

You Are Worthy

Out in nature I find it easier to praise God when the weather's great than when a sudden rainstorm takes me by surprise. On the island backpacking trip I mentioned earlier (see July 16–17), I found myself unexpectedly laughing with delight at the rain and wind, praising God for taking me unawares with his holy power. The question is, will I do the same the next time the weather turns?

> *After a day of sunshine*
> *and rest, heat and quiet,*
> *we wake to the windy*
> *vortex of lake crashing*
> *against shore; sunlight and shadow*
> *a zany tapestry on forest floor.*
> *We hear a roar from the lakeside,*
> *echoing along the bluffs*
> *in great booms and thunder.*
> *We are under siege.*
> *We are at your mercy.*
> *Tents aloft, breakfast scattered,*
> *clouds of blue and gray*
> *send rain in great dollops, and then,*
> *unexpectedly,*
> *a feast of sunshine . . .*
>
> *You are all-mighty, Almighty;*
> *we run for cover,*
> *laughing with holy fear*
> *at the display of such power*
> *and beauty. In the tempest*
> *I'm reminded*
> *how worthy you are*
> *of every waking thought,*
> *every breath and prayer.*
> *You are the Island Maker*
> *at whose feet I pour my*
> *meager treasures of self.*
> *I stand back in awe*
> *and watch you turn my tears*
> *to gold in a forest of light*
> *and shadows and pounding surf.*
>
> *You are worthy.*

Psalm 33:6-12

Unhappy Camper

My husband and I have this joke—which isn't really a joke—that if I'm planning to join one of his hiking trips, he'd better pack his rain gear. It *always* rains when I'm along. Always. Which means I'm not the happiest camper most of the time. I feel entitled to be grumpy.

Several summers ago my husband and I toured the north shore of Lake Superior in Ontario, traveling from park to park and taking various hikes along the way. We decided to give three or four days to one trail in particular, an isolated stretch of shoreline accessible only by foot or boat. So we set out. The sky was blue; the trail was well maintained and easy to negotiate. We hiked an easy four miles to our campsite and had a lovely evening and good night's sleep. The next day we kept hiking, occasionally eyeing the clouds that had begun to gather overhead. Soon it was raining. We plunged on, trying to ignore the fact that the trail was now becoming narrower, rockier, and steeper. Eventually it became so narrow that we found ourselves plowing through a stand of sopping wet pines that acted as a kind of car wash. By the time we got to camp, we were drenched. We pitched the tent at five in the afternoon, got inside, and didn't emerge until nine the next morning for the hike back out—and it was still raining.

But by that point I'd already had my emotional breakdown. Sometime around 8 p.m., I'd begun rehearsing all the things I found disturbing about myself, my job, my life—as if the rain were some kind of punishment for my sins. And my dear husband listened patiently (what else could he do?). Nothing he said could console me, however, and soon I was sobbing uncontrollably. This was way beyond grumpiness; this was existential angst. This was a serious crisis about my place in this world and the seeming absence of God in the wilderness. "Am I doing something wrong?" I sobbed. "Am I supposed to quit my job? What does God want me to do with my life?"—and then, "Honey, is this annoying? Am I annoying?"

Tom assured me I wasn't (which was the right answer). He told me not to worry, and if I was that upset about my vocation, maybe it was time to do something else. He said many other comforting things I don't remember, but the main thing I grasped was that I wasn't alone. Even though I couldn't feel God's presence, I could feel Tom's, and he became a representative of God's grace to me in that moment.

Who do I know who's in a spiritual wilderness right now, and how can I be the presence of God for that person?

Ecclesiastes 4:7-12

The Smooth Road

> Listen! It's the voice of someone shouting, "Clear the way through the wilderness for the LORD! Make a straight highway through the wasteland for our God! Fill in the valleys, and level the mountains and hills. Straighten the curves, and smooth out the rough places. Then the glory of the LORD will be revealed, and all people will see it together. The LORD has spoken!"
>
> Isaiah 40:3-5

This has always seemed a strange passage to me, especially since (at least in my opinion) it's the hilly contours of a land that give it beauty and character. If you level off the mountains and hills and smooth out the rough places, wouldn't that take away the view? Wouldn't that render the landscape fairly uninteresting?

Yet now, after several hiking trips in the mountains, I'm beginning to understand where Isaiah was coming from.

Generally, when hiking on foot, you can plan on covering two miles per hour, possibly three, on normal terrain. But add some elevation gain, such as a tough climb to a mountain pass, and you'd better add an extra hour for every one thousand feet—that's how difficult it is. Sometimes you feel like you've slowed to a crawl and will never make it to your destination. No wonder the ancient travelers valued the flattest, most gentle terrain they could find! Foot travel was their primary means of transportation, and often their livelihood depended on how quickly they could move from Point A to Point B.

Not to mention that on those winding mountain trails you can't see more than a few hundred feet ahead of you. This is somewhat alarming in bear country, where you can stumble upon an unsuspecting bruin without any chance to retreat. I imagine it was even worse in ancient times, when bands of robbers would hide in the hills, waiting to waylay travelers. Flat ground was safer.

Meanwhile, another thing I've learned is just how quickly the sun sets in the mountains—and how slowly it rises. You need to arrive at your destination well before dusk if you don't want to set up camp in the dark, but then dawn seems to take forever. As you sit there sipping coffee in the dim light, you can see the high peaks glowing with glorious sunrise far, far away. Somewhere, a whole city of people is enjoying a beautiful morning. If only the land were flat so you could see the light!

I wonder if that's Isaiah's point. What spiritual mountains must be leveled before the weary seekers of this world can behold God's glory? What barriers have I raised up by my own selfishness?

Isaiah 40:3-5

Sluggish

It's hot. I didn't know Virginia could be so hot. To me it feels like Florida, but of course I've never lived here before. I look outside and observe a squirrel immobile on the branch of a tree, his legs splayed spread-eagle like he has been run over. He just lies there panting in the shade. I've never seen squirrels do this. I've seen them puffed up like cats in subzero temperatures, balanced on a fence with a dusting of snow down their backs, but never this. Just looking at him makes me thirsty. I wander into the kitchen for a glass of water and turn up the air-conditioning.

Hot. My brain feels like melting tar—sticky, slow moving, insipid. My soul, too. I just can't seem to summon the energy to care about anything. I feel like the squirrel outside, like Jonah in the scorching sun of today's Bible story. Nothing really matters. The world's most violent city could experience a massive revival, and I'd be lying on the floor of the living room under the fan, fantasizing about ice cream.

We're such whiners, really. We humans are so governed by our weak and wimpy bodies that the life of faith seems like a Herculean project sometimes, a special track for the spiritual Olympiads, while the rest of us sit on the bleachers under an umbrella, sipping lemonade. Prayer, evangelism, intensive Bible study, discipleship of new believers, serving the poor, living simply . . . only the super-Christians do that stuff, right? The tiniest toothache, a touch of flu, a hungry tummy, a broken air conditioner: We almost welcome the bodily excuses that keep us from having to follow through on our Lord's commands. Like Jonah, we sit under the leafy plant of our discontent and wonder how God could possibly expect us to care about all those *other* people when *we're* clearly suffering.

But the ultimate insult is that, not only does God care mightily about the *other* people, he cares about "all the animals" too (Jonah 4:11). Which is to say, he cares about that squirrel out there, spread-eagle on the bark. And even more, he cares about my animal body, my creaturely self, weak mammal that I am. And rather than insisting I ignore my body in order to reach a higher "spiritual plane" or whatever, God sends the scorching east wind of his Word to remind me to get over myself. If my sluggish body will not rise up and praise him, what good is my soul?

Jonah 3:10–4:11

Even the Animals

I'm on a Jonah kick. Sometimes I wonder if a child helped write the book about him. I mean, who but a kid would ask questions like, "But what about the animals?" I can just picture the scribe who began scribbling it all down, recording the oral history of the famous prophet so future generations would remember. Perhaps there's a small child at his elbow, a son playing with a wooden whale.

"What happened next?" the boy asks. His father pauses. "Well, Jonah gets up from the beach where the big fish spit him up and goes to the great city of Nineveh, as God commanded. And he tells everyone that God will destroy the city. So the people believe, including the king, and they repent of their wickedness. The king says, 'No one may eat or drink anything at all—'"

"What about the animals? I'm sure they were sorry too."

"Oh, um . . ." The father flips through a few parchments. "Well, yes, you're right." He picks up his quill and dips it into the bottle. "Okay, so the king says, 'No one, *not even the animals* . . . may eat or drink anything at all.'"

The boy nods. His father keeps reading, all the way through Jonah's argument with God about the unfairness of God's graciousness and compassion. The leafy plant grows up to shelter Jonah; the worm eats the plant; Jonah wants to die; and God questions if Jonah has the right to be upset about it.

"'You feel sorry about the plant,'" the father reads. "'. . . But Nineveh has more than 120,000 people living in spiritual darkness. Shouldn't—'"

"And also many animals," his son interjects. "God wouldn't forget about them."

The father pauses, reviews his notes. Then dutifully he picks up his quill again. "Okay, so God says, 'But Nineveh has more than 120,000 people living in spiritual darkness, *not to mention all the animals*. Shouldn't I feel sorry for such a great city?'"

His son nods solemnly.

If God cares that much even about the animals, how much he must care for us!

Jonah 3:1-9; Matthew 10:29-31

Alone

I think about Jonah in the belly of the fish—Jonah, who experienced the crushing isolation that comes from rebellion against God's will. First he ran in the direction opposite to the one God intended and experienced the isolation of being cast out of the community of the ship's crew. Then he found himself in the belly of a fish, the heart of the sea, the world of the dead, like an astronaut cut off even from the air other people are breathing. Still later he became annoyed with God for being compassionate with the people of Nineveh and went off by himself to sulk. Even the leafy plant abandoned him after a while.

As I think about Jonah, it occurs to me there are different kinds of isolation. Technically I'm very isolated at the moment, all alone in this air-conditioned bungalow while my husband is at work. But it's isolation by vocation: The writing life requires acres of silence, which for Christians can be a holy solitude. God called me to the writing life; it wasn't my idea.

So mine is not a Jonah kind of loneliness. It's not generated by my stubborn determination to do the opposite of what God desires for me. I know, because I've felt that kind of loneliness before. When I was a hyperbusy full-time youth worker, surrounded by people all the time, I might've perished from crushing isolation if I hadn't answered God's call to a different vocation instead. Rebellion cuts us off from God, who is our only true companion. So it doesn't matter what we're doing or how many people we're with, we're utterly alone whenever we stand outside of God's will.

Jonah 2

Backward

I wonder if this is the first time in the history of devotional writing that an author has worked *backward* through a biblical story. I started with Jonah 4 on July 21 and have steadily counted down to chapter 1. I'd like to say this was on purpose, but that would be stretching things. The truth is, there's little rhyme or reason to the order of the devotions I'm writing until I've written them, and then I go back and restructure everything so it makes some kind of literary sense. And if that means we read Jonah backward, I guess that's what we do.

But I'm only playing with half a deck anyway, since I don't know Hebrew. Last semester my husband, who is a seminary student, was required to translate the entire book of Jonah from Hebrew to English. And even though it's only four chapters long, it took *months*. For starters, Hebrew letters are completely different from ours—more like calligraphic Sanskrit than the ABCs. Second, written Hebrew requires the nifty trick of reading right to left, which takes some getting used to. Third, vowels are generally absent—yep, no vowels. Imagine if this sentence read: mgn f ths sntnc rd. Enough said.

Meanwhile, the Hebrew language has significantly fewer words than English, and the words are far more flexible. They can mean any number of things. For example, the transliterated word *chay*, depending on its use, could mean "live," "green," "raw," "running," "appetite," "revival," or "community" (and that's not all). *Chay* shows up several times in Jonah. So how to decide? But it gets even trickier: In Jonah there are several words that exist *nowhere else* in the Hebrew Scriptures. Last semester I'd overhear my husband and his classmates working on a verse, trying to figure out what a word meant, and one of them would say, "Oh, this notation says the meaning is unclear," and someone else would mutter, "Great." Ah, the joys of translation.

All of this to say, it's easy to get awfully smug in this devotional business, highlighting certain sentences or phrases because they stand out in English while ignoring others entirely. Too often we scope for the quick summary, the simple idea, the ten-second marketing slogan that will give us an easy fix to our problems. But the Bible just isn't like that, particularly the Hebrew Scriptures—and particularly Jonah. Perhaps reading it in its original language is a way to recapture what we've lost in our overfamiliarity with so many stories from the Bible (or maybe reading the chapters in reverse order). Whatever the case, we must guard against thinking we've got God's Word all figured out, when God may in fact have something new to show us. Isn't that what he did for Jonah?

Jonah 1

Adrift

So we've steadily worked our way backward through Jonah (see July 21–24), and I'm still ruminating on the first chapter, the famous flee-from-God story. And what I notice aren't the usual implications of Jonah's rebellion for those who fail to follow God's call but a tiny phrase tucked away in verse 5, which says that while the storm raged on the sea, "Jonah was sound asleep down in the hold" (Jonah 1:5).

Now, I don't know about you, but to me this detail sounds an awful lot like another story from Scripture: the story of Jesus calming the storm (see July 9). In all three of the synoptic Gospels (Matthew, Mark, and Luke, whose plotlines are similar—as compared to John, which stands alone), the disciples, too, were caught in a violent storm, and Jesus, like Jonah, was conked out, asleep on board. In both cases the situation deteriorated, so the sleeper was awakened and forced to deal with the problem. In Jonah's tale, the captain woke him and said, "How can you sleep at a time like this? . . . Get up and pray to your god! Maybe he will pay attention to us and spare our lives" (Jonah 1:6). In the Gospel of Matthew, Jesus *was* the God they prayed to. "Lord, save us!" the disciples cried (Matthew 8:25), and Jesus rose from his berth to do just that. In all three Gospel accounts, the disciples exclaimed, "Who is this man? Even the wind and the waves obey him!"

The Gospels don't answer the disciples' question—at least not directly, nor right away. They leave us hanging, wondering just who this Jesus is. And yet the Gospel writers also expect their readers to have a solid grasp on the Old Testament Scriptures. They expect us to know the book of Jonah. We're meant to notice that little tidbit about Jesus sleeping and say, "Hmm, that sounds familiar. What's going on here?" Our minds start working on the connection, noticing the parallels and the disconnects: Jesus is like Jonah, a prophet, but he's also unlike Jonah, because he can calm the wind and the waves himself. Therefore he must be greater than any prophet—a different kind of man altogether. He is, we finally conclude, the very God Jonah was fleeing from.

All because of a tiny detail about a nap. What other details have I missed?

Luke 11:29-32

Cell Number

I think about Jonah, who was cut off from his community by his own rebelliousness (see July 23), and then I think about our own "communication age," in which e-mail and cell phones are meant to connect us with each other. At the end of important e-mails I write my name, e-mail address, and cell phone number, as if that will somehow make me more real to the person receiving the message. It shows just how available I am, how wired for contemporary communication—when the truth is, I'm sitting all alone at a desk some-where, and so is the other person.

This point was driven home to me the other day when I passed a girl on the side-walk who was talking on her mobile phone. "Yeah, okay," she was saying, "Let me give you his cell number. . . ." And for half a second I thought she was talking about an *inmate*. The image flashed through my mind of a young man in an orange jumpsuit receiving mail from an armed guard at the state penitentiary—inmate number 11685 or whatever, staying in cell D415. Even after I realized she was talking about a cell *phone* number, the image stayed with me. We as a society are trapped by a tiny piece of technology, paralyzed if it loses power or connectivity, frantic if we leave it at home, unable to function outside the four sides of our self-imposed technological prison. "Whatever did we do before cell phones?" said an older woman to me the other day, and I replied, "We talked face-to-face."

The disciple John, writing to the early Christians, made it clear that Christianity is a face-to-face kind of faith. We're dealing with a face-to-face kind of God. He doesn't sit alone up in heaven, texting us from a distance. Rather, as John says, we have seen God "with our own eyes and touched him with our own hands" (1 John 1:1). He breaks us out of our virtual prisons by being utterly real, and thus he leads us into fellowship with one another as real human beings. No longer do we think of each other as just another cell number, flashing on the screen of our disconnected lives, but we greet each other face-to-face, just as God greets Jesus and Jesus greets us.

Dare we break free from our imprisoning cell?

1 John 1:1-4

Virtual Reality

Case in point about living in a virtual age: Just today I communicated with at least ten human beings who were not physically present in this house; I listened to the voices of several others I will never meet; I saw the faces of strangers and celebrities—without literally seeing their faces—online; I read the words of a playwright who died more than four hundred years ago; and I vicariously experienced events in the life of a fictitious character named Hamlet, who seemed as real and alive to me as the birds on the telephone wire outside my window. All this and I don't even own a television.

The sad thing is, these virtual technologies, meant to connect us with each other, actually drive us farther apart and accentuate our sense of loneliness and isolation. To wit: My husband is out of town and called me on his cell phone. He was on his way to a department store, so he finished our conversation in the parking lot. As we were chatting, he suddenly exclaimed with that people-are-so-dumb-they're-amusing tone of his, "I just watched three teenage girls emerge from the same car, and they were *all* talking on their cell phones." I laughed when he said that, but part of me wanted to cry. I had just spent the day with no one but a computer and Hamlet for company, longing for my husband to get home, and here these young women couldn't grace each other with the dignity of attention. They were in each other's company but had no companionship. They were physically present but virtually alone.

(But who was I to judge—me with my earpiece clipped to my collar and the electronic buzz of my husband's voice crackling from some cell tower six blocks away?)

Perhaps this is why Christian practices such as the sacrament of Communion, also called the Lord's Supper, are so very important. They require us to leave the self-imposed prison of our virtual world and interact with living, breathing human beings, to ingest the material realities of bread and juice, and to experience true companionship. After all, that's what *companion* means: one who breaks bread with us (*com* = together with; *panis* = bread). So companionship cannot be done virtually, and neither can Communion. It requires one's fellows; it requires grain and grapes, water and sunshine, maybe a little salt. It requires the audible voice of a real human being who looks you in the eye, offers you sustenance, and says, "This is the body of Christ."

Communion reminds us there is nothing virtual about Jesus.

1 Corinthians 11:20-26

Welcome at the Table

I have a friend who has only recently come back to church after a long and miserable hiatus, during which she truly believed God hated her. For some reason as a child she never got the whole "God is love" thing and instead focused on the "God is unhappy about your sins" part. So the more she sinned, the more she felt God's unhappiness, which she eventually interpreted as hatred, and she gave up on going to church. She'd messed up too many times. Perfect church attendance wouldn't make up for all that, so why bother?

Well, now that she's starting to get the whole "God is love" thing, she's coming to church again. She may sit in the back left-hand corner, hiding from everyone like a little brown mouse, but she's there. She stands when we sing and closes her eyes for the prayers and listens raptly as the Scriptures are read and the sermon is preached. The only lingering difficulty is Communion, or the Lord's Supper. She just can't bring herself to go up front with everyone else—yet.

I ask her why. She isn't sure. It has something to do with feeling unworthy, that she just can't take the Lord's Supper lightly as if it's no big deal. "It *is* a big deal," she insists. "I'd better not go up there and partake casually. Besides, I'm not sure I understand it." Something about her humility and honest fear of God (fear in a good way) gives me pause as the bread and juice are served. There *is* something powerful going on in Communion. Too often we treat it as if it's no big deal, a mere formality like saying "Bless you" when someone sneezes. The truth is, Communion is called a sacrament because it brings us into the presence of the sacred, the holy—a practice that helps us experience the grace of God. We're not worthy to untie the strap of Jesus' sandal, much less sit at his table. And yet he invites us anyway, no matter how much we've messed up.

Dare we treat his invitation lightly?

1 Corinthians 11:27-34

Take, Eat

Eventually my friend has come around to taking Communion again (see July 28). This isn't something she planned ahead, as in, "By Christmas I'll be ready" or "I'll take it on my birthday," but it came as a surprise. One Sunday morning while visiting another church, she found herself going forward for the Lord's Supper without really giving it much thought. And before she had time to argue herself out of it with all the usual objections, she was receiving the bread and taking the cup and sitting back down again. It was as if she had crossed some kind of threshold without being aware and was now able to receive God's grace—grace that had been there all the time, if only she'd allowed herself to accept it. Now she did, and yet she probably felt like she was no closer to understanding what Communion is or why it's vital to the Christian life than she was before.

And I'm not sure any of us are, to be honest. The sacrament of Communion is a sacrament (sacred, holy) precisely because it's not the product of a fallen human imagination but the product of the eternal mind of God—whose thoughts, said the prophet Isaiah, are nothing like our thoughts, and whose ways are higher than our ways (see Isaiah 55:8-9). C. S. Lewis wrote, "I do not know and can't imagine what the disciples understood Our Lord to mean when, His body still unbroken and His blood unshed, He handed them the bread and wine, saying *they* were His body and blood."[38]

The word *sacrament* comes from a Latin translation of the Greek word *mustērion*, "mystery." We're not expected to intellectually understand what's going on. The Lord's Supper was a mystery at the beginning, and it's a mystery now, and it will no doubt be a mystery until Christ returns and we feast with him at his heavenly banquet. This is why part of the Communion liturgy in many churches includes the lines, "Therefore we proclaim the mystery of faith: Christ has died; Christ is risen; Christ will come again." Until then we can't simply put off partaking of Communion until we have it all figured out, nor should we avoid it because it seems obscure. Jesus expects us to participate anyway; in fact, he commands us to. As Lewis said, "The command, after all, was Take, eat: not Take, understand."[39]

Matthew 26:26-30

The Crowds That Followed Jesus: Part 1

I spent a semester working with street children in the slums of Nairobi, Kenya, and it astounded me how quickly some of them could shift from the role of sweet, helpless kid to crass, defiant sinner. They would've betrayed friend or parent if it served their purposes, and they certainly felt no loyalties to us. With few exceptions, most of them couldn't have cared less what message we were preaching, as long as we gave them a handout. Could it be these were the kinds of folks who swelled the crowds that followed Jesus?

We think of them
as the "noble poor"
who slogged through weary days
with little hope
yet still held heads up high
and cleaned their huts
and brushed their children's hair.
But instead they were just the rabble,
a noisy, clamorous throng,
who—looking for a scam—
demanded of the Savior's time.
They hounded him, the thrill seekers,
the bored, the stupid, the hypochondriacs.
They watched him with hawk eyes
to catch the slip, the note of insincerity,
so they could add fuel to the fire
of their boundless self-pity.
And yet they came,
in great milling droves,
drawn by something larger, kinder,
gentler, more genuine
than themselves.
Or, more likely, they came to pass the time,
to shirk their work,
to catch the latest gossip,
to complain.
They blinked in blazing heat, endured,
so later they could add
the juicy details for those who missed it all:
"We walked all day in all that sun;
we trudged ten miles to hear his voice."

But what that voice had said,
they hadn't heard.

Mark 6:30-34

The Crowds That Followed Jesus: Part 2

I remember the first time a group of street children from Nairobi (see July 30) joined us at the ministry center for some bread and juice after a hot game of soccer under the sun. There we were, offering them free refreshments, and they had the audacity to complain that the juice was *too watered down*. Sitting there in the dust, stung by their words, I was suddenly aware of what Jesus must've felt like (and still feels like) as he offered one free blessing after another to the undeserving. Am I any better than they?

> He knew their hearts,
> but still he taught;
> he did not qualify his love.
>
> He touched the noble and the wretch
> while each was still in sin—
> while neither recognized
> whose hands held theirs
> and went away unfazed.
>
> The fools came all that way
> without a crumb of food
> to peer and judge and test
> what he would do.
> And still he took the loaves;
> he blessed and broke them
> while the undeserving watched.
>
> The bread came round,
> the miracle:
> but the rabble dug in
>
> to find the largest piece
>
> and then complained
>
> that it was dry.

Mark 6:35-44

The Greatest Story

August has begun, and meanwhile we're still in the long season of the church calendar known as Pentecost, or Ordinary Time. In some traditions it's also called Kingdomtide, the season in which we live out the reality that the Kingdom of God is indeed near, as Jesus said in Mark 1:15. In the meantime we make our slow and ordinary way through the dog days of summer with nothing terribly exciting on the calendar, few great events to celebrate, few memorable stories to tell.

So I've decided to use this month as an opportunity to explore some of the biblical stories that don't fit easily into the regular church calendar. Over the years, as I've attempted to follow a ritual of morning prayer and Bible study, I've come across Scriptures that sparked my curiosity or inspired my imagination for one reason or another. Usually I can't explain why they do so. Sometimes I find them troubling and that's about as far as I get. Other times I'm struck by a word or a phrase and feel drawn to explore what it means. Often I'm intrigued by a particular character and his or her role and development within the overarching story. Whatever the case, August seems like a good time to crank up the air-conditioning, curl up with the Good Book, and take a rambling, albeit random, tour of the greatest story ever told.

There's a precedent for this kind of approach. The book of Hebrews takes us on its own tour, using chapter 11 as an occasion to rehearse some of the highlights of Old Testament and early church history. The theme of Hebrews is living by faith. And I suppose that's my theme too, though I'm a bit less thorough and organized. This month I'd like to explore those things that spark my interest between the pages of Genesis and Revelation—people and stories that might lead to spiritual insight—or to murkier water, depending on the text. I won't attempt to figure everything out. I may not reach a firm conclusion by the end of each page. But I have a sneaking suspicion God isn't as interested in our intellectual enlightenment as he is in our honest grappling and spiritual engagement. We may not grasp what's going on in many passages of the Bible yet—or ever. But the Bible grasps us, and it's this story we are called to live inside of until we come to the final chapter at the end of days.

Hebrews 11

The Story-Pattern

"History doesn't repeat itself," someone has said, "but it does rhyme."

In other words, the same exact event doesn't happen twice in human history, but over time we notice a pattern of strikingly similar events—such as a popular wartime president's being assassinated while in office, as was the case with Abraham Lincoln in the 1860s and again with John F. Kennedy in the 1960s. Similar echoes happen in literature and stories too. Earlier characters prefigure later characters; final scenes contain the same (or similar) events of earlier episodes, and so on. (*The Lord of the Rings* fans will remember, for instance, that Frodo the Hobbit isn't the first character to lose a finger in the War of the Ring: the evil Lord Sauron did too, thousands of years earlier.)

In short, the sign of a well-crafted narrative is the way its themes echo from chapter to chapter. This is how the author signals to us what's really important, even as it lends the story a memorable and even satisfying "shape," or story pattern, for the imagination— much the same way rhyming words make a poem easier to remember.

If you haven't noticed already, the Bible is a powerful example of this kind of literary excellence. Not only does it contain God's grace and truth for our lives, but it contains some of the most beautifully crafted narrative patterns in the world. For example, the people of God passed through the Red Sea in the Old Testament book of Exodus, leaving their old lives of bondage behind and taking a new path to the Promised Land. If this doesn't prefigure the Christian concept of baptism in the New Testament, what does? And this is only one of many, many examples in Scripture. If we're paying attention, we eventually realize such patterns tell us something important about the nature of God or about sinful, redeemable humankind. And if we're *really* paying attention, we realize the pattern is important for our personal, everyday lives too.

We're part of a story that's bigger than us. We may think that our individual lives are made up of small events that have nothing to do with the wide expanse of human history—or even of God's overarching plan for the world—but that's simply not true. We are part of a great cosmic dance, a pattern of events that continues from age to age.

God's story doesn't repeat itself, but it rhymes.

Hebrews 12:18-29

After the Garden

So in my random ramblings through the Bible, I not-so-randomly begin at the beginning, with Genesis. In June we pondered Creation; now we ponder the created—namely, us. Human beings. The lastborn of all Creation. I've always been fascinated with the first humans, Adam and Eve. I'm intrigued with them not primarily as "literary" figures or spiritual examples but as real people who experienced so many firsts. The first meal; the first sin; the first birth; the first creaking of limbs in old age; the first encounter with death, cold and final; the first heartrending separation from God and from each other. So many firsts . . . including prayer.

Think about it. Until their banishment from the Garden, they must've been able to speak with God face-to-face. Genesis 3:8 says, "When the cool evening breezes were blowing, the man and his wife heard the LORD God walking about in the garden," which makes me think they probably recognized the sound of his footsteps from long experience. Perhaps from the day of their creation, they'd had an evening chat with him every day, just to catch up. "So how was work today?" God would ask, like a loving parent at the dinner table, and Adam the cheerful gardener would reply with some tale about the bumblebees in the clover or the grafting of an apple tree. Eve would show off the honeycomb she'd collected, the clover chain she'd made for her ankle. And God saw everything they had made, and indeed, it was very good.

Or so I imagine. Anyway, the point is, God and his people must have communicated directly in the beginning. So once Adam and Eve were banished from the Garden, it must've been something of a shock to realize that they'd never again hear God's footsteps in the cool of an evening. They wouldn't hear his voice saying, "Where are you?"—nor would they be able to answer him face-to-face. I can imagine Adam, frantic in the midst of his wife's first childbirth, climbing up to the top of a high rock and hollering, "Where are you?!" and hearing nothing but silence. Or at least what he thought was silence. And then, whispering into his spirit like a mysterious evening breeze, the assurance that God was indeed present—that just because they were banished to the wilderness didn't mean God had abandoned them altogether. Only from now on, communication would require a different kind of listening. Eventually Adam, or maybe his descendents, began to call this experience *prayer*.

I wonder if that's why prayer still feels difficult for us today—because originally we were supposed to walk with God and speak with him face-to-face.

Genesis 3:20-24

Walking with God

Okay, besides the bizarre reference to "the sons of God" marrying human women and producing giants (see Genesis 6:1-4)—one of those random, fascinating biblical passages I could write a novel about someday(!)—there's an interesting phrase in verse 9 that throws a wrench in my ideas about prayer. It seemed inevitable that after getting banished from the Garden, Adam and Eve would no longer be able to walk with God or speak with him face-to-face. Well, a little further along in Genesis I stumble upon a tiny biblical phrase, tucked away in yet another tiny little verse, that blows my conclusion wide open. The verse says, "Noah was a righteous man, the only blameless person living on earth at the time, and he walked in close fellowship with God" (6:9)—or, as is elsewhere translated, "Noah walked with God" (NKJV).

Noah walked with God. And just yesterday I made the case that human beings no longer could walk with God after their banishment from the Garden (see August 3)! Yet along came Noah, a righteous man, and communion with the divine was established once again. Sure, it probably wasn't at the same level as what Adam and Eve enjoyed in the Garden, before sin entered the human story, but still—something about Noah's righteousness allowed him to experience God's presence in a uniquely intimate way.

Incidentally, one of Noah's ancestors, a fellow named Enoch, is also mentioned as someone who "walk[ed] in close fellowship with God" (Genesis 5:22-24); his name itself is linked to the Hebrew word for "dedicated." Meanwhile, one of Enoch's ancestors was named Enosh, and it was during his lifetime, the Bible says, that "people first began to worship the LORD by name" (Genesis 4:26)—or, as other versions say, that people "began to call upon the name of the LORD" (NASB) So Noah's religiosity isn't all that noteworthy. But his righteousness is. Not only did his godly behavior open the doors to communication with God, but it led to the preservation of life on this planet. It was Noah who saved a remnant of all creatures during the Flood God sent to destroy the earth, and it was to Noah and his descendents that God made his first covenant, or promise.

So it's a different kind of walking together, but at least God doesn't give up on Adam's descendants entirely. Perhaps, before many generations had passed, God missed their companionship just as much as they missed his?

Genesis 6:1-9

The Friend of God

As for you, Israel my servant,
Jacob my chosen one,
descended from Abraham my friend . . .

Isaiah 41:8

Usually biblical verses end at the closing of a sentence or the completion of a thought—which no doubt made sense to those who originally numbered them. But the above verse from Isaiah ends right there, before the sentence is completed. Perhaps it's because the person who numbered the verses was hit by the same thing that hit me just now: God called Abraham his *friend*. What a great little discovery hidden in this eloquent chapter!

So is that why God chose him? In Abraham's first encounters with the divine, was he so aware of this God that he chatted with him continuously, desiring to really know him, to have an intimate relationship with this mysterious divine Being? Or did God call Abraham "friend" *after* the fact, after they'd journeyed across the desert from Ur to Canaan together? Curious . . .

Anyway, as I woke up this morning and began my usual rambling prayers, I was struck by the demanding tone of the first word I used—*Lord*—and the weirdness of that. Do I really treat him as my Lord? Definitely not. That title, used by me in this hour, is an affront. At the very least, a lord speaks first and the servant listens, then obeys. The servant doesn't approach the throne and start rehearsing the litany of everything he or she needs or wants for the day.

So how do we balance the concepts of God as our *Lord* and God as our *friend*?

I keep coming back to relational imagery, especially after reading this quote by Albert Day: "The Presence is always the Presence-in-the-fullness-of-his-being . . . in the responsibility he assumes for every one of his children." God my father, God my Lord, God my friend. The friend of God! Is that what I am?

Genesis 12:1-9

Don't Look Back

There are beautiful biblical details that grab my attention, such as Noah's and Abraham's closeness to God. And then there are details that are hard and even horrible—the story of Sodom and Gomorrah is one, and especially the fate of Lot's wife. It'd be easy to dismiss this detail as pure legend—a tribal attempt to explain the existence of a strange pillar of salt located near the ruins of an ancient city, perhaps. But then I taste the salt tears on my face and wonder: *If I cried long enough over something God wanted me to give up, would he eventually abandon me to my grief and let my heart harden over for good?*

LOT'S WIFE

I.

They lost her
in the crowded chaos of that day.
Each face became
a twin of every other,
limed in dusty layers, white.
Pushing forward in a frenzied
mass, they dared not
pause to holler her name.
Mimes, they scrambled on,
careful not to turn
and mimic the imploding ruin
at their backs.

II.

Later—as Lot
surveyed the empty theater
of the city's smoking crust—
he found it
standing fixed:
a five-foot stalagmite
rooted in horror to the earth,
petrified solid
with dried and hardened tears."

Genesis 19:15-29

// First published in *The Penwood Review*, Winter 2002—which was, incidentally, the first issue after September 11, 2001.

Degrees of Separation

I think sometimes I use the written word as a kind of shield, as if the letters on the page could somehow protect me from having to deal with people—or even God—directly. There are days when I don't even want to feel God's love and instead push him away. In moments like that I can relate to Jacob, who was surprised and frustrated to find himself wrestling with the divine presence in the dark.

O God, I suppose I write
instead of pray
so I can put a degree or two
of separation between me and you.
Raw soul-encounter is hard, frightening,
and the comfort of the written word
is a refuge. But I miss you
and communion with you.
I confess I have fought against you,
like Jacob against the angel.
I think of the famous paintings
by Doré and Delacroix,"
where Jacob wrestles
head down, straining and red-faced,
while the angel, surprised and amused—
yet dignified and full of power—
strives to lead Jacob in a dance.
If only Jacob would look up!

I confess when I've felt
your love for me I've pushed
it away, focused on the negatives,
let my cynical self drag me
into despair of ever finding joy—
when all along it's right before my face.
Help me to resign myself gladly
to whatever steps you have for me.
Strengthen me by your Spirit
to enter the dance with joy.
Thank you that when I want to challenge
your lead and keep you at arm's length

you wrestle with me anyway
till I receive a blessing.

Genesis 32:22-31

// See http://en.wikipedia.org/wiki/Jacob_Wrestling_with_the_Angel.

God's Face

> Jacob insisted [to Esau], "No, if I have found favor with you, please accept this
> gift from me. And what a relief to see your friendly smile. It is like seeing the face
> of God!"
> Genesis 33:10

What strange magic in this verse! Jacob would not say such a thing lightly, much less to his former enemy, Esau. It was not just an empty formality. Just a few verses before this, Jacob *had* seen the face of God, so he knew it when he saw it (see Genesis 32:30). I doubt his brother Esau *actually* looked like God; it was more Esau's demeanor of grace, forgiveness, and acceptance—that's what reminded Jacob of God's face.

Even though Jacob had wrestled with God only shortly before and had received a wound from him before the end of the struggle, he also received a blessing. Sounds rather like his relationship to Esau, when you think about it. The brothers struggled in the womb (see Genesis 25:19-26) and for the birthright (see 25:27-34), and experienced the consequences of that wounded relationship (see 27:41-45); but Jacob also experienced Esau's forgiveness before the end, a blessing indeed. Even so, Jacob would always walk with a limp from all his poor choices; he was scarred for life, both inside and out.

And now I wonder some more at this curious story. With whom was Jacob really wrestling earlier? I mean, "the man" (or so he's called in the story) never gave Jacob his true name. Jacob later said he had seen the face of God, but it must have been God in human form—a being with very human kinds of limitations—if Jacob could fight him for so long without losing. What if it was Jesus?

Genesis 33:1-11

Stay

I love Elijah, the Old Testament prophet. He was such a wonderful mixture of saintly zeal and human frailty. One minute he was calling down fire from heaven and trouncing the prophets of the god Baal; the next minute he was running for his life from the threats of Queen Jezebel and her henchmen. Like Jonah, he fled alone into the desert and sat down under a leafy plant to die. He truly believed he was the only person left alive who still called upon the name of the Lord, the God of his ancestors. The rest had sold out to Jezebel and her false god. Or so he thought.

God sent him on a forty-day journey back to the mountain of Moses, Mount Sinai, where the people of Israel first received the Ten Commandments. Here, apparently, was where the great leaders encountered God in times of crisis, when idolatry and false worship threatened to undo the very fabric of the nation. Here was where the living God spoke. And indeed, here was where he spoke to Elijah—not in a mighty wind or earthquake or fire—but, famously, in a whisper.

And it's no big task God called Elijah to either. Instead of saying, *You are my great prophet, like Moses, and I will give you another victory in fire and power; indeed, Baal will be vanquished forever,* God said, *Go back. Yep, take the road back to my people and stay there. Start a quiet revolution. Anoint a new king here, a new prophet there, but keep it under the radar, hush-hush. And while you are whispering, I tell you "I will preserve 7,000 others in Israel who have never bowed down to Baal"* (1 Kings 19:18).

How many religious leaders can relate to what Elijah probably felt at that moment? When I was in full-time youth ministry, there was a season when I simply wanted to give up and leave town. Just when I wanted God to flex his muscles and do something awesome, he backed off and kept quietly in the background. And just when I felt like I the only one left who had my spiritual act together, God whispered, *Stay. There are others.* It took all of my willpower to stick it out until spiritual life and health became the norm again.

So just because things are crummy in your faith community, that doesn't mean God wants you to leave.

1 Kings 19:9-18

Run Away: Part 1

> Jezebel sent this message to Elijah: "May the gods strike me and even kill me if by this time tomorrow I have not killed you just as you killed them."   1 Kings 19:2

Imagine what the prophet Elijah must've felt like when he received this message from Queen Jezebel. Where to run? Where to hide? (And we think *we've* got it bad when someone in the media dismisses believers as irrelevant or even crazy. . . .)

Terror, like cold water
washes over my head,
pours through my bones and blood.
I am Elijah, great prophet of God;
yet today I know fear,
just as yesterday I knew power.

Has it been only one setting
and rising of the sun
since I felt the strength of the Holy One,
the faith that comes from victory
in his name? Was it only yesterday
that mighty invocations poured
from my mouth,
through my bones and blood,
spilling onto the altar, saying,
"O Lord, answer me! Answer me
so these people will know that you,
O Lord, are God and that you
have brought them back to yourself"?
The power like lightning fell,
flooding the blood and bones
of that altar, pouring through
the spines and stomachs
and hearts of a people,
of your people.
The unquenchable fire fell
in fury on sacrifice and stone,
wood, water, and trench;
and I was not afraid.

Was that just yesterday?

1 Kings 18:30-40; 19:1-2

Run Away: Part 2

The prophet Elijah was running for his life, and I can only imagine his spiritual anguish at the time. The following reflection from his perspective is a reminder of how quickly we can go from spiritual "highs" to spiritual "lows"—and most of us aren't even faced with the threat of execution. . . .

Now I know fear.
Here I am, the great prophet
Elijah, running like a fox,
humiliated,
with all the hounds of hell at my heels.
Terror grips my throat,
and all I see is her face—Jezebel.
Minutes ago her messenger stood
quivering on the edge of my door frame.
He watched me, wincing,
waiting for the sword to swing
from my hand—the sword that
slew his queen's prophets
just yesterday. He eyed my arm.
And yet all I could do
was turn from him and sprint.
I grabbed my servant's hand—"Come!"
—and my servant followed as
far as Beersheba, terrified by the look
in my eyes. He gathered
our things and we ran,
fear like a dog barking
and snarling at our heels.
Now the image of her fury
rises terrible and conquering
in the desert dust ahead;
and it is as I feared:

the powers of Baal
have won after all,

and I the prophet of the Lord
am nowhere to be found.

But where is God?   1 Kings 19:1-9

AUGUST 12

Follow Me

My random ramblings through the Bible continue, though for some reason I seem stuck on Elijah in I Kings. Each new chapter brings new insight and questions I've never considered before, which makes me wonder if I've ever *really* read any of this stuff. The stories are familiar, but the details are surprising.

For example, Elijah's calling of his apprentice, Elisha, is such a strong parallel to Jesus and the disciples that I'm surprised I haven't heard any sermons about it. I mean, read these texts side by side and see what you think. Elijah places his mantle of succession on young Elisha, who is plowing in the fields, and Elisha says, "First let me go and kiss my father and mother good-bye, and then I will go with you!" And the older prophet replies, in essence, "Fine, but don't be long." By contrast, Jesus tells his prospective followers to put their hand to the plow of discipleship and not look back. Ever. Don't even take a moment—like Elisha—to say good-bye to your family. It's all or nothing.

Luke was no doubt aware of the impact of this story on his readers. They knew their Hebrew history. Most of them had studied the Torah (the books of the Old Testament laws) and the prophets. They knew Elijah was a great prophet, one of the greatest, and that prophecy said he would return one day to announce the arrival of God's Messiah (see Malachi 4:5-6). So for a prospective follower of Jesus to tell him, "First let me say good-bye to my family" was that person's way of saying, "I believe you are a very great prophet like Elijah; and like Elisha, I'm willing to bid farewell to my loved ones for you." And the prospective follower probably thought he was doing Jesus a great honor. But Jesus wasn't flattered. He knew he wasn't simply another Elijah, who would merely announce the Messiah's coming. He *was* the Messiah. He *is* the Messiah.

So while you could have kept Elijah waiting, the Son of God and his Kingdom do not wait. You either jump into the deep end or you don't jump at all.

1 Kings 19:19-21; Luke 9:61-62

No Remedy

> The LORD, the God of their fathers, sent word to them through his messengers again and again, because he had pity on his people and on his dwelling place. But they mocked God's messengers, despised his words and scoffed at his prophets until the wrath of the LORD was aroused against his people and there was *no remedy*.
>
> 2 Chronicles 36:15-16 (NIV, emphasis added)

No remedy. It's a phrase my Shakespeare professor told us to pay attention to in the great plays—the tragedies especially. Whenever a tragedy took its final and inevitable turn toward disaster, one or more of the characters would announce that all was amiss and there was no remedy—no solution, no cure. No chance of turning back.

The Bible, by contrast, is not ultimately tragic, though there are moments when the writers are worried (as in today's text). God doesn't intend for his story to end in ruin for the main characters. We can choose the happy ending. Only by our open rebellion are we thrown into a tragedy.

The Bible is a high romance that ends in a wedding, like Shakespeare's comedies. Before the end, however, God the Bridegroom sees such hard-heartedness, such violent infidelity in his bride, Israel, that it seems there is no hope for her. The relationship is severed, the Groom finally throws up his hands and lets her go her own way—though it breaks his heart. Let her run off to her other suitors, he says; let her sup at their tables until they tire of her and cast her out into the street. Let her wander homeless and hopeless for a good couple of centuries. Let her reach the point of wondering if the Groom was just a wonderful dream, too good to be true after all. And then, just when all is coldest and darkest, and despair has claimed her, *then* break forth with salvation! Then let Christ be the remedy, Jesus the Bridegroom who has come to be with his bride for all eternity.

But of course, the danger is that before this happens, in all her wanderings she will forget her Groom altogether. Will he become so unfamiliar that she does not recognize him when she finally sees him face-to-face? Will she know him when she hears his voice, touches his hand, questions him in the Temple, visits him by night on the rooftop to hear his cryptic words about being born again? Will she recognize that this mysterious man is in fact her long lost lover, come back to woo her once and for all?

2 Chronicles 36:14-21

Words Get in the Way

I'm a bit weary of the triumphant attitude many modern scholars take toward Scripture, as if they've got it all figured out. This goes for conservatives as well as liberals—but especially those who point out (with a sneer) all those places where the Bible is apparently inconsistent or contradicts itself. This is a favorite argument with post-Christian historians and theologians, who find within these inconsistencies proof that the Bible couldn't possibly be reliable. And I say, honestly, *I'm* not reliable—no human being is—so if God was at all involved in the making of that text (inspiring the human writers and the folks who deliberated over the final canon), then the Bible is miles more trustworthy than I will ever be.

This isn't to deny the human element in the writing of the Scriptures—that the scribes perhaps got sleepy as they copied the originals and missed a word, that they may have inserted their theological bias, or that politics possibly played a role in the making of the biblical canon. Speculate as much or little as you like. What I'm saying is that God is bigger. And if God was involved in the making of Scripture—as clearly I believe he was— then we are treading on very thin ice indeed to insist that the human element could trump the Holy Spirit.

Psalm 19:10-11 reads as a kind of argument for the authority of Scripture, particularly as it points to the frailty of the human reader, and challenges us to find any error in God's laws. Because, rest assured, we will *think* we have found errors. But as a writer I've come to recognize that (1) human language is woefully inadequate, and (2) our human understanding is woefully limited. So if we find discrepancies in Scripture, it is because our ability to translate is limited by the languages we use, and our ability to understand is limited by our narrow cultural worldview. If we find inconsistencies in Scripture it is because *we* fail, not because the text fails.

This is not to insult our intelligence or tell people not to use their brains when approaching the Bible. But we need to read it with humility, aware of our own limitations when it comes to communication in general, and to be willing to put ourselves under the authority of what we read in that Book, whether we like it or not.

Psalm 19:9-11

Let Us Argue It Out

Come. Sit down. Let's argue this out.   Isaiah 1:18 (*The Message*)

My husband and his seminary friends have started a debate club of sorts. Their meetings go like this: One of them will pose a theological question, such as, "Must a person assent to the doctrine of the Trinity in order to be saved?" and the group will spend the next hour debating the issue. It's meant to be a lighthearted free-for-all, in which people adopt opposing positions for the sake of argument but will still converse as friends afterward. When they're really on a roll, they'll even resort to cheerful name-calling ("So you're a Unitarian now!"). But sometimes the debate will become serious and quite personal ("So you're saying I'm *not* saved?"). The tension builds in the room, and people study their shoes, until someone tosses out a silly comment ("Well, WWJS: What would Jesus say?"), and the tension dissolves in laughter.

There's something really healthy in all this. Christians will not always agree on everything, and until they learn how to disagree lovingly, they will continue to split into various factions that threaten both the unity and the reputation of the Church. But what happens when a fellow believer's way of thinking is clearly wrong? Does it matter for their salvation? Or are their actions the most important thing? At what point does the historic faith of Christians throughout the centuries trump an individual's ideas or preferences?

I'm not sure what the answer is, but I do know this: There may be lots of things up for debate about our faith, but there are many more things that are *not*. Helping the poor and the oppressed is one of those nonnegotiables. In today's passage, God claims he's disgusted with his people's religiosity, their churchgoing niceness—when in reality they are purposefully perpetrating injustice against the weak and forgotten people of society. So God and man sit down for a great debate. On the one side is God, saying, *This is what will happen if you stand up for the oppressed, and this is what will happen if you don't*. And on the other side is man, saying, "Tch-yeah, I dare you." Finally at the end the passage, God concludes, "I, the Lord, have spoken!"

And what else is there to say after that? No amount of human bluster and bravado can craft a sufficient response. Either we take God at his word or we don't. That's the issue in the life of faith, no matter which side of an argument you land on.

Isaiah 1:10-20

AUGUST 16

God-Breathed

Scripture defends itself most convincingly, but I recognize it's a circular argument. Why do I believe that the Bible is reliable and authoritative? Because the Bible says so. And round and round it goes.

But I also turn to the theological framework suggested by John Wesley, the eighteenth-century leader of the Methodist movement, who challenged people to line up Christian tradition, our ability to reason, and human experience to see how they all plumb with Scripture. Does our intellect support what the Bible says about itself? Yes, my reason sees this book as a brilliant masterpiece full of startling wisdom. Does human experience support this book? Yes, my own experiences tell me that not only do the words of Scripture prove true as I live my life according to their wisdom, but the biblical narratives are hauntingly true to life as we really live it every day—even the accounts of miracles. And does Christian tradition support this book? Of course: Orthodox Christianity has supported the trustworthiness and authority of the text for thousands of years—Orthodox Judaism even longer. We are "people of the Book," and as such we cling to the text as the air we breathe, the food we eat, the world we live inside—even when we don't always understand it.

Because the Bible is the living Word of God, and Jesus is also (preeminently) the living Word of God (see John 1:1-3), this book is essentially a living organism. And how many times have we failed to understand what another living being is trying to tell us, including our closest friends and family? How many times have we ourselves been misunderstood or unable to communicate what we're really thinking and feeling? Then when you begin to jump cultures, continents, and languages, it becomes even more complicated. Add to that the distance of centuries, and you have serious communication breakdown between the reader and the text.

But such breakdowns are not the fault of this Book. That's where the human communication analogy begins to disintegrate. When humans communicate with each other, both parties are capable of misunderstanding and being misunderstood. By contrast, when a human encounters God through his Word, it is the human being and the human being alone who fails. But thanks be to God! He has sent his Holy Spirit to open up the truths of Scripture to us and make it come alive in our hearts. That's what the word *inspire* means: to breathe into, to give life. So if I'm feeling uninspired as I read the Bible, it could be because I'm holding my breath, unwilling to let God in.

2 Timothy 3:14-16

Speak Up

Often when I sit down to write these devos, I'm tempted to hunt around for those select Scripture verses that buttress my worldview or strengthen some argument, rather than engage the Bible on its own terms. I can't imagine God is impressed. He's never been all that interested in telling us what we want to hear, as the wisest prophets know, but prefers to blow open our carefully crafted little worlds and reduce our arguments to dust—even our arguments in defense of his Word.

If I've learned nothing else in my ramble through the Scriptures so far this month, it's that if we read the Bible, we must read *all* of it, and slowly. We must be ready for surprises. We must brace ourselves for something that doesn't sound like Republican or Democratic policies or any of the human systems we like to spiritualize with our political rhetoric, including the American Dream. If I read the Scriptures carefully, I must conclude that, contrary to popular opinion, God *isn't* interested in our pursuit of happiness; he's interested in our pursuit of *holiness*. Whatever it takes, whether we like it or not.

Meanwhile the Bible isn't going to lose its transformative power if I somehow fail to articulate scholarly arguments for its reliability. God is much more concerned about whether or not I'm actually *living* what he says in that Book. If I'm going to expend my breath defending anything, let it be on behalf of the poor. For if I'm not defending the poor, why should anyone listen to my arguments on behalf of the text? It's the text itself that tells me, quite plainly—and in multiple places—to "speak up for the poor and helpless, and see that they get justice" (Proverbs 31:9). If I'm not doing this—*if God's own people don't obey him*—then his Word is wholly unreliable in the eyes of the world, no matter what we may *say* in its defense.

"The LORD has told you what is good," said the prophet Micah (6:8). But since we didn't get it the first time, the Lord came down to show us personally. And so my ramble through the Scriptures now brings me to the New Testament and the Gospel of John. What new things will God speak up about tomorrow that I may not want to hear?

Micah 6:1-8

The Moon

> John himself was not the light; he was simply a witness to tell about the light. The one who is the true light, who gives light to everyone, was coming into the world.
>
> John 1:8-9

The moon was full last night, glimmering like a great lamppost through my bedroom window, silver light slanting in bright swaths across my covers. I have a hard time sleeping when there's a full moon. I'm restless, as if waiting for a thunderstorm or for something magical to happen—for a silent fleet of ships to float slowly over the treetops, maybe. And even when I stand at the window and nothing all that spectacular happens, the world still looks strange. Shadows are tall and deep. Everything is exaggerated. I might, in that moment, confess to belief in giants.

But all that seems like a dream now that it's full daylight. I look up into the sky, and there is the pale outline of the moon's bones, like a misty wreck floating in a blue sea. What dominates the sky now is not the moon but the sun, whose light eclipses all other bright things in the heavens. The moon serves its purpose for a while, but it isn't a true light. It doesn't generate its own luminosity but only reflects that of the greater body that eventually ascends and overtakes it.

So it was with John the Baptist. He was like the moon. People stared at him in awe, marveling at the strange and exaggerated ideas he created by his strange and exaggerated light. And while John was alone in the night-sky wilderness of Judea, he shone brightly enough. But it was because he was reflecting the true Light of Jesus, who at that moment was still below the horizon of people's awareness. Once Jesus entered the scene, John faded into the background—which is why he said, "He [Jesus] must become greater and greater, and I must become less and less" (John 3:30). John, the moon, sank out of sight and ultimately was extinguished, while Jesus, "the Sun of Righteousness," rose "with healing in his wings" (Malachi 4:2).

So am I becoming less and less as the Sun rises, or do I fancy myself brighter than John?

John 1:6-15

The Right Question

> The artist can, out of his own experience, tell the common man a great deal
> about the fulfillment of man's nature in living; but he can produce only the most
> unsatisfactory kind of reply if he is persistently asked the wrong question.
>
> Dorothy Sayers[40]

This curious quote helps me wade through some of the odd and convoluted responses
Jesus gave to many of the questions he was asked. It's not that he was evading the issues
by offering unsatisfactory answers, but that he was "persistently asked the wrong question." He was continually asked to solve people's problems—e.g., "Tell my brother to
divide the inheritance with me" or "Is it right to pay taxes to Caesar?"// etc.—when the
real issue was their salvation. So he never *quite* gave the answer people were looking for.
The paralytic wanted physical healing, but Jesus offered him forgiveness of sins first. That's
because the important question wasn't "Will you heal my paralysis?" but "Will you heal
my spiritual brokenness?"

Sayers wrote, "The artist does not see life as a problem to be solved, but as a
medium for creation."[41] I've made the mistake of looking at the whole story of Scripture in
terms of a problem to be solved, such as the separation of humankind from God, whereas
God may be looking at it through the lens of the artist. No wonder the "solutions" have
always seemed slightly odd! Rather than abolishing sin and death immediately, God is
using those realities as a medium for new creation, not as some sort of flu epidemic that
needs the right vaccine. Each human life is a canvas, and all experiences, both good and
bad, are crafted into the making of the overall picture. God will create something different
of your life than of mine, and it will be beautiful and unique. But it probably will be messy
and rather unsatisfactory too—from our limited perspective, anyway.

Meanwhile, we must not expect all our problems to be solved or our theological
snarls to be unraveled. God isn't in the business of fixing old things; he's in the business of
creating new ones.

Mark 2:1-12

// See Matthew 22:15-22.

Puzzled and Puzzling

How odd Jesus' words must have sounded to the people who first heard them! In John 3:3, for example, Jesus told a nighttime visitor named Nicodemus that one must be "born again." I tend to chuckle at poor Nicodemus for being so confused, but what about me? Do I really get what Jesus is saying? The following poem about that midnight discussion isn't very easy to read, but maybe that's the point. . . .

Like Nicodemus
we are puzzled and puzzling,
peering at you in the dark

["For God so loved the world"]

feeling our way through the murky poetry
of your mind

["that he gave his only son"]

as though looking through
a mirror, dimly.

We hear your words,
not daring to believe

["that whoever believes in him"]

that you might be
redefining mortality
as merely the final chapter

["shall not perish"]

before an epilogue
of eternity

["but have eternal life"]

called

GRACE?

John 3:1-16 (NIV)

Well, Well, Well

Last semester in my husband's Hebrew class, the students began to notice the importance of wells (as in watering holes) in the Old Testament. More than once, a significant man met a significant woman there for the first time. For example, Isaac's future wife was discovered at a well (see Genesis 24), as was Jacob's (see Genesis 29), and later Moses meets his future wife at a well too (see Exodus 2). There in the deserts of the ancient Middle East, where water provided life for the people, the livestock, and the land, watering places also provided opportunities for new relationships to begin.

If we're paying attention to these thematic echoes throughout the Old Testament, we probably should take note when they show up in the New Testament, too. That's because the authors of the Gospels knew their Old Testament Scriptures very well. And so did Jesus. The Gospel of John tells us that Jesus stopped at a well on his way through Samaria—*Jacob's* well, in fact. Coincidence? I doubt it.

So what happened at that well? Yep, a woman showed up. And even though this wasn't Jesus' future spouse, she found at that well the love of her life. The woman believed that Jesus was the Messiah and went on to convert many others to faith in Christ. She who'd had no fewer than *five* husbands—she whose emotional and spiritual well was completely dried up—had finally discovered a source of new and unending life in the midst of the desert. She who was a foreigner, cut off from the household of Israel and from Jesus' own people, found herself and her community married into the story by her simple faith.

Ah yes, God's story doesn't repeat itself, but it rhymes.

John 4:1-41

From Now On We Know God

Poor Philip. He makes such an earnest, innocent request. "Lord," he said to Jesus, "show us the Father, and we will be satisfied" (John 14:8). Like the prospective follower who earlier told Jesus, in essence, "I believe you are as great as Elijah" (see August 12), Philip also thought he was doing Jesus an honor. He was saying, "I believe you are so great that you hold the keys of heaven. Can't you crack open the door and give us a glimpse?" But Jesus basically replied, "Enough of this nonsense. I *am* the glimpse."

This exchange with Philip reminds me of the story about the blind men who stumble upon an elephant, though they don't know what it is. One of them feels the trunk and says, "It's a snake!" while another feels a leg and says, "No, it's a tree," and so forth. The story is often used by postmodern relativists to illustrate how the religions of the world only have a small piece of the big picture—no one has the total truth, including Christianity. And certainly as Christians we acknowledge that human understanding is limited; spiritually speaking, all people everywhere are like the blind men in the story. But as my husband once pointed out, *someone* in the story must be able to see, or how would we know it was an elephant?

So while the blind men are arguing about the snake and the tree, a voice says, "No, it's an elephant." And someone pipes up, "Yeah, but how do you know?" And the voice replies, "Because I'm the elephant, and that's my leg you're grabbing."

Either we believe the voice, or we don't. Either we accept this vision, or not. If we take Jesus at his word, then we do know the Father. We have seen him. No more stumbling around in the dark, Jesus says. From now on you know God.

John 14:7-14

Expectancy

> Cornelius was waiting for them and had called together his relatives and
> close friends.
>
> Acts 10:24

We're pressing forward through the Scriptures, so let's whisk through the Gospels and the first part of Acts until we arrive at the story of Peter's visit to Cornelius in Acts 10. It's a fairly familiar event, since it forced the apostles to recognize that Gentiles were heirs of the Good News as much as Jews—that Gentiles could become Christians too and be called brothers and sisters by Jewish believers. But it's not Peter's spiritual journey I'm noticing this time around; it's Cornelius's.

Here's a pagan Italian officer, stationed in Israel, who had begun to worship the God of the Jewish locals. After receiving the startling vision of an angel, Cornelius sent three of his right-hand guys to Joppa to find this mysterious person whom the angel mentioned, named Simon Peter. They were gone for several days. And what I find intriguing is that Cornelius didn't say to himself, *Well, I'll send them off and then lie low. Best not tell anyone else in case nothing comes of it.* Rather, he opened himself up to the severe ridicule of his family and close friends—set himself up for losing face, losing their respect—and invited everyone over to wait with him for a person who may or may not turn up, who may have been a figment of his fancy, the product of perhaps one too many shots at the bar. And yet Peter *did* show up, and from that point on, life would never be the same for Cornelius or his household.

It reminds me of the story I once heard about a Billy Graham evangelistic crusade at which a young man went to check out the arena ahead of time. Thousands of people were expected; thousands more would be turned away for lack of space. He observed the workers setting up chairs and was surprised that they left such a big open space around the stage. "Couldn't you fit more seats if you filled in that space?" he asked. "Yes," they replied, "but we leave it empty to accommodate all the people who will respond to the altar call."

Oh, to have such expectancy! To trust that God will do what he says! How can I be more like Cornelius and those workers, planning unashamedly for the promises of God?

Acts 10:1-7, 21-33

The Cranky Christian

At a nearby seminary there's a famous theologian who's well known for being a crank. He has little patience with formalities and can't abide sentimentality, especially in church. Properly coiffed ladies sniffling into embroidered hankies as respectful children pass out carnations on Mother's Day—that's his idea of hell. And he makes sure you know about it too. Eventually you either hate him or love him, and either way, he doesn't care. What he *does* care about is that you're following Jesus with every bone in your body and every cell in your brain.

For some reason we have this idea that Christians are supposed to be nice. I'm not sure where this comes from. Jesus was loving, yes; but nice? polite? accommodating? sweet? well-mannered? I don't get this picture from the Scriptures at all. And his followers certainly didn't fit that mold either, especially Paul. All throughout his New Testament letters, many of which seem to have been written in a cranky mood, Paul was chiding the believers for their wishy-washy faith, their sentimentalized Christianity, their halfhearted holiness. He was an expert bargainer; he could wheedle and plead and shame and debate and turn people's own words back on their heads. My guess is you either loved him or hated him, and if you loved him, he didn't make it easy.

For instance, I get a kick out of Paul's petulant jabs at people: e.g., "I won't mention that you owe me your very soul!" (Philemon 1:19) And this is the same man who wrote that love "keeps no record of being wronged"! (1 Corinthians 13:5) Indeed, before he became a Christian he was a Pharisees, a religious zealot who dragged Christians from their homes and took pleasure in rehearsing their record of wrongs before judges and juries. And yet the Holy Spirit used him to change the known world. Only a character like that could speak before governors and kings, synagogues and skeptics. Only a crank could survive stonings, sing boldly in prison, captivate a mob, change the minds of kings, turn the hearts of a ship full of hardened travelers, or convict believers with stinging criticism.

What would happen if the rest of us stopped trying to be nice for once and got cranky about all the right things?

Acts 26:1-23

Perplexed

We are perplexed, but not driven to despair. 2 Corinthians 4:8

How comforting it is to know that Paul and the early Christians were at times "perplexed"! Often I picture them like superheroes, so totally sure of the next step, so confident of God's will that they never wandered in a spiritual fog—the fog of sin or of baffling relationships. Sometimes I feel like that's all I ever wander in rather than the blazing light of God's truth—especially when it comes to my interactions with fellow Christians in the church.

For instance, one Sunday morning an unhappy parishioner accosted me in the center aisle of the sanctuary right before worship began. Apparently I had done something that upset her, and she was determined to unload on me—whether it was an appropriate time or not. This was way beyond cranky; this was downright mean. And though I was stung emotionally, I tried to be nice about it and say, "Well, let's talk after worship." Of course what I really wanted to say was, "Get thee behind me, Satan," because my gut reaction told me this was a purposeful attack, designed to shame me into cowardly compliance. But at the same time I second-guessed myself. What if I was wrong? What if I was being way too overconfident about my role in ministry or my good judgment? The whole thing was perplexing, and I spent the rest of the worship service unable to focus on God at all.

Perplexed. It comes from the Latin word perplexus, which means "entangled." I picture a moth bumbling into a spider's web, unable to break free, or a knitter trying to unsnarl a ball of yarn. All plans are on hold. There's nothing one can do except struggle to untangle the situation. And if things are really ensnarled, it'd be easy to see the whole thing as hopeless and give up entirely.

Spiritually speaking, we can expect entanglements—whether from our own sin or from the sin of others, or even from direct attacks of our enemies. We can plan on being thwarted in our attempts to move forward in the Christian life. And it's only by taking the time to patiently work out all the snarls that we'll be able to avoid despair.

After worship that Sunday, the upset parishioner and I were able to sit down and talk through things. And though we arrived at reconciliation, it didn't happen immediately. But I was determined, like Paul and the early Christians, that even though I was perplexed, I would not give up and quit.

2 Corinthians 4:8-15

Chapter 3,674 of Acts

The book of Acts ends with Paul under house arrest in Rome for two years, awaiting his hearing with Emperor Caesar. Christian tradition holds that he was eventually executed there, but Acts doesn't say what happened. The original readers—including Theophilus, to whom the book is written (see Acts 1:1)—most likely knew those details anyway. But what I find interesting is that the story is unfinished. We're left hanging as to the fate of Paul and the other believers whom we learned so much about in those twenty-eight chapters. If Acts were a stand-alone novel, it'd get lousy reviews.

But Acts isn't a stand-alone novel. Not that there's an Acts II or III out there yet to be discovered; what I mean is the readers *are* the sequel. Wherever the book ends is where the readers are expected to pick up and carry on. Chapter twenty-nine and following would involve the earliest house churches of the ancient world; later chapters would include the martyrs and catacombs; still later chapters would talk about Constantine and the fall of Rome—followed by various councils debating theological issues, monks preserving sacred Scripture during the early Middle Ages, cathedrals flourishing in the medieval era, Martin Luther and the Protestant Reformation, and so on throughout the history of the Christian Church. And eventually it would reach our own generation, here in the early years of the third millennium, Chapter 3,674 or so of Acts.

And I wonder: Will the writers who pen the stories of our time say the same things about us that the author of Acts said about Paul? Will they write that we practiced hospitality? proclaimed the Kingdom of God with all boldness? taught about the Lord Jesus Christ? And that no one tried to stop us, not even our own complacent, materialistic selves?

Acts 28:16-31

Living the Scriptures: Part 1

Before one of our youth mission trips a few years ago, I shared with my prayer partner about my worries and frustrations. I asked, "Would you please pray that we would have peace in our hearts?" (see Colossians 3:15). We talked about how God was already answering that prayer as I prepared a week's worth of devotions for the group—how God was continually giving me Scriptures that were relevant to what each day would likely bring, and we hadn't even left on the trip yet.

My prayer partner then said something I'll never forget. She said, "Sarah, I will pray for your sense of peace, but particularly that the kids would read the Bible verses for each day and think, *This is true! We're living this! We are living the Scriptures.*"

We are living the Scriptures. Her words have stuck with me ever since. We *are* living this story! We're living this Book that we talk about in church each week and read snippets of before we go to work or class or sleep each day. Not only is Scripture alive and active in us, but we are alive and active in it. Not only do the words of Christ dwell in us, in our very hearts, as it were (see Colossians 3:16), but we dwell in the heart of Christ's words. We are living the truths of the Bible every day; we're given bit parts in its ongoing story until God brings all things to their final conclusion at the end of days.

Meanwhile, my original prayer request had been for peace. Through all the crazy preparations for that mission trip—through all the sleepless nights worrying about the things that could possibly go wrong on an international journey—what I needed was the peace I'd read about so many times in the words of Jesus. But the only way that peace would be real was if I invited the author of the story—the Prince of Peace himself—to embed his words in my heart like a living seed.

Colossians 3:15-17 (NIV)

Living the Scriptures: Part 2

On the mission trip I spoke of on August 27, I was invited to preach (thankfully, I was aware of this in advance!). The whole time I was preparing the sermon I couldn't get my prayer partner's words out of my head—that we would "live the Scriptures" while on this adventure. And soon it dawned on me that the text I was invited to preach on (today's passage from Matthew) promotes this very same idea—as does all of the New Testament.

Every time you turn around in the New Testament, you bump into the Old Testament Scriptures. It's impossible to avoid them. Today's passage is just one of many examples. Throughout the story Matthew wasn't just telling us what happened to him and the other disciples; he was explaining how the ancient biblical texts suddenly jumped off the synagogue scrolls and came alive as Jesus rode a donkey into Jerusalem. First Matthew quoted the prophecy in Zechariah 9:9, which says, "Look, your king is coming to you. He is . . . humble, riding on a donkey." Then Matthew recorded the praises of the people, who were quoting Psalm 118 and other verses as Jesus rode into town. Later Jesus quoted Isaiah 56:7 and Jeremiah 7:11 as he furiously cleansed the Temple of crass consumerism. And when the religious leaders expressed concern over the children's high praise for Jesus, the Messiah replied (with a hint of sarcasm), "Haven't you ever read the Scriptures?"—and then he quoted Psalm 8:2 to them.

Had they read the Scriptures? Of course they had! These were the men who were supposed to know Scripture best—who in fact knew it by heart. So what was Jesus getting at?

To them the Bible was just words on paper. To Jesus, if you don't recognize how God's Word is coming true every day around you—if you don't claim that you're living the Word in this very moment—then you haven't really read it.

Matthew 21:12-17

Third Samuel

I suppose it feels like I've gotten way off track in my ramblings through the Bible this month, and I probably have. Each new thought leads to yet another and another, and soon I'm like Alice in Wonderland, leaping down every rabbit hole for curiosity's sake. Where will this journey take us? I'm not sure, but somewhere at the end of it all is the book of Revelation.

But I'm not there yet. At the moment I'm sidetracked in a conversation about how we as Christians are living the very Scriptures we're reading. The book of Acts ends unfinished, an invitation for every Christian since the time of Paul to continue the story—we are, if you will, chapter 3,674 of Acts (see August 26). And like the early disciples, we look around and see God's Word coming to life in our midst every day.

My husband is a great example. Today is his birthday, and, as his mother will tell you, this is a special occasion to commemorate. Like Hannah in the book of 1 Samuel, she had prayed for years to have a child. So when Tom finally came along, she dedicated him, like Samuel, to the Lord. A number of years later he was playing in an empty church hallway while his grandmother was busy elsewhere in the building, and he heard a voice say, "You're being a good boy, Tommy." He looked around. No one was there. So he got up and went to his grandma and asked if anyone was in the building. She said no. He explained the voice, and she said, "Well, it must have been God." Another Samuel moment.//

Tom *is* a good boy; he's a good man. And even though his life has taken various twists and turns since his childhood—including a time in which he wasn't sure he could be a Christian—my husband is now studying in seminary to become a pastor. God honored the prayers my mother-in-law made all those years ago, and the rest of us have witnessed Tom's steadfast loyalty and good-heartedness. I suppose if there were a third book of Samuel, my husband's life would be it.

And why not? Why are we so reticent to speak the Scriptures into each other's lives? Why are we so shy about praying strong prayers for our spouses or nieces or friends, as if we'd be setting them up for failure rather than a life of holiness like their spiritual ancestors? If God's story echoes from page to page of his book, why not from century to century, even to this very moment, into your life and mine?

1 Samuel 1:1-2, 9-28

// See 1 Samuel 3.

True Vision

I once did a study of Revelation with a group of middle school and high school students. The curriculum I used described John's writing to the persecuted Christians as a clever use of symbolic language so the Roman rulers wouldn't understand what the believers were saying to each other. In this way, Christians could communicate in "code," and their words wouldn't seem like a threat to the Romans, who no doubt would persecute them further if John's meaning was understood.

But now I wonder, after reading the first chapter of Revelation again: How on earth could John be speaking in code? The Roman rulers merely needed to read the first few paragraphs, and they would've destroyed the document and sought out not only its author (who stated himself and his location with perfect clarity) but also its intended readership (also stated in detail). Meanwhile, the Son of Man is depicted in royal garb as a great and shining God; his words speak of immortality and power. I can't imagine a greater threat to the Roman Empire than this, seeing as how the emperors themselves were considered divine. John's words would've been pointedly blasphemous to both the Gentiles and the Jews. His time was up; his days were numbered. You can almost hear the soldiers' footsteps approaching his cell.

So John's images and symbols are not an elaborate system like Egyptian hieroglyphics, written in code for the few who were "in the know." He was recording a *real vision* that impacts all Christians everywhere—past, present, and future.

And anyway, who cares if the Romans were ticked off about it? John was already in exile, so what could it possibly have mattered to him if he got in trouble for writing this book?

No, if John said he was recording a revelation from God, then I take him at his word.

Revelation 1:9-19

The Tree of Life

I'm finally winding up this random ramble through the Bible (though I realize I've just barely touched the surface), and for the first time I notice a critical literary image that I previously overlooked—one that both begins and ends the book and in fact seems to be the key to the entire plot. I'm talking about the tree of life.

It's there first in Genesis 2 and 3. When Adam and Eve were told they could eat from any tree in the Garden, this included the tree of life, which wasn't the same as the tree of the knowledge of good and evil, from which they could *not* eat. So once they were banished from the Garden for eating from the wrong tree, they were cut off from the tree of life too, and thus death was introduced for the first time. We don't see the tree again, other than hints here and there, for many millennia.

Then, there it is in the last chapter of Revelation, on the banks of the river that flows through the heavenly city. "On each side of the river grew a tree of life, bearing twelve crops of fruit, with a fresh crop each month. The leaves were used for medicine to heal the nations" (Revelation 22:2). The people once again have access to the tree of life, and this time death is banished forever. How did I miss this before?

Meanwhile, there's a tree in the middle of the story too, or more appropriately, at the climax. The cross of Jesus, often called a tree in medieval times, stands at the pinnacle of God's interactions with humankind. And it, too, is a tree of life, though it comes to us first in the guise of death. Through Christ's death on that tree for our sake, we are reconciled with God and have access to eternal life again. It wouldn't surprise me if, on that last (or shall we say, first?) day at the end of days, we will approach the tree of life that stands in the center of the new Jerusalem and see upon its bark the scars of crucifixion.

Genesis 2:8-17; 3:22-24; Revelation 22:1-2, 14

Same Old, Same Old

I'm home. Well, sort of. My husband and I have returned to North Carolina for another year of graduate school after a summer internship in Virginia, so we're back on a school schedule. Even though I'm more than one thousand miles away from my former hometown in Michigan, separated from family and friends and my old routine, the campus here has begun to feel familiar. I recognize people in the dining hall; I know the folks at my church; I can find my way around the local grocery store. We're back to the same old, same old, brand-new life.

I wish I could say I'm excited to be back, but after a year of so much change, it's hard to care much about anything. Just when I start to care about something, I have to up and leave it, so why bother? Like the Teacher in Ecclesiastes, I'm at the "everything is meaningless" stage. Life feels like it's on an endless loop, a streaming feed of schedules and deadlines and lunch dates and bills. The rivers run into the sea; the wind blows here and there; the sun sets for the billionth time; and no matter how much beauty I see or how many God moments I experience, I feel dull and disinterested.

Perhaps this is why I love the book of Ecclesiastes. The Teacher is so very honest about these feelings. He doesn't hide his discouragement or ennui. He doesn't trip happily into worship, smiling until his face feels like plastic. "As you enter the house of God," he chided his readers, "keep your ears open and your mouth shut" (Ecclesiastes 5:1). In other words, stop being so annoying; God isn't impressed by your pretend enthusiasm for spiritual matters if you're not going to follow through on them (see verse 2). And as for the rest of the week? Be honest: Many of us feel restless and unsettled most of the time. Work and school, friends and family, money and material possessions—why are they ultimately unsatisfying? Because we were made for eternal things (see Ecclesiastes 3:11). We were designed for the heavenly Kingdom of God, the longing for which is planted in our hearts like a great thorn. We will ever be restless and unhappy with the same old, same old routine under the sun, until it sets for the last time and the new dawn of eternity begins.

Ecclesiastes 1:1-11

Out of Mind

Most days during this new school year I've been heading to campus with my husband and writing in the university library. I've decided that part of my job is to people-watch. I often sit at a desk on the "bridge" between buildings, and underneath me is the main walkway through campus that connects one area to another. So all day long, students and staff come and go: short and tall, fat and skinny, young and old, Southerner and East Coaster, Bolivian and Sri Lankan, toting backpacks or briefcases and talking on cell phones. And I can't help wondering where they're from and what they're thinking and how many of them hold some kind of religious conviction or even the faintest awareness of God. If they don't have that spiritual awareness, what do they *think* about all day?

That's something I've never been able to fathom—life without God. On one level, it's impossible: "In him we live and move and exist," Paul said in Acts 17:28, which means we wouldn't be alive in the first place without the Creator. But breathing isn't the same as consciousness. On another level, we're so bound to this physical life that it's easy to ignore the spiritual life: "Out of sight, out of mind," as they say. We can't see it, so we forget about it.

Yet for some reason I've never been able to ignore spiritual realities completely, even when I tried. Even when I'd go through long stretches of deliberate rebellion against God's ways, I was still aware of him. I was raised with the knowledge of his existence as well as his love for me, which is like learning how to read: Once you learn it, you can't really unlearn it, barring some accident or another. Spiritual consciousness, like literacy, becomes so much a part of your life that you can't imagine going through the day without it—in fact, it shapes who you are and what you do, including what you think about.

So for me God is never "out of sight, out of mind"; he's the main topic, the main relationship that fills my mind. Which brings me back to my earlier musings. If the people I see coming and going have no thoughts of God in their heads, what *are* they thinking about?

Ecclesiastes 1:12-18

Quiet Desperation

The mass of men lead lives of quiet desperation.   Henry David Thoreau[42]

I look out of this library window and see students coming and going, going and coming, their minds filled with whatever their minds are filled with. I have no idea how many of them have an awareness of God from hour to hour or what it means to them if they do. And I can't help thinking that if they have no awareness of God, and thus no awareness of their own fallenness or worth, then their lives must be basically desperate—under the surface, anyway.

On the outside they look cool and capable. Most of the girls walk like they're parading down a beauty pageant runway; many guys strut like they've just won a national championship. Even the grad students and scholars walk like they own the earth. And yet Thoreau was onto something 150 years ago. He saw their secret. He knew that deep down, most people are quietly obsessing about their appearance, frantic about the future, miserable about the past, carrying relational burdens that threaten to bring them down, terrified of failure, secretly addicted to any number of vices. We are desperate, if all the statistics about young adult depression and anxiety are correct. Desperate, if some of us are secretly cutting ourselves. Desperate, if we work ourselves into a frenzy over jobs or grades or grad school applications, or if we drink ourselves into a stupor every weekend. The mass of students here at this distinguished university lead lives of quiet desperation.

It's enough to make *me* depressed, and I've been given "a Kingdom that is unshakable" (Hebrews 12:28)! Yet I look out this window and instead of claiming the hope I have in Christ, I find my spirit sinking with discouragement. I'm like the Teacher in Ecclesiastes, who looked down from his palace balustrade in Jerusalem (or so I imagine), watching the travelers on the streets, the merchants in the marketplace, the priests and Levites in their endless parade to and from the Temple. I look out on all this human busyness, this fruitless activity, and I say, "Everything is meaningless, utterly meaningless!" Everything under the sun.

It's a good thing God is *beyond* the sun.

Ecclesiastes 2:17-26

Giant Sticky Notes

I believe in liturgy, those words that are repeated in worship and prayer in many churches from week to week, day to day. Prayers like those in *The Book of Common Prayer* or rituals like the Great Thanksgiving[43] during the Lord's Supper are like speed bumps that keep me humble—especially when life feels mind-numbingly out of control. Repetition makes them a healthy habit, like brushing my teeth or taking a shower, rather than dead words that don't mean anything anymore. Liturgy is like a giant sticky note on my bathroom mirror in the morning, reminding me that I am indeed accountable for the life I lived yesterday and for the life I'll live tomorrow. My days are strung together in a meaningful sequence, and these liturgical words, like the story of Scripture, help stitch my days together into an ongoing pattern. They were here before I woke up and will continue long after I'm gone. It's my privilege to be a part of them for a while.

But for some reason many people in my generation seem to think it's hip to ditch the old stuff, as if we're so incredibly brilliant that we could come up with something better. I find this highly unlikely, especially since our average intelligence has gone *down* in the past couple of decades (or so I've heard). What we've forgotten is that we avoid becoming dumber by learning from those who've gone before us. "It is a good rule," wrote C. S. Lewis, "after reading a new book, never to allow yourself another new one till you have read an old one in between."[44] And I would add, for every new prayer you pray, pray an old prayer too. Sing an old song. Pray the words of someone who lived in a different century yet still knew the same Jesus. Sing the words of someone who walked this road before you and knows where the next bend is headed and which fork to take.

And only *then* sing a new song, pray a new prayer, read a new book. Because the reverse danger is also very real—that we'll become so attached to the old ways that we'll ignore what God is up to in the here and now.

Ecclesiastes 5:1-7

A New Mind

We're encouraged as Christians to have the "mind of Christ," and often we limit this to thinking kind or pure thoughts. But what if that means we are to have the *intellect* of Christ—the same Christ who, as a boy, asked such brilliant questions of the teachers in the Temple (see Luke 2:41-52)? Or on another level, what if we're supposed to think Jesus' thoughts in every situation, in every conversation, as each day unfolds?

I want to have the mind of Christ:

to claim integrity and humility
in my work and studies;
to speak only what builds up;
to be discerning and know
what a person needs to hear;
to think thoughts uncluttered
and perfectly clear;
whether exhausted or wide awake,
to have unswerving purpose;
to fully know that I belong to you;
and walk as if I do—head up;
and talk as if I do—with love;
and eat and sleep and dream and work
and write and fellowship
and laugh and cry,
always mindful that I am your child.

With my mind renewed,
I come before you
each morning, Lord,
not because I am faithful

but because you are.

Ecclesiastes 9:13-18; 1 Corinthians 2:10-16

Somebody Loves Us

The beginning of the school year always makes me think of my mom, a math teacher, whose birthday happens to be today. When I was growing up, our household ran like a well-organized schoolroom: shoes and backpacks tidily arranged just inside the door, lunch food laid out along the counter for the morning assembly line, all of us sitting down for the daily ritual of family devotions at breakfast, and so forth. And despite her own hectic school schedule—especially on those days when she was substitute teaching—my mom still found a moment to write a personal note to both my sister and me, which was carefully stowed in our lunch bags, decorated with stickers and smiley faces. This lasted all the way through high school. In fact, by the time my sister was an upperclassman, her circle of friends begged to see the note every day, passing it around the table like a postcard from a distant missionary. Somebody out there loves us.

And it was not uncommon for my mom to leave little sticky notes or bookmarks or cards around the house for us to find: on the bathroom mirror, slipped inside a textbook, tucked into a jewelry box. She liked (and still likes) to surprise us. One April Fools' Day I stumbled, half-awake, into the bathroom, flicked on the switch, looked in the mirror, and found a poster of a chimpanzee grinning back at me. Then there was the fake grasshopper, alarmingly realistic-looking, that would turn up in our makeup drawers or among the cotton balls—wherever my mom would be guaranteed a startled shriek from one of us. We soon learned to give her a taste of her own comic genius by hiding the creature among her socks or earrings. And back and forth it went. (I still have that grasshopper somewhere. . . .)

All of this to say, my mom made sure we knew, in small but persistent ways, that we were loved. She didn't buy us fancy clothes or cars, or promise us trips to Disneyland; rather, she showed us her love in the everyday things, the little domestic things. She sat with us as we labored through algebra homework, understanding our limitations, our different giftedness. She tucked notes into our textbooks during exam week, reminding us that grades are not everything and that God is bigger. She never let us go on very long without the simple and sometimes startling reminder that Somebody loves us, Somebody cares about the little stuff, and Somebody would be with us even after we left home and she was no longer there to nudge our memories.

That's the kind of person I want to be.

Psalm 92

Back to Port

It doesn't seem to matter what topic I'm exploring in these devos—suffering, summer break, selfishness, Scripture—eventually the discussion turns to prayer. It's like I'm a ship that wanders out to sea for a while but returns to port by nightfall. And I suppose that makes sense. All these topics are good and important for the spiritual life, yes, but if I can't pray about them or if they don't in some way inform our most important task as Christians, then I must question their ultimate significance.

I remember my first assignment in our Christian theology class during my junior year of college. Our professor told us we were to write a prayer and turn it in for a pass-fail grade. Some of us protested: What right did he have to grade our *prayer life*? But he insisted. Because, he said, it's really easy to get caught up in theology as just another academic discipline, like biology or physics or math, when the operative part of the word here is *theo*—"God" in Greek. It's more than just a subject; it's a Person. And if we're not in conversation with this Person throughout the course of studying him, then we've missed the point entirely.

The same is true for *all* the thoughts that occupy my mind. If what I'm thinking right now—I mean *right now*, as I watch the couple flirt at the next table (*That's just gross; must they do that in public?*) or the young mom whisk her screaming child out of the coffeehouse (*Can't she keep him under control?*)—if I can't pray those thoughts, do I really have any business entertaining them? Or rather, what if I were to make a concerted effort to turn all my thoughts, even the negative ones, into prayers? Then if I wander too far out into the sea of selfishness, I'm at least guaranteed to drift back home to the heart of God before dark.

Philippians 4:8-9

Paying Attention

It's curious to me that in the English language the act of attending to something or someone outside of ourselves is difficult to express without using the metaphor of personal sacrifice: We *give* attention, we *pay* attention. In other words, to focus on anything other than our own little lives costs us.

Prayer, as the authors of *The Spiritual Life* wrote, is "a disciplined dedication to paying attention." It, too, requires sacrifice. It costs us our selfish inner ramblings; it requires us to concentrate on someone outside of ourselves—often many someones, if we include intercessory prayer in the equation. In fact, *all* aspects of prayer require us to pay the price of attention. For example:

- In praise and adoration we take our obsessive thoughts off of ourselves, for once, and pay attention to the amazing attributes of our loving heavenly Father.
- In confession we put the spotlight on those things we'd rather *not* pay attention to: we know we're expected to give them up.
- In thanksgiving we take our attention off all the things we don't have or the things that have gone wrong, and instead we pay attention to the details—itemized one by one—of all that God has given us.
- In supplication we let go of our frantic anxieties, our petty problems, our secret sins and obsessions, and deliberately, intentionally place them at the feet of Christ. Then we no longer give them our attention. We let God attend to them. And as we fix our eyes on him, we learn what it is he wants us to do with those things, one at a time.
- In intercession we fix" our attention on the other people in our lives who need healing, forgiveness, grace, or mercy, or to feel the love and presence of God.

Prayer, at heart, is the discipline of paying attention—giving, fixing, focusing; and thus it costs us something—time, energy, pride. No wonder we're so reticent to begin!

Psalm 119:65-80

// Now, there's a slightly different metaphor: to fix attention, as a carpenter applies wood glue to attach two items and then holds those items fast together until they adhere. And then there's "to focus our attention," as a photographer zooms in on a certain item and turns the lens until the blurs turn to well-defined images. . . .

Praying with Jesus

Even though I find it difficult to concentrate in prayer—to pay the price of attention (see September 8)—I find myself wide awake when it comes to wanting to know God's will. Somehow when that topic comes up I can stay unusually alert, repeating the same questions and concerns over and over again, waiting for the teeniest, tiniest sense of direction. Perhaps that's why, of all the prayers in the Bible, I'm drawn to Jesus' prayer in the garden of Gethsemane on the night of his arrest. Each phrase is fraught with tension; each line gives us insight into how we should pray.

1. "Abba, Father . . ." God is our Father; we are his children. We come before him as a child to a parent, recognizing he is our "Daddy" (*abba* means "daddy" in Aramaic). He takes care of us, he provides for us, he protects us. He has the wisdom of a parent who can see down the road to our future and knows what's best for us.

2. "Everything is possible for you. . . ." Whatever we desire is within God's power to give. He isn't thwarted by human sin and decisions; he isn't limited by the laws of nature. Whatever the task, God can do it. This is a critical acknowledgment—not looking at all the obstacles to what you desire, but simply trusting in the power of God and celebrating his power to give.

3. "Please take this cup of suffering away from me. . . ." We can state clearly what we want. Jesus doesn't dance around the real issue or couch his agony in flowery terms or try to sound unselfish or give God several options for fulfilling the request—he just states it plainly. This is what I want; this is my desire; this is what my body, soul, mind, and spirit crave; this is *my* will. God desires our honest assessment of who we are and what we yearn for. How can he grant a request if we say, "That's okay. It's not really that important"? It *is* important. It's important enough to name out loud.

4. "Yet I want your will to be done, not mine. . . ." This is perhaps the most important prayer in all Scripture. God is the perfect one, with perfect wisdom, perfect love, perfect intent. We are human and limited. Even when we know God's will and have a vision of its marvelous outcome for the future, we're naturally incapable of desiring it to be fulfilled if it involves our personal harm or loss. But Jesus is able to pray that he *wants* God's will—which is why I believe we can only pray this kind of prayer if we have emptied ourselves and allowed Jesus to pray *through* us. Otherwise we're not being honest.

Mark 14:32-42

The Inevitable

Whenever there's an unexpected tragedy, such as the events of September 11, 2001 (which we commemorate tomorrow), you'd think we had never heard of death before. Usually we don't give it a second thought until it interrupts our everyday lives with the uncomfortable reminder that this, too, will happen to us someday. There's no such thing as an *unexpected* death. It will eventually happen to 100 percent of the population, including you and me. It even happened to Jesus. Why are we eternally astounded by this?

I wrote this prayer after some of my fellow college students were in a terrible car accident in which one student was killed:

Today I am faced with my own mortality.
This whole community is silenced.
We've been forced to consider the inevitable,
to look into the last room,
to hear the clock chime.
And the chill goes deep.
Certainly this life will end.
Yet nothing is outside of your control.
Even death,
which comes as horror to us—
the very thought of which must sink in slowly
as we wake up tomorrow
and the next day
and the next—
is something you knew and know fully.
That which startles us out of life's comfortable
taken-for-granted-ness, like a sudden sheet of ice,
is an ancient thing to you,
a silent, grim companion:
fixed, yet not eternal.
Even you faced mortality,
but you were not surprised;

you knew the Cross
came before

the Crown.

1 Corinthians 15:21-26

A Time for What?

Someone has decided it's a time for war. That's what I'm thinking on this anniversary of September 11, 2001. Many someones have determined that this new millennium will be more desperate and violent and ruinous than the last, that buildings will come thundering down on the East Coast and in the Middle East, that children on all sides will become orphans, that dust will coat faces of many colors in this wounded world. We are a species bound for violence, from the time of Cain to this moment.// And thus we say, "An eye for an eye, a tooth for a tooth" (Exodus 21:24). This, apparently, is our motto.

But into the midst of this mess comes a young Rabbi who says, in essence, "Turn the other cheek. I know you've heard otherwise. I know you were once given the rubric of a just revenge, which at the time was considered temperance. I know Moses told you, instead of ramping up the violence, to take no more than what was taken from you. If someone took your eye, don't cut off their leg in return. If it was a tooth, don't therefore steal their children's food. Keep the score even so the violence will plateau rather than escalate. But now I tell you, nothing is fair in the Kingdom of God. You have no rights. You are the doormat of the world. If a terrorist strikes you on the one cheek, give him the other to maul. If a gangster steals your coat, give him the rest of your wardrobe. This is called grace, undeserved favor. This is mercy. This is what the true children of the Father are about. If it doesn't make sense to the rest of the planet, that's not your problem. Your job is to be perfect, even as your Father in heaven is perfect."

So under the mercy of this new covenant, is there ever a time for war? Is there ever a time for revenge, lawsuits, slander, dog-eat-dog capitalism? And what role do we play in the making of our time?

Ecclesiastes 3:1-8; Matthew 5:38-48

// See Genesis 4.

War in the Desert: Part 1

It seems many wars these days involve deserts, which lends them eerily biblical over-
tones. One battle echoes a previous battle from previous centuries; violence leads to more
violence. And the desert people of our planet, especially in the Middle East, must be
weary beyond words. So my imagination roams. When the Prince of Peace and his glory
are revealed at the end of time, will the desert and its people—people for whom Christ
died—know joy when they see it?

When all the syllables and sabers
of that ancient dynasty are silent
and all her enemies gone,
the matriarch walks with stately strides
the barren hills,
the wastelands,
the moonscapes of war-torn centuries.
Babylon weeps in great waves of dust,
her prayers rising on the billows of sand,
unheeded, unheard
by the god of her many dead
and dying kings.
Her children huddle, ragged,
against the empty hillsides,
as the planetarium of night
tilts around the North Star.
The sky glows strangely red
where cities once stood.

They long for bread.

Then out of the darkness
comes a voice,
crying in the wilderness.
In mighty earthquakes
the mountains sink
level with the plain,
and all the rough and ragged
ridges of that empty empire
ripple into smooth roads.
Sings the voice triumphant,
"Prepare the way of the Lord!"

Isaiah 21:1-10; 40:3-5

War in the Desert: Part 2

Young soldiers are fighting other young soldiers all over the world, and the media subtly teaches us which faces to hate, which side to take. Meanwhile another young person from a previous millennium looks us in the eye and says, "Love your enemies"[//]—which must mean God loves our enemies too. So which side does that put me on?

Break your hearts
for never-never land,
for the landlocked island
of Lost Boys
in the midst of the great
and heaving sea of sand.
Fatherless,
they wrap in rags
and trudge across the miles,
across the wretched wasteland,
following men whose empty
promises are better
than no promises at all.

Winter approaches,
and deepest night,
while they fall asleep in the sand
cradling semiautomatic weapons,
their faces brown and beautiful,
like chiseled stone.
Boys' hands, boys' eyes
—these are not men.
They are Lost Boys
who ache in the desert
for home, or revenge,
or a noble, foolish death,
whichever comes easiest.

And still the Father of this world
pursues them patiently
until they are finally found.

Isaiah 40:6-11

// See Matthew 5:44.

Under the Mercy

Under the mercy. A great phrase, but I can't take credit for it. I'm borrowing the term from a group of my favorite authors, known as the Inklings, which met during the 1930s and 1940s in Oxford and included guys like C. S. Lewis, J. R. R. Tolkien, their friend Charles Williams, and others. "Under the mercy" was sometimes their signature blessing in their correspondence with one another. It was an acknowledgment that as Christians we live under the mercy of God rather than under the penalty of death; our citizenship is in the heavenly Kingdom rather than any earthly one. Thus we are inextricably connected to one another. Some who knew or admired the Inklings have since continued that tradition."

Think of it as a flag or ensign flying from a ship's rigging. The flag indicates which country the ship belongs to, whose rule it's under. Out on the open sea, in international waters, it's difficult to tell where a ship is from without this indicator. Then once the ship enters waters belonging to a particular nation, such as the Great Lakes, it runs at least two flags up the mast: The top flag belongs to the nation in whose waters it sails; the second indicates which country the ship is from. According to the skipper of a sailboat I once crewed, this is more than just a courtesy: Reverse the order and you could be declaring war, claiming this territory for yourself and your sovereign, or so he explained.

For those of us who claim to follow Jesus, we fly the ensign of mercy above all others—above the flag of nation, state, region, home, family. Mercy is the signature characteristic of Christ's rule. Under this flag we are no longer primarily citizens of the United States, nor a certain race, nor members of a particular family. We belong to Jesus. Thus our first response in war or any other international crisis isn't patriotism to our country above all things, but allegiance to Jesus and his way of mercy. Our challenge is to love others—including our enemies—with the self-sacrificing compassion of Jesus, even when they are at their most unlovable. We're to cover them with a blanket of mercy, just as we ourselves have been covered.

Today is the moment in the church calendar when we celebrate Holy Cross Day.>> If there's any image on our flag of mercy, it's this one: Jesus on the cross, blanketing the world with grace when it really deserved judgment, revenge, and war. Is my own life a flag bearing this image to others?

1 Peter 2:9-17

// See, for example, the closing page of Sheldon Vanauken's memoir, *A Severe Mercy* (New York: HarperCollins, 1977).

>> Holy Cross Day commemorates the discovery of the cross of Christ in AD 325.

The Grace of the Unexpected

The four months I spent as an exchange student in Nairobi, Kenya, were culturally overwhelming, but every few weeks I was given an extra measure of grace in the form of someone who took me completely by surprise. One night it was a British missionary named Peter.

There in East Africa, the British are considered the bad guys. They were the colonizers. Over one hundred years ago they came in and set up modern Western infrastructures that were (and still are) simply untenable. Whenever I'd think of those nineteenth-century colonizers in their safari trousers and jungle helmets, making their proper and respectable way through the savanna to greet the tall Masai man (whose beauty they were unable to see because of his apparent malnutrition, pagan ignorance, etc.), the bile would rise in my stomach.

And yet one evening, along came a man my father's age who suddenly overturned all the stereotypes. At first all I saw was a white man—a Brit, a missionary—not a winning combination in my new African world. And although at first his accent suggested safari, soon his spirit suggested Christ; and I was blessed by a glimpse of God's Kingdom, which transcends all cultures, colors, and stereotypes.

My visitor also gave me the gift of laughter. It's hard to grasp what living in another culture is like, month after month, if you've never done it before. But let me warn you: Humor is the first casualty. The people around you are laughing all the time, but you have no idea why; and likewise when you make a joke, there's total silence. Humor doesn't always translate from culture to culture. So when this man took one look at us American students—with our wacky clothes and unwashed hair and haunted expressions—he knew immediately what we needed.

"It's done me a lot of good to see you idiots," he told us, and we laughed.

"Now promise me you'll never get too religious or anything," he said, with great solemnity. And we laughed again.

Then he gathered us in a circle and prayed, "Lord, may we have fun in your Kingdom down here on earth." And we laughed yet again.

God knew exactly what I needed: to stop taking myself—and everyone else—so seriously, and to actually *enjoy* life again.

Ephesians 6:21-24

Ask and You Will Receive

I've mentioned now and then my fall semester in Kenya, so here's a snippet from my journal at the time. To give you some background, I had landed an internship with an indigenous mission to street children, and on this particular occasion my ministry partner and I were headed to a slum to meet a family. With us came a mischievous street kid named Kamau, who for some reason had taken a fancy to my sneakers.

As we were walking to the slum, it began to sprinkle and then rain, and by the time we reached the market on the main road, drops came like gumballs, hard and fast. We ducked under the tarp of one of the market stalls and watched as the stall keepers frantically attempted to shield their fruits and vegetables with cardboard boxes and plastic bags. The water began to collect in fast pools around the stall and run in small creeks along the cracks in the ground, creating mud on the footpaths. And suddenly I felt a strange camaraderie with all the people who joined us under the tarp: We were all trapped by the rain, all waiting, just waiting and trying to stay dry. There was no difference between us—my white skin would get just as wet as their African skin if we were to stand under the open clouds. There is something about weather that reminds us we're all just *human*.

Anyway, as we sat there, Kamau asked me for the thousandth time if I would give him my shoes. This is a regular conversation between us. I don't know where he got the idea that I would simply give him the shoes off my feet, but somehow he became convinced that this is the sort of person I am. And I'd always offer some kind of excuse, such as the shoes would be too big for him or I'd have to give shoes to all the children, or whatever. Dodge and weave. I did this again, but he kept pestering me, there under the tarp in the rain—probably because he knew I couldn't get away. And just when I'd used up all my arguments (all of them flimsy anyway), the wind lifted the tarp in a whoosh above us, and a big, wet boot came crashing down practically in his lap. I started giggling, but before either of us could say anything the wind deposited another boot and a bunch of muddy water at his feet. My ministry partner and I were now laughing in earnest while Kamau grinned, incredulous. We teased him that he had asked, and so he had received—straight from heaven. He took it all good-naturedly. He didn't keep the boots, but neither did he pester me again.

Which is probably why, on the last day before my flight back home, he looked so surprised and delighted when I handed him my shoes. The humbling part was how long it had taken me to do so. . . .

Matthew 7:7; Luke 6:30-36

Standing Still

I've found that living in another culture can seem surreal at first—and it can become even *more* surreal the longer you stay. This was the case for me while I was a student in Kenya. At first each day seemed like a year: I could've written a novel about the events that happened before lunch. Then periodically it felt like time had stopped altogether. It was as if someone had left the camera shutter open and I was frozen in one spot, aware of every tiny perception. Was God trying to get my attention?

I am a Kenyan now, or so my Kenyan friends tell me. The days are no longer like years, though at times I find that the clock has stopped and the whole earth is standing still—like when I was sitting on a bed in the little hut in the slum near our mission, staring at the spider on the beam above me and wondering how both of us got there. How did this little girl, who waded in the shallows of a pristine lake in northern Michigan, who sketched her imaginative worlds onto sheets of scrap paper and read *Little House on the Prairie* and spent hours swinging under the maple tree at her grandparents' house. . . . How did she get *here*? How did she end up in this smoke-clogged city; this urban youth culture that is neither anarchy nor prison; these big, wide-open, empty grasslands; this tiny closet of a house that one poor family calls home—which has just enough standing room to decide whether you'll sit on the bed by your right knee or the one by your left . . . ?

As I said, the days are no longer like years, though periodically they freeze into moments of timelessness. Yesterday I was sitting in a café in downtown Nairobi with my crazy American friends and an East African percussion group—an outrageously hilarious bunch—and I sat there in the midst of their loud slang, their overpowering Africanness, staring at the tea on the table, thinking, *This moment is exactly frozen somehow, like northern ice. Right now the sun is standing still, and I am in Africa.*

But the moment jumped forward into the next and the next, and sooner or later it became today, and now I sit in the dining hall on the Athi River campus,// watching high clouds create patches of blue and purple on the distant Ngong Hills. There is rain to the south, toward Tanzania, probably a hundred miles away. Mount Kilimanjaro is lost in haze. And somehow I am still me, and God is still God, and even after I return home this moment will remain for him the eternal *now*.

James 4:13-17

// The college I attended had a city campus as well as a rural campus in the grasslands near the Athi River, roughly one hour from Nairobi.

Ugly Ducklings

During my semester in Kenya, I tasted many moments of loneliness, moments of feeling like I didn't belong. Here's an excerpt from my journal during one of those times:

> "We read to know we are not alone."
> From the movie *Shadowlands*

How often I have wanted to curl up with a book here when I've felt most alone! When this African world has so misunderstood me, this ugly, sunburned duckling just wants to hide under a blanket with a book and try to find any other ugly ducklings that might be out there. But for weeks I haven't had a spare moment to do my laundry, let alone read—besides which, there doesn't seem to be a literary work in sight.

A while back someone loaned me a copy of Catherine Marshall's *Christy*, and by some coincidence I caught a stomach virus at the same time and was able to finish the novel in four hours. If only I had dragged it out! Little did I know there wasn't another novel to be found within several square miles. We read to know we're not alone, but if there's nothing to read, we are of all people the loneliest. (It occurs to me that I've just had a taste of what the illiterate must feel like: isolated, cut off from the past, exiled from human fellowship. . . .)

So, lacking any other books, I open Scripture day after day— and lo! here are the ugly ducklings! Except they're not ducklings but gorgeous swans: queens and kings and prophets and evangelists, majestic people of God who rose beautiful and strong out of the waters of grace. Here are the misunderstood outsiders who knew what it was like to be far from home among a strange people. They knew what it was like to be cut off from fellowship with their own kind, and yet they clung to their citizenship in God's heavenly Kingdom anyway. Perhaps that's why the simplest of all creeds, the Apostles' Creed, states that we believe in the "communion of saints"—which is another way of saying we are not alone.

In Christ there are no ugly ducklings.

Jude 1:24-25

Talk Like a Pirate?

Back at the beginning of this devotional (see January 2), I promised I wouldn't forget today's holiday, which is International Talk Like a Pirate Day. At the time I wasn't thinking to myself, *Now, Sarah, what devotional material could you possibly draw out of an obscure holiday like that?* I was simply thinking, *See, I mentioned pirates. I'm cool. I'm a cool devotional writer.*

Right. Now I'm stuck. First, pirates aren't mentioned in the Bible, as far as I can tell, though there are various storms at sea and even shipwrecks, as well as the not-so-subtle commandment "Thou shalt not steal." Second, I can't find any spiritual value in wearing a do-rag on one's head and walking around saying, "Aye, matey"—as much as I love Jack Sparrow and Long John Silver and every other storybook pirate out there. Third, the whole "international" part trips me up. I hate to break it to the folks who initiated this holiday, but no one talked like a pirate when I was an exchange student in Africa (except maybe the people who *were* pirates, in the modern-day sense). My Kenyan friends would've thought I was an odd duck indeed if I had walked around with a patch over my eye, growling, "Argh!" And I, for my part, would have thought they'd taken their obsession with American culture a bit too far if they'd done the same. Life on the streets of Nairobi was weird enough already.

All the same, there's a kind of quirky, creative silliness to the whole holiday that I find appealing. Sometimes I think the world takes itself far too seriously. As children we're allowed to dream and play and invent things; but as grown-ups we're expected to outgrow all that. We're not supposed to play dress up anymore or read children's books or be silly. We're supposed to say the right things and act appropriately and eat dinner with the proper silverware and generally be stuffy and boring.

It's the same expectation the Pharisees had when they questioned Jesus about his disciples' behavior. "Why don't they fast like they're supposed to?" and "How dare they pick grain on the Sabbath!" (see today's text). And I imagine Jesus growling back at them—"Argh!"—and laughing, but then growing serious again. "Do wedding guests fast while celebrating with the groom? Of course not" (Mark 2:19).

So when Jesus is in your life, it's okay to play, to put away the long face, to ignore all those stuffy grown-up rules. The trick is knowing when it's time to get serious again.

Mark 2:18-28

Called You by Name

My first home-cooked African meal was with a young Kenyan couple who were expecting their first child while attending seminary in the United States. They invited several of us who were preparing to leave for Kenya to join them for dinner so we could become acquainted with African customs. As the conversation flowed, we talked about our backgrounds and our families, and eventually the husband asked if I had any siblings.

"Yes," I replied. "I have a younger sister named Abigail."

"Ah," he said, glancing at his pregnant wife with a knowing smile. "Sarah and Abigail. Your parents want you to marry great men."

It took me a moment, but then I realized what he was talking about. He meant the biblical women Sarah and Abigail, who married Abraham, the father of the Jewish people, and King David, respectively. I knew my parents had chosen biblical names for us on purpose, because they wanted to connect us with our spiritual heritage. But I hadn't thought about it in quite that way before. Yes, they wanted us to marry great men—in fact, they'd been praying for our future spouses since before we were born. But first they wanted us to be great women.

"I have called you by name; you are mine," says Isaiah 43:1. At my baptism, the pastor dipped his hand into the water, placed it on my forehead, and called me by name. The sacrament was an "outward expression of an inward grace" that Jesus had claimed me, that my name meant something to him, that I belonged to him no matter whom I married (or not) or how my last name changed or what else happened in my life. When years later I went through confirmation and claimed these promises for myself, my parents gave me a necklace with those very words from Isaiah inscribed on it. No matter whom I spent the rest of my life with, I was God's first.

The funny thing is, in the intervening years since my mealtime conversation with the African couple, my sister and I *have* married great men. We married a Philip and a Thomas, respectively, both named for biblical characters. Both named for disciples, in fact. Followers of Jesus, then and now.

Isaiah 43:1-4

Only One You

Chapel attendance was required at my college, so three days a week the student body would troop into the sanctuary for worship. Usually our seat assignments were determined by some aspect of our student profile—such as street number or home zip code or academic major—and the seating changed each semester. Once it was by first name. There were at least five rows of Sarahs, and my row alone was Sarah *Elizabeth*(!). And here we were, trying to be so unique during our college years, trying to forge our own identities and make our special way in the world. . . . Talk about depressing. But it sure was fun to lean over the balcony and call out, "Hey, Dave!" or "Hey, Chris!" and watch all seven rows of guys turn and look.

Meanwhile, there in the Cs, sitting pretty between the Chelseas and the Chrises, was my roommate, Chloe—the *only* Chloe. Finally, all those years of helping people spell or pronounce her name had paid off. Of course her days as the only Chloe were probably numbered, considering that her name has become one of the most popular for baby girls in the past few years. But for at least one semester she could bask in her uncontested Chloe-ness, knowing that if one of those thirty-seven Sarahs happened to lean over the balcony and holler her name, there was no one but herself to respond.

You may be like Chloe and have an utterly unique name, or you may be like me and share a name with half the building. Whatever the case, there's only one *you* in the universe, only one you in the history of this world. And God knows you by name, knows you inside out, knows the number of hairs on your head.

So when God leans over the balcony of heaven and calls you by name, do you respond?

Luke 12:6-7

Thanks to Frodo?

"I know who your wife is," my husband was told by a classmate one day.

"Oh," Tom said. "Who is she?"

"She's that author who wrote a book about *The Lord of the Rings*. I used to work at a Christian bookstore, so I know these things."

Most of the time I live in relative obscurity, but now and then, for five minutes or so, I'm famous. And occasionally I'm considered an expert. I get random requests for radio interviews or speaking engagements, and I'm expected to know all things Tolkien on the spot. The truth is, I love Middle-earth, but I don't live there. I can answer basic questions and even occasional trivia, but I don't spend my days memorizing the list of kings from the line of Gondor. However, I'm Tolkien savvy enough to know that today, September 22, is the birthday of his two most important characters, Bilbo and Frodo Baggins, whose stories are remembered annually on Hobbit Day."

In true Hobbit fashion, we should offer a toast in honor of these two noble characters: one who unknowingly found the Ring of Power that could enslave Middle-earth and the other who knowingly destroyed it. Their stories have become so entwined with my life as a writer that I can hardly imagine doing what I do without them. In fact, when asked by a news reporter in my hometown why my first book had been so successful, I cheerfully stated, "It's all thanks to Frodo."

And he quoted me. Verbatim. Instead of all the brilliant things I *did* say, he printed *that*. Whatever possessed me to say such a thing? Why didn't I take the opportunity to give credit where credit is due—to the One who gave me great literature to enjoy and hands to write with and a supportive family and a brain? Godless celebrities can stand up in front of millions of viewers and thank Jesus for giving them a Golden Globe or whatever, and I go and thank *Frodo*?

Okay, breathe. My point is, we're shaped by the stories we read, for better or worse, and in my case, it's been for the better. I am grateful for authors like Tolkien and for the stories that have inspired what I do as a writer. I don't know who has inspired what you do in your life, but I've discovered that it's okay to celebrate these people and thank God for their lives. Even the fictional ones like Frodo.

2 Thessalonians 1:11-12

// I don't remember this holiday being celebrated in Kenya either! (See September 19.)

Looking Back

I didn't always know I'd become a writer like I am now. In the fall several years ago, while I was still a full-time youth worker in a local church, I began to sense that God had other plans for my life. But at first I had no clear sense of vocational direction, so I took a personal retreat to begin pondering and praying. Here are some of my thoughts from that time:

> I've spread out my blanket on the lawn of this, my alma mater, next to the sidewalk along which I tromped for four years to class thinking, *How did I come to be here? Where am I headed now?* I pondered these things as I marched along this very same sidewalk at a fast clip sometime during my junior year, a bitter wind sending leaves skipping across the green . . . and now here I sit years later, stretched out on a blanket that is one of many Tom and I have collected in our marriage. I sit soaking up the sun of this fall day, surrounded by blooming things, blue sky overhead, a lovely wind rustling the leaves in the trees.
>
> So why my former college for a personal retreat? Because—as I realized yesterday afternoon while standing in front of the chapel cross—I was given so much here. I was given a faith of my own, rock solid and deep rooted, which can never be taken away from me. I was given friends for life who call Christ *Lord*. I was given healthy Christian adults to model my life after, as well as accountable Christian community to soak my soul in. I was given my spouse here, my life's companion. I was given the very soul of myself in practically every aspect of who I am: faith, fellowship, family.
>
> The one thing I'm still seeking, however—which my undergraduate education gave me in part but without full clarity—is a calling. That's why I'm here this week. For several years now I've served in a vocation that has been a profound and painful challenge, one in which I have felt God's hand, but not necessarily his lifelong call. I'm much more settled in my hometown, in my local church, than I used to be, and I'm certain that God has amazing things in store for this congregation. But I'm lost as to what God wants for me. I've reached the point of ennui. I'm resigned to just "live with it," which I know is not a characteristic of Christ's Kingdom, nor of his people, who are empowered by his Holy Spirit to be salt and light.

Lord, show me how you want me to be obedient to you and what you want me to do. I know you can make a way. Help me to be open to what that is, and grant me the willingness to do it. Amen.

Psalm 139:1-12

Time Is Fleeting

I think God gives us childhood dreams and desires for a reason. For example, I was "writing" before I knew how to form the letters of the alphabet. My parents would give me a pad of lined paper, and I'd fill it with squiggles and loops that looked like cursive. Then, once I *could* write, I'd fashion little chapter books complete with titles, illustrations, copyright pages, and disclaimers.// Years later, as I was in the midst of a vocational transition away from full-time ministry, I remembered those childhood impulses and realized, "Hey, they haven't left me. Is this a hint?" Here are some further reflections from my devotional journal at the time:

> I've been having fleeting thoughts lately about my lifetime goals, namely my goal to be a published author. I can't help wondering with a vague feeling of panic if my dream is slipping further away with every year. And yet at the moment I don't feel like I have anything significant to contribute to the publishing world—aren't there millions of books already? Hasn't everything been said that could possibly be said? But then I wonder if the publishing part even matters. I mean, if I'm committed to writing, shouldn't I be writing anyway, whether or not I'm published? And of course then I wonder, whatever happened to writing just for fun, just to tell a good story or to play around with words . . . ?
>
> O Lord, if your purpose for my life involves writing, then pursue me, drive me, fill my imagination—and give me the self-forgetfulness to accomplish it with delight and effortlessness. For I've begun to wonder how long my husband and I will remain childless in this house, our evenings filled with hours of silence in which to write. Many authors would give anything for such peace and solitude, and here I am squandering it by playing on the computer, reading the newspaper, doing chores! These all have their time and place, but in looking back on these years, what will I wish I had done instead?

I look back on those words and can hardly believe where God has taken me since then. Time is fleeting, but from God's perspective, it's never completely lost. Someday, looking back over your years, what will *you* wish you'd done?

Psalm 139:13-18

// The most notable of these disclaimers read, "My name is Sarah Faulman [my maiden name]. I'm in the third grade. I write books but never finish them." Thankfully this wasn't a self-fulfilling prophecy! (Though my editors *do* get nervous sometimes. . . .)

The Fog of Not Knowing

Eventually it became clear that I couldn't continue in my job as a youth director, as much as I loved my church and the youth. All I knew was that God didn't want me to be a youth director anymore—plus, I was completely burned out. I needed a break. I needed Sabbath rest, a sabbatical. My husband and I decided I would "retire" at the end of the school year and then take six months off from any kind of work, other than the occasional writing assignment from a publisher I'd started freelancing for. I'd simply rest. I'd wake up in the mornings with no clear notion of how I'd spend the day, other than to play and write for fun and work in the garden and give myself permission to not be needed for once. It was a magic time, one of the best gifts my husband ever gave me.

But we knew those six months couldn't last forever. We knew I needed to start working full-time again at the beginning of the new year. The question was, doing what? My friends would ask me, "What will you do next?" and I'd say, "I have no idea. Scoop ice cream, maybe. Whatever God wants." Meanwhile, instead of making me feel like a failure, my wise parents would say reassuring things like, "Sometimes God calls us *away* from something before he calls us *to* something else. And that's okay."

Yet even as I played and prayed and wandered through the nearby river valley during that glorious fall, in the back of my mind was the quiet but persistent idea that my future involved writing. Already I was getting enough assignments to keep up a steady part-time job, but write full-time? *Yes*, my spirit whispered. *Please, God, please.*

And here I am. Less than a month into that new year I landed my first book contract and was off and running with a full-time writing career. And even though it hasn't always been easy, it's clearly the vocation God has for me. But my first step was obedience. I had to walk for a while in the fog of not knowing, before the mists lifted and I could discern where God's path was taking me. I had learned what the seventeenth-century French priest François Fénelon understood: "There is only one way to love God: to take not a single step without him, and to follow with a brave heart wherever he leads."

When have you been in a fog of not knowing? What happened to your faith during that time?

Psalm 37:23-40

The Sound of Panic

What do I hear this morning? The sound of panic, like a trapped bird flinging itself against the walls, beating its wings in blind terror. Whenever I've put off the work needed to complete a deadline, I feel that panic rising. I can hear nothing but the shuddering wings, even though the dawn is lovely, clear, and sunny, and I am beloved of my husband, and all my other work is done. But lurking in the background is the fluttering, beating, rising sense that I am very late, very behind. The beast of my own procrastination prowls near.

And yet today I can silence the frightened bird, send away the beast, remember to be still and know that God is indeed God. It is not I but he who will complete this work, who will provide the words, the inspiration, the stories, the connections. It is his creative Spirit at work in me, and thus it is his work, his manuscript, his deadline. I arise and do my part as his hands at the keyboard.

O Lord, quiet my thundering heart. Give me the inner silence that pours forth from your throne—that glorious, insistent, pressing, covering, filling, lifting, settling, summoning, waking, wonderful silence. Oh, for a world without the noise of fear or ambition or hurry or anxiety or self-assured pomposity! A world? Rather, a heart! Silent as the throne of heaven, deep and still as a mountain pool in the dead of night, calm enough to reflect the moon, the stars, the wheeling constellations, the depth and stillness of space. . . . Help me to move in the unhurried, deliberate, noble dance of the stars, according to your design. The heavens are never rushed. Neither shall my soul be. Amen.

Luke 12:22-26

Keeping in Step

I confess this morning to weak faith and small-mindedness and a recent return to that state
in which I'm determined to do everything in my own power: Forget what God wants—
I don't care. While these changes (from reliance, humility, and spiritual sensitivity to downright disobedience) have been subtle, I know from experience that they lead to wretched
results in the long run if I don't give in to God's desires. It's the difference between keeping
"in step with the Spirit," as it says in Galatians (NIV), or being half a measure off.

I picture a marching band making its way down the street during a parade followed
by the fire engines and Girl Scout troops and a host of floats. For the individual band
members, keeping in step with the drum major and other band members is the sole
concern of the moment. Left . . . left . . . left, right, left. One foot in front of the other at
the same measured pace as your neighbor, or disaster awaits. Half a step off is still out of
step. And if you're out of step, it's worse for everyone than if you're not marching at all. It
throws off the entire formation. I suppose the only thing even worse would be coming to
a complete standstill and causing the whole parade to shudder to a halt as a result of your
insolence.

So I have a choice. I can keep in step with the Spirit and stay in formation with my
fellow believers, or if I'm unwilling to do that, I'd better do the honest thing and step out
of the parade altogether. None of this "marching to the beat of a different drummer" business, in the human sense. Without the Holy Spirit, my drummer is nothing more than the
beat of my self-centered heart.

Galatians 5:16-25

Current

People are always telling me, "You're so full of energy! You're doing such great stuff for God!" And it makes me think of a gerbil running maniacally on a little wheel, or an electrical current zipping around and around. I sometimes wonder if we keep busy with the quasi-spiritual stuff so we don't have to do the really difficult things God is calling us to. What? Help the poor? Sorry, no time. Too busy . . .

The current in me
is strong enough

to power a small life.
See: I zip around

my daily loops
with potential to shock

to make fingers tingle
and hair stand on end.

But if you were to
shut off
my circuit

unscrew the box,
take both ends
of my wires

and scrutinize,
you would find
I only follow

the path of least resistance.

Luke 18:18-23

Don't Give Me More to Do

Lately I've been reading an annotated version of the Bible that has all kinds of suggestions in the margins for ways I can grow in my spiritual life. Most of them involve doing, doing, doing, as if we can't mature spiritually unless we fill every spare minute with activity. After a while, it gets pretty ridiculous. Do I really have the time to paint on a stone or draw chalk pictures on the sidewalk or write a letter to my congressperson? I mean, I barely have the chance to brush my teeth, for crying out loud! Can I possibly add one more thing to my list of stuff to *do*? And besides, if I take extra time to do anything, hadn't it better be on behalf of the poor?

So if I were to send a letter to whoever is writing the next devotional resource I'll read, here's what I'd say:

Dear Devotional Book People,

Please, I beg you—do not give me more things to *do*, such as draw pictures or make lists or write letters. Instead, give me quotes from the saints and classics; give me metaphors to hang my hat on; give me stories to live inside of, to draw my own conclusions from. Give me the great prayers of the Church throughout history. Summarize the lives of the martyrs and prophets. Introduce me to my brothers and sisters in Christ around the world and to those who have gone before me. Help me to seek first the Kingdom. And if you must give me something to *do*, make it specific prayer suggestions that have significant depth, that challenge me in what is perhaps the greatest challenge of any Christian anywhere: to move from comfortable study of the Word to uncomfortable communion with the One who made it.

Sincerely,

Devotional Book Reader

(Now, if only I would follow my own advice!)

Luke 12:27-32

How We Spend Our Days

A dear friend of mine once gave me a card with a quote by Annie Dillard that says, "How we spend our days is, of course, how we spend our lives."[45] It immediately made me stop and ponder: How was I spending my days? Was I spending each day focused on Kingdom values that make a long-term difference in this world, or was I frittering each day away on short-term crises, escapist entertainment, and materialistic impulses? A good question for all of us. If I've spent most of every day on a cell phone, for instance, then that's how I will have spent my entire life. My obituary, if it's honest, would read, "She gave her life to Cingular." Is that how I want to be remembered?

Another quote—this time from the eighteenth-century preacher John Wesley—gets at this same issue. "Do nothing on which you cannot pray for a blessing. . . . It becomes not a Christian to do anything so trivial, that he cannot pray over it."[46] Elsewhere he wrote, "Whether you like it or no, read and pray daily. It is for your life; there is no other way: else you will be a trifler all your days."[47] I like that word, *trifler*. It captures so much of what I see in popular culture. I sit at the hairdresser's, having forgotten to bring a decent book, so I flip through a women's magazine in which the ads and articles are about such trivial, fleeting issues that I can hardly keep from rolling my eyes. A cute handbag here, a smart pair of shoes there, and pretty soon we have trifling down to a science. Because how we spend our money is, of course, how we spend our days. And how we spend our days . . . well you get the picture.

But who am I to judge—me with my nose in a magazine with contents I'd be ashamed to pray about?

Ecclesiastes 11:7–12:1

Honoring Those Who Minister

October is Pastor Appreciation Month, which is of special importance to me because my dad is a pastor and my husband is in seminary to become ordained. So whenever people honor pastors for all their incredible hard work, they're in a way honoring the two most beloved men in my life.

And being in ministry *is* hard work—try job-shadowing a pastor sometime. He's expected to wear a dozen different hats at least: therapist, CEO, financial consultant, psychic, theologian, secretary, emergency first responder, inspirational speaker, van driver, stage manager, biblical scholar, public relations specialist . . . oh, and janitor. I remember the year my Brownie troop leader called our house at the last minute on a Wednesday afternoon and asked if my dad would play Santa at our Christmas party that night. My dad was blitzing off to yet another meeting, so my mom said something like, "Are you crazy?" (though I'm sure she said it nicely). And the lady said, "What—doesn't he only work on Sundays?"

Yeah.

So anyway, October seems like a good month to reflect on what it means to be in ministry—since we're all called to minister to a hurting world, though not all of us are called to be pastors. But I also want to reflect on the Church in general. What does it mean to be part of this thing called the body of Christ? What does it look like? Is Christian community limited to church on Sundays, or is God up to something more radical and life transforming than that?

Stay tuned. Oh, and while we're at it, make sure to send your pastor a card of appreciation sometime this month. . . .

Hebrews 13:7, 17

The Big C

I don't know about you, but my family has always been really involved in church. As I've said before, I'm the daughter of a minister, and I'm married to a guy who is planning to be a pastor when this whole grad school adventure is over. That's why we moved away from our hometown to a big university, and now we're in a strange sort of in-between place when it comes to a place of worship. We attend a small local church when we can, but we also visit other churches sometimes and travel back home occasionally—back to our "home church."

So my center of gravity is constantly shifting. I know church is important to my spiritual journey because that's where I encounter those mentors and heroes I mention now and then. That's where I find the people who've been on this trail for a while. The longer I spend with them as my guides, the more I learn. But I'm beginning to wonder what effect this constant church shifting will have on my spiritual life over time. Know what I mean? Has this ever happened to you?

When life is a little crazy and a spiritual home base seems hard to hold on to, it's helpful to consider what is meant by the word *church*. There are two meanings, and both are right. One is church with a little *c*, the local congregation that I consider my spiritual home. It has a specific location—usually a brick-and-mortar building somewhere—and exists within a specific period of time. But this church is more than a building; it's also a network of people who consider each other family and work to make positive changes in the local community. (Or that's what it's supposed to be, anyway. I'm sure we could trade stories about how often local congregations are just the opposite of that.)

Meanwhile, over and above the local church is the Church with a big *C*, the community of Christian believers throughout all time and history, all over the world. Every person who claims Jesus Christ as Lord belongs to the Church with a big *C*.//

I take comfort in knowing that that no matter how crazy life gets, no matter how often we move or how messed up my local church is sometimes, I'm part of a larger Church of believers that's timeless and unchanging, scattered throughout the entire world from age to age.

Ephesians 1:19-23

// According to most Protestants anyway. Many Catholics have a different spin on things.

Distractions

Some visitors were in church this morning. They came from a local nursing home for folks with mental disabilities. Just as the worship service started, the side door next to the pulpit opened, and they shuffled in with their chaperones to the front pew. A woman in a wheelchair was pushed to the middle of the aisle, right in front of the pulpit.

This kind of thing could've been pretty awkward. The visitors definitely didn't fit in. They weren't polished or well dressed, and they didn't always follow the liturgy. Sometimes they spoke out loud when they weren't supposed to; other times they seemed mostly asleep. When the choir stood up to sing, the woman in the wheelchair became very expressive, wildly bobbing her head and clapping off the beat and waving her arms around. She was even trying to sing along, which almost threw the choir off when they paused before the final note and her voice wailed awkwardly into the brief silence.

For some churches, this would not have gone over well. The choir director could have pinched his lips shut in frustration, thinking the song was ruined. The kids in the pews could've snorted with laughter and embarrassment. The ushers could've gritted their teeth, wishing they'd had the presence of mind to seat the visitors in the back. After all, when we worship we're supposed to concentrate on God, not be distracted by other people in the pews, right? But my church didn't seem to care.

It may sound weird, but I'm not sure "no distractions" is really the point of worship in church anyway. Otherwise, why get together with dozens or even hundreds of other people if we're supposed to concentrate so totally on God that, as the old hymn says, "the things of earth . . . grow strangely dim"? Certainly during our private times of prayer and reading and solitude we need to tune out everything and concentrate solely on God. But when the body of Christ, the church, gets together, something else is going on. There's a reason I can hear the wobbly voice of the woman singing behind me, the one who always sings a bit flat and nasally. There's a reason I can smell coffee on the breath of the old man who shakes my hand in greeting. There's something unique God wants me to experience when the mentally disabled woman in the wheelchair wails into the pause before the final note of the choir's well-rehearsed song, when I'm completely and utterly distracted.

Maybe worship is about being distracted out of ourselves for once. Maybe it's about looking up, looking around at the faces near us. Maybe it's about seeing the world in clearer focus—the people Jesus loves and died for, the body of Christ in the middle of the aisle, bobbing and clapping off beat.

1 Corinthians 12:12, 18-27

Seeking the Doctor

The main employer in my former hometown was the regional hospital, which meant we had more doctors per capita than squirrels. Our town was crawling with surgeons, nurses, physicians, anesthesiologists, radiologists, and specialists of all kinds. You ran into them at soccer games, in the grocery store, on the ski slopes, in church on a Sunday morning.

And yet for all their knowledge and skill, they weren't able to keep our churches from being places where people were hurting—spiritually, emotionally, and even physically. Sometimes our sanctuary felt more like an emergency room than a house of worship, and this was especially true during the sharing of joys and concerns. "Please pray for my neighbor's daughter, who ran away from home." "Please pray for my uncle, who has cancer." "Please pray for me: I just found out my job is being terminated." Please pray, pray, pray.

One Sunday, after a morning filled with many such requests and alarms, tears and trepidations, I wrote this prayer:

O Great Physician,
only you can search the depths
of the hurting.
My wisdom fails.
I don't know how to help
my friends,
this church,
this town,
myself.
We drag the past around
like a bum leg,
limping,
reminded with every movement
of the pain that never goes away.
In a city of physicians,
we are dying.
Our unhealed souls
yearn for you
to take your rightful place
behind the clipboard and ask,
"Are you not well?"
and for us to finally admit, with relief,
"We are unwell. Heal us."

Mark 2:13-17

Cartload of Souls

On October 4, I wrote about my former hometown, a place full of physicians but also full of the spiritually hurting. I was the youth director at my local church there for almost seven years, and sometimes it felt like a search-and-rescue mission: The main task was to search the front lines of spiritual battle for signs of wounded survivors. My students were under fire from all sides: families falling apart, friendships leading them astray, addictions holding them hostage to so-called pleasures that had long since ceased to be pleasurable. And in the midst of it all were my own spiritual wounds, running deep in the tissue of my past. How could I possibly help others if I, too, was hurting? I couldn't. All I could do was carry the people I could to the only One who can truly help.

So here's part 2 of the prayer-poem from October 4:

Limping myself, I come
with my cartload of souls
and lay them at your feet.
They lie there crumpled
at the foot of your throne of grace,
beneath your throne of mercy.
These wounded ones
are within your reach, O Lord;
and so I beg you:
Heal these children.
Draw them to you in a way
so attractive, so unavoidable,
so heart-wrenchingly beautiful
that they can hardly dare to turn away.
Tame their rebelliousness,
their strong-spirited, free-willed souls.
Blast through their apathy,
astonish them out of their boredom,
shock them out of their self-centeredness.

And do the same for me.

Jeremiah 3:21-22

Shaking the Dust from My Sandals

Sometimes serving in church leadership (say, on a mission trip) can be exhausting and even infuriating. People are opinionated. They don't want to follow. They'd rather stick to their old ways, even if those ways aren't biblical or even remotely healthy. They resist your work every step of the way. You wake up each morning bracing yourself for the next conflict, even as you battle bitterness from the last confrontation. And yet somehow all that cumulative anger must be dealt with in your heart, or it will sabotage your ministry. I wrote this prayer after several months of frustration with my job as a youth worker in a local church:

I wake so often with
the deep fog of this ministry
already descending
upon my tired mind. I'm lost
in a swirl of activities and programs
and promises and failed opportunities
and wandering people.
I am wounded.
I am angry—still.
Advent on the far-distant horizon,
and yet I'm still nursing
the old life,
rejecting your healing,
hardening my heart
against the people and situations that hurt,
giving in to the lies
that I have failed,
that I have no future here.
And what am I waiting for?
Waiting for the day
when I can shake the dust
of this town from my sandals, I suppose.
But you won't let me.

I hurt. And yet
I know you've taken care of it.

Help me to let go.

Luke 9:1-6

Broken Vessels

By now you've picked up on a major theme in my life, which is that it's not always easy or delightful to serve in ministry. In fact, it's really, really tough most of the time. The tasks of ministry often push you to do things you'd rather not do, such as talk to a homeless person who smells like urine and cheap liquor or counsel a friend who is so self-obsessed she can't even hear what you're saying—and most of the time you're not even qualified for any of this anyway. Not to mention it's often a thankless job in which you hear more complaints than kudos about the work you're doing. (I can just hear the blind man telling Jesus, "Could you use lotion or something? Your fingers are kinda rough on the eyelids.")

And in the midst of all this, we find ourselves drying up spiritually because we're not replenishing our spirits from the well of living water, Jesus himself (see John 4:4-14). I began reflecting on this the other day in terms of how God uses us to pour life into a hurting world, and it hit me that it's not *our* lives that we're pouring out. Our own lives dry up eventually, which means we must become vessels for *God's* life to pour through us. Otherwise we have nothing to offer the world.

So here's my prayer:

*Trickle your Spirit
through the cracks of our lives
until these broken vessels
can sustain the pressure
of your presence
no longer
but burst into wells of
healing and joy
—into springs from which
the Spirit pours
unlimited.*

2 Corinthians 4:5-7

The Missing Piece

Okay, this may sound ridiculous, but I have this thing about the last bite of dessert.

Seriously. Without looking at my plate, I can tell you how much pie or cake or ice cream I have left, especially if it's only one bite. If I'm at a party and I put my unfinished plate down somewhere, I'll hunt until I find it. And if someone throws it away or eats the rest without asking? I'm thrown completely off-kilter. I'll roam around looking for it, simply *positive* I had one last bite left. Granted, most of the time I'm totally unaware that I'm even doing this. If you sit next to me at dinner, you won't hear me muttering, "Three down, two to go," nor will you run into me at a party only to have me ask, "Hey, have you seen my plate? I swear I had one last cookie on there." But in the back of my mind I'm doing the math.

The funny thing is, I also have a bad habit of wandering around the house while I munch on stuff and then leaving the food on the dresser or the counter while I do something else. Usually I come back to it, but one time my husband found what looked like cat poop on a storage bin only to realize it was an unfinished Tootsie Roll. Is that gross or what? When he confronted me about it (laughing), I was amazed. How could I have misplaced or forgotten something so important? What happened to my interior calculator that I didn't notice the missing piece of chocolate and go looking for it? How could I have forsaken that last bite?

This is all in fun, of course, but it brings up a simple point. If I—a simple, selfish little human being—can be that diligent about a treasured bite of food, it's no big stretch to think of God's diligence in keeping track of each precious person on this planet. God knows how many children are starving in sweltering Saharan refugee camps. He knows the number of hairs on the head of each migrant worker in the fields of California. He keeps count of the elderly folks forgotten in the ghettos of America's cities. He never, ever loses track.

So what if I became that diligent about seeking the forgotten of this world?

Luke 15:8-10

No Place Is Godforsaken

After church a few months ago, a young couple invited everyone to their house for lunch and an informational session about a new ministry. So Tom and I went. We drove five blocks from church into the rough part of town, where almost half the homes are boarded up or condemned and many residents live in bondage to addiction and prostitution. It's also where the graceful old porches and tall shade trees speak of happier times, both in the past and—by God's grace—in the future.

This is what our friends hope, anyway. They recently bought a large old home on a relatively quiet street. They envision the healing of old wounds in that neighborhood—wounds caused by racism, by negligent stewardship of the land and its resources, by addiction and hopelessness and all the things that keep people in bondage. It has nothing to do with gentrification, which entails fixing up old neighborhoods until the former residents can no longer afford to live there. Rather, this vision is for relocation (following Jesus into the abandoned places of this world and making a home there), reconciliation (between humans and God, between people and races), and redistribution (of resources, so that there may be "no needy people among them" [Acts 4:32-35]).

So they've established their house as a place of intentional Christian community and hospitality. The Christians who join them commit to live in fellowship with one another—sharing communal meals, household responsibilities, and worship—as well as welcome those who are temporarily homeless. But why the ghetto? Why not do this in a safer place? Because they believe, as one of our favorite teachers has said, that *no* place is Godforsaken.

We believe so too, or we wouldn't be moving in with them this month.

Isaiah 61:1-4; 62:2-4

Intentional Christian Community: Part 1

Have you heard of them? Your parents might have called them "hippies" or "Jesus freaks." Your grandparents probably thought they were communists. A couple of hundred years ago they would have become monks or nuns. Nowadays they're labeled the "new monastics" and are interviewed for Christian magazines like they're some hip new trend. Whatever the case, they're the Christians who have chosen a lifestyle known as "intentional Christian community"—believers living together in the same household, baldly speaking."

It's rather like a fraternity or sorority house, come to think of it. Those are intentional communities, true; but they're not intentional *Christian* communities (with very few exceptions). On the flip side, the houses and apartments I lived in while I was an undergraduate were certainly Christian communities, because we were Christians attending a Christian college, but they weren't necessarily *intentional*. There wasn't a set "rule," or list of spiritual commitments, that we made to one another, such as keeping the Sabbath or joining in daily evening prayer or reaching out to our elderly neighbors. We came close to such a lifestyle sometimes (like the year my roommates and I visited a nursing home on Monday nights), but it was never formalized.

I look back now and it seems something was missing from that experience. It's one thing for Christians to live in the same location, coming and going as they please. It's quite another to commit to living *in certain ways* in the same location: praying and worshipping together, living simply, sharing common resources, serving the poor, seeking unity, obeying one's spiritual leaders, and so on. And yet this was the lifestyle of the first disciples. Sure, they were itinerants with Jesus, taking their "household" on the road, so to speak. They never stayed in one place for very long. But once they committed to following Jesus, he expected them to live as brothers and sisters, as one family.

Though not everyone is called to "intentional Christian community," it's worth asking the question: Why are we so eager to talk about the "family of God" on Sunday morning when we live like strangers the other six days of the week?

Luke 8:1-3, 19-21

// For more information on this and similar Christian movements committed to sustainable living and social justice, visit www.newmonasticism.org, www.catholicworker.org, or www.sojo.net.

Intentional Christian Community: Part 2

This week my husband and I are packing up our worldly goods and moving into an intentional Christian community with some friends from church. Some people might call this kind of lifestyle a new trend, but it's really an ancient concept going back at least as far as Acts 2, if not further. Verses 44-46 give us a glimpse:

> All the believers met together in one place and shared everything they had. They sold their property and possessions and shared the money with those in need. They worshiped together at the Temple each day, met in homes for the Lord's Supper, and shared their meals with great joy and generosity.

This kind of shared living still happens today. At some point a group of Christians may begin to wonder why they live in their separate little worlds when God might be calling them to greater ministry and Christian witness by living in the same household or the same neighborhood. This goes way beyond attending the same church. It means sharing daily life together as a family—preparing and eating communal meals, tag-teaming on household chores, taking turns with the washing machine, worshipping together through morning or evening prayer (or both). And by pooling their resources and living simply, they're able to reach out to the neighborhood, even as they are a powerful example of true Christian unity, through the power of the Holy Spirit.

In theory anyway. I'm about to learn the nitty-gritty details.

If those first Christians from Acts 2 were here, what advice do you think they'd give us?

Acts 2:41-47

Moving Again

As I said earlier, we're moving *again*. This is the fourth move in fourteen months since we started this grad school adventure, more than all the moves in our previous ten years of marriage combined. And I'm beginning to feel it. I'm tired. I'm tired of all our *stuff*, especially. I keep packing up the same books, the same clothes, the same office supplies, the same dishes—and pretty soon I just want to dump it all.

So I've trained myself to pause and think, *Why am I keeping this again?* If I can't come up with a good answer—as in, "I need this for work" (such as my books) or "I need this for survival" (such as the first aid kit)—then it goes. It lands in the pile of giveaways or in the trash or on the curb for recycling, and that's that. End of story. End of my material madness.

But it's not easy, in our consumerist culture, to simplify our lives. We learn at an early age to say, "Mine! Mine! Mine!" like those seagulls in *Finding Nemo*. And even if we eventually reach the point where we desire to live simply, our families and friends inundate us with stuff at birthdays and holidays—because they love us, right? More than half of the things I've been lugging around were given to me—and, quite frankly, this is why I treasure them. I don't have piles of things because I'm a big spender; I have piles because I'm loved.

I'm moving into a communal home where some of my roommates were recently homeless. They struggle to make ends meet. They don't have a lot of stuff of their own—not just because of money problems, but because they don't have the extensive network of loving relationships that I do. So I'm beginning to wonder: Will my piles create an unnecessary rift between us? After all, in many Asian and Eastern countries, simplicity is a sign of holiness. (What must those people think, anyway, when Christian missionaries arrive and build nice houses behind gated communities?) Is it all that different in our country?

What will my roommates think of me?

Matthew 19:16-26

House Rules

Well, we're slowly settling into life at our new community house, which is an exercise in chaos management. For starters, we've downsized during the past year from an entire house to just *one* bedroom with two closets and a bathroom, so I feel like I've been playing Tetris all week, trying to cram everything perfectly into the right slots. Rule #1: Get rid of at least two-thirds of your material possessions if you wish to be taken seriously in this kind of situation. (Or better yet: Get rid of *all* of it, as a certain Rabbi once proposed. . . .)

Second, all three of the guest rooms in the house are now full, which brings the total household population to twelve, including three children under the age of three. Rule #2: Lock the door when you go to the bathroom. (Three-year-olds don't comprehend that closed doors mean "Do Not Enter.")

Third, there's no clothes dryer, so laundry is a major undertaking—especially the fine art of hanging cold, wet sheets on the line without dragging them through the dirt. Rule #3: Use clothespins on pillowcases so they don't end up in your neighbor's yard.

I could go on and on. And of course none of these rules are written down, so I'm learning it all by trial and error. But once I get the rules figured out, life is much saner and I'm able to concentrate on the important things, like listening between the lines to what a single mom is really saying or being available to keep the three-year-old focused so everyone can eat in peace.

The Christian life comes with its own "house rules," many of which are written down ("Give, and you will receive" [Luke 6:38]) and some of which we learn by trial and error along the way. In time, it dawns on us that if we let our personal lives continue in a swirl of chaos where there are no rules, we risk missing out on what God is really up to in the rest of the world. If we're unable to see beyond our own selfish messes and mishaps, how will we ever be able to see Jesus in our midst?

Psalm 119:33-40

Natural Laws

The more I progress in the Christian journey, the more I realize there are certain unchanging spiritual truths, or "natural laws," that operate like gravity on the human spirit. We may push against those laws, particularly since so many of them seem counterintuitive at first, but the longer we're on this road with Christ, the more we realize just how unchanging those laws are. Here are some I've begun to notice lately:

- Obedience is the next step if I'm to make any headway toward growth, health, or transformation. Where are the unresolved sins in my life? I will never move forward spiritually until I deal with them. What broken relationships need to be addressed? I will never have healthy relationships in the future until I deal with the ones I have now. What (imagined) obstacles stand in the way of my obedience? I will never progress in maturity until I address these obstacles one at a time.

- Practicing the spiritual disciples—such as prayer, Bible study, worship, fasting, silence, and solitude—is a must in order to continually experience God's grace and presence. The apostle Paul tells us to "work hard to show the results of your salvation, obeying God with deep reverence and fear" (Philippians 2:12). The spiritual life takes work, period. But that's why these practices are often called the "means of grace"—because this is how God meets with us daily, and we with him.

- Life is precious; relationships are precious; our days are fleeting. Therefore we should never take for granted the gifts of health and wholeness, nor the gift of relationships with the people whose lives intersect ours. An attitude of thanksgiving is the key that unlocks the door to joy in the here and now.

- Pride is the greatest obstacle to all of the above. It stands in the way of obedience, of sticking it out in the spiritual disciplines, and of true gratitude.

What makes us think we can live like Jesus if we don't follow his spiritual rules?

2 Timothy 2:3-7

Not Being the Greatest

Of course one of the first things that rears its ugly head when people live in close proximity is pride. Ah, yes, I'm a bit of a specialist in this area, unfortunately.

My freshman year of college was a shock in the self-esteem department. In high school I had been good at everything: drama, music, art, writing, leadership, you name it. I was constantly winning approval from adults and students alike, earning awards and titles—in short, being recognized. But at my college, *everyone* was incredibly gifted. I remember walking into the student lounge of my freshman dorm one afternoon, and there at the grand piano was a nondescript pre-med student playing Tchaikovsky like a concert pianist. All around me on campus were operatic vocalists, award-winning dramatists, dedicated visual artists, first-rate student teachers. In all the areas I'd previously excelled, there was someone far more talented than I'd ever be. I began to doubt my abilities.

Even in English classes, which I loved, I remember one of our professors telling us, "I know most of you are accustomed to getting straight A's in high school. That's because you were above average there. Well, now that all of you above-average people are together in one place, you're back to being simply *average*. So don't complain to me if you get Cs on your papers—C is *average*, after all. If you want to get a B, you must plan on doing above-average work; and if you want an A, you'd better be some kind of prodigy. Any questions?"

Not a very heartening speech. But it sure made me appreciate those A's when I got them. And as they kept coming, I began to wonder if this was an area I really excelled in after all. Then there were all the extracurricular things that I discovered I really enjoyed, such as gospel choir and intramural Ultimate Frisbee(!). Eventually I learned to play to my strengths. But my sense of identity took a tremendous blow that first year, and it took me two or even three years to recover any fragments of self-worth.

Sometimes I wonder if we're affirmed a bit too often in our youth. Well-meaning parents or teachers praise us for every little thing we do, giving us rewards for mediocre work because they want us to have strong self-esteem. Pretty soon we think we're geniuses at everything. But the truth is, we're not. God has gifted us with many abilities, but only a handful of human beings could ever claim to be the "greatest." The trick is finding the one area where your interests and unique abilities cross paths with God's will for your life. Then when people look at you, they don't think, *She's the greatest*, but *How great God must be!*

Matthew 23:11-12

Because I Said So

Most days I work on my writing projects at the university library, where I can pretty much guarantee I'll find utter silence. Often the person in the seat next to me is collapsed over a laptop, sound asleep—a casualty of one too many late-night study sessions or keg parties. But sometimes I'll end up at a table next to a group that's working on some project or another, talking in whispers regarding a subject I know nothing about.

Take the Math Geeks, for instance. They meet together on Friday mornings and discuss things like integers. One time their voices became really animated, so it was easy for me to overhear their conversation. Apparently two of them were having a disagreement about which theorem they should use to solve a particular problem. One guy insisted on a specific theorem, while another was questioning where he got it.

"But where did you get that?"

"I'm telling you. This is the one we should use."

"Yeah, but which one is it? I mean, who said we should use it?"

"Dude, just trust me."

"I still don't get it."

And so on, until finally the other said in exasperation, "We should just use it, period! It's the Because-I-Said-So Theorem."

Aha. Now we get down to it. Forget the class textbook. Forget what our professor has to say. Forget group protocol. This is what we're doing. *Because I said so.*

How many times have I wanted to say that in my life when it comes to spiritual issues? I may know full well what the Bible has to say about a subject. I may know exactly what Jesus would have me do in this or that situation. I may even be part of a Christian fellowship that has committed to living in a particular way. But if I'm really honest, I'm living by my own rules. I don't really care what other people think. I don't really want to do what God has in mind. I want to make things up as I go along, create my own set of principles and theories to live by. And you better not question me about it, either.

How often do we live according to the Because-I-Said-So Theorem rather than God's way?

Proverbs 21:2-4

Arrogance vs. Self-Confidence

We have this idea from popular culture that Jesus was somehow a wimp. I'm not sure where this comes from—maybe because he was so loving, which some people miscon-strue to mean "pushover." But a close reading of the Gospels gives us a very different picture. No one pushed Jesus around and got away with it (see Luke 11:37-54). In fact, at times Jesus sounded downright arrogant: "Follow me," he said, "Believe in me," "Come to me." And people probably wondered, *Just who does he think he is?*

But there's a great deal of difference between arrogance and self-confidence. Arro-gance is the assumption that you are superior to everyone else—and therefore more valu-able. Arrogant people do not know when they have reached the limit of their abilities. They presume they can handle anything that comes their way, and they don't need anyone else's help, thank you very much.

Self-confidence, on the other hand, is the belief that you are well equipped for the work God has given you to do. It usually develops after your personal strengths and qualities have been tested and refined in the fires of adversity. You succeed at something once, and you're more willing to try it again the next time. The more times you succeed, the more confident you become with yourself. Then you're able—when faced with other, bigger challenges—to discern when you're in over your head, and you have the humility to ask for God's help or to let someone else step forward.

Jesus told his followers, "Let me teach you, because I am humble and gentle" (Matthew 11:29). If we have the same attitude as Christ, we will have self-confidence without the arrogance. And that's not wimpy.

Psalm 138:4-6

Pride Checklist

I was reading a Christian magazine once that provided a checklist for readers to assess whether they were prideful or not. I usually find such quizzes shallow and annoying, but this one hit so close to home that I found myself using it as a kind of prayer of confession. In my journal I wrote:

> Of these things I am guilty, Lord:
>
> - a spotty prayer life (which indicates self-reliance)
> - weariness (which indicates that I'm trying to do more than God intends instead of letting him order my days)
> - anger (which means I'm not letting God be in control of what happens in my relationships)
> - a critical spirit (which indicates that I'm bringing others down in order to lift myself up)
> - a defensive reaction to criticism, despondency after failure, and the inability to laugh at my mistakes (which demonstrates that I take myself too seriously and look upon myself too highly)
> - taking responsibility for success, accomplishment, or financial prosperity (which means I've lost sight of God's gracious and undeserved provision)
> - impatience about having to listen, wait, serve, be anonymous, or be led by someone else (which indicates an overdeveloped sense of importance)
> - when honestly confronted by others, I . . .
>
>   - ✓ flare up
>   -   face it honestly
>   - ✓ lie
>   - ✓ mislead
>   - ✓ try to talk myself out of it
>   - ✓ defend myself
>   - ✓ blow them off
>   - ✓ deny it to myself
>   - ✓ ignore them
>   - ✓ make promises I don't intend to keep

Ouch.

> *Forgive me, Jesus. As John Wesley, said, "Let me be nothing, and Christ be all in all!" Amen.*

Proverbs 11:2; 13:10; 16:18-20

More Than Just "I Know"

At some point during my childhood, Grandma decided to make audiotapes of my sister and me at play. Often we had no idea the cassettes were rolling—Grandma would slip the tape recorder behind the couch or just outside the door, and we'd play contentedly for hours, blissfully unaware.

Well, mostly contentedly. I'm afraid to say that little Abbie, who is three years younger than I am, was often swept along in the drama of my overdeveloped imagination without much say in the matter. Whenever she attempted to assert her independence or change the course of events, her input was immediately dismissed. Here's a typical exchange, now preserved forever for posterity, to my chagrin:

[Sounds of two small girls reenacting the story of Hansel and Gretel. Running footsteps, yelling, and a loud bump.]

Younger Girl: Sarah, you knocked me down.

[Older Girl keeps playing.]

YG [louder]: Sarah, you knocked me DOWN.

[OG plays on, oblivious.]

YG [louder, in stern reproof]: SARAH, you KNOCKED me DOWN.

OG [annoyed]: I *know*.

Yes, you heard me. I said, "I know." No apology. No "Are you okay?" No chastened backtracking. Just "I know," as if my time were being wasted by such trivialities. If apologies are accepted years after the fact, I offer mine now, confessing to Abbie and everyone else that—in all honesty—I'm still an unthinking and self-obsessed little girl most of the time. The only difference is that I've learned to mask my inveterate selfishness by conformity to the general rules of niceness, as has most of so-called "polite" society.

But niceness isn't good enough in the end. Nor is the mere acknowledgment of our actions, as if "I know" were sufficient. No, God calls us to that old-fashioned word *contrition*: deep regret that comes from spiritual self-reflection, which leads to humility and greater awareness. My grandma didn't realize that's what she would eventually bring about by documenting my sins, but I'm grateful for it. It makes me all the more aware of how much I need Jesus to form his character in me—otherwise, how could I possibly love as he loves?

Today is my sister's birthday, and so I shall say, for posterity, "I'm sorry I knocked you down. I love you!"

Isaiah 57:15-21

The Prodigal

Whenever I read the story of the Prodigal Son in Luke 15, I feel a closer connection to the older brother—the one who stayed home and fulfilled his duties, albeit grudgingly—than the younger. I'm the child who does what I'm supposed to even when I find no joy in it. I'm the one who takes pride in my "righteousness" and feels annoyed at any suggestion that I might not have it all together after all. I stick close to the Father, true, but deep down inside, I'd like to think I don't really need him. Sound familiar?

The back screen door
bangs shut and this eldest one
comes into the kitchen,
her hands dirty from the field,
an angry sort of scowl on her face.
The Father is leaning against the counter,
his face calm, expectant, kind.
"Hi," he says, as she begins to wash
her hands in the sink.
"Hi," she says, her face turned away
as she punches soap into her palm
and begins scrubbing.
The water runs into the sink,
clatters down the drain
as she, scowling, tries to keep her composure.
The Father has that sort of
huggable presence about him
that both repels and attracts her
(though she's relieved
he isn't annoying about hugs
as some affectionate people are).
For several moments she keeps scrubbing,
frustrated that her eyes are beginning to brim.
"You'll never get it off," he finally says,
gently—
and she sobs,
"I KNOW!"

Luke 15:11-32

Unplug My Heart

For some reason lately, I don't feel compassion or love for the people around me. It's as if those emotions have been plugged; they've been stopped up and shut off.

I keep wondering why that could be. I mean, I come from a wonderfully loving family—when did I become the Pharisee? What was it that shut up my heart? I know that Jesus has the power to dramatically change my warped perspective about people, but my emotions won't let me *feel* anything—I can't quiet my cynical, hypercritical, analytical mind. I know the Holy Spirit is like a plumber, working on the clogged pipes of my soul, but there is some serious blockage there. There is a part of me that no one touches, no one nears, no one is allowed to intrude upon.

Where did this part of me come from? It wasn't from some past experience or childhood trauma. It wasn't from a rocky relationship that left me wounded. So it must have come from inside me—my fallen state, my inherently crumbled and corrupt spirit. And even though I've been considered something of a melodramatic person for most of my life, I think in the past I allowed my emotions to be expressed only in the world of my imagination. Loving people is so much easier to *imagine* than to *do*: feeding crowds, making children happy, visiting widows, saving the lost, crying over tragedies . . . with none of the endless, endless defeats. My imagined world excluded Jesus because I was capable of making all those things happen myself.

So when I responded to pain in this world, I responded from a Christian worldview but without recognizing my need for the power of Jesus to make my response even possible. But now that I'm experiencing the depth of my inability to love others in real life, I'm keenly aware that a strong imagination and a Christian worldview are not sufficient. I must have Jesus.

In the end, I'm only able to love others if Jesus unplugs my hardened heart and loves others *through* me.

1 Corinthians 13:1-3

Never Wasted

Serving the needy is exhausting. Here I am in a Christian community that's committed to hospitality—to welcoming the stranger, the homeless into our house—and I feel all my energies recklessly expended on daily domestic duties. Wash the dishes, mop the floor, change a diaper, take out the garbage . . . on and on it goes. But somehow I must remember that nothing I do is wasted if it's done for Jesus.

> Lord,
> you are so full of mercy
> that it wells up and overflows
> my heart, spilling into the lives
> of the people I'm here to serve.
>
> It pours out, even when no one
> really notices and this servanthood
> business is all rather thankless
> and the overflow seems a waste.
> Help me to remember the woman
> pouring oil by lamplight
> under the anxious gaze of Judas,
> surrounded by skeptical men
> with raised eyebrows
> and doubting hearts.
> Weeping at your feet,
> she poured out the oil,
> she pulled down her hair
> and dried your sunburned toes.
> And that's when you said
>
> tears of repentance are never wasted
>
> —and neither is the oil of mercy.

Luke 7:36-48; John 12:1-8

Time-Out

> Your people are saying, 'The Lord isn't doing what's right,' but it is they who are not
> doing what's right.
>   Ezekiel 33:17

We've had a lot of time-outs at our community house lately. The resident three-year-old
is still learning that he can't have his own way all the time. No, he *doesn't* get to make a
mess of the board games or throw LEGOs around the living room or eat cake instead of
dinner just because it strikes his fancy to do so. And if he persists, he will get a time-out—
a grown-up will pick him up and plant his little bottom on the chair in the hallway, and he
will sit there for three minutes with nothing to do.

Of course he hates it. He yells and kicks and says the meanest things he can think
of, and meanwhile the grown-up isn't exactly enjoying the experience either. Somehow the
little "bad guy" has turned the tables and made the *grown-up* feel like the big bad guy, as
if this time-out is somehow the grown-up's fault rather than the result of the child's own
behavior. The child sulks and whines, but it's the grown-up who's made to feel like a loser
before it's all over.

I imagine God can relate. All throughout the prophetic books of the Old Testament
(such as Isaiah, Jeremiah, and Ezekiel), God was like the dad giving his children a time-out.
His people kept messing up in big ways by worshipping other gods and oppressing the
poor and generally being stupid. So God stepped in and said, in effect, *That's enough. I'm
fed up with this behavior.* They lost most of their privileges, including their freedom as
a sovereign nation, their house of worship (the Temple in Jerusalem was sacked by their
enemies), their homes and livestock, and much, much more. And yet, even though it was
their own fault, whom did they blame? Yep. They blamed God. They insisted that *he* was
the bad guy—that he'd abandoned them, that he wasn't listening to their cries for help,
that he brought all this injustice upon them.

But if only they had repented and taken responsibility for their own actions, God
said, he would have given them back their freedom.

So. How do you react when God gives you a time-out?

Ezekiel 33:17-20

Divine Discipline

Sins have consequences. We can't ignore God's rules—by lying or shoplifting or sleep-ing around, for example—without feeling the negative ripple effects of those choices for a long, long time. And it doesn't matter whether or not we get caught. Our own characters are maimed for life. This is one of the spiritual realities of the universe, like the law of gravity or the fact that you'll trash your retinas if you stare too long at the sun.

But for Christians, sinning results in more than just natural consequences. We also experience God's intentional discipline. Think of it this way: If a child puts his hand on a hot stove, the parent doesn't need to punish the child in order for the child to learn a lesson. The child will experience the natural consequence of his behavior. But if a teenager deliberately lies to her dad, he will discipline her by removing certain privileges or adding certain responsibilities. Why? Because he loves her. He values their relationship. He wants her to grow up to be a trustworthy person. But most important (if he's a Christian), he wants her life to be a testimony to the rest of the world about the love of Jesus. After all, how will the world know that Jesus is trustworthy if this teenager (who calls herself a Christian) isn't?

So the loving parent disciplines the child, and thus the rest of us learn an important lesson about God's relationship with his children. When we mess up (the operative word being mess), God steps in. He doesn't just let us go on with our sinful behavior, blithely ignoring the ways we destroy our own characters and ruin his reputation in the eyes of the world.

No, God loves us too much for that. The question is, do we recognize his discipline when we're in the middle of it?

Hebrews 12:5-13

Lost in Translation

I've shared how there's a three-year-old who lives in our community house right now. He's capable of talking in full sentences, which are mostly decipherable, but sometimes I feel like a missionary trying to hold council with a tribal chief. He's got the tone and even the diction of language, but I'm clueless about the sense.

For example, last night during evening prayer he kept struggling in his mother's lap, saying, "I want my sah, I want my sah"—so of course I was touched, thinking he wanted his "Sarah." But when his mom let him go, he marched straight over to the two-liter of Pepsi under the coffee table. He wanted his *soda*. (And what am I? Chopped liver?)

So anyway, many of our conversations are like that. He reaches for something far above him on the counter, saying, "Peez," and I say, "What do you want?" and he says, "Nana." And I say "What?" and he says it again, louder—"NANA"—like I'm hard of hearing. And I say, "I can't understand you, sweetheart—*what?*" And he scrunches up his face and starts to wail. This is as far as we get before his mother walks into the kitchen and says, "Oh. He wants a banana." Then his face miraculously lights up, and he jumps up and down. Mommy gets it. She understands. Life is good.

I'm glad I'm not a three-year-old, though sometimes I, too, feel like no one around me understands what I'm really trying to say. Language is such a funny business that it often takes several passes before there's direct contact, even with the people who love me the most. You probably can relate. The great thing is that God never wonders what we want. He never looks at us with that puzzled, blank expression that says, "Um, I didn't catch that. What did you say?" And even though his thoughts are higher than our thoughts—and even though he's fluent in thousands of languages—he never gets hung up on our inability to express ourselves. He knows what we want even before we ask. He's like the mommy who comes into the kitchen just when everyone else fails to comprehend what we mean. God gets it. God understands. Life is good.

Isaiah 55:8-9

Small Faith and Difficulty

Life in our community house isn't always easy. There are a dozen of us, for starters, including three children under the age of three (and a baby on the way). So the simple logistics of running a household become rather complicated. You can't just do a load of laundry whenever you want; you must wait your turn. And the bathroom might be in use when you need to shower. Or the thermostat might not be set at the temperature you like best. Or the granola cereal you left in the cupboard last night won't necessarily be there for breakfast. If you come from a large family, you know exactly what I'm talking about. (Rather like dorm life, actually. . .)

It's tempting to get caught up in these small details, which become big details when you're in a hurry or have a cold or just plain feel crabby. It's amazing how quickly our human impulses and desires can trump all those lofty spiritual goals we set for ourselves. We prefer to *imagine* life in Christian community rather than live it. And thus when the community doesn't live up to our expectations, we sabotage the whole effort by our pettiness and complaining.

The twentieth-century German theologian Dietrich Bonhoeffer knew these issues well. He, his students, and his faculty—who lived together for a time in seminary housing—no doubt struggled with some of the same pettiness that we do. Thus he challenged them to "give thanks daily for the Christian fellowship in which we have been placed, even when there is no great experience, no discoverable riches, but much weakness, small faith, and difficulty."[48] So don't focus on how things aren't what you expected. *Give thanks.*

What his students (and Bonhoeffer himself) didn't realize was that their beloved leader soon would be imprisoned for resisting Hitler's Nazi regime. He eventually would have to write from an isolated cell, alone and cut off from his beloved community of believers. His letters indicate that he longed for Christian fellowship again. But he never came back. Bonhoeffer spent the rest of his life alone in prison and was eventually executed by the Nazis mere weeks before the end of World War II.

May I never take the gift of Christian fellowship for granted, even when there's "much weakness, small faith, and difficulty."

Galatians 6:9-10

The Art of Celebration

The prayer of confession from *The Book of Common Prayer* asks that, for Jesus' sake, we might be forgiven so "we may *delight in [his] will*, and walk in [his] ways, to the glory of [his] Name" (emphasis added). We say those words almost every day during morning prayer at the seminary chapel, and whenever we do, I feel awed and convicted at the same time. How often have I done God's will—such as holding my tongue or reaching out to a stranded motorist—and treated it as a "daily grind" rather than a delight? How often have I felt annoyed by spiritual interruptions rather than thrilled by the opportunity to serve?

And yet *celebration* is considered one of the spiritual disciplines, like prayer, Bible study, worship, silence, and solitude. It's the willingness to take delight in the tasks God asks us to do. Richard Foster wrote, "Celebration is central to all the Spiritual Disciplines. Without a joyful spirit of festivity the Disciplines become dull, death-breathing tools in the hands of modern Pharisees."[49] So when one of my housemates leaves all his or her dishes in the sink, do I take the role of the Pharisee and serve grudgingly, grumbling with irritation—yet still proud of my own righteousness—or do I take up the task with cheerfulness?

The art of celebration isn't easy. But neither is, say, getting used to the taste of beer. And yet millions of Americans willingly drink gallons of the stuff, right? So buck up, campers! If your friends can get plastered cheerfully, weekend after weekend, by drinking a substance that tastes like urine and battery acid, then there's no excuse for your crabby attitude when it comes to the spiritual life.

(!)

Okay, so I'm partially kidding and partially not.

Philippians 4:4-5

The Theology of Enough

It's been unseasonably cold here lately, and I often worry about the pregnant mommy in our house, who doesn't really own any winter stuff. Just the other day her friend gave her some money to buy shoes and boots at a thrift store, but as her belly gets bigger it doesn't seem realistic for her to buy a winter coat that won't fit in a few months.

So at breakfast one morning, when the grass in the yard was covered with frost and the furnace was working extra hard, I said with a burst of generosity, "Take my coat when you go out today." I was referring to the multilayered winter ski coat my husband bought me a few Christmases ago—the one with a lot of white trim that I always have trouble keeping clean. And instantly I envisioned the grubby buses she has to ride all day and her three-year-old, who often spills things, and all the possible ways my coat could get trashed. *Great.*

Anyway, we finished breakfast, I did a load of laundry, and everyone got ready for the day, and somehow my offer completely escaped my mind. So there I was, getting ready to go outside and hang my laundry on the line—getting ready, in fact, *to put on my coat*—when my housemate comes along, sees the coat, and says, "Oh, thank you so much!" And before I had time to think, she was turning around so I could help her slip into it (not so easy when you're pregnant)—which of course, I did. I had offered, and she had accepted. Duh.

"If you have two coats, give one to the poor," said John the Baptist when people asked how they should repent from their sins (Luke 3:11, TLB). Dorothy Day put it this way: "If you have two coats, one of them belongs to the poor." Some have called this the "Theology of Enough"—the idea that "God did not create too many people or not enough stuff. Poverty was not created by God, but by you and me because we have not learned to love our neighbor as ourselves."[50]

So did I freeze? Of course not. I had another coat in my closet.

Luke 3:7-11

Fall Back

The days are growing shorter as October winds down, though I must say I've always had an appreciation for fall lighting. There's something about the way the sun hangs low in the sky all afternoon, creating long shadows through the leafless branches of the woods, that makes me feel wistful and nostalgic. When we "fall back" through daylight saving time every autumn, each day slides slowly into a long dusk as we drift toward winter, and I'm more aware than usual of the passing of time, of growing older, of the loss of childhood places and people.

Right now in human history it feels like we're stuck in the long autumn dusk of our world. We are the victims of our own technological advances, living under the threat of global pandemics and weapons of mass destruction. After many millennia in which our formerly agricultural society lived close to the earth and to each other, we're now more familiar with the seasons of our favorite television shows than the way the earth changes under our feet from month to month. We have no option to "fall back," either. We have made our machines and damaged our world, and we must somehow live graciously with the sins of our past before spiritual winter descends.

But we can put our hope in what the sixteenth-century poet John Donne called "the last and everlasting day," when Jesus will return in final victory and vanquish the spiritual darkness of this world forever. We're on a slow slide toward spiritual winter, but one day Jesus will return to renew all things—one day we will "spring forward" into the new season of his heavenly Kingdom—and there will be no more need to "save" daylight. The Lord himself will be our Light!

May then sin's sleep, and death soon from me pass,
That waked from both, I again risen may
Salute the last, and everlasting day.[51]

Revelation 21:22-25

Freak Snowstorm

It's one thing to feel all nostalgic and dreamy about the approach of winter while basking in the sun of North Carolina, where I temporarily live; it's quite another to do so while winter is growling in my face. I've just flown home to Michigan to visit family and participate in my all-time favorite cultural event, the C. S. Lewis Festival,// and we've already had to reschedule events because of the weather. As my father drove me through a blizzard to an event that probably *should* have been canceled, I couldn't believe this was the same planet I live on the rest of the year.

All the same, there's something glorious about watching the world be completely transformed by a substance so clean and pure that for a little while we forget how dirty our cities are. To me snow is a physical symbol of God's grace, reminding us that the world won't always be as it is now, poisoned by our destructive impulses and thoughtless waste. All of creation is waiting for Christ's return, when the world will be renewed like a sudden snowstorm and we humans will no longer maim the earth by our sinfulness but will rule it with grace and wisdom.

But snowstorms also remind me of God's power and majesty—especially when the frigid north winds come blasting across Lake Michigan and slam into my former hometown like a freight train. It's tempting to treat that kind of weather as a nasty interruption to our everyday lives, a major inconvenience. But I suppose that's how many of us think of Christ's return, too—if we're honest. Perhaps we'd better reconsider our attitudes, starting with the weather?

> Praise the Lord for snowfall,
> when the dirt-brown mud
> underground disappears
> and he magics out his love
> in powder and ice.
>
> Praise the Lord for North Wind
> that blasts its breath
> across the high places—
> across the fast, flat waves,
> driving all things before it.
>
> For red cheek and cold eyelashes
> and the sting of all airborne things:
> Praise the Lord!

Romans 8:18-25

// See www.cslewisfestival.org. Their tagline is "To Narnia and the North!"

What Else Would It Be?

I'm at my parents' house in Michigan for a visit, and tonight is Halloween. We're taking turns answering the door while we attempt to eat dinner, which is always a challenge. My mom is a teacher and my dad is a pastor, so we have lots of kids stopping by to say hi and show off their costumes. And then there's the usual gaggle of neighborhood children ringing the doorbell every few minutes. So first my mom jumps up and dashes to the door, then my dad, and now it's my turn.

The little guy on the front porch looks to be about seven or eight years old—dressed up like a Jedi Knight, I think. As I open the door, he simply holds out his bag without a word.

I grin and say, "Is this a trick or treat?"

He gives me a look like I'm crazy and replies in a droll tone, "What else would it be?"

I laugh. "Well, you're supposed to *say* 'trick or treat,' you know. That's what you do at Halloween."

"Ohhhh," he says sarcastically. "I've never heard *that* before."

The little twit is still holding out his bag, so I put in a few pieces of candy (fewer than normal) and say, "Well, there you go. Happy Halloween," and I close the door.

My parents and I have a good laugh about it. But I'm also a bit miffed. Of *course* I know that if someone is standing on the front porch on October 31, in costume, holding out a bag of candy, it's got to be a trick or treat. What else would it be? And yet there's part of me that *likes* to be asked. I don't just want to be a candy dispenser; I want to interact with the kids, have a conversation, enjoy their presence.

I wonder if this is how God thinks of prayer. Sure, he knows all our needs before we ask; I mean, we're standing at the threshold of heaven with our hands held out—what else would we be doing? And yet I think there's a part of God that *likes* being asked. He doesn't want to be some sort of cosmic Wish Granter; he wants to interact with us, have a conversation, enjoy our presence.

When was the last time I really *asked*?

Matthew 6:7-8

All Hallows' Day

Halloween is fun and everything (though a bit bizarre, if you ask me), but the celebration Christians really should be excited about happens today: All Saints' Day, or in old English parlance, All Hallows' Day. This is the time in the ancient church calendar when we remember the saints, or holy ones who have gone before us. That's what *hallow* means— "holy"—and thus the night before is called All Hallows' Eve or *E'en* (which is short for *even*, which is short for *evening*). Hence *Hallow-e'en*. Got that?

So anyway, back in the fourth century when the first Christian missionaries arrived in the pagan islands of Ireland and Great Britain, they found a culture that celebrated its new year at the start of winter, on November 1, through a festival known as *Samhain*. The pagan priests and priestesses believed that on the night before the year ended, the veil was somehow thinner between the living and the dead, between the real world and the otherworld of the spirits. Ghosts roamed the hills and valleys, they said. Demons prowled the streets. Even today, many pagan traditions regarding Samhain have lingered, including the lighting of jack-o'-lanterns and the wearing of costumes—all originally designed to keep the demons at bay. (Apparently they wouldn't carry you off to the otherworld if they thought you were, say, a Teenage Mutant Ninja Turtle.)

By contrast, the church insisted that Jesus has conquered the powers of hell once and for all. We have nothing to fear from the world of the spirits on Samhain or any other night of the year—Jesus is our protection. We trust in him alone, not jack-o'-lanterns or costumes or anything else. So the church decided to make November 1 All Saints' Day, when we remember those who went before us and trusted in Christ alone for their salvation.

As November begins, the start of the Celtic New Year, my mind turns to things "in the sky above or in the earth below" (Romans 8:39). Demons and angels, heaven and hell. . . . We tend to make Halloween out to be a silly romp, and yet it seems to me that the stakes are rather high in the battle between the powers of darkness and the powers of light. How can our lives, like those of the saints, witness to the truth of Romans 8:38?

> I am convinced that nothing can ever separate us from God's love. Neither death nor life, neither angels nor demons, neither our fears for today nor our worries about tomorrow—not even the powers of hell can separate us from God's love.
>
> **Romans 8:38-39**

Angels and Demons

I've always been fascinated by angels—not those silly fat cherubs with harps that you see in cartoons, but the real angels from the Bible: the ones who look like giants and warriors with flaming swords who paralyze people with fear. They are their own unique spiritual species (no, we *don't* become angels when we die), and they go by different titles—cherubim, seraphim, archangels, powers—depending on their "rank" or role in heaven. Long before the first chapter of Genesis, the angels were, according to Christian tradition, created to be God's personal assistants, like courtiers and guardsmen in the castle of a king.

But something happened. Christian tradition tells us that before human beings entered the story, there was rebellion in heaven. An angel named Lucifer desired to be as great as God. Subsequently he was thrown out of heaven along with all the angels who had joined his rebellion. This was his mighty fall. Lucifer (also known as Satan or the devil) established a stronghold on earth, and his first act of power was to inspire the first human beings to rebel against God (see Genesis 3). This led to *our* mighty Fall, and Satan has been wreaking havoc on God's creation ever since—though he will one day be defeated.

Of course, this is only what we can piece together from miscellaneous scraps of information the Bible provides. The story isn't fully told in Scripture. But Jesus gave us a fascinating little tidbit in Luke 10:18 that's just enough to get me thinking: What happened to the angels before we came along? What did Satan do to get kicked out? Is that story over? How do we know we can trust the good angels now?

The poems on November 3 and 4 use two different metaphors to think about fallen angels. The first metaphor compares these angels to falling stars. The second likens Satan to a self-obsessed symphony conductor.

What metaphor would you create to describe the fall of those angels?

Luke 10:17-20

A Priori[//]

One day while reading Luke 10:17-20, I began to ponder the contrast between falling "stars"—which aren't really stars at all, but meteors—and true stars that stay fixed in the heavens, trustworthy and unchanging. Could this be one way of thinking about the untold story of how the bad angels rebelled against God at the beginning of time and how we can trust the good angels now?

> We view the angels
> like constellations,
> eternally fixed
> in the final pattern of their choosing
> (whereas we mortals
> drift like cosmic dust
> from one orbit to another—until
> the universe stops expanding).
>
> But before they settled into place
> the seraphim must have spun
> like meteors 'round the sun, till
> one of them felt the sudden
> gravitational pull of earth
> and fell like lightning
> from the sky,
>
> a third of heaven with him."

Philippians 2:14-18

// A priori is Latin for "that which comes first."
<< First published in *Time of Singing*, Spring 2002.

First Half, Second Half

A couple of years ago I read *The Silmarillion* by J. R. R. Tolkien (of *The Lord of the Rings* fame). *The Silmarillion* gives an exhaustive fictional history of Middle-earth, from its creation all the way to when Frodo enters the scene. In the beginning, Ilúvatar (Tolkien's name for the Creator) is directing a symphony of the subgods—or angels—a beautiful, harmonious work of music that could go on for eternity. But then one of the angels, Melkor, rebels against the melody and desires to play his own tune. He creates discord in heaven, is kicked out, and eventually takes the newly created Middle-earth for his own domain.

I suspect Tolkien was well aware that, according to ancient Christian tradition, Satan was the top angel in charge of heaven's worship music before he fell. Puts an interesting spin on all those arguments that take place during praise band rehearsal or church choir practice, eh?

I.
As the curtain rises,
all heaven is in harmony;
the instruments of cherubim
are tuned to perfect pitch.
Music pours from center stage,
from mighty Mount Olympus;//
the maestro smiles approvingly
at symphony, at excellence.

II.
Yet, without warning,
the forbidden fruit
of dissonance
becomes too tempting
to resist.
Before the piece is finished,
maestro falls
to the orchestral pit of earth,

dragging the curtain
down with him.

Job 38:1-7

// According to Greek mythology, Olympus was where the gods lived.

Was Free Will Worth It?

O Lord, all my ramblings about good and evil, angels and demons now make me wonder: Was free will really worth it? When I think of all the horror that we humans unleash upon each other and upon this planet—the abuse, the torture and torment, the pain and disfigurement and aching loss—was it really a fair trade-off for our freedom?

Somehow I must believe it was, and is . . . I must fling myself upon your grace and cling whimpering to your feet, burying my frightened face into the edge of your robe. Your reason for allowing evil makes no sense to me as yet, but I know you are both almighty and compassionate. Your answer to all our suffering lies somehow, somewhere in the brutality of the Cross: that in your life on earth you were no stranger to the consequences of free will. You took those consequences upon yourself, through your own torturous death, and somehow through the Resurrection you turned all the horror into something glorious.

This is a mighty mystery, Lord, but one that only deepens my love for you. May I never be so bewildered by this world of sin that I lose sight of your loving grace and thus begin to hate you. And for those for whom hate is the only comprehensible response to the horrors they've witnessed, O Lord, forgive them; they don't know what they're doing. Teach me how to be a part of their healing, Lord, in whatever way you choose.

Such a weary, soul-battered time. . . . There is a war going on—not only for souls to be won or lost but for spirits to be nurtured or maimed, effective or ineffective, fruit bearing or barren. Show your power to transform and heal, O Lord, that we might once again rejoice in the freedom we have in Christ. Amen.

Romans 1:28–2:4

Picture This

Lately I've been thinking about the vividness of evil, how our movie portrayals of it are so much more powerful than our portrayals of good. For example, I remember one film critic complaining that the evil places and characters in *The Lord of the Rings* are so much more convincing than the good ones. Rivendell, the dwelling place of the good elves, looks more like "Ye Olde Woodshoppe," he said, than a place of haunting beauty.

My guess is that we rarely see any examples of true goodness, so we have a hard time picturing it as anything but cheesy and unconvincing. The exception is when we witness someone's heroic actions in response to incredible evil—such as the young Christian doctor giving up a comfortable career in order to help suffering children in Africa. There we have an image of goodness that is not somehow separate from a backdrop of evil but happens in spite of evil, in response to evil, and thus shines with an even greater luminosity.

Likewise there is nothing cheesy about an elderly nun roaming the streets of an American ghetto with food for the homeless and hungry. There's nothing unconvincing about a youth group standing shoulder to shoulder as they raise the walls of a Habitat for Humanity house in Biloxi, Mississippi. There's nothing Ye-Olde-Woodshoppe-ish about a real-life cathedral in the heart of an urban metropolis. The difference between these examples and all the silly renderings of supposed "goodness" we see in movies is that these people and places exist *to the glory of God*. Goodness will never appear convincing unless it has a worthy subject.

So if that's true in the movies, what about your life and mine?

Psalm 112

Nameless Fears

In peace I will lie down and sleep,
for you alone, O Lord, will keep me safe.
Psalm 4:8

I'm disturbed that I'm becoming more and more fearful as I get older. For example, I have this sudden terror of big dogs that I never had before, thanks to a near miss with a chained pit bull in Juárez, Mexico. Then while volunteering at a mission warehouse in southern Michigan, I had this bizarre dislike of the freight elevator, as if I were being suffocated. I've also become afraid of drowning lately—after growing up on the Great Lakes, swimming and sailing all my life!

These are unexpected fears that are not residual from my childhood but unique to my young-adult life. I'm jaded, maybe. People have earned my distrust. I'm scared of my own lack of good judgment, which makes me cautious (well, compared to what I used to be). I'm not at ease when pushed past my comfort zone or ushered along in someone else's culture. It must have something to do with feeling out of control, manipulated, helpless, whereas when I was younger I used to be more adventurous, trusting in God and other people. My four months in East Africa as an undergraduate were a case in point. What happened to the young woman who wasn't afraid to eat dinner with strangers, learn a new language, take a city bus into the slums?

Perhaps back then I was ignorant, innocent, and young in my faith, and God was gracious to me. Perhaps he simply took care of a fool? "Ignorance is bliss," the saying goes. Now that I'm older, does he expect more of me?

One thing I do know: No matter what, whatever decisions I make or actions I take, I must take the next step in faith rather than fear. My father, a wise and experienced minister, taught me that. I must not act on my fears but take the next move in the full awareness that God alone will keep me safe.

Psalm 4

Something Amiss

One fall afternoon, as Tom and I lay peacefully in the field near Pigeon River, basking in the unusually warm sun—the sky gorgeous and blue above us, the sound of the wind in the tall grass whispering as we read and napped—along came people, somewhere down the trail, hollering and laughing and generally being obnoxious. I kept expecting huge dogs to come bounding up, snarling, or to hear gunshots, which we'd been hearing anyway in the distance at what must have been a shooting range. The unseen intruders launched a canoe from the opposite bank, making a ridiculous amount of noise, and eventually drifted away.

Robbed. We were alone, the sun was warm, the day was beautiful, and suddenly a nameless fear robbed me of any sense of peace, security, joy. Perhaps I've watched too many *X-Files* reruns or read too many newspaper crime logs. Rural America has its own terrors. Whatever the case, my mind conjured up frightening scenarios of what could happen to two people napping in a field. I no longer felt safe.

I think of Adam and Eve, before they sinned, walking in the dusky garden at evening, having no sense of disorientation or anxiety at the coming dark. What would it be like to have no fear—not any *cause* for fear, mind you, but the genuine absence of those nameless, childish terrors of the dark or of being left utterly alone? What would it be like to be so aware of love, so sure, so wrapped around by God's presence, that you become a friend of all creation and lord of it too—even of the dark? What would it be like to have no awareness that something is amiss with the universe? What would it be like not to fear being left alone, helpless and defenseless, by your own broken humanity?

In moments like this, I want the Garden back.

Genesis 2:15-25

Safe or Unsafe?

I find great comfort in the promise that God alone "will keep me safe" (Psalm 4:8). But it strikes me that I need to explore this word *safe* a bit—because I don't believe it means God will keep me from all bodily or emotional harm. Obviously God doesn't always keep us "safe" in this way, or we wouldn't know Christians who've been injured in car accidents or been victims of crime or worse.

Recently I attended a retreat for women in ministry in which I began to notice that the buzzword for the weekend was *safe*. The participants and facilitators alike would talk about not feeling "safe" in their churches or not feeling "safe" around certain people— especially around men who didn't respect them in leadership. And finally I asked, "What do we mean by 'safe'?" Because it strikes me that I regularly feel emotionally and even physically *unsafe* doing the things God has called me to do. Moving to the inner city is definitely not safe. Confronting a friend who needs to get her life back on track isn't all that safe (emotionally speaking), because I might get my feelings hurt. Humbly putting myself under the leadership of someone who doesn't respect me is not exactly safe. Confessing my sin to a mentor isn't safe—as far as my pride and reputation are concerned. But these things must be done in order for me to grow spiritually or reach a hurting world. The apostle Paul's second letter to the Corinthians makes this clear (see today's text).

In short, sometimes it's safer to do the "unsafe" thing God is calling us to do than to stay where we are spiritually.

And yet in the midst of all this is God's promise that our lives are in his hands. We aren't attempting all these things alone. His hand of protection is upon us. His traveling mercies go with us. His mighty power has guarded us time and time again. His angels stand at the ready. Which means that even in those unsafe moments—when the car flips or we become prey to random crime—God is near anyway. We will never be completely abandoned.

2 Corinthians 11:23-30

The Peaceable Kingdom

A few days ago I wrote about how my peaceful nap by the river was disturbed by a nameless fear (see November 8). Something about being alone in the wilderness is alarming—and this is especially true at night. I suppose most of us were afraid of the dark when we were kids (I once called my parents into my pitch-black room because I was convinced there was a cat sitting on the bedside table, staring at me through the darkness). But what's really troubling is that we truly aren't safe anywhere on this planet; evil is alive and well and has a vested interest in injuring us.

I suppose if my river scare had happened inside a chapter of *The Lord of the Rings*, I might not have fooled myself into feeling so secure in the first place. J. R. R. Tolkien's epic fantasy depicts an imaginary world called Middle-earth, where evil is actively seeking to destroy all peace-loving people. Tolkien paints in vivid detail just what the stakes are in the cosmic battle between good and evil: The Dark Lord is searching for the magic Ring of Power so he can control the world, and those who stand against him, such as Frodo the Hobbit, risk being destroyed completely. Nowhere is safe.

But there is one character who seems unmoved by the war for Middle-earth or the power of the magic Ring. His name is Tom Bombadil—and incidentally, he didn't end up in the film version of the story. In fact, Tolkien's publishers wanted Tom removed from the original book too, but Tolkien insisted on keeping him. He considered it vitally important to retain one corner of Middle-earth that evil couldn't touch, one character whose memory went all the way back to before the darkness. When Frodo asks Tom Bombadil who he is, Tom replies:

> Eldest, that's what I am. Mark my words, my friends: Tom was here before the river
> and the trees; Tom remembers the first raindrop and the first acorn. . . . He knew
> the dark under the stars when it was fearless—before the Dark Lord came from
> Outside.[52]

This is a hopeful moment in the story, even if it doesn't really matter to the overall plot in the end. At least to me, Tom Bombadil symbolizes the spiritual reality that darkness hasn't always been the property of the evil one—and one day we'll reclaim the dark as part of the nighttime beauty of God's peaceable Kingdom.

The end of all our earthly fears? The end to our terrors of the night? This is good news!

Revelation 21:1-4

Crowd of Witnesses

I skimmed through John Foxe's *Book of Martyrs* last night, not realizing until I was partway through that it was written in the 1500s as he witnessed multiple burnings at the stake and was often in danger himself. I was fascinated, sobered, ashamed, strengthened, and encouraged. Two things strike me about the stories of the martyrs, particularly those who lived during the pre-Reformation era in England in the late 1400s, on through the Reformation in the first half of the 1500s.

First, these men and women died defending the Word of God. They insisted on reading it for themselves in their own language and insisted on the truths found within it as opposed to the distorted doctrines and practices of the medieval church. And in some ways, isn't this something we still need to do? I feel like I am constantly having to defend the Word in today's culture, sometimes within the walls of the church, and especially in our pluralistic society. Would I be willing to die for it though? Would I be willing to stand my ground if someone asked whether I truly take Jesus at his word when he claimed to be "the way, the truth, and the life" (John 14:6)? In what ways are the truths of Scripture being distorted, denied, or dismissed today—and what am I going to do about it?

The second thing that strikes me is that these men and women are now included in the "huge crowd of witnesses" mentioned in Hebrews 12:1, that host of ordinary men and women—saints—who possibly even now witness our lives and struggles here, and whose legacies and dreams and ministries are continued through us. I am part of a rich heritage, an awesome family of faith. Not only is Jesus watching me as I run this race, but there's a whole stadium of people watching as well. They've passed the baton and have taken their seats in the stands to witness how I'll pass it on to others for the homestretch. Am I worthy of these people? Or is my life like flabby muscle in comparison? Am I only moping along in this race, much to their bewilderment and distress?

The second Sunday in November is the International Day of Prayer for the Persecuted Church. Even now, as I write this devotional, there are Christians in other countries who are being persecuted, arrested, beaten, and even killed for their faith. These saints and martyrs are counting on *us*. Will we make sure they haven't lived and died in vain?

Hebrews 11:35–12:2

Imagining Heaven

After several years of teaching youth Sunday school, I've begun to expect that at some point each year I'll be asked the standard set of "God questions" that plague the preteen mind. These concerns usually pop up at random moments, between long stretches of comatose behavior, and are almost always *way* off whatever subject we're discussing at the moment. For example, in the middle of the story of the Crucifixion, someone will suddenly wake up and ask, "How can God be three people?" Or "Did Adam and Eve have belly buttons?" Or "What happens to people who die without hearing about Jesus?" (Not for the faint of heart, my friends!) Or my personal favorite: "What is heaven like?"

I've eventually learned that these questions point to deeper issues at the heart of all spiritual development. But not all of them are of equal import. The concept of the Trinity and the issue of belly buttons are not on the same plane. The question about the salvation of others is a powerful segue into discussions of evangelism, prayerful intercession, and the grace of God. But the question about heaven—about life after death—has the most at stake for these kids personally, at least in their minds.

Let's be honest. Heaven is the carrot on the stick when it comes to choosing Jesus. Certainly, forgiveness comes as a great relief to the average messed-up seeker. Empowerment by the Holy Spirit is definitely cool. But without the promise of life after death, those other things don't really matter. Imagine if John 3:16 said only, "For God loved the world so much that he gave his one and only Son"?

It would beg the question, "So what?"

John 3:16-21

What Will It Be Like?

Generally speaking, we (the Church) have failed to adequately answer the question, "What will heaven be like?"// In the absence of clear scriptural statements, we're so leery of sharing what we *think*, *imagine*, or *hope* that we avoid speculation altogether, even when our hopes have good grounding in Scripture and are the product of reasonable thought and balanced experience. We stick with "safe" and accepted images—such as the vision of worship at the throne of the Lamb in the book of Revelation (see 7:9-17)—but only barely touch the surface of all that God might have in store for us. Meanwhile, popular culture seems more than happy to depict the afterlife with luminous detail, though it's usually based on quasi-reincarnation theories and sentimental schlock (the silly film *What Dreams May Come*, starring Robin Williams, comes to mind).

It's time for us to stage a coup. We need to bring our creative imaginations—shaped and sanctified by the Bible—to bear on our understanding of heaven and present heaven in a way that shows that life after death is worth living. That's what I'd like to tackle in the next week or so of devotions.

So what does heaven look like, anyway? Let's start with a little myth debunking. First, we need to ditch the whole clouds and harps and halos stuff, okay? That sounds more like hell to most people anyway, especially those who aren't exactly musical. Heaven is home, not some cosmic opera in the sky where everyone lives on clouds. It's the presence of God—God, who is our home (see Psalm 90:1). For followers of Christ, this is a current spiritual reality that we'll one day experience as a physical reality (though the issue of where remains unknown). This is why we speak of life with God in both present and future tense: the "already but not yet" Kingdom of Heaven.

What heaven will physically look like is not certain, though we get a sense from Scripture that it will be familiar to us, like a city on a hill, shining in a glorious sunrise (see Revelation 21:10-11). It may have some semblance of an organized landscape—perhaps, as C. S. Lewis wondered in *The Last Battle* (the final book in The Chronicles of Narnia series), a landscape that looks strangely familiar, as if all the beauties of earth were merely a reflection of the Kingdom. Maybe all this time what we've really loved about earth is its very heavenliness.

Anyway, that's a start.

Revelation 21:10-21

// One exception is Randy Alcorn's book *Heaven* (Tyndale, 2005).

We'll be Doing What?

Most seekers can resonate with the concept of heaven as home, a safe place. They like the idea of no more sin, no more death, and God wiping away every tear from their eyes (see Revelation 21:4). They're thrilled about the prospect of seeing loved ones who've already passed away (though not so thrilled to find out this is limited to believers), and they cling to the fact that our bodies will be whole and perfect. But most seekers also want to know, "What will we be doing?"

Isn't that the question most people ask before committing to anything (after "Who's going to be there?" of course)? This is exactly where many seekers lose interest in heaven (or instead invent their own version of it), because few Christians seem willing to offer a compelling description of what will be going on there. If it's just the Worship Music Channel, 24-7, then no wonder the unchurched seem disinterested.

Imagine if a pastor or worship leader were to give every member of the congregation a canvas, paintbrushes, and a box of paints, explaining that every week from now on, each person would paint during the service—as an act of worship. Some people would be thrilled. Others would head for the door. Still others would put up with it, believing that art is an important form of worship expression even if they personally aren't very good at it. Now imagine if the pastor, after several weeks of artistic productivity, burst out in the middle of the worship service, "Isn't this wonderful? Isn't this a beautiful act of worship? Just think: When we get to heaven, it will be like this! All of us standing in front of canvasses, painting and painting and painting, forever and ever. Doesn't that sound fantastic? I can't *wait!*"

Stop there. What's your gut reaction (particularly if you can't paint)? How about the reaction of the average teenager—say, the benchwarmer on the eighth-grade basketball team (particularly if *he* can't paint)? He would react the same way he does when he's told that heaven will be one big worship service for all eternity, with everyone singing and singing and singing around the throne, world without end, amen. Sure, music will be going on in heaven. But is music the sum total of worship?

So what about you: What's your vision of heaven? Is it a place you want to be? And where did that vision come from, anyway?

Revelation 4

Heavenly Worship

Music lovers, take heart: There will be music in heaven. The image of Jesus enthroned, surrounded by singing worshippers, is portrayed most vividly in the book of Revelation (see chapters 4 and 5). It's a glimpse of what's going on in God's presence, even as you read this. According to John and other writers of Scripture, the Kingdom does include music and singing and a host of angels (possibly even with harps). But we shouldn't therefore assume that music or liturgy will be the sum of heaven's activity, particularly if we understand that all kinds of human activity, including creative expression, can be acts of worship.

Let's think concretely. Picture a king on a throne in a castle that sits on a hill overlooking a vast kingdom. Of course there is activity around the throne: People are bowing down before the king and offering gifts and pledges of service or fidelity. There's no doubt some music going on. But there's also activity in other rooms of the castle as well as on the castle grounds—the preparation of food, the beautification of the building and gardens, the writing of stories in the king's honor, the practice of archery for upcoming festival competitions, and so on. And there's still *more* activity in the village near the castle and in the surrounding countryside—architecture, bridge building, exploration—all of which is being done in the name of the king and for his sake.

Wouldn't the king be just as pleased with those other kingdom activities as he is with the worship happening before his very throne—as long as it's all being done to his glory?

Luke 14:15-24

The Perfect Game

If we're not strumming on harps for all eternity, what will we be doing in heaven? Here are some musings inspired by one of those goofy youth group games. . . .

One night in my youth group leader days, we were playing Giant Four Square, in which the entire youth room was broken into four quadrants and there were multiple people defending each quadrant. (The ball could be played indefinitely off walls, ceiling, furniture, and body parts but could only bounce once on the floor of each square—rather like racquetball except on steroids.) At some point during the game, we hit perfection. If you've ever played sports, you know exactly what I mean. It lasted for only about eight seconds. But it was eight seconds in which every player, from the most athletic jock down to the most timid freshman, hit the ball just right: one bounce in the square, then a mind-blowing sequence of ricochets off of various arms and hands and sofas and walls until we collapsed onto the floor, laughing at the sheer brilliance of it all. Then, just as quickly, we lapsed back into our usual uncoordinated bumbling and went on to set a new record low.

But there was something about those eight seconds of perfection that got me thinking. What if those eight seconds stretched into ten minutes, ten minutes into an hour, an hour into eternity, in which every player loved God *with all their strength* and gave him the glory? Scripture says that someday we will "run and not grow weary . . . walk and not faint" (Isaiah 40:31). The concept brings to mind the young Olympian Eric Liddell, whose true story is portrayed in the famous movie *Chariots of Fire*: He ran every race as an act of worship. Is it possible to play some (perhaps not all) sports that same way now? And if so on earth, then why not in heaven?

Maybe in heaven we'll finally be able to fulfill Christ's commandment to love the Lord our God with *all* our strength (see today's text). We'll hit the perfect game, to his glory. While the angels and martyrs are singing around the throne, perhaps our renewed bodies will jump and stretch and run and play a living sacrifice of praise.

Mark 12:29-31

Exploring God's Country

Whenever an adult is unable to answer a child's questions about, say, the origins of the universe or some other spiritual conundrum, what does the person usually say? "Well, why don't you ask God when you get to heaven?"

But *will* all our questions be answered the moment we get to heaven? I suppose it's possible. But doesn't it sound more interesting to anticipate having all eternity to discover more and more of the new heaven and new earth around us—each "day" a new experiment to try, a new skill to learn, a new (or perhaps ancient?) language to study, a new (or old) book to read?

And what other sorts of adventures will heaven provide for us? What will be the landscape and backdrop of eternity? We can be sure it'll be far grander and more stunning and gorgeous than anything we've seen here on earth. The apostle John, in his vision of the new heaven and the new earth, was taken to "a great, high mountain," from which he could see the holy city of Jerusalem (see Revelation 21:10 and following). He recognized it as Jerusalem, but it wasn't like the city as we know it today. Instead, it was filled with precious gems and guarded by angels, a vast and glorious place that would take an eternity to explore. We can imagine that the surrounding countryside is just as amazing.

As C. S. Lewis portrayed in *The Last Battle*, the new arrivals to Aslan's country are immediately launched on a marvelous adventure, climbing "further up and further in" to the new landscape. Up into the mountains, past waterfalls and rocky peaks, higher and higher until they can see the whole world stretched out before them.

What mountains will there be to ski down or waves to surf or oceans to navigate or cliffs to jump off when we get to "God's country"? What new knowledge and insight will we have all eternity to discover? This vision of heaven is becoming more and more interesting!

Isaiah 11:6-10

Telling the New Old Story

An old rabbinic saying goes, "God created people because he loves stories." I love stories too. In fact, I can't imagine existence—including eternity—without them. So in all this discussion of what will be going on in heaven once we get there, I'd like to know: Will the Great Story of God's saving work in human history still be worth hearing, or will we move on to bigger and better things?

I doubt our stories will end at the gates of God's Kingdom. The rehearsal of the stories of God's loving faithfulness is the core of Scripture. This could hardly be shelved when we get to heaven without each of us losing our sense of who we are and who God is. It would be like trying to read the last fifteen chapters of a book without reading the first. Instead, I imagine heaven will be our opportunity to tell the story of God's grace over and over again, as a child begs for the same stories each night and feels safe in the hearing of them—for all eternity.

Meanwhile I imagine the story of eternity will keep moving forward, even as the plot will be tied in some way to what happened here on earth. And there *will* be a plot. There must be. After all, no story can continue without a plot. When the plot ends, the story ends. But what will the plotline of heaven look like—especially if you remove conflict (as we know it) from the mix? How could there possibly be a plot without conflict?

Perhaps the best clues are to be found in the first chapters of Genesis. The plot device of that story, before the Fall (before *conflict*) was the activity of creation. If we apply that same principle to the story of the new heaven and the new earth, it's not hard to imagine that the main characters will work to bring order instead of chaos, to create rather than consume, to build rather than destroy, to trust rather than disobey. That will be our plot.

But the whole tenor of the plot will have changed from Genesis 2 and 3. No longer will the threat of rebellion or hubris lurk in the background. God alone will get the glory for any creative act—all activity will be an act of praise. And if there is any learning curve, it will be due to lack of practice, not rebellion. But this time we'll have all eternity to try again and get it right.

Just as the activity of creation is what began our human story in the first chapters of Genesis, my guess is the activity of *new* creation will drive the heavenly story long after the last chapters of Revelation. That's the kind of story I want to be a part of!

Psalm 145:1-7

Keeping House

In the past few devotions (see November 12–18), we've been exploring what heaven will be like, especially what we'll be doing once we get there. Now we come to that wonderful image of heaven as home, our final dwelling place.

"There is more than enough room in my Father's home," Jesus told his disciples on the night before his arrest. "I am going to prepare a place for you" (John 14:2). The King James Version says, "In my Father's house are many *mansions*" (emphasis mine)—which is delightfully strange. How can there be mansions within a house? And yet for those of us who've bought into the upwardly mobile lifestyle of popular culture, we rather like that word *mansions*. Finally, we think: We'll get our hands on some prime real estate; we'll enjoy the comforts and luxuries we've been pining after all these years.

Maybe we tend to focus on the wrong aspect of this promise sometimes: The key is the home part, not the mansion part. *Mansion* is the luxurious place reserved for the very wealthy, staffed by dozens of servants and filled with exotic, useless treasures. *Home*, by contrast, is the intimate setting where we are valued and loved. If I am to spend all eternity somewhere, quite frankly I'd rather be in a warm and loving home, however small, than in a cold, isolating mansion, however vast. Home to me is a cozy room and a comfy chair by a warm fire, enjoying a simple meal with good friends. This seems more like the sort of thing a poor stonemason from Nazareth would prepare for us anyway. An upper room. A simple supper. Memorable conversation and fellowship around a table.

"When everything is ready," Jesus told his disciples on that last night, "I will come and get you, so that you will always be with me where I am" (John 14:3). Mansion or hut, palace or cottage, home is wherever Jesus is.

John 14:1-6

Eternal Life Starts Now

Too many Christians talk about heaven and eternal life as future realities, as if the Kingdom of God were all very nice in its own way but not terribly relevant right now. We're super-busy and important here on earth, you know. We have places to go, people to talk about, trivia to invent, shopping to finish. We have our heavenly reservations, so we don't need to worry about it anymore. But in John's Gospel I hear Jesus saying something else entirely. "I tell you the truth," he said to the religious leaders of his day, "those who listen to my message and believe in God who sent me have eternal life. They will never be condemned for their sins, but they have *already passed from death into life*" (John 5:24, emphasis added).

Wait—you mean heaven has already started in our lives? Eternal life has begun? What about the glorious city, gold streets, singing angels, and our own corners of the throne room in which to strum our harps and praise him? Perhaps all that will happen someday (though as we've already discussed [see November 14–17], a great deal *more* will happen as well). But if we're reading John correctly, it becomes clear that eternal life starts *right now*—not when we die, but in this very moment, in this quiet morning with the sunlight streaming through the windows on this very ordinary day. Eternal life has been here all along, ever since I knelt at whatever age and "asked Jesus into my heart," as they say. The great dance of heaven, of knowing Jesus, has already begun, so that by the time we're physically ushered into his presence for that last and first joyous banquet, we will already know the steps of the dance. We will know it so well that we'll feel finally at home.

We step into the stream of eternal life *now*, and from it we draw our nourishment until it will carry us finally into the sea of forever.

John 5:19-24

All Will Be Revealed

During my sophomore year in high school, my parents went on a trip to Israel and invited their friend Kathy to stay with my sister and me. I don't remember a specific moment in that week, mostly just the strong impression of a fun-loving, warm, and earnest adult who was genuinely interested in us and unashamed to talk about spiritual things. We laughed a lot, as I recall, and it usually began with Kathy's sudden exclamation of "Oh!" when struck by a startling new realization, which she then elaborated on with wide-eyed astonishment before erupting in a fit of giggles.

Meanwhile, her respect for my parents was obvious. My sister and I had lots of fun moments with Kathy, but she would never undermine, question, or bypass any of the household rules. On this she was both enthusiastic and unwavering, and thus she earned our trust.

It must have been about a year later when we had the conversation I remember so vividly. I can't recall the circumstances that brought us together or even what problem I was worrying about, but we somehow ended up talking on her couch one afternoon while I poured out my heart. Kathy listened and spoke of God's love for me and prayed—and while she prayed, she had one of those sudden revelations, except this time it wasn't loud and giggly but teary and full of awe. She saw me in ministry to my peers; she envisioned many people coming to know the Lord through my witness. I will never forget Kathy's face when she prayed. She was like a little girl in the presence of a loving daddy. It made me want to be that kind of Christian when I grew up, someone who rejoices with childlike awe when God reveals something new that we'd never realized before.

Recently I learned that Kathy died unexpectedly. I don't know the circumstances, and I was too far away to attend the funeral, but I am assured of this: Kathy is finally in a place where she sees her Father face-to-face, where all will be revealed that she only dimly understood before. Somewhere in the midst of the amazing sounds and silences of God's heavenly Kingdom, there is an awe-filled voice exclaiming with childlike surprise, "Oh!"

Colossians 3:1-4

Rest in Peace

Somewhere in heaven there is a former Oxford don named C. S. Lewis enjoying a cup of hot tea and a good book in peace—or so I imagine. Today is the anniversary of his death in 1963, or shall we say it's the anniversary of the beginning of his last and best adventure?

Often we think the famous author of The Chronicles of Narnia must've lived a quiet, bookish sort of bachelor life with his quiet, bookish, bachelor brother. But in fact Lewis had a rather zany household.[53] For starters, there was the divorced mother and teenage sister of his buddy Paddy Moore, who had died in the trenches of World War I. Apparently "Jack" Lewis and Paddy had made a pact that if one of them should die, the other would care for the surviving family—and Jack kept his promise. Mrs. Moore and her daughter, Maureen, were part of the Lewis household for almost thirty years, until Mrs. Moore's death.

And it wasn't an easy thirty years. Mother and daughter didn't always get along. Jack was continuously interrupted from his writing or studies to take care of some menial domestic task that could've waited. In time, due to some estrangement, he became the object of Mrs. Moore's growing spite and resentment. Meanwhile, his brother, Warnie, despised Mrs. Moore's very presence—and turned to alcohol more than ever. Add to this the odd housekeeper and even odder gardener, and you had a veritable zoo.

How did he have the time, focus, and energy to write his literary works? I haven't a clue. All I know is that whenever I'm tempted to believe that life in this community house will never mesh with my solitary vocation of writing—that I'll never, in fact, finish this very book—then I remember C. S. Lewis. Hospitality is not a special calling for the gregarious, domestic types who love spending all day scrubbing floors and embroidering doilies and baking strudel from scratch. Hospitality is the call of Christ, no matter what our vocations or personalities. "For I was hungry," Jesus tells us, "and you fed me. I was thirsty, and you gave me a drink. I was a stranger, and you invited me into your home" (Matthew 25:35). This means a lifetime of holy interruptions until we finally rest in heaven's peace.

If a bookish Oxford bachelor could answer that call, what's holding us back?

Matthew 25:31-46

On Life's Brevity

Today is my birthday, and it seems appropriate that Psalm 90 is on the agenda for daily prayer. It's one of the oldest known works of literature in the world, a psalm of Moses, as it says at the beginning, which means it was probably written while the people of Israel were wandering in the desert on their way to the Promised Land. That makes the opening line especially poignant: "Lord, through all the generations you have been our home!" There the Israelites were, homeless, living out of tents like nomads (because they were nomads), and their prayer affirmed that God himself was their dwelling place. Given how often I've moved in the past year, it's no wonder I wake up with this psalm running through my head, rehearsing all the ways God has been faithful "through all the generations" of my life.

But on this, my birthday, Psalm 90 also appeals to me in a different way. In the past few years I've become more and more conscious of how I'm aging. My limbs and joints respond to lying on a hard floor (and getting up from it) like complaining children. I've counted the gray hairs on my head, observed wrinkles around my eyes, and felt stiffness in my knuckles when I first awake. Lately I've become uncomfortably aware of those days when I dither around in meaningless activity, lacking productivity—especially at work, where time seems like a boomerang, winging away through the air of my projected to-do list, only to come full circle again without a single item completed. I feel extremely busy, but when I add up everything I've accomplished, it seems pathetic somehow.

The story goes that someone once asked the famous evangelist Billy Graham what surprised him most about life, and he said, "Its brevity." He has been one of the most hardworking ministers in the world, and yet he, too, felt life slipping through his fingers like sand in an hourglass. But Psalm 90:12 assures us that this awareness of our own mortality is what gives us wisdom. It prompts us to give God the credit for any work we've actually accomplished, since he alone can "make our efforts successful" in the long run (verse 17). And what greater joy could there be on the day of our resurrection than the knowledge that, in Christ, our earthly work—though brief—was not in vain?

Psalm 90

Return to Me

Funny how at the beginning of the school year I have all sorts of good intentions—to get up early for prayer, to read soul-stretching books, to join this or that Bible study—but within a few months I'm back to my usual dithering. I don't pick up my Bible for weeks except when I'm using it to write one of these devotions. What must God think of me? The same thing he thinks whenever his people lose sight of his Word, I suppose. . . .

Here's an example. In the ancient days of the kings of Israel, there were only a few copies of the Book of the Law (the scroll containing portions of the first five books in the Old Testament) in existence. So whenever there was a bad king in the palace and lazy priests in the Temple, people kind of lost track of those scrolls. In fact, at one point the scrolls were essentially forgotten, bricked up in a dusty old closet somewhere. They weren't discovered again until the Temple was being cleaned out and fixed up during the reign of young Josiah, a righteous king. So Josiah gathered the entire nation together to hear the Law read aloud—words that had been so long unread that they were almost entirely forgotten. And as the people listened, they suddenly realized what they'd long since forgotten: God had given them rules to live by, and they'd been breaking them all these years.

Sometimes I feel like the people of Israel in this story. I put my Bible on the bookshelf or the bedside table, and if I don't remember to read it every day, it gets buried under the clutter of my life, collecting dust. I go on my merry way, thinking all is right with the world, when in fact I'm sinning against God every time I turn around—because I've forgotten what's in that Book. Then when I finally pick it up again, out of guilt or a sudden burst of spiritual energy, I'm simply stunned by the words I read in those pages. I *swear* I've read them before. And yet it's like my brain is a sieve, sifting out those things I don't want to hear. I read the words anew, and my first reaction is to grieve. I'm ashamed of all the ways I've failed to live up to God's expectations. I'm crushed when I realize how casually I've treated him.

Even so, his Word contains more than just warnings; it contains many beautiful promises too. Here's one of my favorites: "Return to me," God says through the prophet Zechariah (1:3), "and I will return to you." In fact, when I'm not reading my Bible, what I'm *really* missing out on are more than just the rules to live by—I'm missing out on the lifelines to cling to.

2 Kings 22:1-13

The Novembers of My Life

The ancient people of the Middle East had a custom in which they'd tear (or rend) their robes in a moment of great grief or fury to symbolize the magnitude of the situation.// In a culture where clothing was handmade from scratch and often woven from top to bottom out of a single piece of cloth, this was a significant and irreversible act. You couldn't simply go out and buy another robe. Everyone who saw you knew that some great sin or loss had occurred. So what would happen today if we wore our spiritual condition for all to see?

> *As usual, the Novembers of my life*
> *begin with great commitment to you*
> *but then taper off*
> *into worlds of my own making,*
> *seasons of self*
> *that prove only what I can't do*
> *when left to my own devices.*
> *Every year I return with your people*
> *to the dusty, unused Temple*
>   *(my bedside table)*
> *to hear the Word again,*
> *that book long silent on the shelf*
> *or lost in the storeroom,*
> *boarded up and forgotten*
> *until some prophet pulls out the nails,*
> *clears away the dust,*
> *rolls out the aged scrolls, and says,*
> *"Hear, O people."*
> *And every year I want to rend my garments.*
> *I weep at the words I'd forgotten*
> *and renew my covenant*
> *to be good and read the Bible*
> *and not wait another year*
> *or generation*
> *before I read it again . . .*
>
> *. . . But lurking in the background is that small voice*
> *from somewhere in the prophets that whispers,*
> *"Rend your heart and not your garments."*
>
> *O Lord, change me from the inside out.*

Joel 2:12-13 (NIV)

// See 2 Samuel 13:8-19 (not an easy story); 2 Kings 22:8-11; Job 1:13-22; and Mark 14:60-64. Actually, none of these are easy stories.

Praise Him Always

It's Thanksgiving weekend, when the entire country turns itself upside down and inside out in order for families to get together—even though it's a major inconvenience and there really isn't anything to do once we gather except stuff ourselves and watch football. Too often we ignore the main title of the day: *Thanks*giving, or giving thanks to God for all he has given us. But of course the real question is, why aren't we doing this *every* day? Why don't we praise him for *right now*, for this moment, wherever we are?

> Praise the Lord for now,
> for right here:
> for these curtains
> on these lovely windows
> in this dear old house
> in this quiet room
> on this wintry, empty day.
> Praise the Lord for all the people
> I haven't yet talked to,
> who are precious to him,
> to whom I should give
> my wholehearted attention.
> Praise the Lord
> for all the things about himself
> I haven't yet learned
> but can't wait to learn.
> May I be conscious enough to give and receive
> what I should out of every encounter
> with people and ideas today.
> Praise the Lord for the meals I'll share,
> the folks I'll meet.
> May I seek to truly serve them
> with my words and actions.
> Praise the Lord!

Psalm 106:1-5

Ambassador

Well, it's hard to believe the second long season of Ordinary Time, that time in the church calendar when nothing "special" is going on, is winding down. Ever since the celebration of Pentecost in late spring, the focus of our spiritual growth has been less on the story of Jesus and more on living the Christian life—living like Jesus in the everyday, ordinary moments. But now we're approaching one of my favorite times of year: that glorious stretch from Advent to Easter when we rehearse the stories of the birth, death, and resurrection of our Lord. And the last hurrah before this happens is "Christ the King Sunday," when we celebrate the promised return of Jesus in all his glory as Lord and King of the universe. As Handel's *Messiah* says, "And he shall reign forever and ever . . . forever and ever . . . forever and ever. . . . Hallelujah! Hallelujah!" (and some people complain that *contemporary* praise choruses are repetitive!).

Anyway, here's a little psalm about living as a citizens of the King while waiting for his return. How does our citizenship in his Kingdom change the way we spend Ordinary Time?

You are the King.
Today I am an ambassador
from your Kingdom of light,
bringing your message
to those who stumble around in darkness.
I will love the people I meet
and have meals with
and laugh with
and argue with.
May your words break like sunlight
on their hearts
and fill their imaginations
with good things.
Awaken their desire
to be under your kingship,
to live by your rules
and to love you with all they are.

May they transfer their citizenship
to your Kingdom,
today and always.

2 Corinthians 5:18-21; Colossians 1:12-14

The Day of Rest

At our community house lately we've been trying to be more intentional about keeping the Sabbath. After all, it's a *commandment*, not merely a suggestion, and it ranks number four overall in God's original Top Ten list. In Exodus 20, God tells the people, "Remember to observe the Sabbath day by keeping it holy" (verse 8) and then clarifies this by saying it's to be "a day of rest" (verse 10). Just as God took a break after the six days of Creation, God's people take a day off on the seventh day. Specifically, God says, "No one in your household may do any work" (verse 10).

Okay, let's pause there for a moment. Notice that this doesn't say, "No one may work except Mom, who must prepare an awesome Sunday dinner with all the fixings and then spend three hours cleaning up afterwards." And it doesn't say, "No one may work except the kid who forgot to start his science project that is due Monday." It doesn't say, "No one except Dad, who loves working in the yard on his day off" or "No one but the convenience store clerk or the golf caddies or the lady at the grocery store checkout lane."

God says *no one*. Period.

That's tricky, isn't it? Because often we view Sunday (the Christian Sabbath) as a day to play or catch up on everything we didn't do on Saturday. We come home from church—if we go to church at all—and then hit the ski slopes or the Internet; and when we're done playing, we think, *Yikes, I didn't finish that essay that's due tomorrow* or *I never did pick up those groceries*. And the day is shot. No more rest. No more Sabbath.

What if we finished everything we needed to on Saturday so that we could truly rest on Sunday? And I mean *rest*: go for a walk, read a book, play games with others (not just alone on the computer), take a nap. What if we decided we wouldn't spend any money on Sundays—because spending money means someone *else* has to work on what should be a day off? You know—not going out for brunch, not shopping at the mall, not even stopping to get gas after church.

What if we took God's commandments seriously?

Exodus 20:8-11

No Work of Any Kind

I've been thinking about the commandment to keep the Sabbath holy, and I'm fascinated by the difference between Exodus 20:8-11 and Deuteronomy 5:12-15. (I had no idea the Ten Commandments are listed twice in the Bible: first in Exodus 20 and then again in Deuteronomy 5.) Anyway, God gives two different reasons why his people are to rest. In Exodus, they're told to rest on the seventh day because that's what God did in the Creation story: He worked hard for six days creating the world and then took a break. But in Deuteronomy, God tells his people to rest on the Sabbath because they must remember they were once slaves in Egypt. They don't need to be slaves again—even to the work they enjoy and get paid to do.

Hmm, puts an interesting spin on how we spend our Sunday afternoons, eh? I mean, it's one thing to take the day off from work or school and actually stay home. And it's one thing to take a break from all your household tasks. But it's quite another to take a break from the work you really love to do (for those of us who love working). For instance, I could write all day, every day, and never get bored. And some people actually like doing household chores(!).

The other thing I notice about the passage in Deuteronomy is that God gets really specific about not enslaving anyone *else* on the Sabbath either. Back then it was common practice for family households to have male and female slaves. And we could easily pride ourselves that there's no such thing as slavery in this country anymore. But is there? What about the waitress at Sunday brunch? What about the clerk at the gas station? What about the workers in the mall who clean the bathrooms and take out the trash and sweep the floors after the weekend crowds? If it weren't for our greediness as a nation, they wouldn't have to work on Sundays. So in a way, they are slaves after all.

What if we made sure they didn't have to work on Sundays—or at least not for us?

Deuteronomy 5:12-15

From Sunset to Sunset

It's late Saturday afternoon at our community house, and we're rushing around finishing chores and projects before Sabbath begins. And I don't mean we're getting ready for church tomorrow: I mean we're anticipating the approach of sunset *today*. That's when Sabbath begins for us: on Saturday night, as the sun sinks below the horizon and the winter sky gradually darkens to a rich blue. We come to the dinner table having turned off our computers, folded the laundry, closed our textbooks, and taken out the garbage, so we can sit in the approaching dark and experience the grace of not being needed to run the world.

As a community, we've decided to follow the traditional Jewish approach to marking time, which holds that a twenty-four-hour day begins at sundown and ends the following sundown. We don't do this all week long—just from Saturday night to Sunday night. As we gather at the dinner table, we greet the approach of sunset by lighting candles and praying a traditional prayer ("Blessed are you, O Lord our God, King of the universe""). We also bless the children and thank God for the elements of our meal. Then after dinner we enjoy one another's company or watch a movie or rest quietly in our rooms, preparing our hearts for worship with God's people in the morning. Ideally, we even go to bed early(!).

On Sunday evening the process is similar. We meet at the table, light candles, and pray the traditional prayer—except that after dinner we bid farewell to the day of rest and acknowledge a new day, a new week of work and school and all the tasks God has given us to do. It's the deep breath before the plunge. Now we can turn our computers back on, check our upcoming schedules, answer e-mail, throw in a load of laundry, and generally prepare ourselves for the week ahead. Rather than frantically dashing about on Monday morning, cursing our ill-preparedness, we're able to face the week refreshed.

You wouldn't think such a small change would make such a big difference, but after several weeks of practicing the Sabbath—I mean, *really* setting it apart as something unique and precious—I'm beginning to suspect our spiritual ancestors were onto something.

Ezekiel 20:10-12

// For deeper insight into traditional Jewish Sabbath—or *Shabbat*—practices, Lauren Winner's *Mudhouse Sabbath* is a great place to start (see "More Spiritual Caffeine" at the end of this book for publication details).

In This Together

One of the reasons our community house has been discussing how we can keep the Sabbath is because it truly takes all of us to make it happen. We share a communal meal together, even on Sundays, so someone has to plan ahead with the groceries, and someone has to plan ahead with the meal, and someone has to clean up afterward. And meanwhile it's easy to start projects around the house or the yard, or to do a few loads of laundry, and pretty soon everyone is looking industrious. It's hard for one person to have a day of rest while everyone else is working.

But if we've *all* made the commitment to keep the Sabbath as a day of rest, then ideally the groceries have already been bought and Sunday dinner has already been prepared by Saturday night. The bulk of the pots and pans are washed before we eat, rather than left for later, and we throw the rest in the dishwasher rather than wash it all by hand, as is our usual water-conserving practice. The clothesline is empty. The vacuum cleaner is silent. The computers stay turned off.

So what are we doing instead? Well, wander through our house on a Sunday afternoon and hopefully you'll find people reading, napping, playing games together, or chatting on the porch in the sun. This past Sunday we decorated the house for the holidays. Advent begins this week, so we pulled boxes out of the closets and went through them one by one, reminiscing about our families and past Christmases. We played Christmas music while stringing white lights on the mantel and lighting candles in the windows. We brainstormed how we could acquire a Nativity set that children can play with (why are these so hard to find, anyway?). We taught our resident three-year-old that we decorate with evergreens to remind us of God's eternal love and we light candles to remember that Jesus is the Light of the World. And next week we'll probably decorate some more.

In the end, when it comes to keeping the Sabbath, we're in this together.

Isaiah 58:13-14

About to Happen

Advent begins this week—that season in the church year when we look forward to Jesus' birthday—and my Sunday bulletin reads, "The word *Advent* comes from the Latin *adventus*, which means 'coming.'" As I'm reading, I realize that if you add three letters to *Advent* you get *adventure*, which means the two words must be related somehow. Which is odd, because I've always thought of Advent as a time of *waiting* for something to happen, whereas an adventure is about going out and *making* things happen. But now I wonder.

So I crack open my Oxford English Dictionary (affectionately known as the OED) and find out what the connection is between these two strikingly similar words I've never noticed together before. (By the way, the OED is really cool if you're a word geek like me—it gives the root language and the original meaning of stuff.) I find out that both *Advent* and *adventure* are from the Latin verb *advenire*, meaning "arrive"—from which we get ancient nouns like *adventus* and *adventurus*: "about to happen."

My mind is mulling this over now. Suppose Advent isn't only about waiting for something to happen but also about joining the adventure God has in store—the thing that's "about to happen," that only God knows?

The wise men saw the night sky and knew something was about to happen, so they packed their passports and hit the road in the general direction of the star. The shepherds saw the angels, heard something was about to happen, and took off running to see if it was true. Joseph had dreams in which angels told him things were going happen, so he did what they told him to do. Even the baby John, mostly asleep in Elizabeth's womb, woke up and kicked for joy when the voice of Mary murmured through the walls of his warm little world. Nobody just sat around waiting during Advent.

And neither should I. Where did I ever get the idea that I must wait and have the next step figured out before I take it? As long as God knows what's just around the corner, I can keep moving forward. It's about diving in before I'm even quite sure what's about to happen. That's the adventure. That's Advent.

Luke 1:39-45

Please Stand By

I have to tell you about Justin the Theologian, who goes up front for the children's sermon at our church each Sunday. I think every church has a Justin, the one with the loud voice who answers all the questions with "God!" or "Jesus!" and never lets any of the other kids get a word in edgewise. It reminds me of the joke about the pastor who asks the children, "What's small and furry and has a fluffy tail and lives in trees?" and one kid responds, "Well, I know the answer is supposed to be Jesus, but it sounds like a squirrel to me." That's Justin.

Anyway, so the other day the teacher was talking about how Advent is all about waiting. She asked, "When are the times we have to wait for things?" Amid the various responses about waiting at stoplights or checkout lines, Justin launches into this random story about playing a video game that morning that was on the TV, not the PlayStation or whatever, and how he turned it on and plugged it in and set up the joystick and clicked on all this menu stuff and this happened and that happened and then—just when we all thought the teacher would have to interrupt—he said, "And then the screen said, 'Please stand by.'"

And he got it right. That's exactly what Advent is all about. That's what waiting on God is like. I think of Simeon and Anna in today's Bible story, those wonderful old saints who spent most of their lives worshipping and praying in the Temple of Jerusalem, waiting on God's promised Messiah. Sometimes God asks us to act, to get up and do something, but other times we're simply supposed to sit tight and wait for God. And we wait because that's what the instructions said, even if nothing seems to be happening, even if we keep seeing the same thing and hearing the same thing and it looks like nothing has changed and our hands get tired clutching the joystick and we're ready to go do something else. We were politely instructed to please stand by, and if we trust the process(or), that's what we do.

Luke 2:25-38

Waiting Room

Today I don't feel so great, but honestly, I'm not fond of going to the doctor. I'll make myself completely miserable before I'll admit something's wrong and I need help. Usually this means I'll only feel worse before I feel better, and part of feeling worse is sitting in the waiting room at the doctor's office inhaling other people's germs and trying not to touch things like door handles. There's always some kid with a runny nose, rifling through the children's books in the corner and making sure he slimes everything, including *The Berenstain Bears Visit the General Practitioner* or whatever, infecting all the other kids in town. Meanwhile, the nurses seem to call everyone else's name but mine.

When I'm miserable, waiting is worse than anything else I can think of. All I want is to go home and curl up in my bed with a big box of tissues and sleep for twenty-six hours. But this doesn't mean I'll feel any better when I wake up. Instead, the real progress seems to come when I make myself even *more* miserable by first going to the doctor's office and sitting in the waiting room all afternoon until someone calls my name, inspects my tonsils, and says, "Yep, you're sick." I'm prescribed some ridiculously expensive meds to take with food every four to six hours, and by the next day I do, indeed, begin to feel better.

I suppose waiting on God is sometimes like being sick. Things are miserable. We want our circumstances to change now. We want an instant fix. And just when we're feeling as crummy as possible about the situation we find ourselves in, that's when God calls on us to act. More often than not, it means getting up and doing something we'd rather *not* do. And most likely, it means things will get worse before they get better. But then— and this is the weird part—things *do* start to get better, all because we did what he said.

During Advent I think about Mary and Joseph and how difficult things must have been for them, waiting on God. Waiting for him to smooth things out between them when it became clear that she was in fact pregnant, but not with Joseph's child (it was God's baby, but who would believe it?). . . . Waiting on God to deliver this baby safely, even though they were many miles from home and family. . . . Waiting on God to save them from Herod. . . . Always feeling more miserable before they felt better but needing to get up and do something about it anyway. . . . Never really resting until they were finally home again after sitting in the waiting room of God's promises. How can I learn to wait like that?

Matthew 1:18-25

The Sleeper

Sleep overwhelms me as I sit with my Bible and prayer book this morning. I nod in and out of consciousness, my mind attempting to produce some kind of thought, which—upon starting to wake again—I realize is nonsense, the stuff of random, incoherent dreams. Conversations drift through my head, absurd in their unrelatedness to the Scripture or to the readings or to anything having to do with my real life, much less this attempt to pray. Since prayer eludes me today, I'll have to put it on paper. . . .

This morning I struggle
in my groggy half-awakeness,
in my dark fog of dreams
to remember something . . .

. . . And, oh yeah: I praise you.

It's easy enough to write,
but it's like molasses in my mind.

Breathe the wind of your Holy Spirit
and dispel the fog, O Lord.
Disintegrate the mist out of me.

Call me to awake, this sleeper,
and rise from the dead;
to crawl and claw my way
from under the covers
of this hectic, headachy sleep,
where my dreams wear me out
and I wake up tired.
Call me forth, blinking,
into the sunrise of your grace.
Let me see you and rejoice.
Rejoice!

Praise the Lord!

Ephesians 5:8-14

The Fear of the Lord

A visiting professor once told my human development class a story about her little nephew. Apparently this child was afraid of the dark and would do anything to make sure he wasn't alone at bedtime. So his parents would attempt to put him to bed, and he'd spend the next few hours hollering for someone to bring him a glass of water or sing him a bedtime song or read him a book, and so on. Once his aunt figured out he was afraid of the dark, she came in and sat by his bed and assured him he didn't need to be frightened. "God is with you," she said. And he nodded soberly as she kissed him good-night. So she left the room, thinking *finally* everything would be all right.

But before long he hollered for his aunt again. She went in and found him cowering under the covers.

"What's wrong?" she asked.

He replied, "God is scaring me."

God is scaring me! Our first instinct is to laugh, because the child's reaction is the opposite of what his aunt wanted. We hope our children will know how much God loves them—that he's watching over them and takes care of them like a loving parent. But when we stop and think about it, we realize there's a great deal of honesty in his response. Here's this tiny child, alone in the dark, suddenly aware of another Being in the room. And yes, this Being is supposed to be loving and protective, but he's also really, really big. And powerful. And mysterious. And not like us. There's something unsettling about that.

I think the child was aware of something important that night. God is not someone we mess around with, like Mommy or Daddy or Auntie who comes running when we call. God is there for us, yes, but he's in charge. He loves us, yes, but he also holds our lives in the palm of his hand. He's not there to feed us chicken soup; he's there to save our souls. Without him we are nothing.

If that doesn't teach us to fear him, what will?

Proverbs 9:10-11

Rejoice with Trembling

The Old Testament people made a much bigger deal than we do about the "fear of the Lord." Most of the time we'd rather think of God as a kind of "cosmic therapist"[54] who patiently listens to our needy babblings and then helps us work out a solution. But this doesn't sync with what the Bible says. Instead, when God shows up, people's first instinct is to fall to the ground and hide their faces. Even in the presence of the angels—God's mere messengers—people act like it's the end of the world. They know something about God that we've forgotten.

God is more than a comfy buddy we pal around with. Sure, he loves us like a daddy, but he's also the emperor and judge of the universe, holding the power of life and death in his mighty hands. He punishes entire nations for their deeds of injustice, for their oppression of the poor and vulnerable. Presidents and kings quake in terror when God shows up. Angels bow before his throne. And Scripture tells us that no human being can look upon his face and live (see Exodus 33:18-20).

So what has changed since ancient times? Why don't we fling ourselves to the ground anymore when we come before God in prayer? Why don't we hide our faces when we suddenly realize that God is in the house? I think part of it is because we've forgotten just whom we're dealing with. We've gotten too comfortable, too proud of our personal status as God's beloved children, too wrapped up in our modern democratic ideals to realize that God has veto power over every single human life.

Yet at the same time, Jesus made God accessible in a way he never had been before. We can walk with him, talk with him, experience his love and grace. Because of what Jesus did for us on the cross, we are no longer separated from God but will be brought "with great joy into his glorious presence without a single fault" (Jude 1:24).

So somehow we must strike a balance between abject terror and casual unconcern in our relationship with God. We must, as the poet said in Psalm 2:11, "serve the LORD with *reverent* fear, and rejoice *with trembling*" (emphasis added). But how?

Psalm 2

Look to God

Last summer, when I was on staff for a youth camp, we learned a worship song titled "In the Lord I'll Be Ever Thankful," which originated from the Taizé community in France.// We must've have sung it at least three hundred times, especially as we walked into chapel every morning for the daily prayer service. Some days I wasn't feeling terribly thankful—especially if we'd been up late the night before or I had a headache or I was anxious about leading my workshops—so it took me a couple of rounds before I could really mean it. But there was one line that always stood out because it seemed so foreign to our situation: "Look to God, do not be afraid."

There we were in the glorious chapel, enjoying the peacefulness, soaking up the sunlight pouring through the myriad stained-glass windows, and if anything seemed to be far, far away it was fear. And yet the song instructed us to not be afraid, as if we were singing in the middle of a hurricane with the waters rising around us. I suppose some of us felt that way with the various circumstances in our lives, but at least for me, in that moment, the words seemed somewhat out of place.

It's now many months later, and I'm still singing the song every day. Except this time I'm singing it at night in our community house, surrounded by new friends who come from all walks of life—including women and children who are in need of temporary housing until they get back on their feet financially. So there we are, singing about thankfulness by candlelight, and I can't help but wonder what the future holds for my new friends. Each day brings new worries. And suddenly I get it. Suddenly that simple line, tucked away in the middle of the song, actually seems relevant. I look around at the faces of my friends and sing, "Look to God, do not be afraid," and I really mean it.

Isaiah 41:9-10

// For more information about this ancient-future Christian monastic community, visit www.taize.fr/en. Many of their song lyrics are posted in full under the "Prayer and Song" section.

Do Not Be Afraid

"Don't be afraid," the angel Gabriel said to a young Jewish girl named Mary (Luke 1:30). "Do not be afraid," an angel told Mary's fiancé, Joseph (Matthew 1:20). "Don't be afraid!" said the angel to the shepherds on the night Jesus was born (Luke 2:10). Every time an angel showed up in the Bible, the looks on people's faces must've indicated just how terrifying the presence of these beings could be. And yet our culture depicts them as fat little cherubs or sweet young supermodels! As C. S. Lewis said, "In Scripture the visitation of an angel is always alarming; it has to begin by saying 'Fear not.' The Victorian angel looks as if it were going to say, 'There, there.'"[55] Has no one else ever read what Scripture says about angels and archangels?

The other night during evening prayer in our community house—right after we sang, "Look to God, do not be afraid" (see December 8) and I had begun reading aloud the assigned Scripture passage—we heard gunshots. They were just a few blocks away. My voice faltered for a moment while everyone sort of blinked at each other. But I kept reading. After a moment, our house leader quietly stood up and stepped onto the front porch to see if there was anything worth calling the police about. Nothing. We went on with the worship service, eventually blew out the candles, and then stood around for another half hour talking about the realities of inner-city life.

"Do not be afraid," we sang that night. "Don't be frightened," the angels tell the women and men whose hearts pound in their chests, whose voices falter in the middle of evening prayer. "Look to God," the angels sing when the darkness of the world seeks to drown us. Radiant with glory, they silence our pounding hearts and strengthen our feeble voices and overwhelm us with a power more steady and eternal than the violence of this world could ever overmatch.

Angels stand to our left and to our right with flaming swords. Cherubim and seraphim are our rear guard. The hosts of heaven go before us like an army with banners, not like a bunch of fat little babies with harps. Thank God!

Psalm 34:1-17

He Who Watches Over You

I wonder if anyone has ever done a study on how many times the average American hits the snooze button in the mornings. I'm sure I've bumped up the average over the years. Even now my husband will come into the bedroom in the morning after having eaten and showered and spent time in prayer (and probably waxed the car, for all I know), and I'm still there, slumbering away. He sits on the edge of the bed and watches me for a while, and as I slowly drift into consciousness, he sings little morning songs to get my attention. Those are God moments, when I feel like a small child whose parent has been watching over her through the dark night—the magic parent who miraculously never sleeps.

I wrote the following prayer while thinking about the contrast between the God in Psalm 121, who "never slumbers or sleeps," and the Jesus in Mark 4, who crashed in the back of a fishing boat, exhausted. There's something both comforting and alarming about the idea of Jesus falling asleep like any ordinary human being. And yet isn't there something both comforting and alarming about the idea of God never sleeping at all?

> *Father, you are wide awake.*
> *You never sleep*
> *or drop from exhaustion, powerless.*
> *But you know what it feels like*
> *. . . don't you . . . ?*
> *to be wakened out of oblivion*
> *to a plunging deck*
> *and a panicked crew*
> *who frantically call your name,*
> *their hair wild and drenched,*
> *their eyes pleading, fearful.*
> *You rolled out of that berth*
> *and rocked your way—*
> *still groggy and drained—*
> *across the heaving surface of a boat*
> *to the bow above the waves;*
> *you grasped the halyard*
> *with the spray in your face*
> *and summoned words from the depths*
> *of your spirit.*
> *And your awakening out of that slumber*
> *was Power enough*
> *to put a storm to sleep.*

Psalm 121; Mark 4:35-41

Flying

Generally speaking, I don't have trouble flying. I do it a lot, and most of the time it's a smooth ride. But the other day as I buckled myself into the tail section of a jet bound for Detroit, the pilot came on the intercom saying we could expect some turbulence due to winds. And of course the first thing that came to my hyperactive imagination was that scene from the TV series *Lost*, where the tail section of the plane breaks off in midair and various passengers and crew get sucked out the back. *Great.*

Now, I love that show. I'm hopelessly addicted to watching past episodes on DVD. But thinking about it while I'm at ten thousand feet isn't exactly the healthiest exercise for my imagination. For starters, I was in the wrong section of the plane; I should have picked the middle with Jack or Kate. Then, as the plane dipped and bucked in the predicted turbulence, I glanced sideways at my fellow passengers and thought, *Even if we did survive, would I want to be stuck on a spooky island with these people?*

I felt on the verge of hyperventilating until I remembered something important. I wish I could say it was a Scripture verse or the mental image of angels under each wing, but I'm ashamed to say it was merely a statistic from the National Transportation Safety Board, which is that many more people die from car accidents than from plane crashes every year. For some reason this calmed me down. I don't hyperventilate every time I get in a car, do I? And yet technically I'm in more danger on the road than in the air. With this knowledge, I began to relax. The plane gave one last bump, and the turbulence was over.

Strangely enough, *that's* when my mind turned to God. Gratitude, relief, humility— these were the emotions that washed over me. I felt awed by the power of the air. It was almost exhilarating to know how small I was in relation to the planet God had made. Why he would choose to love me—even when I am so panicked that I forget him completely— was a mystery I couldn't fathom. All I could do was thank him over and over again.

In the end, what other response is there?

Psalm 62

Skeptics

The holidays are upon us, that season when we think a lot about family. For many of us, these are good reflections; but others really struggle this time of year.

Perhaps you've experienced firsthand how your own relatives can sometimes be the most skeptical and discouraging people you know. Maybe it's because they love you so much that they don't want to see you get hurt. So before you even have a chance to try something new, they offer words of caution and maybe even rebuke. Certainly, they know your weaknesses better than anyone else, giving them insight into what you can and can't do. But sometimes, lingering jealousies and resentments—or the desire to control—give their skepticism a cruel edge, more like a calculated campaign to crush your self-esteem so you can't strive for anything without being mocked or shamed in front of everybody. I've done that to my own loved ones, which I can't recall without wincing. Where does such cruelty come from?

Our families also know when we're bluffing in public, and they'll call us on it. "You never did that," they'll say, or "That's not what happened." Because they know our history, they keep us from becoming the people we're not—and when we're headed down the wrong path, that's a good thing. That's part of family accountability: keeping us from living a lie. I need my family to do this for me sometimes.

But we see few of these same cautions or concerns at the beginning of Jesus' own story—particularly with his second cousin (or so) John the Baptist. Many Advent stories have to do with John, the "voice shouting in the wilderness" (Matthew 3:3), the prophet who prepared the way for the coming of the Messiah, instead of a birth narrative. In addition to John, the key players in Jesus' family not only seemed to embrace Jesus' unique sense of call, they trusted his character. Mary believed, Elizabeth believed, John believed and even used his celebrity status to tell everybody about it. They went public about him before he went public about himself. And if we can't trust their judgment as to what kind of person he was in the privacy of his own home and family—when the rest of the world wasn't looking—then whom can we trust?

Luke 3:15-18

Once and for All

The book of Hebrews has always struck me as odd. I mean, it's not written like any of the other New Testament letters; we're not even sure who the author is. From the very first words, it signifies a timeless approach, almost like a father reading bedtime stories to his children, rather than the compelling urgency of Paul's letters, which begin with brief greetings and earnest prayers and then quickly get down to church business. Yet the author of Hebrews is up to something eternal, unshakable. There's nothing superfluous in his (or her?) words. And in this season of Advent, I want to be paying attention.

"Long ago . . ."
What an odd way to begin.
No "dear beloveds . . ."
no exhortations or personal notes.
Just Theology 101
answering the ultimate question—
"Can God be known?"—with
a resounding yes!
He has revealed himself first
through the prophets,
mouthpieces of the Almighty,
frail and imperfect messengers;
but now—oh, now!
In these last days there is nothing
but glory,
nothing but God himself
revealed in his own likeness, begotten
as his own thumbprint,
an autobiography, line for line,
spelling Son.
No stream of verbiage
from a messenger in the desert;
no page after page
of ink-spotted judgments;
simply one Word—

Son (salvation)—

and then silence.

Hebrews 1:1-4

The Bleak Midwinter

Winter is here for good. It's funny how we treat it like some kind of nasty cold that we want to shake as quickly as possible. Even when someone lives in a lakefront house, like the one I'm visiting today, it's tempting to tell guests, "Yeah, it's pretty, but you should see it in the summertime." Most people would probably think, *What's the use of a house on the lake when you can't even play in the water this time of year?* No swimming, no boating, no swinging in the hammock with a good book. . . . Nothing but ice and cold and shoveling snow for months and months. Summer is the real point of living here. Winter is something we want to get over as quickly as possible, like the flu.

And yet here I am, sitting in the sunny family room, looking out on a frozen inlet surrounded by snow-covered woods and hills and houses, and I'm struck by how lovely it all is. I was here once before, in the summer, when the trees shaded the house and the leaves hid everything else from view. The strange part was that I couldn't really tell the lay of the land around me at all. But now I can see everything: each tree along the ridgeline, each deck and porch and rooftop, the way the sunlight slants across the hill on the other side of the inlet. And despite the fact that everything is essentially dead and barren and ugly this time of year, the whole scene has its own poignant beauty.

Sometimes I feel like my faith has entered a season of winter. God, like the sun, feels cold and distant; I know he's there, but I can't feel the warmth of his presence in my life. I'm not growing in any of the areas I'd hoped, not improving my attitude, not guarding my tongue, not learning anything new from the daily Scriptures or books I read. I want this season to be over as quickly as possible so I can return to the old days—back to the comforting sense of God's warm, loving presence without having to think much about it, back to the fun adventure of new life and growth all around me without having to work so hard. Instead, everything feels frozen and barren and bleak.

Even so, it's amazing how much clearer the view is when my soul is in winter. I'm keenly aware of God, or rather, how far away he feels. I'm able to see the bare ridgeline of my own frailty, the limits of my own abilities—which of course forces me to cry out to God for help because I recognize that I can't do any of this on my own. In spiritual winter I'm able to see things as they really are, the contours of my own sinful soul and the wide expanse of God's grace, arching like the blue sky behind it all. I take nothing for granted, which gives this season of my life its own poignant beauty.

Why do we try to rush through winter when it shows us things as they really are?

Psalm 65

Advent in Michigan[//]

In time
the sons of men
filled the world
with their evil deeds.
And God beheld
the desolate waste,
the soiled streets,
the bitter brown of barren fields;
and the sin of the world
cut him to the heart.
"I will blot from the earth
the memory of these things.
Behold, I will make all things new!"

So he gathered up the clouds
from the four corners of the sky,
their billows pregnant with promise.
He gathered them in great, dark piles
on the horizon of hills
while the weathermen watched,
the grandmothers gazed,
the schoolchildren pressed
their noses against the glass.

And God said,
"Let there be snow."
First, small white flakes,
like lace, drifting.
Then—wind, driving
snow before it, a blizzard
hiding hills from view
(and the tops of church steeples,
and the streetlights, too).
For forty days and nights
the world was covered in white,
the wretched lines of a wretched world
blurred soft overnight—
      buried, forgotten,
      as God birthed grace upon the earth.

Isaiah 43:15-19

// First published in *Time of Singing* (Winter 2002).

Snow Day

I am nine years old. Lying in the dark, hearing the wind crash around the eaves of the house, I can feel the chill air on my face as I curl deeper under the warm blankets. Snow was falling when I went to sleep the night before, falling in great feathers and piling like powdered sugar all over the brown December of this wintry, windswept farmland. Footsteps downstairs, muffled in slippered feet, join the sound of low voices—my parents are talking in the kitchen. Periodically I hear words like "school" and "snow day" through the cracks in the furnace ducts. A muffled radio joins the waking sounds of the farmhouse-parsonage.

Shivering, I slither out of bed and dart to the window, which sits low against the slope of the ceiling. I pull the thin curtains aside. It is still dark on the fields across the country road, but closer to the house, where the kitchen windows cut swaths of light across the yard, a pale luminosity hovers over the lawn, blurring lines and shapes into a moonscape of snow. The yard faintly glows. As I stand there, dancing from foot to foot, quivering like a squirrel, a distant thunder approaches, rumbling along the highway. Headlights appear over the top of the hill, and a snowplow suddenly roars by in a swirling gust of snow. Its beams confirm what I hoped was true: Snow has fallen many inches deep and continues to fall even now. The road is a beautiful mess. If the weather holds, the school buses cannot possibly get through.

But I must wait for confirmation. Grinning, I dash back to the sleigh bed, where the sheets are still slightly warm. I slide inside again, anticipating the approach of my father, the bearer of good news, coming up the stairs from the lighted kitchen. The mere fact that he takes his time this morning only feeds my growing excitement. My one hope in all my nine-year-old world is that today will be a snow day; today we will have grace.

His footsteps make their way up the stairs at the other end of our rambling house. He walks across the bare boards of the master bedroom and pauses on the landing to switch on the light. He then walks down the few steps into the room—one, two—and makes his way to my door, open just a crack. It creaks open wide. "Good morning, girls," he says. It's his usual morning voice. I hold my breath for more. He shuffles through my room to reach my sister's door, where he speaks gently again: "Good morning—don't worry about getting up just yet. There's no school today."

I let out a whoop and leap out of bed.

Grace! Grace!

Romans 10:13-15

Christmas Break

It's Christmas break, and we're lying around like slugs. My roommate (also known as husband, Tom), currently a Very Important Graduate Student, is enjoying not having classes for three whole weeks. Meanwhile I, the brave, hardworking breadwinner of the family, have devotions to write. Needless to say, it's a lot easier when he's not around distracting me with old *Lost* episodes and the MP3 player hooked into our new sound system. So rather than consider this entire afternoon a wash, I decide to enlist him in brainstorming ideas of topics for this devo. The conversation goes something like this:

Tom: You want my ideas for the whole *book*?

Sarah: Tch-yeah. What did you think I meant? [I get up and go into the bathroom. Note: We have one room to ourselves in this communal house, so it's nearly impossible to get away from each other.]

T: Hey, come back. I wasn't sure what you meant by *devo*. Are you talking about *this particular* chapter or the whole book?

[I come back with my laptop and start typing.]

T: Are you writing down what I just said?

S: No.

T: Why not? You said you'd record this conversation.

S: Look, let's just go back to the topics, okay? Do you have any ideas?

T: But you didn't write down what I just said.

S: I'm not going to.

T: Then I'm not continuing this conversation.

S: Fine, I'll record it. [I start typing again. It looks like this: lasldfl j;f algfghguepoq-ikhasjfh ldv nbakjhslkjhdf gbbncnalsdhgf hgkjhalkjhdf.]

T: Hey, wait a minute. Let me see that.

You get the picture. The conversation goes nowhere. Probably because we have no brain cells left after a semester of work and school. And now I wonder: What's my problem that I can't focus on God when my usual routine is all messed up? Why do I let even the smallest things distract me from spending time with him? If God doesn't fit into my life when I'm on Christmas break and have all the time in the world, then what makes me think I'll fit him in when I'm back to my usual busy schedule?

Psalm 119:9-16

It Will Come to Pass

Christmas is right around the corner, so we're reading all the Advent Scriptures during morning prayer. Today it strikes me how Zechariah's prophecy in Luke 1:68-79 is essentially a political speech, promoting the destruction of Rome and the return of Israel to the Jews—and perhaps that's how he understood it at the time. And quite honestly, my first thought in reading it is that none of it came true, at least not in Zechariah's lifetime. Rather than being saved from their enemies or being able to "serve God without fear," those who chose to follow this "mighty Savior" suddenly became the target of their enemies and couldn't even worship in public for more than three hundred years.

By contrast, I have the rare privilege of living in a time and in a land where that prophecy could be seen as having been fulfilled in human history. As a Christian in twenty-first-century America, I don't fear for my life every day, nor do I have to worship or serve God in secret. And yet there are many Christians around the world who don't have such freedoms. I'm acutely aware of the rare privilege this freedom gives me, as well as its particular dangers to the state of the soul. After all, other things can still rule in my heart, and other gods can still be on the throne of my life, including Self. So in spite of all our civil freedoms, we're not truly free until Christ comes again and permanently makes all prophecies come to pass. And in the meantime, we can assume that hardship will be a fact of life and that many Christians around the world will be unable to worship freely, without fear.

> O Lord, help me to accept with gratitude the rare gift of being employed in a Christian vocation without fear of reprisal from the state. Help me to use my time, my resources, and the money available for ministry wisely. Help me by the power of your Holy Spirit to do only those things that you desire and to eliminate those things that are not within your plan. Give me a radical sensitivity to your prompting, I pray, that I may be uneasy operating outside of your will. I ask for your vision and purpose to infuse all I do this day, so all that comes to pass will happen with excellence and give you glory. In Jesus' name, Amen.

Luke 1:57-79

Flame

I'm awake and alone in our darkened room with only a candle to light this page. At first I lit the candle simply to combat the smell of burned falafels from dinner, but then I happened to turn off all the other lights too, and I was reminded in that moment how much I enjoy firelight. So I thought, *Well, this is nice. Let's keep it this way for a bit.*

There's something about a solitary flame that is calming and gentle, yet strong and somewhat eerie too. Such a little thing, this flickering fire, but it illuminates the entire room. It's also dangerous, which I don't want to forget. It could tip over and catch my tablecloth on fire and then engulf the room and ultimately this building. One flame—that's all it takes. Such power contained in so tiny a thing.

As I putter around by its small light—folding laundry, putting things away at day's end—I'm aware of how ancient fire is, how people have used it in the dark of winter like this for thousands of years. I feel connected, suddenly, to those people of the ancient world, as if candlelight reminds me of what we human beings once knew about the elemental and most important things in the universe. We cannot fully function without fire. We need it for warmth, for light, for cooking, for heating the water by which to sanitize the things we use. We need it to live.

But because it is so dangerous, flames are usually hidden in our modern world. The pilot light of the stove or furnace is carefully positioned out of sight. Electricity is channeled through wires, and we never see the blue flame of its power unless something has gone wrong. If we build a fire in a fireplace, it's generally for fun, to create atmosphere, not because we need it to survive.

What would happen if we put fire back in its proper place, at the center of our existence again, its flames continually reminding us of how small and dependent we are? How would that change our understanding of Jesus' birth, as it was prophesied in Luke 1:78-79?

> The morning light from heaven is about
>   to break upon us,
> to give light to those who sit in darkness
>   and in the shadow of death,
> and to guide us to the path of peace.

Isaiah 9:1-7

Stars

Recently my husband surprised me with a trip to a nearby planetarium, where the instructor demonstrated what the night sky looks like to most of us city dwellers: the orange glow on the horizon from acres and acres of streetlamps and parking lots and well-lit neighborhoods, with the nearly invisible stars in the background. Then she said, "But what if we take away all the light pollution? What did the sky look like to people thousands of years ago?" As she spoke, the orange slowly faded and the sky began to grow dark like velvet until I could no longer see Tom's face. The stars leaped into clarity, glittering like precious gems, and the hidden star clusters—normally too dim to see—filled the empty spaces between the constellations until the whole dome was dancing. The schoolchildren around us gasped in astonishment.

I think of the wise men, traveling at night. In order to follow the star, they must have had to sleep during the day, which meant that for weeks—possibly months—they rose at dusk when the first stars began to appear and then plunged into the oncoming night to follow the one unusual star that blazed low on the horizon. At the first light of dawn, when the star set or faded, they made camp and went to sleep, waiting for the darkness again so they could resume their strange journey. What wonders they must have seen in the sky while traveling along the desert road at night! And what terrors they must have encountered too: the lurking bandits, the prowling lions, the deteriorating trail crumbling away into canyons or disappearing into clefts of rock. No streetlights to guide their way, either.

When Jesus gazed at his people two thousand years ago and said, "I am the light of the world" (John 8:12), what did they know about light that we with our modern electricity have since forgotten? Such a small thing, a flame, and yet it conquers even the deepest corners of space—for stars are fire and flame, and their light illuminates dark pockets of the universe that no human eye has seen. He is a Light like that. He is the Morning Star, that glorious planet sparkling on the horizon before the sun comes up. He is the Sun of Righteousness itself, rising as the greatest star of all to conquer the darkness of our world.

Have I, fooled by the false light of this false world, forgotten what the wise men once knew?

Matthew 2:1-12

DECEMBER 21—
WINTER SOLSTICE

Darkness

Today is the shortest day of the year, the official start of winter, though for most of my family in the North, winter started months ago. I remember in high school getting up in the dark and dashing to the shower, where I'd let warm water pour over me until I could move without shivering. We ate breakfast with the lights on in the house, darkness pressing at all the windows, and no hint of sunrise for hours yet. We were at the western edge of the eastern time zone and almost as far north as the 45th parallel—halfway between the equator and the north pole—which meant I wouldn't see sunrise until my second hour of classes.

So I went to school in the dark, sat in class looking out at the streetlights and falling snow, and wondered what sort of crazy institution would require human beings to function effectively before the sun came up. First hour was basically a wash, all of us blinking in the light like bats startled out of their cozy caves, unable to process anything the teacher was saying. (Whoever decided teenagers can function before 8 a.m. should be impeached.) It wasn't much better in the afternoon, either. Walking in the wintry dusk to my five o'clock volleyball practice, I remember thinking, *Doesn't the sun set at like ten or something in the summer? This is just wrong.*

And there *is* something "wrong" about the dark, in the sense that it's not the normal state of life as we usually envision it. Unless we're vampires or something, we don't stay up all day and then greet the approach of night with a sigh of relief: "Ah, finally. It's dark." But if we stay up all night from insomnia or terror, we greet the dawn with joy: "Hurrah! The night is over." Darkness feels unsafe somehow. Strange things happen in it—nightmares and crimes and crazy things people wouldn't dare do in the daylight. Even from ancient times, dark has been associated with evil because it is the realm of shadows and deception and nameless fears. And all throughout the Bible, we see darkness at war with the Light. Instinctively, even as we go about our daily winter routines, we know this.

Inside me, the same battle is going on. Part of me doesn't want God's searchlight of truth and righteousness to probe the areas I wish to keep hidden from him and from everybody else. I want those dark areas, those shadows. I don't want to be startled out of my cozy, comfortable worldliness and thrust into the light, where I'm forced to function as the person God wants me to be. And yet something deep inside me knows that darkness is wrong, darkness is doomed, because eternal dawn will come someday. Will I embrace it like I do the sunrise on this, the shortest day of the year?

1 John 1:5-7

Not Fair

Tonight my husband, Tom, and I helped my in-laws wrap gifts—hundreds of Christmas gifts—for all the various members of the family, including the young grandchildren. Wrapping for everyone else was fairly easy, but wrapping for the kids was a nightmare. We had to pay scrupulous attention to every package so that each child received the same number of presents as his or her siblings. The last thing we want is a meltdown on Christmas morning if Junior discovers that his sister has received a total of seven presents from Grandma and Grandpa while he has only six. Forget that one of his presents costs more than three of his sister's packages combined; little kids see the world through the lens of quantity, not quality. Seven equals seven; fair equals fair.

The same thing was true in my family when I was growing up, I'm ashamed to say, and I know we weren't the only family like that. What is it about gifts—those undeserved and unearned items meant to express unconditional love—that turns us into howling, hissing, grumbling, crabby brats? And who ever made us kids the family accountants, keeping track of who gets what and who owes whom and whether or not things are fair?

I glance through the New Testament and find all kinds of grumbling about the unfairness of things. There's the parable of the workers in the vineyard, who complain when the ones who arrived last are paid the same as the ones who arrived first (see Matthew 20:1-16). There's the story about the rebellious son, whose older brother gets annoyed when the father throws a party celebrating his brother's return (see Luke 15:11-32)—I mean, why doesn't the good son get a party? *He's* the one who has been there all along, doing his father's will, hasn't he? Elsewhere, a condemned and dying criminal receives a pardon; prostitutes and tax collectors are given tickets to the Kingdom; the poor and the outcasts are thrown a party by the king." What sort of parenting does God think he's up to, distributing such extravagant gifts so arbitrarily, and especially to the "kids" who least deserve it?

But he turns the tables on us. "Should you be jealous because I am kind?" asks the owner of the vineyard (Matthew 20:15). These are God's words to us, of course—to every crabby kid who ever complained that so-and-so got more presents, to every sibling who ever sulked in his or her room after Christmas morning, to every Christian who ever felt a flash of jealousy when a friend landed a great job or got engaged or bought a nice new car. Technically speaking, as the Bible reminds me, the only things I *deserve* to find under God's Christmas tree are punishments for my sins. That I receive any good thing at all is pure grace: undeserved, unearned, because my Father loves me—just as he loves all my brothers and sisters. What business do I have getting angry if God shows his love to them, too?

Psalm 103

// See Luke 23:39-43; Matthew 21:28-32; Matthew 22:1-14.

At the Inn: Part 1

During the Christmas season one year, I went with my husband to the local homeless shelter, where he was a volunteer "innkeeper" once a month. Our town was small enough that the shelter was really just a house with enough beds for maybe seven people, so it was much cozier than you might expect—though the guests themselves were rather rough around the edges.

That particular night was unusual because a young family had checked into the shelter: a father, a mother, and their adorable baby girl. As I watched the other guests and volunteers interact with this child, I was suddenly aware of the Bethlehem moment unfolding before my eyes. Here's the first part of my reflections from that night:

> It was quiet there at the inn
> when along came Amy and Ben,
> traveling the Bethlehem road.
> Homeless, helpless,
> without family,
> with child,
> unmarried—
> they were on the fringe.
> So these two sometime innkeepers
> stepped in to the role
> of drawing them in, offering room,
> setting extra places at the table,
> lest they be turned away into the cold and dark.
> We unloaded the donkey,
> bustled around with dinner,
> made jokes, tried to put them at ease,
> tried to overlook
> their unmarried-ness,
> their with-child-ness,
> their helplessness;
> while they, at our mercy,
> accepted it all with the
> strange humility and trust
> that come from poverty.

Luke 2:1-7

At the Inn: Part 2

Here's the second part of the reflection I wrote after our Bethlehem evening at the homeless shelter (see December 23):

And then there was Moira,
the baby—beautiful, shining,
crawling around, alert and cheerful.
She drew us in. We forgot
all the awkwardness of homelessness.
We stopped bustling.
My innkeeper's hands
reached out as she cooed and grinned
and I pulled her onto my lap.
Oh, joy! Such unconditional love,
such wonder and curiosity
on the rosy, precious face!
And meanwhile the other guests came and went:
the shepherds who shuffled in
from their AA groups,
Danny with tattoos up his arms,
telling story after story
of his amazing, impossible life.
They oohed at the baby . . .
The phone rang.
The young couple ate their dinner.

Then entered the wise man,
Simeon, big and bearded and kind.
Moira's face lit up
in fascination and expectancy
as he crouched next to her,
his gray eyes sparkling.
Her tiny hands grabbed
at the white beard, the glasses,
the wrinkles around the eyes.
He had a new love, this wise man—
couldn't hide his adoration.
He lifted her to the ceiling
with those big, gentle hands,
his face fulfilled, wondering.

And I was blessed in Bethlehem.

Luke 2:8-20

Absurd

You'd think it'd be easy to come up with something profound to say on Christmas Day. There's a ready-made topic at hand: the birth of God, the coming of Jesus, our Savior. But by now all the great ideas have been used up already, all the profound stuff has been said over the last two thousand years. And at least to me, the story has become so familiar that it has almost lost its sense of power, of mystery, of wonder and amazement. Instead, the only thing that amazes me anymore is how absurd this holiday has become.

Exhibit A: Yesterday in a store window I saw a stuffed mama snowman next to a daddy snowman with a baby snowman between them in what looked like . . . yes . . . a manger. The Word has become snow and dwelt among us.

Exhibit B: Next door to my in-laws' house, where we're staying for the holidays, is a giant, glowing, blow-up Santa like the kind you once saw only in department stores or the Macy's parade. He's waving toward the cul-de-sac as if hordes of small children are driving by. (Note: *Cul-de-sac* is another way of saying A DEAD END THAT NOBODY DRIVES DOWN EXCEPT THE SIX PEOPLE WHO LIVE THERE.)

You get the idea.

Part of me thinks this kind of absurdity might be excused on the grounds that, long before Jesus arrived, the pagans celebrated winter solstice with all kinds of festivals and feasts and pageantry. Which means that as our culture loses its memory of the true Christmas story, it reverts back to those older, darker roots, focusing less on the holy mystery and more on the materialistic impulse to "eat, drink, and be merry, for tomorrow we die." Perhaps this is to be expected.

But then another part of me wonders if we've heard the story so often that we've deliberately grown deaf to it. The original root of the word *absurd* in Latin is *absurdus*, meaning "deaf, muffled." It's like the whole world has put its hands over its ears and is hollering at God, "Whatdya say? Something about a baby?" Because if we take the story seriously, it might make claims on us that we'd rather not have to deal with, such as letting God be in control of our decisions or giving up the material things we ravenously desire. The angels sing God's Good News from the sky, but thanks to the absurdity of this world, no one's listening. A baby cries in a feeding trough, but he cries into the darkness, and no one hears.

No wonder Mark began his Gospel with "a voice shouting in the wilderness" instead of a birth narrative (see Mark 1:3). He knew his audience would grow stone-deaf to the mystery of it all. I hope I can still hear at least a little bit of what God is saying on this holy night.

Mark 1:1-3

Strangers

My husband and I are on the road traveling home after Christmas with family. Wherever we travel, I'm always amazed at the sheer volume of people in the world. We drive for hours and then come upon a city like Columbus, Ohio—one of those cities you learn about in fifth grade when you study the fifty states, but that's about all you know about it—and as we get closer, we see more and more development—suburbs and businesses and factories and malls—and the traffic gets heavier, and the exits and on-ramps more frequent. And then all of a sudden, we're snaking through a spaghetti bowl of expressways right downtown, surrounded by thousands of people in cars and buildings and streets as far as the eye can see. *Who are they all?* I wonder. *Where are they going? What thoughts are running through their heads? How does our God keep track of every human heart in just this one city, let alone the entire world?*

All those people have an interior life just as I do. They look out at the world from their small window of self, through eyes that can take in only a little bit at a time, just like mine, and they are just as obsessed with their own issues and problems and relationships as I am. Inside their heads, they are thinking and dreaming and observing, just like I am. Which means that what I see when I look at them is only a small part of who they really are, because who I am when others look at me is only a small part of who I really am. And yet the amazing thing is that if God knows me to the depths of my being, as I believe he does, then he knows each one of these people too. All these strangers, zooming around in cars and riding up elevators and shopping at the mall—none of them are strangers to God, though he may be a stranger to them.

Then here comes our God, into the midst of it—our Savior, Jesus. He arrives smack in the middle of this mess of expressways and urban malls, looks each person in the eye, knows him or her by name, understands the thoughts and dreams and hopes and fears of each one, and says, *There are no strangers in my world.* He pushes through the mob of needy hearts, through all those who follow him in desperation, begging for help with their problems—he pushes through in order to seek the orphan, the widow, the foreigner, the one who gets lost in the crowd on the streets. He seeks them, stretches out his hand, and says, *You are never forgotten. You are never alone.*

If that thought doesn't change my view of the stranger next to me, what will?

Psalm 146:6-10

Grace Place

Once again I'm longing for our old home, the one we left behind when we began this grad school adventure eighteen months ago. And yet my guess is that I'm longing for more than just home, but rather for a true heavenly rest, the room in God's house that Jesus promises (see John 14:2). An image of some unknown place comes to me in waking dreams sometimes—a vision of grace as a place, a rest for the soul. The overall impression is of a rambling old farmhouse with hardwood floors and ceilings. I'm always standing in the same spot, looking through a dark kitchen with its great stone fireplace to a many-windowed dining room with a long table and high-backed wooden chairs. The most striking thing about the windows, besides being many, is that they give way to a view of deep, new-fallen snow and small pines overburdened with white. The daylight is dim and white and shadowless, as if several more inches of snow could fall any moment. There is not a breath of wind, nor any sound or movement whatsoever, except the crackle of a fire in the fireplace. It is a serene, perfectly still place, and my heart leaps when my mind goes there.

As the holidays pass, I'm reminded of how content I could be as a child, how many hours I was given to simply sit and be at peace and observe my world. What a gift that was! I would trace the outline of a tree with my eyes or absorb the particular beauty of books lined up on shelves or memorize the pattern of wallpaper in a bedroom I will never be in again . . . tracing, always tracing the world with my eyes that I might reproduce it on paper or simply keep it in my memory. I could be entertained with the slightest things, including little sticks and pebbles and feathers that I used to create tiny fairy villages. I didn't have every want satisfied, but I grew to appreciate small surprises.

So all in all, I can train myself to be content, to delight in where I live (it's not hard) and become creative with organizing and rearranging our stuff. Because there's no reason why I shouldn't have a happy adulthood and make each new place my grace place too. And perhaps that rambling farmhouse in the new-fallen snow is my heavenly "mansion"— for which I'm willing to wait!

Jesus, teach me to make my home in you and not become restless without a house of my own. When it's time to move again, make it obvious for a good reason. Have patience with me as I learn the secret of being content and how to dwell in you, even as you dwell in me. Amen.

Philippians 4:11-13

Go Deeper

I don't always agree with the religious material I read. For example, I once came across a poem whose basic premise was that while some extra-special holy people may enter into the inner chambers of God's presence, the poet will "stand at the door" to welcome those who are passing by. He wants to help seekers in their groping blindness to put their hands on the latch and enter, but by contrast, those who are already deep inside may risk forgetting about the others who are lost.

And I think, *Eh—what?* The beautiful paradox of life in Christ is that the closer we come to God, the closer we come toward our fellow brothers and sisters. We have nothing to offer a hurting world if we ourselves aren't sitting at the feet of Jesus. There was no possible work Martha could do to match Mary's choice; Mary found the better way. Jesus himself spent entire nights in prayer that he might fully meet the needs of the poor and hurting the next day. Mother Teresa, the great twentieth-century missionary of Calcutta, India, rose for prayer at 6 a.m. and followed that with several hours of worship and study before she went out into the streets.

So were Mary and Mother Teresa out of touch with the world? Was Jesus so "heavenly minded" that he was no "earthly good"?// Speaking from personal experience alone, I can say that the more spiritually minded I am—the more time I spend in the innermost chamber in the presence of Christ—the greater clarity with which to truly see my fellow human beings. The greater wisdom I have to address their needs, the deeper my love and compassion for them.

People are drawn deeper into the presence of God because they see great beauty in those depths. They see people whose hearts and minds and wills are utterly devoted to God, and they desire that kind of life too. They are like the early Christian converts who, before their conversions, observed the believers in the Temple and wanted whatever they had (see Acts 2:46-47). They were drawn further in, not because someone stood at the door, but because of the magnetic beauty of Jesus as shown forth in the lives of those closest to him.

So if we're really serious about helping the lost, we must go deeper into the spiritual life with God.

Luke 10:38-42

// These phrases compliments of Oliver Wendell Holmes.

Hearth and Home

Here I am, a beggar standing at the very threshold of peace, gazing into the warm coziness of a home. I see the gold firelight flickering on the walls, smell the wholesome food, catch a glimpse of the Master of the house. He smiles and beckons me inside. But instead of stepping across the threshold to be fed at the table, to be wrapped in warm clothes and gathered close to the fire with a delicious loaf between my hands, I hover just outside in the cold, an angry scowl on my face. I hear my thin little voice protesting that grace just isn't *like* this—this warm fire, this free food—it isn't real enough. Yet all the while my heart aches at the simple truth of what I see.

So I hover there, crabby and annoyed that I'm shivering, my cold nose running, my neck stiff, my clothes too thin, and my stomach rumbling. I am a beggar too proud to beg, too full of myself to be filled by him, too suspicious that it will all melt away into a gold puddle on the concrete that then disappears between the cracks.

Oh, let me shake my persistent pride and come quaking into this warmth, my toes beginning to tingle, my eyes searching out the Master, whose love fills the whole house! Oh, let him feed me, clothe me, speak to me in that comforting voice—not because I deserve it, but because to refuse would be to dishonor him. To refuse would be to ignore the One who paid so dear a price for this warm fire, this nourishment, this assurance that there's a place the sordid world cannot reach. He has given me a home into which the cold cannot seep, which remains untouched by all the busy, chilly, windblown, doubting, frustrated, and irritated days of drippy noses, freezing fingers, quickly snatched meals, and flyby conversations.

He has welcomed us, undeserving, to his table in his house. How could we refuse?

Psalm 23

Honored Guests

For a couple of years my husband, Tom, volunteered at the local homeless shelter in our small town. One year he discovered that the guests at the shelter didn't have any kind of New Year's Eve party. There wasn't a TV for them to watch what was happening at Times Square or to count down until midnight, and obviously there wasn't any drinking allowed, since some of the guys were recovering alcoholics. (Not that there has to be drinking in order for something to qualify as a party—far from it! But that's what many of the guys were used to.) So Tom decided to have a New Year's Eve party at our house, even though we didn't have a TV either. But he figured, "Hey, we have food and games and sparkling juice, and we know how to count down from ten, so why not?"

So the director of the shelter agreed, and plans were made to bring the guys over around dinnertime on New Year's Eve. Now it's important to remember that Tom is a great cook. Having a bunch of guests over is no big deal; he loves to go all out and make several courses and create desserts from scratch and that kind of thing. And he certainly wasn't going to scrimp this time. But as he was setting the table, he paused to consider how he'd serve the sparkling juice. Would he use all our wine glasses, including the irreplaceable antique pair we received as a wedding gift? Weren't they too fancy for these guests? What if the guys accidentally broke one?

For a moment he even considered giving himself one of the antique glasses and putting the other away rather than risk having them get broken. Then it hit him. What made this occasion any different from hosting the Queen of England or any other honored guest? Who was he to make those kinds of distinctions?

So he welcomed the guests and served dinner using all the special serving dishes. Many hours later, after the dinner was eaten and the games played and the last of the sparkling juice gone, my husband said good-bye to the guys and started washing up. And it was while he was scrubbing away, his hands all slippery with soap, that he accidentally shattered one of those antique wine glasses.

Luke 14:7-14

Alpha and Omega

I can hardly believe it, but we've arrived at the final page of this *Daily Grind*. After a year of daily sips, we've reached the bottom of the mug, the dark little granules in the dregs of the cup. And yet there's more spiritual refreshment to be had. The pot is full on the counter of God's grace; tomorrow in the new year we can be filled again. And whether we turn back to the beginning of this book and start over, or launch new explorations of the spiritual classics or other devotionals, we are sure of this: The very same God who started us on this spiritual journey will be with us to its end.

Praise the Lord!
He is the BEGINNING.

Praise him for old things:
ancient sky and antique earth,
endless sea,
and all those timeless promises
that upheld our ancestors
long ago in love—
promises to one day
make all things

NEW!

New sunrise and
green grass and
cloud shapes
that have never been before;
new mercies
and snowflakes
and children,
a new heaven and new earth.

He is the END.
Praise the Lord!

Revelation 22:12-14

NOTES

1. Don Postema, *Space for God: The Study and Practice of Prayer and Spirituality* (Grand Rapids, MI: CRC Publications, 1983), 17.
2. Evelyn Underhill, *The Spiritual Life* (New York: Morehouse Publishing, 1937), 12.
3. Ibid., 29.
4. Ibid., 93–94.
5. Ibid.
6. C. S. Lewis, *C. S. Lewis: Letters to Children*, Lyle W. Dorsett and Marjorie Lamp Mead, eds. (New York: Simon and Schuster, 1985), 45.
7. Author of *Passion and Purity*, a book on romantic love that I was reading at the time (Grand Rapids, MI.: Baker Publishing, 1984).
8. Harry Emerson Fosdick, *The Manhood of the Master*, quoted in Rueben P. Job and Norman Shawchuck, eds., *A Guide to Prayer for Ministers and Other Servants* (Nashville: Upper Room Books, 1983), 283.
9. C. S. Lewis, "The Weight of Glory," quoted in Wayne Martindale and Jerry Root, eds., *The Quotable Lewis* (Carol Stream: Tyndale House Publishers, 1990), 352.
10. Fosdick, *Manhood*, quoted in Job and Shawchuck, *A Guide to Prayer*, 283.
11. Urban T. Holmes III, *Spirituality for Ministry*, quoted in Job and Shawchuck, *A Guide to Prayer*, 204.
12. Translated from the Gaelic and put into verse by Cecil Frances Alexander, 1889.
13. Richard J. Foster, *Celebration of Discipline: The Path to Spiritual Growth* (San Francisco: HarperSanFrancisco, 1988), 45.
14. Sarah Arthur, *Walking with Frodo: A Devotional Journey through The Lord of the Rings* (Carol Stream, IL: Tyndale House Publishers, 2003).
15. Oswald Chambers, *My Utmost for His Highest*, entry for October 17, www.myutmost.org/10/1017.html.
16. Elizabeth Goudge, *The Scent of Water* (New York: Coward-McCann, Inc., 1963), 115.
17. C. S. Lewis, quoted in Martindale and Root, *The Quotable Lewis*, 499–500.
18. Chambers, *My Utmost for His Highest*, entry for August 6, www.myutmost.org/08/0806.html.
19. Dietrich Bonhoeffer, *Life Together* (New York: Harper and Row Publishers, 1954), 46.
20. Holmes, *Spirituality for Ministry*, quoted in Job and Shawchuck, *A Guide to Prayer*, 203.
21. Ibid., 204.
22. C. S. Lewis, *Mere Christianity* (New York: HarperCollins Publishers, 1980), book 2, chapter 4.
23. Thomas Merton, *The Seven Storey Mountain* (New York: Harcourt Brace and Company, 1948), 217.

24. Ibid., 123.

25. Carlo Carretto, *The God Who Comes*, quoted in Job and Shawchuck, *A Guide to Prayer*, 198.

26. J. R. R. Tolkien, *The Silmarillion* (Boston, Houghton Mifflin Company, 1977).

27. I'm indebted to William J. Bausch in *Storytelling: Imagination and Faith* (New London, CT.: Twenty-Third Publications, 1984) for this reading of Genesis.

28. Humphrey Carpenter, ed., *The Letters of J. R. R. Tolkien* (Boston: Houghton Mifflin Company, 1995), letter 213.

29. Ibid., letter 142.

30. The Rutba House, eds., *School(s) for Conversion: 12 Marks of a New Monasticism* (Eugene, OR: Cascade Books, 2005), 166.

31. John Donne, *Divine Poems*, number XXI.

32. Daniel Taylor, "In Praise of Stories," in *The Christian Imagination: The Practice of Faith in Literature and Writing*, ed. Leland Ryken, 407–426 (Colorado Springs: WaterBrook Press, 2002), 422.

33. Warren W. Wiersbe, ed., *Developing a Christian Imagination* (Grand Rapids, MI: Baker, 1995), 282.

34. Kurt Bruner, *The Divine Drama: Discovering Your Part in God's Story* (Carol Stream, IL: Tyndale House Publishers, Inc., 2001), 13.

35. First published in 1880.

36. The Rutba House, *School(s) for Conversion*, 166.

37. Annie Dillard, *Holy the Firm* (New York: Harper and Row, 1977), 58.

38. C. S. Lewis, *Letters to Malcolm: Chiefly on Prayer* (New York: Harcourt Brace Jovanovich Publishers, 1964), 102.

39. Ibid., 104.

40. Dorothy Sayers, *The Mind of the Maker* (New York: Harcourt, Brace, 1941), 188.

41. Ibid., 188.

42. Henry David Thoreau, *Walden* (Boston: Houghton Mifflin Company, 1949), chapter 1.

43. The full text of the Great Thanksgiving liturgy can be found in *The Book of Common Prayer* (see "The Holy Eucharist: Rite Two," starting on page 361 of most recent editions, published by Oxford University Press); or visit www.bcponline.org (click on "The Holy Eucharist," then click on "Rite II," and then scroll down until you find the Great Thanksgiving).

44. C. S. Lewis, *God in the Dock* (Grand Rapids, MI: William B. Eerdmans Publishing Company, 1970), 201–202.

45. Annie Dillard, *The Writing Life* (New York: HarperCollins Publishers, 1989), 32.

46. John Wesley, "On Conscience," The Sermons of John Wesley, Global Ministries: The United Methodist Church, http://new.gbgm-umc.org/umhistory/wesley/sermons/105/. Apparently Wesley was the king of double negatives.

47. John Wesley to John Trembath, 17 August 1760, The Letters of John Wesley, Wesley Center Online, http://wesley.nnu.edu/john_wesley/letters/1760.htm.

48. Bonhoeffer, *Life Together*, 29.

49. Foster, *Celebration of Discipline*, 191.

50. The Rutba House, *School(s) for Conversion*, 30–31.

51. John Donne, "Resurrection" (revised), from the cycle of sonnets entitled "La Corona."

52. J. R. R. Tolkien, *The Lord of the Rings*, (Boston: Houghton Mifflin Company, 1983), chapter 7.

53. Lewis's stepson, Douglas Gresham, highlights these details in his biography *Jack's Life: The Life Story of C. S. Lewis* (B&H Publishing Group, 2005).

54. Christian Smith, with Melinda Lundquist Denton, *Soul Searching: The Religious and Spiritual Lives of American Teenagers* (New York: Oxford University Press, 2005), 148.

55. C. S. Lewis, *The Screwtape Letters*, quoted in Martindale and Root, *The Quotable Lewis*, 46.

MORE SPIRITUAL CAFFEINE

Some of the following resources are referenced in *The Daily Grind*; others are just plain good reading.

Augustine (354–430), *The Confessions* (New York: Vintage Books, 1998).

Dietrich Bonhoeffer (1906–1945), *Letters and Papers from Prison*, edited by Eberhard Bethge (New York: Collier Books, 1953).

Bonhoeffer, *Life Together* (New York: Harper and Row Publishers, 1954).

The Book of Common Prayer (New York: Oxford University Press, 1979).

Frederick Buechner, *The Alphabet of Grace* (HarperSanFrancisco, 1970).

Carlo Carretto (1910–1988), *Letters from the Desert* (London: Darton, Longman & Todd, Ltd. 2002).

Oswald Chambers (1874–1917), *My Utmost for His Highest*, www.myutmost.org.

Annie Dillard, *Holy the Firm* (New York: Harper and Row, 1977).

John Donne (1572–1631), *Divine Poems*.

François Fénelon (1651–1715), *Talking with God*, modern English translation by Hal M. Helms (Brewster, Mass.: Paraclete Press, 1997).

Richard J. Foster, *Celebration of Discipline: The Path to Spiritual Growth* (San Francisco: HarperSanFrancisco, 1988).

Richard J. Foster and James Bryan Smith, *Devotional Classics: Selected Readings for Individuals and Groups.* (HarperSanFrancisco, 1990). This is one of several Renovaré resources for spiritual renewal, www.renovare.org.

Elizabeth Goudge (1900–1984), *The Scent of Water* (New York: Coward-McCann, Inc., 1963). Many of Goudge's books are out of print, so keep your eyes peeled at used book sales and old church libraries. Or, if you're lucky, occasionally they can be found online.

Rueben P. Job and Norman Shawchuck, eds., *A Guide to Prayer for Ministers and Other Servants* (Nashville: Upper Room Books, 1983).

C. S. Lewis (1898–1963), *God in the Dock* (Grand Rapids, Mich.: William B. Eerdmans Publishing Company, 1970).

Lewis, *Mere Christianity* (New York: HarperCollins Publishers, 1980). First broadcast as a series of radio addresses on the BBC in 1943.

Lewis, *C. S. Lewis: Letters to Children*, edited by Lyle W. Dorsett and Marjorie Lamp Mead (New York: Simon & Schuster, 1985).

Lewis, *Letters to Malcolm: Chiefly on Prayer* (New York: Harcourt Brace Jovanovich Publishers, 1964).

Lewis, *The Screwtape Letters* (New York: HarperCollins Publishers, 1996). First published in 1942.

George MacDonald (1824–1905), *Diary of an Old Soul* (Minneapolis: Augsburg, 1994).

Wayne Martindale and Jerry Root, eds., *The Quotable Lewis* (Carol Stream, IL.: Tyndale House Publishers, 1989).

Thomas Merton (1915–1968), *The Seven Storey Mountain* (New York: Harcourt Brace and Company, 1948).

Kathleen Norris, *The Cloister Walk* (Riverhead Books, 1996).

The Rutba House, eds., *School(s) for Conversion: 12 Marks of a New Monasticism* (Eugene, OR: Cascade Books, 2005), www.newmonasticsm.org.

Dorothy Sayers (1893–1957), *The Mind of the Maker* (New York: Harcourt, Brace, 1941).

Evelyn Underhill (1875–1941), *The Spiritual Life* (New York: Morehouse Publishing, 1937).

Lauren Winner, *Girl Meets God: On the Path to a Spiritual Life* (Chapel Hill, N.C.: Algonquin Books, 2002).

Winner, *Mudhouse Sabbath* (Brewster, Mass.: Paraclete Press, 2003).

Luci Shaw, *Polishing the Petoskey Stone: New and Selected Poems* (Wheaton, Ill.: Harold Shaw Publishers, 1990).

Sheldon Vanauken, *A Severe Mercy* (New York: HarperCollins, 1977).

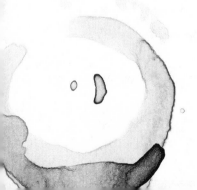

Do-able. Daily. Devotions.

START ANY DAY THE ONE YEAR WAY.

Do-able.
Every One Year book is designed for people who live busy, active lives. Just pick one up and start on today's date.

Daily.
Daily routine doesn't have to be drudgery. One Year devotionals help you form positive habits that connect you to what's most important.

Devotions.
Discover a natural rhythm for drawing near to God in an extremely personal way. One Year devotionals provide daily focus essential to your spiritual growth.

For Women

The One Year Devotions for Women on the Go

The One Year Devotions for Women

The One Year Devotions for Moms

The One Year Women of the Bible

The One Year Daily Grind

For Men

The One Year
Devotions for
Men on the Go

The One Year
Devotions for
Men

For Couples

The One Year
Devotions for
Couples

For Families

The One
Year Family
Devotions

For Teens

The One Year
Devos for Teens

The One Year
Devos for Sports
Fans

For Bible Study

The One Year
Life Lessons
from the Bible

The One Year
Praying through
the Bible

The One Year
through the
Bible

For Personal Growth

The One Year
Devotions
for People of
Purpose

The One Year
Walk with God
Devotional

The One Year
at His Feet
Devotional

The One Year
Great Songs of
Faith

The One Year
on This Day

It's convenient and easy to grow with
God the One Year way.

The One Year
Life Verse
Devotional

THE ONE YEAR WAY

Teach Truth.

MEET JESUS EVERY DAY THE ONE YEAR WAY.

For Kids

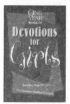

*The One Year
Devotions for
Girls*

*The One Year
Devotions for
Boys*

*The One Year
Devotions for
Preschoolers*

*The One Year
Devotions for
Kids*

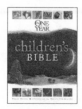

*The One Year
Make-It-Stick
Devotions*

*The One Year
Bible for Kids:
Challenge
Edition*

*The One Year
Children's Bible*

*The One Year
Book of Josh
McDowell's
Youth Devotions*

THOUGHTFUL. PRACTICAL. AFFORDABLE.

The One Year Mini for Women helps women connect with God through several Scripture verses and a devotional thought. Perfect for use anytime and anywhere between regular devotion times. Hardcover.

The One Year Mini for Students offers students from high school through college a quick devotional connection with God anytime and anywhere. Stay grounded through the ups and downs of a busy student lifestyle. Hardcover.

The One Year Mini for Moms provides encouragement and affirmation for those moments during a mom's busy day when she needs to be reminded of the high value of her role. Hardcover.

The One Year Mini for Busy Women is for women who don't have time to get it all done but need to connect with God during the day. Hardcover.

The One Year Mini for Men helps men connect with God anytime, anywhere between their regular devotion times through Scripture quotations and a related devotional thought. Hardcover.

The One Year Mini for Leaders motivates and inspires leaders to maximize their God-given leadership potential using scriptural insights. Hardcover.

CP0161